D1296361

Wyndham Lewis titles published by Black Sparrow Press:

The Apes of God (novel) (1981)
BLAST 1 (journal) (1981)
BLAST 2 (journal) (1981)
The Complete Wild Body (stories) (1982)
Journey Into Barbary (travel) (1983)
Self Condemned (novel) (1983)
Snooty Baronet (novel) (1984)
BLAST 3 (journal) (1984)
Rude Assignment (autobiography) (1984)
The Vulgar Streak (novel) (1984)

Forthcoming:

Rotting Hill (stories)

WYNDHAM LEWIS

RUDE ASSIGNMENT

AN INTELLECTUAL AUTOBIOGRAPHY

ILLUSTRATED BY THE AUTHOR

EDITED BY TOBY FOSHAY

WITH SIX LETTERS BY EZRA POUND
EDITED & ANNOTATED BY BRYANT KNOX

LEE COUNTY LIBRARY
107 HAWKINS AVE.
SANFORD, N. C. 27330

BLACK SPARROW PRESS
SANTA BARBARA—1984

RUDE ASSIGNMENT. Copyright © 1950 by Wyndham Lewis. Copyright © 1984 by the Estate of Mrs. G. A. Wyndham Lewis by permission of the Wyndham Lewis Memorial Trust.

NOTES and AFTERWORD to *Rude Assignment*. Copyright © 1984 by Toby Foshay.

INTRODUCTION and NOTES to "Six Letters by Ezra Pound." Copyright © 1984 by Bryant Knox.

SIX PREVIOUSLY UNPUBLISHED LETTERS BY EZRA POUND. Copyright © 1984 by The Trustees of the Ezra Pound Literary Property Trust.

All rights reserved. Printed in the United States of America. No part of this book may be used or reproduced in any manner whatsoever without written permission from the publisher except in the case of brief quotations embodied in critical articles and reviews. For information address Black Sparrow Press, P.O. Box 3993, Santa Barbara, CA 93130.

LIBRARY OF CONGRESS CATALOGING IN PUBLICATION DATA

Lewis, Wyndham, 1882-1957.
  Rude assignment.

   1. Lewis, Wyndham, 1882-1957—Biography.   2. Authors, English—20th century—Biography.   3. Artists—Great Britain— Biography.   Foshay, Toby, 1950-
II. Title.
PR6023.E97Z477   1984   828'.91209 [B]   84-16837
ISBN 0-87685-604-0
ISBN 0-87685-603-2 (pbk.)
ISBN 0-87685-605-9 (deluxe)

EDITOR'S NOTE

The text for this edition of *Rude Assignment* is that of the first (and only) edition, published by Hutchinson of London in 1950. The British style of the original has been preserved, with minor emendations of typographical, spelling and a few stylistic oversights. A list of these can be found at the back of the book.

As in the original edition Lewis's own note are indicated by symbols and given at the foot of the page, at times with additional matter by the editor in square brackets. Editorial annotations are indicated by superscript numerals and placed together at the end of chapters.

A fresh group of illustrations (all self portraits by Lewis) has been chosen for this edition. The greater availability of and acquaintance with the broad spectrum of Lewis's pictorial canon permitted a different approach here. At any rate, as is known from a letter to Hutchinson's at Cornell (Lewis to Sutherland, 29 Jan 1949), Lewis was restricted in his selection to the small sampling of adequate reproductions of his work then in his possession. A list of the illustrations in the first edition is given at the back of the book.

As is perhaps indicated by the original sub-title to *Rude Assignment*, "A Narrative of My Career Up-to-date", Lewis intended to write a more conventional autobiography than the one he published. (The sub-title of the present edition, more accurately representing the nature of the book, is an editorial addition.) He twice in the text refers to important matters too sensitive for his publisher. The suppression of three of his books in the 1930s and the fiasco of his sympathetic book on Hitler in 1931 were vital to the impulse behind *Rude Assignment*. Having to pass these events over seemed to lessen the narrative element in the composition of the book. Early drafts of two chapters, one written in a more personal narrative vein, the other unused and incomplete, are given here as appendices. Interesting in their own right, they also reveal a more candid Lewis, one not so exercised by either a personal or a public censorship.

Toby Foshay
Dalhousie University
Halifax, Nova Scotia

ACKNOWLEDGEMENTS

The editor would like to thank Dr. Donald Eddy of the Department of Rare Books, Cornell University Library, for permission to quote from unpublished material in the Lewis Collection. Thanks also to the staff of the Department for their help and cooperation. Appreciation is due to Claudine Bertin and Deborah Bulmer for help with French translations. I would like especially to thank Rowland Smith, Omar Pound, Seamus Cooney (who contributed several notes and the bulk of the emendations), Paul Edwards and John Martin for their interest and helpful suggestions, and my wife, Ann Wetmore-Foshay, for her encouragement.

The first three *Rude Assignment* letters from Pound to Lewis printed in this volume are held in the Contemporary Literature Collection, Special Collections, W.A.C. Bennett Library, Simon Fraser University and are reproduced with the permission of Percilla Groves, Special Collections Librarian. The second three *Rude Assignment* letters from Pound to Lewis printed herein are held in the Department of Rare Books, Cornell University Library and are reproduced with the permission of Dr. Donald Eddy. All six of these previously unpublished letters by Ezra Pound are Copyright ©1984 by the Trustees of the Ezra Pound Literary Property Trust and are used by permission of New Directions Publishing Corp., Agents.

CONTENTS

PART ONE
THREE FATALITIES

SECTION A. THE INTELLECTUAL

SECTION B. SATIRE

SECTION C. POLITICS

PART TWO
PERSONAL BACKGROUND OF CAREER

RUDE ASSIGNMENT

An Intellectual Autobiography

PART I
THREE FATALITIES

SECTION A

The Intellectual

CHAPTER I

INTRODUCTORY

THIS is an account of my career as writer and artist up to the time of writing. The work is implicated in the life of the worker, so as a rule it is difficult to treat of the former in isolation. When it is purely the work, as work, that is in question, only so much concerning the individual responsible for it is relevant as furthers an understanding of the work. Here the work does not quite occupy that position, however, as I shall presently explain. In one sense, even, this book is more about the worker than the work.

Some men's work is all background — is all man: whereas with some poets, for instance, you need no more than to think of them as a bird, whose song was sweet. But the term work is out of place with such as the latter — as you would never speak of 'the work of the nightingale'. There are other poets who are extremely different from this. Their song is *about* something. It is packed with human history. To take one case only, the most illustrious and perhaps the most obvious; how necessary it is to an understanding of the work of Dante to know that he was a refugee politician, that the Popes were his great enemies — to go into the party-feuds of the Guelphs and Ghibellines, check Dante's part in them: why he was sentenced to be burned alive. The fires of his Hell, and the particular direction the flames took, acquire more meaning when that is known.

With a novelist it is the same as with the poet: there are some who spin stories as the larva of the bombycid moth spins its cocoon. You do not have to know, any more than with the silkworm or the songbird, what they thought or why they thought it. Others differ from these extremely: such as Gustave Flaubert, where the spinning of the yarn is purposive. In such a case it is well to trace back to its source the imprint of German pessimism, and to allow for the strains induced by epilepsy. — As to critics, of them there are none in that class in which the work speaks for itself: and the critic is about as impersonal as a village policeman. His criticism is only of value if you know the natural-history of his taste.

This is not, as I have said, purely an account of a career, however. It has not been primarily to speak of my work that I have undertaken to write this book. Indeed, it would never occur to me to pass my time so unprofitably as in the indulgence of an historic mood. — Certainly it is about my work, and especially that side of it that has raised up difficulties for its author. But it is also about *the nature of this type of work*, and about the paradoxical position of the workman — not myself alone — engaged in it. And, more personally, it is about the nature of my thinking (as illustrated in my work and otherwise) which has resulted in my life being so difficult a one to live. Lastly, this book is itself a work — a new work.

Why I should, at this time, have given priority to this particular work in place of the novel which is now destined to follow it, or the new critical survey I have in mind, I will make as clear as I can. In the first place, a writer who is a novelist, a critic, a political pamphleteer, as I am: who has been engaged, as in my case, in the analysis of what is obsessional in contemporary social life; in composing satiric verse; exposing abuses in art-politics; celebrating in fiction picturesque parasites; in weighing, to the best of his ability, contemporary theories of the State (few made known to us without a pistol at our heads); who has often found himself in conflict with the inveterate prepossessions of his age and country; who, as an artist, has come at a time of great change, and has, without reserve, entered into the controversies arising from this embittered struggle between the old and the new: anyone extending himself in so many directions, with such a maximum of informality, and disregard of consequences, will find, as time goes on, that more and more people and things are mixed up with his work, so that to speak of one is to speak of the other.

In the course of controversy, in order to discredit an opponent (and after the controversy has died down this does not stop) many disobliging fictions gain currency. A picture of a man is in this way handed down which is a very bad likeness, one that corresponds only slightly with the original. After his death, even, the painting goes on. Something, I suppose, of this kind always happens to the polemical. And controversy has been my lot — not because I have any love for it. That must be put down to the times.

This sensation of malaise with regard to the scurrilous 'likeness' for which enemies are responsible has a history. Those who have invited reprisals, as the result of some action inflaming contemporary opinion, must often have experienced it: but there is of course a classic instance. Newman, who moved over from the anglican catholic into the roman catholic communion (surely a harmless enough proceeding, one would say), on this account the recipient of much intemperate abuse, at last turned upon an attacker. 'Better,' he wrote, 'that he should discharge his thoughts upon me in my lifetime, than after I am dead.'

And it is a strange thing how satisfactory it is when some malevolent person 'discharges his thoughts', a discharge which one is free to answer. When more than one do it, that is delightful. For if only the spurious portrait of oneself gets painted in public (and not surreptitiously, so that one never sees it, though one may hear that the work is going forward and will be there some day — to be gazed at in shocked astonishment by another generation — weighed with that deceptive authenticity which things contemporary have) — if it is brought out into the open to be painted there, then all is well. 'The phantom may be extinguished which gibbers instead of me,' as Newman said. 'I wish to be known as a living man, and not as a scarecrow.' And so long as the living man is still there he can annihilate the phantom: whereas when a phantom himself it would be too late.

What I am saying is that strong personal motives have dictated the writing of this book. It is not any one particular thing: it is a small mountain of ever increasing nonsense, which has to be shovelled away — deposited by many hands, for a great number of petty reasons. Some action at last has been imposed on me.

Questions of how deserving I am of such flattering attentions aside, I have in a servile society uncovered my mind too often, provoked too many people by defending myself or my craft with an unwelcome determination, to escape the obligation of a cleansing operation on the grand scale, such as this is. And were I not to use my pen for this purpose, these matters would be set down, some day, with important facts left out, and some others introduced which were never there until some kind person put them there. To this public narrative of mine — from which in order to publish it at all much material evidence must be omitted — I shall write a fully documented Supplement, containing the most important items I am debarred from imparting at this time.[1] Sealed copies of this unprintable Appendix will be deposited at the national libraries here and in America (a step taken, I understand, by Yeats, on the occasion of his controversy with his fellow countryman George Moore) to be opened at a later date. Thus I shall feel more comfortable: although naturally it would be preferable, if one had the money, to put a stop to defamation as it occurred.

For a number of years I have felt that such a book as this, in justice to myself — as citizen rather than as author — should be written. — Actions of mine have been accounted for in many different ways, most of which I have known to be mistaken, or misleading. Sometimes this has been the result of ignorance, at others there has been wilful inaccuracy.

I would rather have a few bad failings. I do not wish to be one of those perfect people, of which we all know such great numbers that often we cannot but experience deep astonishment — seeing how much sheer perfection there is in the world — that our time is so filled with disorder and stupid violence. All I would like to bring out in the course of this book is that at times failings have been attributed to me which I never possessed. I shall be satisfied if I can do that.

So much for the personal impulse, responsible for the first step, but which does not alone give the book its life. For there is nothing I treat of here that is simply my private affair and that of nobody else. Quite the contrary: throughout matters are discussed which are, in the most tragic sense, everybody's business. The question, as an instance, whether man should maintain himself upon a civilised level, or return to lower levels of life; or again, how much, and what kind of, freedom he should possess (or *will* possess).

Of the three Parts into which the present volume is divided, it is my object in the first Part to make clear the conditions, adverse in the extreme, under which such books as mine must be written. Any harassment meted out by fate to the individual, is superadded to the great initial handicap of being an 'intellectual', for instance, and is not improved thereby. It is from that weak position that he must face any extraneous opposition. The first few chapters are impersonal to the extent that they treat of vile conditions which are not peculiar to me.

This is the necessary groundwork for an account of my career: for one would not set out to describe a house without first supplying the information as to what it was built on, especially if that happened to be a bog. Having done this I pass on to the problems of a more special order belonging to the satirist. And finally, in this Part, I reach politics; the problems of (1) the satirist, and (2) the political writer building themselves up, pagoda-like, upon the massive initial drawback of 'intellectuality'. So, at the outset, I expound these crushing handicaps, rather as a general might expound (not without a certain gloomy pride) the handicaps under which he fought: as (1) the sea at his back; (2) the sun in his eyes; and (3) a considerable hill, in the occupation of the enemy, suspended immediately over his position.

Part II is autobiography — so much as is required to set forth the circumstances, economic and otherwise, which made it possible for me to be here at all, writing and painting as I do. I cannot of course say how, but at least I can indicate when, I became among other things a satirist. On the other hand I know when, and why, politics came into my life. The outline of the events responsible for these developments will be found in Part II. The third and last Part of this book is a biography, and in some cases a restatement in different terms, of a number of my books. Perhaps I should add that already in the section devoted to Satire (Part I) the career material begins, in the form of answers to attacks, and in the section immediately succeeding it (the subject of which is politics) other personal attacks meet at last with a rejoinder. — This will afford some guidance as to the respective functions of the three Parts into which this book is divided.

Notes

[1] In the "fully documented Supplement" Lewis presumably intended to discuss his three suppressed books of the thirties — The Doom of Youth, Filibusters in Barbary, and The Roaring Queen — as well as to name and answer his hostile critics and to refute the defamatory accusation of Fascist sympathies arising from his early book on Hitler. However no such Supplement survives among the Lewis papers at Cornell. Draft versions of a discussion of the Hitler books do exist and are printed below as Appendix II.

CHAPTER II

THE HIGHBROW, AND THE TWO PUBLICS

I AM what is described as a 'highbrow'. That is the first thing about me; it underlies, and influences, all the other things that I am — all the things that it is not desirable to be. And this part of my book is to take the form exclusively of a catalogue of my personal handicaps.

But this term — half abuse, half of derision — is not *me*, it is not an attribute of mine, or anything personal to me. It is just something that happens to any writer or other artist, to be described in this ridiculous fashion — one who is not a bestselling or potboiling hack.

There are two distinct kinds of writing, or of any other art, at the present time. Such conditions have never existed before, and will perhaps never be present again; we are uniquely cursed. The 'highbrow' is one of these two divisions into which humanity has been cut — for the use of these terms extends beyond the artist to the Public catered for. It has come to describe a human category — the 'highbrow' and the 'lowbrow'.*

This clownish American term, 'highbrow', is more than just a label. It is a *uniform*, as much as the garment stamped with arrows worn by the convict. For a man is a 'highbrow' all over, from head to foot, or not at all. He is somebody set apart from other men — for thinking in a peculiar way. He cannot mix with them without their at once detecting the difference, and feeling embarrassed. Even he uses a dialect — long and funny words and expressions — as unpopular with the solid citizen as is thieves' slang. He is regarded as 'standoffish', but people stand off him, his company as much wanted as that of an escaped budgerigar by a cluster of sparrows.

The Philistine once felt diffident in the presence of the 'clerk' or Gelehrter — of his intellectual betters. But he knows now that they are only 'intellectuals', or 'highbrows' — *jokes*! He knows, too, that the Philistines are really the Chosen People: the Nineteenth Century was the 'Century of the Philistine'. The Twentieth is called 'the Century of the Common Man': but it is turning out to be the Century of the Philistine again, just the same as the last. (Someone meant to go to town with the Common Man, but they lost him on the way.)

Why on earth should an intellectual, however, wish to associate with the Philistines? Surely that would be most uncongenial company for him! — He does not, of course, wish to do that. The best variety of intellectuals, on the other hand, are by no means enamoured of the Ivory Tower. They do not want to speak to the stars, but to men. They merely object to their being Philistines; especially they resent people deriving merit from their barbarity: their social conscience recognises in them a vast infected area, which should not be permitted to remain as it is. They object to being denied (by means of the branding described above) the missionary's privilege to go

---

* This classification does not extend beyond the bourgeoisie. The working class of course does not count. The typical 'lowbrow' would not like to think he shared his brow with *them*. They might, if it came to the point, be described as the 'no-brows'.

amongst the Philistines and bring civilisation to these modern middle-class savages. And, then, if as seems very probable, this badly-infected middle class is economically wiped out: if golf-courses are put under the plough, bridge clubs converted into something more useful, the commercial theatres turned over to the State, the culturally-destructive monopolies controlling them dissolved — what then? Will the Philistine perish with the Bourgeoisie?

A danger that is patent enough is that the 'lowbrow' virus will infect the working mass underneath it, into which Philistia will sink — if the virus is not there already, transmitted by the Moving Picture industry. The division into 'low' and 'high' would thus be perpetuated, with an added militancy: or what is derisively labelled 'high' be wiped out. — The unity thus obtained would be a cultural zero as injurious to the social body as any other organic atrophy. For the Anglo-saxon is not the Slav, or even the Celt: he does not dance or sing *for preference*, he is strong but he is silent, and we have the most conclusive evidence, in certain parts of the world, of what he is capable when left to his own devices, in the way of a cultural desert.

Do not let us be distracted, however, by speculations as to what may come to pass in the fullness of time: it is what is here now, irrespective of what may be here tomorrow, that is the subject of this and the succeeding chapters. *The Two Publics* I have collectively named them. And for a writer the Public is of critical importance, as it is for the actor.

Though already in Dickens' day the Public was too big, it has now broken into two very unequal parts: a 'popular' and a 'highbrow', the latter being so insignificant in size as to be practically a private audience, such as a group of friends and relatives would provide.

As the cities grew, and privilege rapidly gave ground, the Public altered, from the compact, alert, educated Public of moderate size, that of the aristocracies, to the swelling mass of readers of the Victorian shopkeeping and mercantile classes. It became so large that writers were a little uncertain for whom they were writing. The focusing became blurred. The immediate result was a falling off in quality. The beautifully written books of the Eighteenth Century were succeeded by books the style of which was coarser and looser. To come down to our own day, such writing as that of H. G. Wells (I am not speaking of the matter, only the manner, if one can make such a distinction) could not have been handed by any bookseller to the Public which currently read 'The Sentimental Journey' or 'The Tale of a Tub.'*

It was hoped by good-hearted people that 'popular education' would elevate the new multitudinous society to a plane where it would equal in understanding and appreciation that of the privileged classes. Because 'popular education' was a sham, if for no other reason, this did not occur. There was another deadly factor: the flattery of the 'sovereign people' by politicians tended to erect bad taste, or no taste, into a position where it

---

* In comparing, as I am about to do, these two types of Public, although certainly I would agree that the aristocratic Public was the better of the two, no *partipris* for that social order need be surmised, for it is not there. I, no more than de Tocqueville, would recommend a return to that, or anything like it.

became above criticism: and, as I have remarked, the word 'highbrow' was coined slightingly and damagingly to describe those who persisted in employing their critical faculties.

Then the commercial gentleman, at a certain moment, stepped into the picture. He had been held in check under the aristocracies. (I have written somewhere that the only conceivable use I could think of for the fox-hunter was to keep the businessman in his place.) This predatory money-spinner saw very clearly that the multitude was a goldmine. The fact that it was uninstructed, sentimental, greedy of sensation, did not trouble *him*. The What the Public wants' principle it was called. – He, too, assisted in confirming the zero-mind (which is what the human mind is like until you have put something into it and trained it to function) in its position of cultural arbiter. Hollywood is the most perfect expression of this.

One might have supposed that among the political class – I speak of the era which ended with the advent of the present social democratic administration – however rotted it might be by Victorian philistinism through which it had passed, something would remain of the better earlier standards: the popular press, the many temptations to illiteracy, notwithstanding. Anything but that happened. Except in a few cases, nothing whatever was left. There are no throwbacks to the habitués of Button's Coffee-House among Twentieth Century London clubmen.

Detective fiction has for long been the cabinet minister's habitual reading, with Mr. Wodehouse's ghastly butler as an alternative to Poirot and Lord Peter Wimsey. In the States it is much the same. One of my personal experiences which have a bearing upon the question of the cultural level at which the politically or socially prominent live relates to the young wife of a multimillionaire. Wishing to display her cultivation, she informed me she had been reading 'Forever Amber'.[1] She did not seem to know any other book of the same cultural range, although I could see she was trying to remember one or two. As her chauffeur drove me back to my hotel, he, too, I learnt, had been reading 'Forever Amber'. There was a note of self-importance in his voice, as there had been in hers, as he alluded to it. – Then Herr Hitler, according to reporters accompanying him, was wont upon long plane journeys to read crime stories. – Another illustration of these tendencies: in Public Libraries in the New World 'Western Stories' occupy whole blocks of bookshelves. This for adult reading.

But the roster of backslidings into juvenilia, or related phenomena, is endless. Nor of course do I say that there is any harm in 'mystery' and murder, our debased form of Arabian Nights Entertainments (nor the literary sex stimuli which could come under the same head) except when it represents a literary monopoly. W. B. Yeats once told me that he never used detective fiction until he was forty: but he assured me that all men at forty did so. Yeats read other books as well, however.

––––

The Majority Public, to return to that, is not one solid mass, ten million strong. There are layers, as it were. But even the top layer is far too low for, say, 'The Way of All Flesh'. Contemporary man is allergic to the masterpiece.

He is allergic, that is, to other than superficial matter between the covers of a non-technical book. One way of gauging by analogy the extent of his literary toleration is to observe how much, if any, of serious matter he will suffer on the radio, before switching off. In practice he never is obliged in Great Britain to switch off anything, however, unless by mistake he should tune in to the Third Programme. All his cultural allergies are locked away in the so-called Third Programme, which, because of the wave-length reserved for it, can only be heard in London and its neighbourhood. So, in Manchester or Nottingham he is perfectly safe.

Our present-day Minority Public is not a half, probably only a tenth, of the Eighteenth Century Public. It is the Public of the Intelligentsia. Although much smaller, this Public of the Intelligentsia might be expected to compare favourably with the Public of the aristocratic era. That is, however, not the case. It is too specialised: an unrepresentative fraction of the whole. And it *is* the whole, in some form or other, that is required by a writer.

Notes

[1] *Forever Amber* (London, 1944) by Kathleen Winsor made the best seller lists in 1944 and 1945 (no. 1 in 1945). The first novel of the much publicized and photogenic author, it was set in Restoration England and emphasized the bawdiness of the period. As of 1982, it was still in print in both England and America.

CHAPTER III

THEY STEAL THE HALOES FROM THE
STATUES OF THE SAINTS

THE existence of two distinct communities, such as those of Highbrowland and Lowbrowland, owing their origin, as distinct entities, to irreconcilable differences of taste and of opinion, cannot but involve hard feelings: and hard feelings there are. The smaller community is so small that what in the end this must lead to is the suppression, the liquidation, of the intellectual groups altogether. It will come about as the result of pressure upon the feebler to conform. Let us start, however, by imagining what must be the sensations of a gilded hack, as he watches the degraded products of his nasty brain being contemptuously trampled underfoot by the seedy but conscientious critic. This occurs every time, his latest bestseller having appeared, he peruses his press-cuttings.

Critics of books, pictures, or plays, are as often as not 'Highbrows': but many of the books, pictures, or plays they are paid to write about are 'lowbrow'. As might be anticipated, sometimes they say wounding things about them. The general Public regards critics as a pernickety and spiteful class. It shuts its eyes and ears as far as possible to what the critics say. With the lowbrow writer, painter, or actor it is another matter. Their lives are often embittered by ridicule and censure, for although they sell their books by the hundredweight they are respected by nobody: or though a play has a run of six hundred nights, the critics are apt to provide an opprobrious chorus. A film gets such terrible press notices (especially if it is American) that one would think the Public would stop away. Mercifully, from the standpoint of the box-office, the average movie-lover is not in the habit of looking at newspapers, much less the weekly periodical press.

Before the war, there was scarcely an art-critic who did not reprove, ridicule, or scold the Royal Academy Exhibition, when every Spring it displayed, according to custom, its meretricious wares — its glittering diamonds, its juicy satins, its glittering brass-hats, and sketchy peeps at nature. (An institution of the same order and quality as Madame Tussaud's — though this is rather unfair to the waxworks, where the waxen effigies have a certain Douanier-like charm.)

If in the book-world, or in the theatrical profession the critic can be to some extent disregarded, this has not proved to be the case with painting, sculpture, and design. Perhaps because oil-paintings cost much more than books, bad pictures have almost ceased to sell.

The intellectualist barrage of the last thirty years has had a great effect in the sale-room, and, in the matter of the visual arts, the Minority has won the day in that sense. In literature, even when the writer has had every critic in the press acclaiming him, it has made very little difference financially — until, by some extraneous means, he came to the attention of the Public. Since the establishment of the two water-tight Publics this has been a fairly rare occurrence.

The author of 'Lady Chatterley's Lover' only reached the Plain Man of today by way of the bedroom window. In all his attempts prior to that, Lawrence remained outside, an intellectual's hero, that was all. And the bedroom or lavatory window is the intellectuals' best bet (or, I should say, was). Hemingway showed the children how to play at a 'stick-up' and how to strap their popguns under their arm-pits: *he* got in that way. Neither Lawrence nor Hemingway departed from their high standards as writers. It was a question of subject-matter, not of style.

Enter by the front-door and you go dressed accordingly. And it is a very cheap outfit indeed that you will wear; or a cowboy get-up, or masked and with an ill-concealed Smith-Wesson. If a woman, with a tiara and a haughty stare; or as a 'womanly woman', with Mrs. Beeton's Cookery Book under your arm or with a story of how you were seduced. There is no dignified or decent way of going in.

The invisible line separating the two Publics cannot be crossed with impunity by one of the Minority. So fine a preraphaelite painter as Millais ended his career with 'Bubbles' and a baronetcy.* As to the dangers that beset the Minority Writer, it is enough if he transgress in his heart. So fine a mind as Hudson's (I suppose toying with thoughts of popularity) was guilty of Rima.[1] To produce anything so sickly there must, I suppose, have been some native rot. There are very few cases, if any, however, of a great artist like Henry James committing intellectual suicide.

The advocate of 'highbrow' values, as against the values of the good easy man, who 'knows what he likes', must always appear pernickety. The label 'highbrow' contributes to this impression. Whereas the two-party character of criticism gives to the opinion of the *outs* — the permanent Minority — a suspect and merely partisan appearance.

———

There is another result of this separation of the bright from the dull, the intellectual from the non-intellectual, namely the exclusive encouragement of opposite orders of extremism. Thus in the United States Frank Salisbury, R.A., was to be official artist.[2] At the other extreme stands picassoan or other extremism. Nothing gets much chance in the gulf that yawns ever wider between these extreme positions. If there were no gulf and the extremes drew together, then many artists who are not by nature extremists (of whichever kind) would produce what is the finest and maturest type of work.

The gulf widens and deepens, however, and the conditions favourable to the production of the best intellectual extremism (such as Paris provided for those mercurial masters who now are old) disappear. In writing, the same shrinkage of opportunity may be recorded. One day soon all of *that* kind of extremism will be engulfed. But what an extremism will have meanwhile been built up at the other end of the scale!

A hundred years ago, or even half as long, it was a generally accepted belief that the poet or philosopher, shivering in his garret, was a better man than the sleek bestseller, basking on his terrace at Cannes. What the

* A poster advertising Pears' Soap, showing a curly-headed boy blowing bubbles.

latter produced had no value except in terms of L.S.D.[3] whereas the former was 'loved of the gods' and would no doubt 'die young' — but *how glorious!* It was almost like dying in battle, for England, Home and Beauty. Browning expressed all this type of feeling on numerous occasions. 'What porridge had John Keats' he exclaims with dramatic emphasis — and all his readers, invariably well-fed and well-heeled, applauded.

Apart from the fact that there was an unmistakable tendency to let everybody die of starvation who displayed any unusual talent, and much talent must have been lost through hunger and neglect, nevertheless the respectful attitude was *something*. It was better than being sneered at, as a 'highbrow', and starve just the same, or to live on charity. The emergence of socially valuable personalities at least was not obstructed: for their values were not questioned. Those valuations are today under attack: even a tendency exists — a primitive Christian impulse — to say that what has been considered high is really low, and what has been thought low is high. It is the democratic levelment that de Tocqueville foresaw, extending far beyond merely social particulars.

I would now like, having prepared the way, to draw attention to a distinction, which is perhaps the key to what is novel in the situation I have been describing. — Changing values, representing a see-saw of taste from decade to decade, affecting the reputations of the inhabitants of our pantheon — from Shakespeare downwards — is one thing. Such movements are going on continually. They are changes that emanate from reactions within the ranks of the small Minority groups alone. These are the keepers of the pantheon, as it were. They engage in arguments constantly about the relative importance of their idols.

These changes affect very slightly, if at all, the great Public. The early Victorian romantic poets lose standing: Shelley and Keats decline, Dryden and Crabbe go up. The Majority is unaware of such fluctuations among the unread authors dustily huddled upon the library shelves.

The values involved in these periodic adjustments are of a totally different order from those which distinguish a contemporaneous 'highbrow' and 'lowbrow' work. And this is the fundamental distinction to which I referred above. In the latter case it is *a difference in the essential nature* of the respective works. The difference between something self-evidently trivial or shoddy, and something self-evidently engaging all the energies of a considerable mind and sensibility. And there measurement is possible — as much as it would be possible to measure and compare the brain of Isaac Newton and that of a fieldmouse. Taste is not really involved at all. Only the cash-nexus blurs the verdict: only that and the automatic reflection in our department of life from violent political readjustments elsewhere.

The word 'self-evident' uncovers the essential humbug in the position. For the two Publics would never have come into being; there would be no labelling 'highbrow' what is work seriously undertaken — in order to distinguish it offensively from what is *not* serious — were *the self-evident inferiority* of work done to soothe the tired businessman, or to provide sensations for the bored matron, not disputed. And there is today unquestionably, in however veiled a form, this novel dispute. In America I have heard the matter openly canvassed, and bold claims made for the purely commercial article.

No dispute should ever have developed as to *ultimate* values: for that is what it means. Were the potboiler and bestseller content with the purely monetary reward all would be well. But he, and even more his promoter, wishes to enhance still more the profits accruing, by gilding the notoriety obtained in this (quite legitimate) traffic, by stealing the haloes from the statues of the saints: by appropriating the homage formerly reserved for great achievements of the mind, and putting it to commercial uses. In this way the cash-value of what they have to sell is notably augmented: and our binary system of two cultures, with distinct Publics, came into being. And gradually the 'low' Public — the commercially promoted Majority — has come to claim that is is the real, the best, and the only, one.

Notes

[1] W. H. Hudson (1841-1922), Argentinian-born novelist and naturalist, spent his adult life in England. Rima is the central figure in his best-known novel *Green Mansions* (London, 1904). Epstein's sculptured panel of Rima in the Hudson Memorial in Hyde Park created a great stir at its unveiling in 1925.

[2] Frank Salisbury (1874-1962), painter of portraits, historical and ceremonial subjects, did portraits of royalty, prime ministers and church dignitaries. He portrayed many leading Americans, including the five presidents from Coolidge through Eisenhower, and such figures as J. Pierpont Morgan and John D. Rockefeller.

[3] I.e., pounds, shillings, pence.

CHAPTER IV

THE CRISIS OF MANAGERIAL CONCEIT

WHAT is to be predicated of a civilisation that has cut itself in two, and driven into an abusively labelled pen (the minor and despised one of the two unequal parts) all that is most creative and intelligent in it? Any member of this 'intelligentsia' who challenges the justice and the wisdom of this division, collects bad marks against himself, as *extra-pernickety*. Yet all the population suffers (since no man gains anything from misusing, or not using, his mind) because of the isolation and stultification of its most intellectually energetic and imaginative individuals. Were these not relegated to what is little better than a concentration camp, and condemned to impotence in this way, the cultural standards of the English-speaking societies would be very different from what they are.

Responsibility for the Majority Public must in the first place be laid at the door of monopoly-capital and mass-production. Then there is a psychological explanation, too. The ubiquitous power-bug has a part in this herding, and in the low quality of the herd. — To deny to other people the means of understanding obviously gives great satisfaction to many, as is sufficiently demonstrated by the orgy of unnecessary censorship, when war comes. *They* know what is going on: 'The Public' does not.

Again, to keep other people in mental leading-strings, to have *beneath* you a broad mass of humanity to which you (although no intellectual giant) can feel agreeably superior: this petty and disagreeable form of the will-to-power of the average 'smart' man counts for much in the degradation of the Many. And there is no action of this same 'smart' man that is more aggravating than the way in which he will turn upon the critic of the social scene (who has pointed out the degradation of the Many) and accuse him of 'despising the People'.

The instinct to be 'big' at the expense of the Many, to acquire superiority by means of impoverishing others mentally, turned the other way round — upwards instead of downwards — accounts for much of the hatred of the 'intellectual'. — In a thoroughgoing analysis a number of minor causes would have to be considered: but these two factors, with all their ramifications, are the decisive ones: namely (1) the perennial instinct of man to feel superior, and (2) the discovery by monopoly-capital of this novel eldorado, the democratic mass-public.

So people have deteriorated. They have neither the will nor common sense of the peasant or guildsman, and are more easily fooled. This can only be a source of concern and regret, to all except 'the leader of men'.

The Russian People, who have never had to pass through the cheapening process to which for a hundred years the English and Americans have been subjected, respond to art stimuli of a more severe and serious order — plays, ballets, books — than would be possible for our Public.

It is not our Public that is to blame, then — any more than it is the fault of the English labouring man, of the navvy type, that he is like an artificially preserved prehistoric creature. He no longer signs his name with a cross—as he still did when first permitted to vote. But they were very careful in giving him the vote not to give him at the same time the mind (which education supplies) to use it with understanding.

The mind of the 'petit-bourgeois' Public (and in this we must include the rank and file professional man) is not much above the labouring man. This bourgeois Public have been denied education as much as he has— or, better, cultivation: that most valuable part of education, such as is provided by good books or good plays, beautiful buildings, intelligent recreations, travel and leisure. These it does not possess—because it has been supplied profusely with 'what it wants'. And 'what it wants', its mentors and purveyors decided, was all that is most banal and platitudinous, the sugary and the violent. — It would be wholly absurd if it were held responsible for being what it is: for remaining in the low I.Q. category. How could it be otherwise, seeing that it has been locked up in that category by the purveyors of cheap sensation, sob-stuff, 'glamorous' sex? — Just as the 'highbrow' — in his compulsory divorce from the People — has been locked up in his 'high' attic, or in his Ivory Tower.

———

Thus prepared, we may now speak of what may grow into a crisis of respect for human kind — let alone a crisis of altruism, for altruism cannot survive in the existentialist atmosphere of these times, pervading the ruins of Europe. But this crisis is in part the outcome of the existence of the 'lowbrow' mass, whose origins I have been considering. Also playing its part, is the deliberate brutalisation of the 'lower orders' by the Victorian, and the post-Victorian. The new men as a rule are intellectuals. Whereas their opposite numbers in Russia, whatever may be said of stalinism, do not suffer from a *lady and gentleman* complex. There are few Englishmen who do not. Will the new men here since 1945 retain a decent respect for the 'little man' of the capitalist cartoon; the small suburbanite, the football and dog racing crowds, the ant-like swarms on the summer beaches, suddenly become his clients?

I will digress in order, in passing, to examine the specifically *national* factor. Men who make revolutions are, through it all, Frenchmen, Russians, or Englishmen. The worst blemish in the English character is not, as many people would have it, hypocrisy: it is that the Englishman is a congenital snob. This fact seems to me of importance to socialism — though I am often told it is not. Will the Englishman divest himself of his snobbery, as he passes over into the new social order: or will he take it with him — assuming, in its new environment, horrible and unexpected forms? Will the Stalin of England insist that he is of an awfully good family, and will it be high treason to remind him that his papa hawked fish in the New Cut? Will the shoddy genius of the Old School Tie go hand in hand with this British version of the Commissar?

There has been 'Labour', but in England socialism has mostly existed as salon-socialism, up till now: a middleclass monopoly. I know and have met great numbers of socialists but only two or three issuing from the working-class. — You would think that a young middleclass man, when he decided to dedicate himself to the emancipation of the working-class, would lay aside for good the old school tie, and with it the degrading emotions of idiot-pride in the not very interesting fact that his 'people' floated at a respectable middleclass distance above the gutter. You would think he would dump all that into the trash-can and try and be serious.

But this as a rule does not happen: among Popular Front acquaintances I have met with more straight social snobbery than anywhere else. Where one had thought only to find a passion for social justice, one so often discovers nothing but an unlovely little power-complex. Snob and socialist are not regarded as mutually exclusive terms in England. And this feudal atavism, or, as it usually is, hangover from the Servants-hall, has not been by any means confined to the small-fry. — When, many years ago, I met Prince Kropotkin, I detected no sign that he remembered that once he had been a Prince. That he had left behind, along with his fortune, when he went into a most honourable exile. Perhaps this is easier for an aristocrat: it is easier to leave a great deal, possibly, than to turn your back upon something insignificant.

It is abashed that we learn — in the book of her friend and biographer — that Beatrice Webb could not manage to like the working-class.[1] Was she just an interfering middleclass Victorian lady, then, troubled with a power-complex? That great Irish gentleman, Mr. Bernard Shaw, in his obituary notice of H. G. Wells (*New Statesman*, Aug. 17, 1946), goes on like some snobbish schoolboy about Wells's parents, who, it seems, were not so rich as Mr. Shaw's. Oh dear me!

Now I will return to the crisis of respect for human kind — present, or rapidly developing. In politics this can have terrible results: for those in power then begin pushing men around as if they were chessmen, not of flesh and blood. The 'managerial' type are exponents of an advanced inhumanity. Some have seen in the present social democratic administration in England examples of the 'managerial' type. — With that view I am not in agreement, though it is too early to come to any final conclusion. All government is management. Because these more honest men do not govern in a smart underhanded way like their predecessors, they expose themselves to partisan misrepresentation as *over* governing that is all.

James Burnham gave a name to a class to which he belonged himself, by temperament.[2] And no feudal class ever acquired so superior an attitude towards its dupes and dependents as the 'new managerial' type shows towards its prospective, or actual, clients, the multitude. Herr Hitler (picked by Burnham as a heroic and *successful* 'manager') produced, in his notorious treatise, what was among other things a handbook as to how most scientifically to fool the Many. In it he studies with a chuckling rapture the demagogy of Lloyd George — whose speeches he regarded as models of demagogic perfidy and sleight of hand.[3]

The crisis of respect for humanity is only assuming universal proportions today. But with world war i and its sequel it began already to appear. It has been immeasurably aggravated by world war ii and *its* sequels. The cheapening of human life — until we all have grown rather like doctors in our necessary callousness about the human animal, whose 'ideals' look sillier at every fresh homicidal outburst: the lowered standards of life ensuing upon war — all of this conspires to dethrone homo sapiens and to put in his place homo stultus, or the Yahoo of Swift. No one is to blame for this. It is human nature accomplishing its destiny. — The enemies of man do not point these things out, since they profit by them. And the friends of man get called his enemies.

Those engaged in publicity services or in popular entertainment — to go on with the catalogue of dehumanisation — cannot retain much respect for the million-headed Baby, whose mouth it is their job to make water, or from whose big blue eyes their job it is to extract buckets of tears. (Only a hypocritical propagandist would dispute the accuracy of this account of the mind of the publicist, or entertainer, always hard-boiled and professionally sardonic.) It is difficult to see how politicians, whose function it is to feed and to clothe it — to the accompaniment of howls for more food and more silk-stockings — can feel as warmly as they should towards it. And the people who best sell and potboil for it feel much the same. The pressman studies with entire detachment his paper's clients, whom he baits with titbits of highly flavoured news. And now, since the shortages in consumer goods and foodstuffs, there is yet another division of our society, namely that between shopman and customer. In England the queueing herds of shoppers, receiving their tiny ration or being fleeced for some absurdly over-valued article of household necessity, or ill-fitting preposterously priced garment, do not inspire respect, and certainly do not receive it. I speak particularly of the English scene and Europe generally.

There are, when you come to think of it, great numbers of people almost obliged to feel little respect for man in the mass: respect for what I have called — not out of disrespect but as a means of obliging the reader to focus the situation in all its horrible bleakness — the million-headed Baby.

It is impossible, Renan believed, *d'aimer 'le peuple' tel qu'il est* — to love the People the way they are. They have first to be trained. But training has not been forthcoming for the one class, and has been taken away from the other — for the professional classes once shared in the cultivation of their rulers. Rather than cure that great big Baby 'the Public', as is done with children, of its worst habits, it has deliberately confirmed it in them. And just now its stocks are lower than at any period since its birth — lip service notwithstanding. The puny minority of creative men too, let me repeat, enjoy less consideration than at any former time. How identical are the destinies of these two categories of men, separated seemingly by an abyss.

Notes

[1] Beatrice Webb (1858–1943) was the wife of Sidney Webb (Fabians both) with whom she wrote the comprehensive history of *English Local Government*, 9 vol. (London, 1906-29). See Margaret Cole, *Beatrice Webb* (London, 1945).

2 James Burnham, *The Managerial Revolution* (New York, 1941). He discusses Hitler in chs. 11 and 15.

3 Adolf Hitler, *Mein Kampf*, trans. Ralph Mannheim (London, 1969), p. 433 on Lloyd George: "Precisely in the primitiveness of his language, the primordiality of its forms of expression, and the use of easily intelligible examples of the simplest sort lies the proof of the towering political ability of this Englishman."

CHAPTER V

THE THICKENING TWILIGHT OF THE ARTS

HAD Milton or Voltaire been born in Carthage, they would never have given literary expression to their thoughts. Only the State spoke there. It did not speak of social justice, either, or of the sanctity of the human soul. No one had ever heard of the Individual in the city of Hannibal. And this would apply of course to Tartary and Turkestan, and many other places.

A 'public' is a feature of Graeco-roman civilisation. — But *two* Publics is the beginning of no Public at all.

With my account of the Two Publics — not a parable but a fact — I have explained the great fundamental handicaps with which all creative intelligences in the Twentieth Century are born. It may be compared to a physical disability, lameness or curvature of the spine. It affects them as radically.*

Had Lord Byron been writing *à coeur ouvert* about himself he most likely would have started by speaking of his lameness — and how in spite of it he swam the Hellespont. H. G. Wells (seeing that this is England, where there are things worse than a hump or a club-foot) would begin with the poverty of his father and mother. With the author of 'The Idiot' it would be his epilepsy. — These are first things. So I began by showing you the English writer or artist finding himself restricted to a Public not much larger than that possessed by the research worker, or that existing in the academic field. A botanist's audience is no smaller or more specialised than the author of 'The Way of all Flesh' secured, or 'The Dubliners', or an early Lawrence.

If a writer complains of this situation, the retort is as follows: 'If you say your Public is unrepresentative and small, write books like Daphne du Maurier and you will have a Public as representative as that of Dante.' If it is a painter, here is what is said: 'Paint pictures like Brockhurst and you will have a Public as wide and representative as Titian's.' — All this is something not of our making: our will is not engaged, I wanted to begin by getting down the things that are as remote from the individual volition as being English or being such and such a height in your 'stocking feet'. The Public influences everything: Joyce's 'Finnegans Wake' was conditioned by it, or the pictures of Paul Klee.

The two artists I happen to have mentioned suggest a postscript to what I have been saying regarding the two Publics. The first named is a specialist's book, the second are a specialist's pictures. Neither has any organs for the outer atmosphere of the market-place, or where 'the brute male force of the wicked world which marries and is given in marriage' has its being. Both inhabit the thickening twilight of the arts, both are creatures adapted to that twilight: or call it if you like an interior or a

---

* The troubles of the man of science take a rather different form, and with them I leave it to someone better qualified than I am to deal.

subterranean world. For specialists in literature and painting they exist for no one else, except students who hear them lectured about by highbrow professors, and a few dozen curious minds here and there. Yet is one to pretend that the audiences that rocked or wept in the Attic Theatres in response to works by Aristophanes or Aeschylus were in the presence of an inferior truth; and is a work of art more profound because its meaning is mysteriously wrapped up in however dexterously packed a verbiage?

There are many intellectuals who say that the artist should inhabit the same world as the saints, or at least one as secluded from 'the brute male' extroversions of the human average. It is but another case — although they would not admit it — of shyness of the 'common man', of the market-place. For these the Two Publics arrangement does not seem amiss. They might perhaps say that what I am describing as a 'reservation' would be justified if only because it enabled the cultivation of such esoteric beauties, in the half-lit antechambers of the Unconscious, as those produced by Joyce in the last phases of his life, or those for which the precious and exquisite *petit-maître* of the Bauhaus was responsible.[1]

Enjoying as I do this kind of work (being a specialist) I am as alive as any pundit to the fact that this exclusive 'highbrow' workshop, catering for a small Public, has something remarkable to show for itself. Out of its very limitations and frustrations, it has created something. Its little dark and stony desert has flowered. Like a prison-art, or the introspection of the recluse, or the strange genius of the demented, it will survive in some form, as an integral part of our cultural expression. Some people would treat it as a permanent institution; and why not?

These considerations, however, in no way cause me to qualify my indictment of the Two Publics. The Russians are correct when (for their own purposes) they condemn the art of the *avant-garde* in Western countries — 'unrealistic, romantic, and mystical' — for its 'separation from the people'. But it should be recognised that the 'people' here has been degraded by commercial standards, or, lower down, by its relegation to the status of a beast of burden; and indeed that the artist has been, in the manner described above, *kept away* from them.

Art of the first order must be lost in this cul-de-sac. A whole society, not an unrepresentative fragment, is demanded by great gifts of speech and great interest in public affairs such as Dante or Milton possessed, for instance. The public stage, with live actors — in contrast to the private Mystery, staged in a rich patron's cellar, for an audience of cognoscenti of shadow pictures of an obscure emotional underworld — is what now stands empty. With his architectonic appetites, requiring air-filled spaces, for Buonarotti[2] there would be no place today, nor would there be for most of the so-called 'great masters' of the past.

The artist has not 'escaped', or 'fled from', the outer world of men in general, of reality: he has been *driven* from it. There the philistine business-man and his satellites have it all to themselves. A materialism such as Rome at its worst never knew has invaded everything: we only speak of 'culture', as of religion, when engaged in a world-war now: and then it is only the bureaucrats brought into being to promote 'culture' who get any-thing out of it, not the artist.

Before leaving the subject of the Two Publics I should like to say something with reference to life within the small highbrow compound, or, better, Reservation; more especially that part of it inhabited by the painters. Traditionally impecunious, it exercises a fatal attraction of a social order for moneyed outsiders. Then it offers an excuse of idleness and temperamental behaviour too. All of which represents a most unwelcome complication for more serious artists.

We artists do rather live like an Indian tribe, the relics of another civilisation, in a Reservation. Rich visitors can come among us: they are initiated into the tribal mysteries, becoming 'blood-brothers' — just the way it happens with the Indians of Taos, or some other dusty centre of exotic tourism.

The Indians, you will recall, from what you have read of such resorts, begin to turn out art-objects for sale to these seasonal intruders. When they do that, naturally the work so produced loses greatly in artistic value. So long as a totemic object is carved or painted in response to the demands of a tribal cult, it has the power inherent in all belief. Producing it for sale to tourists — or to 'blood-brothers' who have bought their way in — is another matter. And so it is with the 'Highbrow' tribe.

It has always been my feeling that these patrons are a curse. I have not concealed my feelings, much to the rage of the patrons. These people intrigue, too, and interfere in tribal affairs. — As if without such extra irritations it were not bad enough being little better than a motheaten Indian, and living in the equivalent of an Indian Reservation!

But the choice of this 'romantic' imagery, for some readers perhaps, clothes with a misleading glamour what is in fact very squalid. The patron now is apt to live — as a privileged member of that small impecunious society — among his protégés. As may be conceived, in a calling so depressed and impoverished, he exercises much power. Quite small sums of money, expended in the purchase of pictures have an action like dynamite. Even, in certain cases, the rich intruder becomes a sort of dictator, which is not only undemocratic but undesirable for many reasons.

The indulgence of these instincts, on the part of a wealthy dilettante, might be beneficial if it were not for the fact that, unlike the dealer, his social preferences enter into it. As a rule these direct him, as do his other tastes, to what is second-rate, and to a lavish advertisement of what is not very good. The introduction of the less exacting values of the potboiling world outside may accompany such a régime: in Anglo-saxon countries this always is the danger.

Since, as I have said, he *lives* with those he supports, our Maecenas is repelled by personality, and attracted by the lack of it. So rebarbative a genius as Cézanne, or so uncomfortably intense a one as Van Gogh, or so arrogant a master as Whistler, would not make the ideally subservient dinner-guest. So, in such a little world, the handicap upon any over the light-weight class is formidable.

Renaissance patrons, who are the models generally for ours, were more robust. But what is involved is completely different. That was a great public matter, this a small private one. The patrons of other centuries were popes and princes, whose patronage altered the whole appearance of the world they lived in. Ours are small-time collectors.

Another troublesome feature is the hundreds of idle people who are drifting around, with or without money. Displaced persons, in truth, who find it convenient to live with the artists. They have swollen to unnatural proportions the ranks of Bohemia. The fact that during the last two decades this has come to be recognised as normal does not make it any better. It has again to be put on record to complete the picture here.

It is not yet quite a 'World Without Art': but Art is flickering out among these unrealities. A small body of people are still attempting to produce fine art and good literature; but it is impossible to exaggerate the difficulties. The artistic impulse, with no outlet in the public life of the community, has been consigned to what is, as I have called it, nothing but a Reservation: not of Indians still supplicating ancestral divinities, but of writers and other artists persisting in their devotions — very substantial sacrifices demanded of them, with terrible consequences if withheld — as under happier circumstances commanded the devotion of those who are now our 'classics', the great humane intelligences of the past.

Notes

1 The Bauhaus, a school of architecture and the applied arts inspired by William Morris, became the centre of modern design in Germany during the 1920s and established itself as almost a symbol of modernity in the thirties and forties. Klee taught there from 1920 to 1930.

2 I.e., Michelangelo Buonarotti.

CHAPTER VI

INTUITION VERSUS THE INTELLECT

OR IS THERE SUCH A THING AS AN 'INTELLECTUAL'?

SO far I have made no attempt to examine the term 'intellectual'. There was no occasion to do so. In the division of people into intellectuals, on the one side, and just nice ordinary decent people on the other, this colloquialism plays its part. Everyone knows what it means, and it means the same thing to everybody. For the purposes of describing and criticising that unhappy division I have accepted it as the approved counter. But now, in this long chapter, I am turning my back upon the popular scene: I shall enquire to what extent the Intellectual may be said to exist, except as an abusive figment of the popular mind.

In France — as is the case with so many other things — the term 'intellectuel' has greater definition and much more intellectual content than it has with us. And it is to an acrimonious battle of wits in the literary world of Paris that I now shall turn: for, as it happens, the term 'intellectual' plays a prominent part in this particular polemic.

———

Julien Benda's 'Trahison des Clercs' is a book which received a great deal of attention in England and America in the Thirties.[1] It is almost a modern classic. Here is a case in which a famous intellectual arraigns other intellectuals for their treachery to the intellect. And indeed, as I see the matter, his denunciation was, and is, fully justified. Benda employed the word 'clerc' (or clerk) however — at least for the title page. We generally find that archaic and Chaucerian word is used in French controversy when one writer is being disparaging about another, as so to speak a reserve epithet.*

The date of publication of Julien Benda's book is 1928. (I speak of course of the original French edition.) But there was another book published in 1914, which seems to have a great deal to do with it — although it is not referred to by M. Benda. This book was entitled 'Les Méfaits des Intellectuels.'[2] This latter is full of a doctrinaire violence: it is in fact an anti-intellectual verbal convulsion, whose author, Edouard Berth, was a disciple of Georges Sorel. And Sorel is a man of considerable importance: he was responsible for one of the most famous French books of the century, 'Réflexions sur la Violence', which was supposed to have inspired fascism, it being the *livre de chevet* of the first fascist, Mussolini.[3]

Berth's principal contemporary target was precisely M. Julien Benda, upon whom he delivers an attack of the most florid and clamorous pugnacity — and I cannot believe that it reached my ears but not those of

---

* As for instance: 'Je conçois la haine que nourissent pour cet Etat guerrier nos clercs laïques, etc.' — BERTH.

M. Benda. It seems therefore extremely likely that from 'Les Méfaits des Intellectuels' came the impulse for the writing of 'La Trahison des Clercs'. *Clercs* being, as I have said, another way of saying intellectuals, by the substitution of *intellectuels* for the former word one arrives at 'The Betrayal by the Intellectuals'. That and 'The Misdeeds of the Intellectuals' as titles are so very like as to suggest a close parentage. To my mind M. Benda's book is simply an answer to M. Berth's. In spite of the fact that 'La Trahison des Clercs' is in another class entirely, the two books can be most usefully studied together.

We will take Benda's first and I will employ throughout the word intellectual rather than clerk — which in English-speaking countries has not retained, as in France it has, something of its original status of scholar. — Benda's book is not directed against the intellectual, as such, at all. He has not — as have his opponents — any quarrel with the intellect, or objection to its free and indiscriminate use for the liquidation of pretentious humbug and the hundred other jobs it alone can perform. It is the *false* intellectuals only he wishes to castigate: not 'le vrai clerc', of that order of high and incorruptible intelligences to which belonged Malebranche, Goethe, La Bruyère, Renan. (Of this century I noted that he mentioned Proust and Valéry and that I think was all.) It is a novel type of intellectual, which at the time of writing had been there for little more than half a century, at which this great pamphlet is aimed.*

One of the dominant subjects in 'La Trahison des Clercs' is war; it is critical of the bellicose professors and bloodthirsty men of letters who were such a novel feature of the years immediately preceding world war i — and they were by no means absent from the scene in the years ushering in world war ii. The intellectual, he argues — meaning by intellectual or 'clerc' just any figure in the history of literature, since that is what any person writing a book is called today — that kind of man has always observed a proper detachment regarding matters of current controversy and to partisan passions of the moment. Remembering that earlier party-struggles turned at least as much upon religious as upon political issues, one is obliged to ask M. Benda whether Pascal's 'Lettres Provinciales' were really so blamelessly aloof from the controversial passion as all that: and as for pure politics, whether Voltaire's judgements showed that sublime impartiality that, according to Benda, those of a true 'clerc' should exhibit.

With great justness he accuses the latter-day intellectual, however, of being engaged in a very different type of work from that which occupied Pascal in exposure of abuses in the 'Lettres Provinciales' or that in which our own early pamphleteers so zealously indulged. He accuses them of going over, with all their apparatus of learning and literary magic, to the side of the political power-addict — the man-eater, the firebrand: further of as good as accepting the standards of the philistine. This he does not say in so many words, though the following amounts to that, it would seem to me — 'humilier les valeurs de connaissance devant les valeurs d'action'. The 'values of action' are always philistine values. And Berth's writings are, like his masters,

---

* Since that time, and very recently this writer has, I believe, engaged personally in politics. In that, of course, he has not observed his own teaching: but that does not make the teaching less good.

a long panegyric of action — of the sword at the expense, expressly, of the pen, the tommy-gun contrasted favourably with the typewriter.

The curious obsession of the modern intellectual with the warlike virtues is a subject to which we owe some of the best pages in this book.* The veneration for action, and for men of action, is a feature of Twentieth Century thinking. Hemingway is an obvious instance of a writer whose muse is married to Action. But in France and the continent in general some of the men most influential in this century — Nietzsche (for he belongs to the Twentieth), Sorel, Péguy, Maurras, Malraux, have exalted the life of action — and, what is also to be noted, have been followed because they did so. And it has not always been the most masculine or active who have responded to this vitalist gospel.

With all the energy at their disposal a majority of the modern intellectuals have striven to excite to passionate action — not to exhort to reflection or moderation, not applied to the reason, but always to the emotions: they have pointed passionately to the battlefield, the barricade, the place of execution, not to the life of reason, to what is harmonious and beautifully ordered. This is in fact *the betrayal*, specifically indicated by Benda.† Even to have served as a soldier, or to have followed the profession of arms, establishes a special claim, in some mysterious way, to literary honour: from which such men as Vauvenargues, Vigny, Péguy, are seen to benefit.

Benda insisted that this was something entirely new. Victor Hugo, for instance, was by no means a man to disparage action: yet he would not, as Benda says, have preferred Napoleon to, say, Galileo, or Shakespeare, or Erasmus.

———

Picking up some days ago a book of Léon Bloy's, the somewhat unexpected subject the soul of Napoleon Bonaparte,‡ I found myself attempting to plough through a bubbling mass of the customary inflated metaphor. Neo-catholicism and chauvinism were so indissolubly mixed that it was impossible to distinguish the Cross from the Sword.

Then I turned back to the title-page to discover the date of its publication. 1912 it turned out to be: two years earlier than Berth's 'Méfaits'. This pious old war-dog could smell the carnage shortly to begin: so he was building an ornate little shrine to Napoleon — bringing out the battle flags of Austerlitz and the Pyramids. Two years later Berth — his colleague in choleric neo-catholicism — would be composing his attack upon all those apt to interfere with the development of the war-psychosis. Bloy is a different proposition to Berth: he was one of the principal heroes of the catholic renaissance in France. Maritain and Raissa sat at his feet in the early days of their conversion. 'La Femme Pauvre' was a considerable book.[4] There is a sort of writing, however, that the French can tolerate which to the English reader is like melted chocolate cream and cotton wool thrust into the mouth at the same time. For my part I can only admit

* In a volume entitled 'Les sentiments de Critias' [Paris, 1917] it appears that Benda concentrates exclusively upon this.

† Cf. p. 195. 'Trahison de clercs'. [In the Norton issue of Aldington's trans. (New York, 1969), p. 158.]

‡ 'L'Ame de Napoléon.' — Léon Bloy. Mercure de France [Paris, 1912. No English trans.].

Bloy to my mind a few pages at a time. When a hundred lines or two of such vermiform verbiage as 'aussi inconnaissable que le tissue de combinaisons infinies de la Solidarité universelle' has wound its way into my mind, all cerebration stops, and I am obliged to put the book down. It belongs so much, however, to the same type of thinking (or better of feeling) as Berth's, that it will help to an understanding of the latter to quote two particularly apposite passages here. The first of these can be found on the second page of 'L'Ame de Napoléon'.

'Napoleon! We have there the Face of God in the shadows. . . . Napoleon is inexplicable and, without doubt, the *most* inexplicable of men, because he is, before all and above all, the Prefiguration of Him Who is to come and Who is not any longer perhaps very far away. . . .'

After another page or two I put the book down. When I opened it again it was at pp. 96–97, and there I found something about 'this naif great man of genius . . . sleeping under his "Star" '. But he had dreams: and eventually we find him a *sleep-walker* like Herr Hitler.

'Napoleon was a sublime sleeper, a somnambulic conqueror that the sufferings of others and his own caused to cry out during his sleep – whose cries brought terror to the extremities of the earth.' Beside this demigod – whose cries of suffering as he sleeps make the Polynesian quake, make the Hebridean shudder, cause the Mexican peon to catch his breath, and the hearts of the very whales in their polar retreat to miss a beat – the modest divinity to whom he was compared cuts a rather poor figure; being after all on the quiet side (and it has never yet been claimed that when Jesus died the Greeks and Romans in their cities experienced a wave of inexplicable terror).

Bloy's hero was a highly successful little Corsican gangster, whose fate and that of his lieutenants would have been much the same as that of Hitler and his ministers and Gauleiters, had Napoleon's enemies been better organised and had the English been Twentieth Century men, toughened by Twentieth Century anti-humanitarian propaganda, instead of Eighteenth Century men, softened by humanist philosophy.

This worship of the Man on horseback, the Man of Destiny, of the Man of blood, can be studied in Bloy as well as in Treitschke and Nietzsche, though I have never heard of anyone doing so, since he is a professional of the most convulsive piety.

Aggressive Frenchmen – Sorel, Barrès, Maurras,[5] Péguy – were, as much as the Prussian professors who usually get all the blame, pepping up the French for the slaughter.

Let my first quotation from Edouard Berth's 'Misdeeds of the Intellectuals' be read while Bloy's paeans to Napoleon are still ringing in our ears.

'From our humanitarian dream we were awakened, after 1905. We are patriots: since Tangiers, the preparation for a war with Germany has given renewed force to the French soul and as is natural has revived the religious spirit – war, this grandiose, sublime, and terrible reality, imposing an heroically pessimistic conception of life, a conception which it is impossible to reconcile with the insipid optimism of Eighteenth Century thought.

'One may observe the ideological consequences of the reintroduction of that great fact, *war*, into the contemporary consciousness. The bourgeoisie, in a national sense, reforms its ranks. Will it proceed to the restoration of the monarchy — thus confirming the dilemma of Sembat's book: namely, *Faites un roi, sinon faites de la paix.* Make your choice: either a King — or Peace!'*

That is Berth in 1914. His words had a quite different ring eleven years later, in 1925. But let me quote from something he wrote at this later date.

'That we are witnessing the *ruin of the modern world* — ruin which the "great war" (1914-18) will have helped not a little to precipitate and to consummate — about this there can be no doubt in the mind of any well-informed person.'†

So the excitable little child — going bang! bang! bang! with his toy pistol in 1913-14 — has learnt his lesson. And the noisy little German children, a hundred thousand marks worth a penny or two, had momentarily learnt their lesson as well.

———

To speak of Berth is to speak of Sorel; and indeed the best way to discuss 'Les Méfaits des Intellectuels' — which is Sorel and a great deal of soda-water, plus neo-catholicism — is simply to substitute for the Sorelian arguments of which it is full, the master himself. The meaning attached by Berth to the word 'intellectual' is precisely that which we find — expressed with more vigour — in various works of Sorel's.

Of all the apostles of dangerous living, pure action, 'heroism', blood and iron, Georges Sorel was the worst — the most shrewd and irresponsible. If not at his instigation it was under his inflammatory influence that Berth, in 1913-14, attacked everything and everyone capable of bringing a little moderation into the over-heated atmosphere. The same repressive propaganda, on the German side of the Rhine, proceeded from the harsher pens of pangermanist professors.

Sorel's masterpiece of incitement to violence was not, however, directed to inflaming chauvinism but to providing for the maximum of class-hatred. But there is no reason to suppose that he was a good socialist. Indeed, it was a matter of complete indifference to him which class got charged with hatred first: bourgeoisie or proletariat, it was all one. The bourgeoisie were all right, provided they loathed the proletariat so much that it increased the natural dislike of the poor class for the rich class. There was a beautiful detachment about Sorel. And Berth expressed himself as well pleased with the French bourgeoisie — they were getting splendidly warlike — though this was for another purpose than that envisaged by his master.

Sorel insists that 'the people' must retain their proletarian attributes. About this he is adamant. He shows extreme displeasure at Condorcet's mental habits,‡ where that Eighteenth Century worthy is found proposing to cure the people of their superstitions, so that the helpless Many may

---

* 'Méfaits des Intellectuels', p. 275.

† 'Les illusions du progrès' (p. 60). Georges Sorel.

‡ 'Les illusions du progrès' (p. 60). Georges Sorel. [*The Illusions of Progress*, trans. John & Charlotte Stanley (Berkeley & Los Angeles, 1969), pp. 27-28.]

cease to be the eternal dupes of their masters: so that a workman would be able to defend himself against political salesmanship, ballyhoo or charlatanry, or cure himself of prejudices and superstitions, 'by the use simply of his reason'. Sorel is rather like those lovers of the picturesque who resent the idea of hygiene and pedagogy, automobiles and telephones being introduced among those divine bug-ridden, half-idiot, backward populations — laden with junk-jewellery, and operatically costumed.

But just as it is important that *classes* should remain as they are, so should *nations*. And it is not only the proletariat or bourgeoisie which should be pumped full of hatred: he has plenty of venom left for the nations as a whole. It is obviously a good thing for the nations to preserve their hatreds and rivalries intact, and that still more of such combustible matter should be artificially generated. They should be full of 'race', and full of fight. He sees life as a kind of bear-pit or place where spirited cocks tear and scratch each other to pieces. — Like his master, Nietzsche, he is, in the last analysis, romantically Darwinian.* — Human society is red in tooth and claw. They are part of the murderous zoo of nature.

Berth announces in his 'Méfaits des Intellectuels' that he has become a royalist: and Sorel latterly had, one feels, from time to time to remind himself that he was supposed to be left of centre. But it would be very bad marxism, he explains† to treat the bourgeoisie with anything but admiration: even veneration. In devouring the bourgeoisie, as it is your marxian destiny to do (he tells the proletariat), you must accord them god-like honours. Did not the 'Communist Manifesto' declare that the bourgeoisie had been responsible for marvels beside which the Pyramids, Roman aqueducts, or gothic cathedrals were child's play? The bourgeois are people worthy of the highest honor.

Before, approximately, the year 1847, historians, philosophers and moralists were in the habit of demonstrating that Europe was in a bad way because of the inadequacies for centuries past, of governments in the hands of the rich classes. It had been a record of crimes and follies. The new society, they taught, which was in process of being born must correct all that, basing itself upon the humanities and the precepts of the classic sages and fathers of the Church. Then came Marx and Engels. From that moment the above view became out of date. Thenceforth history has been taught quite differently.

Far from there being anything wrong with the behaviour of the rulers of Europe, the reigning bourgeoisie, they were perfect miracle-workers. Of course they had to be devoured, just as they had devoured the feudal ruling class who preceded them. That was the law of nature, killing and devouring (the only unfortunate thing being that there would be nothing left afterwards to devour the proletariat). But 'the revolutionary workers must find their inspiration in the works of bourgeois economy, in order to realise similar marvels themselves'. This is why practically all socialism to-day is a tough capitalist-socialism.

* Just as all the Russian writers were said 'to come out of the Cloak of Gogol', so this strange Gallic litter of intellectual fire-eaters derive from Nietzsche, whose influence in France, in the first decade of the century, was enormous.

† 'La Ruine du Monde Antique' ([Paris, 1925; 2nd ed.] p. xxiv). Georges Sorel.

From this it can be seen that a disciple of Sorel's would not find it very difficult to get a little absent-minded about the proletariat and to feel quite warmly towards the bourgeoisie. Even he might okay a king: which was what Berth did. All the wars, usuries, tortures, inhumanity, oppressions of the rich classes and rulers of the immediate past, far from being crimes (as the humanitarians and rationalists had taught) were perfectly normal form for a healthy and vigorous society. But we may really now let Berth take up the tale and offer us his definition of the term *intellectual.*

Berth's book breathes war from the first page to the last. One of his definitions of an 'intellectual' would be 'a man who does not love war'. In justifying his adherence to monarchism his main argument is that kings love war. In fact, they *are* war. Thus:

'The State, of which Maurras's monarchy would in effect be the reinstatement, is of the following kind . . . a State that is *non-intellectual*; a State, I mean to say, restored to its essential functions and true nature, which is *to be War incarnate.*' This kind of State would cease to be 'the prey of Intellectuals' and 'the instrument of their rule . . . the modern democratic State'.*

A State is, in other words, a society organised for war. What is natural for all States is to be bracing themselves to spring upon another State. But the Intellectual is always attempting to defeat the ends of nature: is in his essence *anti-natural.* Because he knows it is natural to engage in war, he of course proposes a society that would never go to war, and would subsist in an unnatural state of peace. — So the first thing to remember about the Intellectual is that he abhors the natural, and attempts to replace it by something ideal and artificial. The State-form that is typical of him is democracy — the most artificial theory of the State extant.

Berth's neo-catholicism is so deafeningly noisy (like that of Bloy) that any not of his opinion are bludgeoned with his minatory diatribes. Religion, for this foolish dervish, is merely an excuse to roar. He is a *neo* and more royalist than the royalists and the uproar of his devotions fills the Parisian firmament. He is nothing if not traditionalist. True aristocracy, he tells us, has nothing intellectual about it: 'it is warlike and heroic — traditional, historic. It rests upon carnal realities: upon the *blood,* upon *physical heredity,* upon *race'.* — We are in an atmosphere of hitlerite Blut und Boden; but at the same time ferociously catholic, royalist, and still a little marxist. It is, in fine, a curious piece of French political baroque.

Where Berth tells us what Democracy — his bugbear — really is, it sounds like a lowbrow credo in reverse. Democracy is 'profoundly intellectual: it is anti-traditional, anti-physical, . . . anti-realist, idealist: it will only recognise *des esprits purs,* a detachment from all historic and natural links, floating above time and space, in the contemplation of *des idées claires* — ideas *clear* and *distinct'.†* And needless to say, adds Berth, people of this kind have nothing to do with the *people,* who are much nearer to a good old carnal King; with a dozen fat mistresses, adoring war and fond of *la chasse* (when he can't be killing men he kills as many animals as

* 'Les Méfaits des Intellectuels'. — Edouard Berth.
† 'Méfaits', etc. (p. 43).

possible), and, in fine, doing all the things the People would like to do if they had the opportunity. No beastly *intellectualism* about your King, or Noble, or Priest, as there is about the modern democratic ruler — the Intellectual!

So let us note, before proceeding, that the Intellectual, in addition to being anti-natural, is anti-traditional, anti-physical (which is included no doubt in being anti-natural), anti-realist: is anti-historic (no respect for time), and, in conclusion, unsympathetic to the ordinary hearty specimen of humanity, who is of course too near to nature to suit him.

———

The key-word which releases the full flood of Berth's wrath, however, is the word *reason*. For it is the function of the Intellectual to reason, he deals in the *rational* — unlike Berth who relies entirely upon his intuitive equipment, and regards the Reason as the arch spoil-sport and the principle that stands in opposition to nature.

Complications arise, notwithstanding, for Berth. Maurras is for him a master only second to Sorel. Yet, alas, 'Maurras loves to exalt Reason, to defend the Intelligence; he has for romanticism in general, and *intuitionist* philosophers in particular a profound contempt. One knows what he thinks of Bergson!'

Now Bergson is a god of Berth's as well as Maurras. You can easily conceive therefore how extremely awkward this is for Berth. But he surmounts it by showing that Bergson's 'intuition' is really identical with classic Reason (a very different matter, he tells us, to plain Reason) without any difficulty. As to the damaging fact that Maurras is always defending the Intellect — and indeed it is glaringly obvious that this eminent royalist is an arch-intellectual — that is solved in a similar manner. 'The rationalism of Maurras is a *classical rationalism*, that is to say realism: it is in complete opposition to democratic rationalism, which is idealism.' Maurras, like Proudhon, or like Sorel, has attacked idealism as it exists today. The *idea* has become impregnated with 'anarchic sentiment'.

But he has so little difficulty in overcoming little inconsistencies of that order for a very good reason. He advertises the superbest doctrinaire contempt for logic. The *pensée maîtresse* of Proudhon — the revered ancestor of Sorel — was decisive for him. It had provided him as it were with a carte blanche* to commit himself to any statement some passing emotion had suggested, without having to stop to consider whether it contradicted some statement he had made the day before. For the 'master idea' of Proudhon's was that consistency was made for slaves. Berth took the fullest advantage of this.

If you add the fact that the famous 'idée claire' of Descartes was one of Sorel's particular bêtes noires — and consequently one of Berth's — you

---

* The reference is to Proudhon's attitude to antinomies, which caused the head-on collision of opposite theories of property.

can imagine the facility with which the latter disposes of any antinomy —
and the chaos that reigns in the pages of the 'Méfaits'!

With the name of Descartes — and with the introduction of this new
counter, logic — we get nearer to the clarification I was seeking when I
undertook the writing of this chapter. Sorel — with his customary clarity —
expounds his intuitional principles. 'In our day,' he writes,* 'the belief
that everything is susceptible of a perfectly clear explanation is not by
any means less strong than it was in the time of Descartes. If one takes it
into one's head to protest against this illusion of rationalism, immediately
one finds oneself regarded as an enemy of democracy.' Sorel insists, and
his disciple Berth after him, that democracy and rationalism must be
bracketed, since one is merely the political expression of the other.
'The great question today is to teach men to reason well,' he points
out. 'From that proceeds the extraordinary importance attached to logic.'
— But the objective of the criticism undertaken by Sorel (and so of that
of Berth) is not philosophic, but ideologic. Sorel obviously is not interested
philosophically in the contrasting minds of Descartes and Pascal. It is
to the successful and self-assured society to which the teaching of Descartes
would lead — and did in fact lead — that he objected. In such a society there
would be no scope for all that *heroism* which was his stock in trade and
which you could not have without a great deal of 'the tragic'. A sultry
and catastrophic landscape was to Sorel's liking, for it was such conditions
that were propitious for his genius. Looking backward, the Eighteenth
Century greatly disgusted him: the Age of Reason, with its attempt to
eliminate everything from life which produces misery and violence, and
so tragedy (which in its turn produces heroism, of which there must be
a professor named Sorel).
So he was not at all concerned with questions as to whether as Descartes
believed the individual mind is competent to gauge the validity of its
deliverances: or whether, on the other hand, we are, with Pascal, content
to avail ourselves of what is there, responsive to our techniques, without
'useless definition' — unreally existing as we do between two mysterious
infinities.†6 No: his partisanship (and so that of Berth) in favour of the
mysticism of Pascal, as against the rationalism of Descartes, was not because
Sorel himself was a mystic. Anything but. His mind was not only extremely
rational, he was described as being — privately and socially — a relisher, in
a cynical spirit, of the droller aspects of human controversy. Mysticism
and its enigmatic and shadowy regions were more propitious for crimes of
violence — that was all. People were more open to take the tragic plunge

---

* 'Les illusions du progrès' (p. 50). [Eng. trans., p. 22.]
† 'Elle suppose donc que l'on sait quelle est la chose qu'on entend par ces mots: mouve-
ment, nombre, espace: et, sans s'arrêter à les definer inutilement, elle en pénètre la nature
et en découvre les merveilleuses propriétés. . . .
'La principale comprend les deux infinités qui se rencontrent dans toutes, l'une de grandeur,
l'autre de petitesse'. *Pensées. — Pascal.*

required of them in such a mental atmosphere, than in the bland and sunlit world of Eighteenth Century thought.

———

Returning to Berth the 'socratic Greeks' share that gentleman's scorn with the men of the Eighteenth Century. *Intellectualism* is inseparable, as he sees it, from the notion of *intelligibility*: both made a great point of an intelligible universe. To want things clear-cut and consistent is to be an *intellectual*: so far we are still with Sorel. (The criticism of the 'socratic infatuation with knowledge', was a Nietzschean theme.)

Berth's rampant neo-catholicism, however, is directing him when he tells us that 'christianity' has, in place of the clarity and dull serenity of hellenic culture, 'substituted the *clair-obscur* of vast cathedrals: the enormous and half-lighted vessel' (for one of the cathedrals has become a majestic ship) 'seems to point its prow into the infinite, borne upon a tempestuous sea and guided in the night by the solitary *étoile du Berger*'.

In M. Berth we see Faustian Man at his most floridly Faustian. He exults in the 'abysses' which have opened for our profounder vision as Christians, delights in the huge sable shadows cast by the doctrine of original sin, and in the grandiose pessimism which imposes on us the sensations of the most unrelieved tragedy. With that he will scornfully contrast the pitiable optimism of Classic Man, or Eighteenth Century positivism, or Doubting Descartes, that positivist before his time; or lastly such despicable contemporaries as Julien Benda. (Everything with him exists as a superlative. All he approves of is grandiose, staggering, superb, or formidable: no one is merely 'wrong-headed' or uninteresting, but *despicable*.) He never ceases to marvel how *anyone*, with such superb misery and so much glorious tragedy to be gloated over on all hands, should be found to give a thought to so second-rate a thing as *happiness*!

I began by outlining the argument of 'La Trahison des Clercs': and now I have given some idea of what Berth and his master Sorel stood for (attempting to transmit, as I went along, a little of the empty clatter of the former). The type of criticism levelled at Julien Benda in 'Les Méfaits des Intellectuels' it is easy to guess.

Actually the treatment of Benda is on the 'tough' side. He is referred to by Berth as 'our fakir lost in the contemplation of his intellectual navel', as a 'gutless monster', a 'cissy' or *femelle*, a 'metaphysical Jew', a 'cur' (roquet), the 'quintessence and the fin du fin of modern intellectualisme'. — He is treated, in fine, as the arch exponent of all that Berth and those of his way of thinking detest: the champion of the 'idée claire', as one opposed to the intuitional and the mystical, apostle of the pacific as opposed to the pugnacious — of optimism as opposed to pessimism.

My reason for selecting these particular controversialists will I think be obvious. On both sides 'intellectual' (or 'clerc') is not used in a complimentary sense: for both knew the power of the written word, and neither likes to see it employed against the principles he professes. For myself, Benda seems to have the better case. On the other hand Berth and Sorel have a precise meaning for this term when they make use of it (which is no doubt why Benda preferred the word 'clerc', for his rejoinder). When these literary bravos hurl it at somebody, they signify a person who attaches an undue importance to the deliverances of the *intellect* — and so may appropriately be designated as an *intellectual*. I am not at all suggesting that this charge can be dismissed as an empty one. Quite the contrary: it seems to me that people are much too intellectual quite frequently. But when these criticisms are used in the interests of violence and emotional excess, that is a different question.

I should like to make this clear. Were it simply the old cartesian quarrel that was in question, I should go over to the side of the Sorelians: not because I should object to the prospect of a habit of universal doubt — not because Descartes supplied a ready-made rational equipment for the enlightened layman — no harm in that: but because I should agree with Pascal and with Newton that the human reason is a toy of very limited availability.* But, as I have already pointed out, Sorel is a political polemist and is not interested in the matter from that standpoint at all (and as for Berth, a *pensée* of Pascal is merely a convenient brick to throw at an opponent). The use Sorel and his satellites make of their anti-cartesian technique I regard as dangerous and childishly irresponsible: whereas Benda used his rationalism to humane, sensible, and social ends.

Insensibly I have been led into discussing things, however, which seem to require more than a footnote, if my own position is to be understood. So let me resort to an image, and so describe my general reaction to the central problems emerging from the polemics of these people. Those of the intuitionist persuasion, as much as exponents of the 'idée claire', commit one to this. For they attach their usually frivolous arguments to fundamentals: and I am afraid that one cannot arrive at an intelligent judgement upon their use of the world 'intellectual' (which is our ultimate purpose in this chapter) if you ignore the values involved in their credentials, which refer us to the great sources of our thinking, as modern men.

Making use then of an image (not elaborated — not to be leant on too heavily or it would collapse) it might be said we are performing our several parts in an intricate play, of doubtful merit, upon a stage the lofty and cavernous wings of which lead immediately into the darkest night. We know if we move into them there awaits us a precipice we should not see, but suddenly there would be nothing solid there under our feet — a chasm limitless in depth, literally with *nothing* at the bottom of it. How do we know there

---

* The above, needless to say, is no more than a hasty pointer. For all speculations or surmise, or exercise of the imagination, to be under an interdict (on the ground that nothing can be known, so why guess?) would be rather a bleak and lifeless situation. When one reads Mr. Ayers ('Language, Truth, and Logic' [London, 1936]) one admires Mr. Ayers' logical toughness: but the positivism of Descartes comes to look a quite lively affair by contrast, for all his rule of rigorous incredulity, by comparison with this homely, impassible, intellectual detective-sergeant.

Again, if one immemorial myth obtained a monopoly, and it was accepted that if you were to dream, or to indulge in fictions, it must always be *that* dream and *that* fiction, all others being tabu: then the imagination must experience an inevitable revolt.

is nothing — that it is a fall that can never end? That is one of the things we know. Such, in physical terms, is our situation.

Who we can be, incredible cast of ratiocinatory animals that we are, how we got upon this narrow, infinitely precipitous peak (if that is it) — why we play the piece we do — to all such questions there is no rational or even imaginable answer.

But that we should not make ourselves passably comfortable, or 'happy', while we are here, for this brief performance, I can never see, nor why we should be hysterical, or glory in our lot. Comedy perhaps is a better *genre* for such a situation than tragedy: and because we are tragic beings, whatever way you look at it, is it a consistency imposed on us to drench this stage with our blood and with our tears? Since we are all condemned to death, *à bref délai*, is that a reason for brutally and murderously attacking one another — does that make it any better?

———

By dint of careful analysis of this group of books the word 'intellectual' has acquired at least a distinct meaning for us. The 'intellectual', as seen I think by Sorel or Berth, is the man of theory, who deals in abstractions rather than in concrete and smoking-hot realities: who applies a rational rather than an emotional standard of value to everything: who would bend and distort nature until it conform to his ideal. He is theorist, rationalist, and idealist.

In politics he is the 'planner', in religion the ascetic, or puritan or purist, in art the 'abstractist' (the purist there also). Accordingly the jansenist, calvinist, or puritan would seem to belong to the same intellectual type as the cubist or constructivist; or the latter to that of jacobin or 'Babouviste' or any whole-hogging contemporary 'planner'.

As to his *name*, the intellectual derives that, as we have seen, from his display of an inordinate belief in, and reliance upon, the human intellect. Sorel bestows upon him a genealogy which would indicate Descartes as the first of his line in the modern age: the cartesians, with their reliance upon the human reason, their contempt for the romantic, the mystical, and intuitional, were the first 'intellectuals', Sorel would say — those monsters who have gained control of the modern world.

The term 'intellectual' *can* be provided with a clear — and even useful — significance of this kind, I believe. But the above formula narrows it down too much, excluding several types of men who would qualify in a classification such as I should draw up, for instance. Something rigorous, hard, and cold in the way of thinking: the rational rather than the emotional approach — without limiting it historically in any way — would be the first steps in identification.

It would never be a term the definitiion of which could be pushed too far. There are so many kinds of intellectual. In thinking of those writers I have been closest to — Eliot, Joyce, and Pound — all would answer to that description; very fastidious minds, each in his department very rigorous, each accommodated with a private critic, as it were, in attendance upon his creative faculty, who would make composition a stern labour. They are people who would be immediately identified as 'intellectuals', of course in Anglo-saxon countries. Yet there is no classification of the genus that would include them but exclude Rupert Brooke or Hardy, say.

These three contemporaries of mine would answer to some, but by no means to all, of Sorel's requirements. Eliot, for instance, would be justifiably indignant should he hear Descartes described as his intellectual progenitor. Joyce was hardly a democrat. Pound is nearer to the intuitionists than to the rationalists.

For none of these three writers of remarkable genius — to signalise yet another complexity — was war a question that ever particularly exercised their minds, I believe I am right in saying. — No great christian teacher since Tertullian has regarded it as amiss for a christian to bear arms, in a just cause.* But what war that was ever fought was an 'unjust' war, except of course that waged by the enemy?

Speaking of course with some diffidence, I should imagine that Eliot's view would be that of the great doctors of the Church: whereas Pound has lived too long with the *trouvères* to regard war as anything but a romantic institution. As to Joyce, he took no interest in such matters, one way or the other. I never discussed those problems with him, but if I had I know what would have happened. He would have searched in his memory for what Aristotle has said on the subject, and we should have ended as far away from the contemporary scene as Archimedes, or the Trojan Horse.

It is a curious fact, but there is no great English writer for whom war was a subject of major interest, as it was with Tolstoy. Much less is there one who was sufficiently possessed of it to have made of it a master work, as was 'War and Peace'. And if there had been such a man, he would have been of the Doughty or Col. Lawrence type, and the work would not have been undertaken to denounce war, but to glorify it. — Then, of course, the English did not overrun half the world for nothing.†

The subtitle of this chapter reads: 'Is there such a thing as an Intellectual?' So let me, in concluding, summarise my answer to that question. — If you, for the purpose of belittling him, affix the term 'intellectual' (or more familiarly 'highbrow') to any man of conspicuous intelligence, or whose standards notoriously are not those of the market-place, then there is such a thing only in your stupid mind, or on your foolish lips. But there is another and more serious sense, in which such a term may be admitted, and even serve a useful purpose.

The definition of 'intellectual' would be no easy task, as this chapter has proved. Julien Benda — deliberately ignoring all who did not fit in — would have defined it as a learned man prostituting his high function and inciting others to violence. His polemical opposites would say (scowling at Benda)

* Suarez apparently saw clearly that war was hopelessly unchristian (De Caritate. Disputatio, xiii) [*Selections from Three Works of Francisco Suarez, S.J.* The Classics of International Law, No. 20 (London, 1944), pp. 799-865] but he reasoned that war does not in itself involve hatred: 'punishment of a crime is quite consistent with goodwill towards the criminal'. Consequently you may, as a soldier, plunge your bayonet into the heart of an enemy, while still loving him as a christian should.

† The only English writer I can think of who, under other circumstances, might quite well have written a 'War and Peace' was the greatest of all, namely William Shakespeare.

that it denoted a democrat in an Ivory Tower, preaching peace and plenty — in contrast to war and want. All I need say, as my final word on this subject, is that few intellectuals are to be found who are prepared to oppose the Zeitgeist. The latter is committed to courses which, if pursued to their logical ends, will wipe out all that the human intellect has contrived, distinguishing us from cattle and pigs, and still more from bees and centipedes.

Notes

[1] Julien Benda, *La Trahison des clercs* (Paris, 1927); trans. R. Aldington, *The Great Betrayal* (London, 1928). Lewis cites the original publication date wrongly in the next paragraph.

[2] Edouard Berth, *Les Méfaits des intellectuels* (Paris, 1914). No English translation.

[3] Georges Sorel, *Réflexions sur la violence* (Paris, 1908); trans. T. E. Hulme, *Reflections on Violence* (London, 1912). *Livre de chevet:* pillow book.

[4] Leon Bloy, *La Femme pauvre* (Paris, 1897); trans. I. J. Collins, *The Woman Who Was Poor* (New York, 1939). "Raissa" is the wife and collaborator of Jacques Maritain, the Catholic philosopher.

[5] Charles Maurras (1868-1952), poet, essayist, journalist, politically an extreme monarchist, was editor of the ultra right-wing weekly *L'Action française.*

[6] The passage Lewis quotes is not in fact from the *Pensées* but from *De l'Esprit géometrique et de l'art de persuader,* from which source Lewis's errors of transcription have been corrected. In the translation by G. F. Pullen it runs as follows:

> She [i.e. geometry] therefore assumes that the inquirer knows what is signified by such words as movement, number, space, and without pausing for superfluous definitions she penetrates into their nature, and discovers their marvellous attributes. . . .
>
> The chief of these is a twofold infinity, comprising those two infinities which find in all created things a point of contact: the infinitely great and the infinitely small.

(From "Reflections on Geometry and the Art of Persuading," in *The Essential Pascal* [New American Library, 1966], p. 306.)

SECTION B

Satire

CHAPTER VII

EXPOSING AND DISCOURAGING VICE AND FOLLY

UP to now I have been describing a handicap that I share with all non-commercial practitioners of the various arts. My next concern will be with one I have in common with an even more restricted number of people. – I have said I am a 'highbrow' – for we are back now in the Anglo-saxon scene. Next I come to the fact that I am, among other things, a 'satirist'.

The dictionary[1] describes *satire* as 'a composition in verse or prose holding up vice or folly to ridicule . . . use of ridicule, irony, sarcasm, etc., in speech or writing for the ostensible purpose of exposing and discouraging vice or folly'.

When Dryden was looking for a definition of Satire, he went for it to Heinsius, in the latter's dissertations on Horace. It begins: 'Satire is a kind of poetry, . . . invented for the purging of our minds; in which human vices, ignorance, and errors, and all things besides, which are produced from them in every man, are severely reprehended. . . .'[2] – This says a little more than the dictionary – as 'invented for the purging of our minds'. To the ancients and their Renaissance disciples it connoted a *purgation*, as did the performance of a Tragedy. But here the purgation would be by means of laughter. – Let us, however, remain with the dictionary definition for the present.

Of course the dictionary's definition, as would be that of Heinsius, is far too circumscribed to comprehend all that we would now class as satire. It belongs to the age of Juvenal or Persius, or the classicism of the Seventeenth or Eighteenth Century, rather than to the present time. Taking that definition, however, as a starting point, let us consider *speech* first, and *writing* afterward.

According to the definition supplied by the dictionary there are few people – at least I know only a few – who are not 'satirists' in their *conversation* most of the time. Their subjects are found among the immediate circle of their friends and acquaintances. Some of this marks a mere appetite for mirth; but not a little we have to admit – unless we wish to be hypocrites – must be put down to 'malice'. Men irritate one another; they relieve their feelings in that way. Or they are in competition, to some extent, socially, sexually, professionally or what not, and they seek to gain an advantage over a friend by means of private ridicule. – 'Vice and folly' do not come into such satirical activities as this.

(It is my experience that among those who reprove the satirist for his

47

'malice' there are none so quick to do so as people whose tongues in private are loaded with spite. — Hard as it is to believe, one who has himself written satirical pieces causing genuine suffering to quite harmless members of his circle, is capable of viewing Satire, when it is *other people* who have written it, as a most pernicious practice, the proof of a mean, depraved, malignant, vain, and antinomian disposition.)

As to *writing*, if there are very few persons who are not satirists all the time in private life, then, using satire in that sense, there are very few writers of fiction, or playwrights, for instance, who are not part-time satirists. Fielding, the first fictionist, was a satirist: Dickens and Thackeray likewise. The clergy of Barchester Towers are figures approached in a most satirical spirit. Meredith and Butler were satirists. H. G. Wells was apparently such a satirist (though I, personally, was not aware of it, having read only his fantasies inspired by science) that even death did not still the last of the angry tongues. Mr. Shaw is a satirist, as is the author of 'A Passage to India', as also the author of 'The Informer', and both D. H. Lawrence and James Joyce. The greatest French novelists, Stendhal, Balzac, Flaubert, down to Gide, Proust, Mauriac, must all be classed as that too. But for the most part the novelists I have mentioned, the English, French, and Russian, are of mixed type. Few are whole-time satirists. Almost none answer strictly to the dictionary definition. In the theatre, where you would begin your list with 'Troilus and Cressida' or Ben Jonson, the accounting would be very similar to that of the novel.

———

There is a most important distinction to be made between the classical conception of Satire and our own. Visual demonstration is more effective with some people, as it is with children. Accordingly, to illustrate this distinction I will take two cartoons, one by David Low, and one by Vicki.[3] Translated into verbal terms, both would answer to the description, 'Satire'. Low's conforms to the contemporary model (of more, or less, heightened naturalism), Vicki's is closer to the classical.

You will observe that I have not chosen one of the Colonel Blimp series: for in those — as far as the figure of Blimp is concerned — Low goes over into the classical, or conventional, idiom. Blimp is a fat doll, with button eyes and a stuck-on moustache. He is not quite a human being, although usually the other figures in the cartoon are.

The type of drawing employed in the first place, by Low (as by Phil May) is that of a *quick sketch from life*. Secondly, the exaggeration is very slight: it is little more than the student in a Sketch Class will use to 'get character'.

The two methods, that of Vicki, and that of Low, are very different in the reactions they produce. Vicki's is the more purely aesthetic; and as political satire it is far less devastating. One appeals to the intellect, the other to the passions. Low is more personal, because his figures are much more *people*. If I were a politician, planning the slaughter of a rival, I should pick Low.

The drawing in Vicki is so fanciful and amusing that one does not think of the subject as a creature of this world. It is much more impersonal: this is the type of Satire demanded by an audience in a time when the classical standards obtain. It was this order of Satire which flourished in our Augustan Age: or was that demanded by those who applauded 'Le Bourgeois Gentilhomme' and 'Tartuffe'. The figure pilloried is the incarnation of a Vice, or of a Folly: it is not a *person*.

Low's versions of prominent parliamentary or social figures, were 'candid camera' snapshots, rather than specifically cartoonesque: although naturally he possesses a great talent for arrangement, too, and, above all, an uncanny ability to make the figure portrayed move and speak — gesture, run, scratch his head, or go into violent action. The *lifelikeness* in his visualisation of a scene is extraordinary. This is perhaps his most notable gift. When he did a cartoon of myself and Mr. Augustus John, for instance, the latter holding down the President of the Royal Academy upon his lap, for me, brush in hand, to portray, the likeness was remarkable, and the scene so vividly conceived that one felt it had happened.

It was said that by his satirical portraits Low actually killed a certain statesman. Although this was no doubt a pleasant exaggeration, certainly as one saw in the pages of the Evening Standard, week after week, the dissolute-looking figure, one felt it was a living man who was being shown to one: not funny in any way, but just curious and lamentable: and it is easy to see how it may have been depressing to the original, even if he did not regard it as a portrait. It was what is called 'cruel'.

When a statesman or other public figure is cartooned by the gentle Vicki, generally with the head far too large for the body — a convention which at once precludes the illusion of reality — the whole man is transformed into a manikin existing upon a different plane to that of life. The offence is not so great — the political effect is less insidious. The victim need not lose his composure. He can smile as he regards the little manikin, and observe appraisingly: 'Very clever. The fellow is remarkably clever.' It is not *him*: it is a little figure, a grotesque — a distortion of his face, obviously done to provoke laughter; but it is not *his actual face*. — They would find it more difficult to be superior with David Low. — Low told me once that when he met one of his subjects they took it very well as a rule; but with their *wives* it was another matter.

In Fielding, where satire in creative fiction has its beginning, as has the novel itself, the types are very near to life, all but those of young ladies, which have of course a conventional uniformity. I cannot see that Squire Western is other than a living country magnate of that time. If we could go back into that century, and live with such people for a while, they would behave identically — exploding into language bristling with the word 'Pox' — as do the characters in the books. Should we describe it as Satire (merely because it does not refine the truth) or should we call it realism? The latter would be the term I should prefer, but for many people this is Satire.

The Dublin scene in Joyce's 'Ulysses' is what life is like, neither more nor less, projected with the added realism secured by the impressionist technique. It is, however, described as Satire. On the other hand, of course, Mr. Jingle, Mr. Snodgrass, Scrooge, Mr. Pecksniff, the Veneerings, Uriah Heep are all comically *named* as they are unnaturalistically conceived. They belong specifically to Comedy, or to Satire.

These are not merely questions of terminology. An interpretation of life is involved as well. Probably it would be sufficient to say that in a work of art, in writing or any other mode of human expression, *where there is truth to life there is satire.* That, however, implies the less strict use of the word. The most logical thing would be to confine the use of it to work where, as with Dryden, or in Swift a conventional machinery is used, and the characters as embodied ideas, are rendered incapable of breathing the same atmosphere with us, so that we know that they are not people such as ourselves, but a symbolic company.

Next, comedy and humour introduce a complication. — The whole-time satirist would, according to the dictionary, be a man whose task it was to portray, and if possible to cure or to destroy, fools and evildoers. His logical aim would be a society of the wise and the good. — The aims of pure Comedy, on the other hand, contain none of this ethical impulse. Indeed, Comedy, in its fresh appetite for the absurd and the foolish, implies complete satisfaction with the world as it is. Remove all folly from it, and all fools, and Comedy would take its departure, too. The complication makes its appearance when you begin to ask yourself where Satire ends and Comedy begins, unless you insist upon confining Satire to the classical formula.

No comedian, professional or otherwise, promoting laughter at the expense of others, can very well do that without passing over into the satirist's domain — where he begins, that is, to do something to the person who is the occasion of the mirth. Anybody whose character or whose person has been laid under contribution in the interests of the comic muse would be likely to say that he had been the target of satire. The pejorative nature of comedy where our personal feelings are involved would not admit of such distinctions as the dictionary would allow.

I will now turn to another major difficulty. — There was no more typically satiric mind, surely, than that of Gustave Flaubert. He answered all the requirements superficially of that type: he boiled with indignation equally at the 'malfaisance foncière' and at the stupidity of man. But for him there were few if any exceptions. Every class of man was equally to be despised. 'L'ignoble ouvrier, l'inepte bourgeois, le stupide paysan, l'odieux ecclésiastique.'

Can one say that Flaubert, for whom all this mass of folly and of crime was a source of perpetual stimulation, did not relish his self-appointed task of purging and scavenging? He suffered, unquestionably: in 1870–71 his sufferings reached their maximum, when man seemed to him to have surpassed himself. But on the whole can one say that this great satirist and master of the highest comedy would have been as much in his element in a more virtuous and intelligent society? Rather than a great moralist he was a great intellectual. — So Satire itself differs greatly in the proportions in which vice and folly respectively enter, as a stimulus, into its creation.

We might decide upon the following formula in a case where the intellectual passion overpowers the moral. — When (we could assert) a very strong moral element is present, as in the pictures of Hogarth, where it is *vice* rather than *folly* that is the target, or folly so noxious as to amount to vice — and provoking reactions that vice engenders but not mere folly — we are in the presence of Satire.

Flaubert is almost in a class by himself — perhaps the first member of a new class. For him human life in its entirety is composed of folly and crime in one degree or another. 'Nos vertus ne sont le plus souvent que des vices déguisés',* could have been a saying of his. As for the Christian, there was for him pervasive and universal sin. For Flaubert, however, any taint of Christianity (such as he found in the socialism of Louis Blanc and even thought he detected in Baudelaire) aroused his hostility. So we should not, in any case, expect to find a moralist basis to this bleakest of satires. Nor was there the gaiety which accompanies Comedy. It was the Satire of nihilism.

For Flaubert it was not a few men selected here and there for attack, as especially wicked or particularly foolish. It was mankind that was chosen. Nothing so comprehensive as this is envisaged by any respectable lexicographer; in whose view those guilty of folly or of vice are exceptions, inviting castigation at the hands of that functionary, 'the satirist'.

* ['Our virtues are most often only vices disguised'. Epigraph to] De La Rochefoucauld [Maximes (1678)].

Notes

1 The Oxford Concise Dictionary.

2 Essays of John Dryden, ed. W. P. Ker (Oxford, 1926), vol. II, p. 100.

3 Sir David Low (1891–1963) caricaturist, illustrator and cartoonist; he did a cartoon of Lewis at the time of the rejection of Lewis's portrait of Eliot by the Royal Academy in 1938, reproduced on the cover of Lewisletter #6 (Newsletter of the Wyndham Lewis Society). Vicki — Lewis must mean "Vicky" — pseudonym of Victor Weisz (1913–1966), cartoonist and painter, successor to Low on the Evening Standard. Philip May (1864–1903), illustrator, contributor to Punch.

CHAPTER VIII

EVIDENCE OF A CHANGED OUTLOOK FROM THE PORTRAITS OF THE PAST

FROM what has been said in the preceding chapter let me refer you to one remark, which I should like now to enlarge upon: namely that, in whatever department of human expression, *wherever there is objective truth there is satire*: which is to say that there is something (whether more of it or less of it) which we call truth. To state this differently: all 'realism' is apt to be classed as 'satire', or as 'caricature' — all that is unemotional and objective. It would follow from this that for us *the true* must (1) always be emotional, must (2) be favourable to the object.*

In our day the above mentioned standards are at a very different level than formerly. They have been jacked up, bit by bit, until their level is lifted abnormally high above the 'real'. In all the arts this change is reflected — in letters, in acting, in the visual arts, in building. Anywhere, except where 'highbrow' values prevail, there is far less of the real: in its place is an inflated, conventional, 'improved' substitute.

As a portrait-painter — I mean in oil-paint, not in words, and in that capacity I am certainly no satirist — I am uncomfortably familiar with these changed conditions. Experiences gained in that capacity of which I now shall speak furnish one with an insight into the mind of a generation obtainable perhaps in no other way.

You can render a person's physical appearance with great accuracy, putting down feature by feature what you see, without flattery but with a beauty deriving from the technique, and you will at once discover that that is not what people call a portrait at all. It is what Queen Maria Luisa, or King Charles IV of Spain, when Goya painted them, regarded as a portrait. But they were a couple of unassuming little people. It is not what our contemporaries understand as a portrait. They are much grander people and much more particular.

What average persons, in our time, think of as the *truth* about themselves, pictorially (and what goes for the face goes for the spirit too), is, as a minimum, something with all their weak points omitted. If the chin recedes, that recession must be corrected, if the face has an unbecoming flush it must be quietened down to a gentle glow, if the legs are disproportionately short, they must be lengthened. What the eye sees is for them a caricature. You are, as an artist, either incompetent, or 'cruel', if you remain upon the objective plane. Which is of course why no straight photographs are published in the papers today, at least of women: except for 'candid camera' shots by snooping cameramen.

No tyrant in the Twentieth Century would tolerate such a rendering of himself as that at Rimini of Sigismondo Malatesta. He looks tough, and apparently did not mind at all. Whereas I remember doing a portrait

* I am here defining two 'truths', nothing more of course.

of a redoubtable magnate in which I made him look the 'strong man' that he was, and that I supposed he would like to appear to posterity. I soon found out my mistake. His family, with one voice, objected that I had not brought out the 'kindliness' which was, they averred, so notable a feature of his personality.

I doubt if a Lionello d'Este of today would accept what Pisanello did of him, though it is by no means displeasing. They would exclaim, 'is my ear really so enormous as that — and is it necessary to leave it sticking up above the cap in that ridiculous fashion? And, oh, that *underlip*! Do I stick it out like that? I am sure it is not so big as you have made it!' As to the terracotta bust of the Condottiere Niccolo da Uzzano, in the National Museum at Florence, no contemporary artist who put such a work on exhibition could hope for any further commissions (*no more* in America, and very few in England). In this connection it is interesting to recall that Stresemann refused to give Mr. Augustus John any further sittings, and so one of that artist's best portraits remains unfinished, though beside that of Niccolo da Uzzano the face we see, while certainly porcine, is normal enough. It is that, at all events, of a *nice* pig. (The modern politician is apt, however, to believe his own press-agent's version of himself, and the condottieri were less delicate and not so vain.)

Picasso's portrait of Miss Stein is an example of portraiture that might be placed among the Renaissance portraits I have been considering. Evidently the sitter approved of it. But she was a 'highbrow'. And so we come again to the division, to the Two Publics: and what it is essential, of course, to note is that neither Lionello d'Este, nor the tyrant, Sigismondo Malatesta, nor Niccolo da Uzzano, was a 'highbrow'. They were what today would be members of the Majority Public. Yet they behaved as only 'highbrows' do today in their response to the artist's view of them. Their outlook upon life was more robust and realistic. They knew that famous captains and tyrants led a harsh life, and did not expect to look like Santa Claus. They knew that life deformed us all a little.

It would be impossible to exhaust the evidence available to demonstrate the extraordinary change that has occurred in people's outlook: not merely what they expect of the portraitist, but — for that follows from this evidence — where they would place the line separating objective truth from 'satire', or caricature. The Italian Renaissance is the best period to select for the demonstration, since nothing earlier would lend itself to comparison, unless you went as far as antiquity. With Italian Renaissance portraits — that of the Doge Leonardo Loredano, or the very beautiful one of Cardinal Bibiena, or those selected above — we are dealing with an art free of any primitive awkwardness; as free as a portrait by Sargent. — The only difference is in the minds of the people involved.

Before leaving this cloud of painted witnesses from another age, I will cite, for anybody inclined to follow up this subject, three portraits of the same woman — for we have almost as many renderings of her person as that of Queen Maria Luisa — namely Caterina Cornaro. First, that by Veronese in the Kunsthistorisches Museum in Vienna, second that (by Gentile Bellini) even more 'brutal' and 'cruel' according to contemporary standards, in Budapest, and thirdly where she appears, with a crown, among the Venetian

noblewomen, in Bellini's 'Recovery of the Relic of the Cross'. — All I need
say is that had this lady been put on canvas by a popular portrait painter,
in England or America, in the Twentieth Century, we should not know
what she really looked like as now we do. You may regard it as more
desirable that human beings should not be portrayed as they really are: but
that scurrilous opinion has nothing to do with the subject of the present
enquiry.

———

It will be evident from what has transpired in the course of the above
demonstration that we cannot do without the Time factor in discussing
Satire. What in another age would have been described as truth would
today be called caricature, or satire. Again, we have seen that that cardinal
fact, the existence of Two Publics — of two canons of thought and feeling —
cannot be dispensed with in arriving at a definition of Satire.

CHAPTER IX

A DROPPER OF MOLTEN IRON

MY purpose up to now has been to show that the frontiers of what we call
Satire have been immensely enlarged, on account of (1) the more general
use of the word, to denote anything of a critical and sardonic nature, and
(2) the fact that much that our forefathers would have considered merely
factual, we look upon as exaggerated and verging on Satire, if not altogether
'satirical'. In the small 'highbrow' community alone the appetite for the
real survives: and it is there only that something of the classical standards
is encountered. Outside all is *niceness.** And because of that, of course,
true Satire cannot, at this time, exist. For Satire is never *nice.*

Two minor explanations seem called for here, one considerably overdue.
— To expound is to simplify: but there are not, of course, two neatly
demarcated worlds, one small and 'highbrow', the other large and 'lowbrow'. Like the Jew, 'highbrows' have not a territorial habitat. They are to
be found everywhere, dwelling among the Philistines. What I have called
their Reservation is not, except in a minor way, a geographical reality, only
a cultural one.

The second thing is this. Satire is often political; has a somewhat sensational side. And people enjoy Satire (directed at others). Consequently
even good Satire has, or can have, a public larger than the purely highbrow:
more extensive than any 'Ivory Tower' art, either literary or pictorial. It
benefits by a sizeable accretion of the popular public. The upshot is that
Satire has to be regarded from a slightly more popular angle.

———

But I have not set out to write an essay upon Satire — since it has almost
become that — for the pleasure of the thing; or for the sake of Satire, but
for my own sake. All that I have said so far has had a very concrete personal
motive. For being *a satirist,* unlike being *a highbrow,* is in the nature of a
personal matter: and has caused me considerable personal inconvenience.

So I have been preparing the ground, merely, for what I shall now have
to impart. If I considered at such length the tender-mindedness of my
contemporaries, for example, it was but to show how, since the plain unvarnished truth may be classed by them as an offence, or a satirical attack —
since what is only objective truth meets with this reception — then *deliberate,*
barefaced, Satire must be received, by the same people, as an instance of the
intervention of the Fiend in human affairs — prompting a person of peculiar
malevolence, meanness, venom and scurrility to traduce and slander a
number of peculiarly noble people, who until that moment scarcely knew
what Satire meant, and, in a word, in whose mouths butter would not melt.

W. B. Yeats, who had a great liking for Satire, and who showed much

* Politically I have, elsewhere, described that Majority world as 'the Great Soft Centre' [in
The Mysterious Mr. Bull (London, 1938)].

appreciation for mine, told me that I would be *stopped*, for in England that was what had always happened. He seemed under the impression that I was embarked upon a career as a satirist. But that was far from my intention. Indeed I should be very sorry to have nothing but that mode of expression to my credit, as it is not my favourite one.

It has been said of Dryden that he 'was not lightly moved by light things; and while his adversaries howled and gnashed and gesticulated, he swam steadily above on an easy wing pouring molten iron upon them.'* But I was a dropper of molten iron but once, and winged my way elsewhere, never having regarded such an occupation as more than a gigantic episode.

'The Apes of God' is the only one of my books which can be described as pure Satire (unless we wish to speak of verse): there is much farce, comedy, and other things there too, but as a satire it must generally be classed. The violent abuse of which I am the object still, even today, must, I surmise, belong to the aftermath of this book; although it was first published a decade and a half ago.[1]

I should be the last person to expect the satirist to be allowed to pass his life in peace. If I aim a blow at *a class* (the 'upper class', in this instance, where it laps and droops over, like an expiring plant, into the none too spacious Reservation afore-mentioned) I expect retaliation. One must expect literally anything from the outraged nobodies or their buddies, whose class is dying and they with it. In their death-agony they are capable of delivering some nasty kicks. I have made it my habit never to go to law, but to shoot back when shot at, and frighten them away, once in a while.

Do not let us call the being a satirist a handicap exactly but perhaps an impediment — as slander (with which I have been plastered from head to foot) always is: and let us place it beside my handicap as 'intellectual' — a lesser difficulty but one in its way quite troublesome. — I am an 'intellectual' who has been once, but on rather a massive scale, a 'satirist'.

———

Now I will, in conclusion, very briefly consider the justification of Satire. Irresponsibly to attack, in pieces that hold them up to ridicule, this person and that, just for fun, or in ill-natured play, or to acquire a sense of personal power, is in the same order of things as playing pranks on harmless people. It is a cruel and detestable sport. Much petty Satire, occasionally written, is of that kind: I have in mind one or two past offenders, though of not very recent date. Such semi-private squibs or smears should not be dignified with the name of Satire. But a book like 'Cakes and Ale' cannot be classed with these: though I heard at the time that a victim, real or imaginary, wept upon a bookseller's neck, gasping that he could never show his face again.[2] — As I happened to think it would have been a good thing if he hadn't, it seemed to me that that little masterpiece was morally justified. It all depends, in a case of that nature, whether you think it is a *good thing* or not.

Persius, I have just read, founded his Satire upon the precepts of the

* George Saintsbury [*A Short History of English Literature* (London, 1898), p. 475].

Stoic philosophy: his sanction was The Porch.[3] Dante, no doubt, felt amply justified by Christian principles in roasting his enemies: and, on the same principles, had they been in his place, they would have roasted *him*. Whether Stoics or Christians, their minds are quite at ease, for in their personal enemies they have no difficulty in detecting vice: and it deserves the severest punishment, they feel. As to their personal license as executioner, there is no difficulty about that, for are they not divinely appointed, or do they not derive their sanction, via their immediate master, from Cleanthes?[4]

For those of us who can but feel very imperfect Christians (perhaps even of a Laodicean habit, as is so usual today) or with no Stoic backgrounds, or other good excuses, it is another matter. How does a cartoonist like Mr. Low square it with his conscience, for the bloodthirsty life he has led — driving his *banderillas* into so many hides, year after year? Or Mr. H. G. Wells, or Mr. Maugham, or, to take a Frenchman, M. Gide?

In the case of two of the Englishmen I have mentioned, it was political Satire. All social Satire is political Satire. And in the case of my solitary book of Satire, that is the answer too. If anyone smarted because of it (and it seems that they did, for although the personal identification may have been unfounded, the class identification was probably accurate) they smarted for a political reason. As a class, they had outstayed their usefulness and had grown to be preposterous parasites.

As once upon a time, according to English law, it was the duty of any man, observing another rustling a horse, to apprehend him (if he could) and to hang him (if he had a rope) to the the nearest tree (if there were one thereabouts): so it was incumbent upon all good citizens to turn satirists on the spot, at the sight of such as those exhibited in 'The Apes of God' — if they had any Satire in them, of which I happened to have an adequate supply.

Notes

[1] *The Apes of God* was published in 1930. Lewis was writing this in 1947.

[2] Somerset Maugham, *Cakes and Ale* (London, 1930). Lewis may be referring to Hugh Walpole, who felt himself caricatured in the character of Alroy Kear in Maugham's novel. See Rupert Hart-Davis, *Hugh Walpole* (London, 1952), pp. 316-17.

[3] Persius (A.D. 34-62), Stoic satirist. "The Porch" is the Painted Porch or *Stoa Poikile* in Athens, which gave its name to the Stoic school founded there by Zeno, c. 315 B.C.

[4] Cleanthes (c. 330–c. 231 B.C.), successor to Zeno as head of the Stoic school.

CHAPTER X

MALICE

EXAMPLES of direct, or indirect, retaliation because of my book of Satire it has not seemed worth while to furnish. Such things we take for granted. But there is something that I will put in evidence, to demonstrate how the mere fact that, at one time of your life, you have wielded the satirist's lash against a class of offenders – or 'slapped them in the face' with your wing – makes you liable to insults in *other* departments of your work. When I was discharging the functions of a critic to the best of my ability, because that criticism did not please it has been treated as if it were Satire. – Here is my illustration of how handy a thing it is to somebody seeking to combat Mr. Lewis the *critic*, to have Mr. Lewis *the satirist* in the background.

A Mr. Levin wrote a little book* about James Joyce, upon whose work he lectures at Harvard University. It is a book treating Joyce extremely seriously, I am glad to say, for in my view, also, Joyce was a writer of great importance. However, those elements in his work which especially recommend themselves to Mr. Levin, have the opposite effect on me. I have as much right to disapprove of those particular aspects of his work, clearly, and to consider that their influence would be bad, as has Mr. Levin to approve of them, and recommend them to his students. We cannot all think alike.

My book, 'Time and Western Man', contains an elaborate analysis of the writings of James Joyce, and more especially 'Ulysses'.[1] As to 'Time and Western Man', it will be sufficient to say that in my view, at the period at which I wrote it, the philosophy in the ascendant was destructive, and that it should be combated. In its pages – and it is a book of considerable length – I provide a very detailed answer to that disintegrating metaphysic.

In contemporary literature several authors came under review, in the first part of my book, as having plainly abandoned themselves to those influences. Some were philosophers, or physicists, others writers of fiction: Joyce was one of these, and at the moment the most considerable. In spite of my extremely friendly relations with him, I had no choice – if I were to carry through my plan with thoroughness – but to assign his work a prominent place in my critical analysis. – Perhaps one ought not to frequent writers or other artists whose work one regards with a critical eye. But when I first knew Joyce I was not possessed of that clear picture of the contemporary scene which I afterwards acquired. I had just come out of the army and I had not yet abstracted in my mind the philosophic pattern of the various movements in the midst of which I found myself.

My critical appraisal of the work of Joyce was, however, unambiguously partisan. It derived from a set of principles which were clearly enunciated. Its validity depended upon the validity of those principles. If you did not agree with the philosophical premises you would not agree with the criticism, and could disregard it entirely. Of how much critical writing can this be

---

* 'James Joyce', by Harry Levin. Faber and Faber [1944].

said? There was, in a word, none of the offensive omniscience from which criticism generally suffers. Indeed, all people who set themselves up as critics should be obliged, before they begin, to provide a statement of first principles, to which their criticism can be referred: just as in politics one is generally aware of the specific theory of the State favoured by the writer in question—tory, stalinist, catholic, old-style liberal, or what not. Then we should all know where we stood.

It was because my position was defined so circumstantially and with such unmistakable plainness that I did not regard what I said as in any way personally offensive to Joyce: nor did I anywhere imply that he was not worthy of the greatest attention and respect—the space I allotted to him is evidence of that; or that his work was other than *of its kind* a masterpiece. It was the *kind* I did not like so much as some other kinds.

Mr. Levin uses the very just word 'impressionistic' to describe the technique employed in 'Ulysses'; and—to go over into another art, where Impressionism took its rise—when I leave the National Gallery, in Trafalgar Square, where I have gazed at Van Eyck, Raphael, Bellini, Cosimo Tura, and so on, and visit immediately afterwards an exhibition of the work of, say, Topolsky,[2] though I note the skill and bravura of the latter—and the same would apply to other work of that order—I recall the company I so recently left, the order, the dignity, the formal purity of the great masters of the past and I know which manner I prefer. I appreciate impressionism, some of it much more than Topolsky's melodrama. But I should never hold it up as a model.

So all Joyce had to say was: 'I like and follow Vico, and Bergson, and Freud. My friend Mr. Lewis does *not*. He has a perfect right to his opinion: and naturally, with his views upon those masters and teachers by whom I have been guided, he would not like what I do as much as otherwise he might. As it takes all sorts to make a world, there is room for Mr. Lewis and those of his predilection: and for me, and those who think as I do.'—But he did not say that. He was a man who heard criticism with difficulty. On my side, I feel I should have been more circumspect: I warmed to my subject. I was perhaps too forcible. At that time I was about the only writer in English-speaking countries who gave utterance to such opinions, and I had to insist in order to be heard.

In Mr. Levin's book there is a bibliography. It includes 'Time and Western Man', with the following note, for the guidance of the student: 'A vigorous attack on—among others—Joyce, well timed and badly aimed, penetrating and exasperating'.

It would have been a good thing to add, 'but very useful to others engaged in writing about this author'. For all I need do now is to quote a few lines from his book and with what I have already said the issue will be plain.—Mr. Levin is summarising the main formative influences (p. 67) in the life of his subject.

'The international psycho-analysis movement, under the direction of Jung, had its headquarters in Zurich during the war years while Joyce was writing "Ulysses", and he could scarcely have resisted its influence. And, although philosophy could not have offered him much in the way of immediate data, it is suggestive to note that Bergson, Whitehead, and others

— by reducing things-in-themselves to a series of organic relations — were thinking in the same direction. Thus the very form of Joyce's book is an elusive and eclectic "Summa" of its age.'

But it was precisely the fact that Joyce's work was such a 'Summa' that caused me to write about it as I did. It was a compendium of all the wrong things. And elsewhere in 'Time and Western Man' — oddly enough — is a careful critical analysis of the philosophy of Bergson, Whitehead 'and others'. — In other words, Mr. Levin has merely taken a few of my examples of *bad* doctrine, and re-issued them as examples of *good* doctrine: doctrines which were either formative influences for Joyce, or else contemporary examples of the same order of thought as that dominating Joyce's work.

There was another major weakness as I saw it, in 'Ulysses', quite apart from the philosophy implicit in it, namely its *form*. Mr. Levin cites Jung as saying that there is no beginning or end in 'Ulysses': that you can cut it in half, and the half would be as organically complete — or incomplete — as the whole. That was one of my objections: an objection that applies even more to 'Finnegans Wake'. It seemed to me rambling and structureless. In detail it was brilliantly executed, and packed with first-rate observation of manners, of the most delightful humour and even passages of original beauty. But it had no firm and logical linear structure. Rather it was a chaotic mosaic.

Odds and ends of words or phrases were always floating about in his pockets: he would put his hand in his pocket to take out a packet of cigarettes and bring out with them a scribbled scrap of conversation scratched on an envelope, or notes of the names of objects. Joyce carried about with him from one country to another a trunk full of such fragments, bits of paper, newspaper-cuttings. The resulting book was too much a patchwork of these.

We were talking once, I remember, when I first got to know him about the cathedral at Rouen; its heavily encumbered façade. I had said I did not like it, rather as Indian or Indonesian sacred buildings are a fussy multiplica-tion of accents, demonstrating a belief in the virtue of *quantity*, I said. All such quantitative expression I have at all times found boring, I pointed out. I continued to talk against Gothic altogether, and its 'scholasticism in stone': the dissolving of the solid shell — the spatial intemperance, the nervous multiplication of detail. Joyce listened and then remarked that he, on the contrary, liked this multiplication of detail, adding that he himself, as a matter of fact, in words, did something of that sort.

Now these, surely, are serious differences — differences as fundamental and well-recognised as that between the classical and romantic sensibility, between the pagan and the christian world, or any other traditional opposites. So what is there strange, or improper, in someone adhering to one of these natural groupings advancing carefully reasoned critical objections to work deriving from the opposite aesthetic and intellectual principle? — I can see nothing strange or improper in this: but apparently Mr. Levin can.

Not long before his death I met Humbert Wolfe at dinner, and he observed: 'I *admire* what you write. I do not *like* it.'[3] That was a highly civilised remark. A saying that is perhaps the most famous illustration of that type of mature intelligence is Voltaire's — 'I detest what you say, but I would defend with my life your right to say it'. In a review Wolfe wrote of

'Time and Western Man', where, in his review, framed in terms of the most generous praise, he observed that *this* was the plane upon which it was proper to contend. And I am perfectly certain that Wolfe experienced as little innate sympathy as Mr. Levin for my kind of mind, and I was personally acquainted with him no more than I am with Mr. Levin.

———

Let me quote a page from Mr. Levin's book. He has said that 'the emergence of this method in fiction' — the *monologue intérieur* — has been hailed as nothing less than a 'scientific discovery', but proceeds to point out that 'even within the traditions of the novel, the internal monologue appears to be less of an innovation than Joyce or Dujardin would have liked to believe'. — I was mainly responsible, I think, for dispelling this belief. But here is the page (p. 69) which I propose to extract, by way of evidence.

'André Gide has found instances in Dostoievsky's "House of the Dead". Fanny Burney wrote tolerably conventional novels, a hundred years before Dostoievsky or Dujardin, but in the privacy of her Diary she set down a page or two that ask demurely for comparison with the last words of Molly Bloom:

' "Well, I am going to bed — Sweet dreams attend me — and may you sympathise with me. Heigh ho! I wonder when I shall return to London. — Not that we are very dull here — no, really — tolerably happy I wish Kitty Cooke would write to me — I long to hear how my dear, dear, beloved Mr. Crisp does. My papa always mentions him by name of my *Flame*. Indeed he is not mistaken — himself is the only man on earth I prefer to him. Well — I must write a word more — only to end my paper — so! — that's done — and now good night to you. . . ."

'Fenimore Cooper, one of the least adroit novelists who ever won lasting fame, somehow flounders into the stream of consciousness. Cooper follows Scott in taking over a Shakespearian *entourage* of clowns and fools, one of whom is an old Negro retainer Caesar, in "The Spy". When his young master takes leave of him and jocosely suggests that Caesar convey a farewell kiss to the young ladies of the household, Cooper's racial feeling sinks into Caesar's subconsciousness:

' "The delighted Caesar closed the door, pushing bolt after bolt, turning the key until it would turn no more, soliloquising the whole time on the happy escape of his young master.

' " 'How well he ride — teach him good deal myself — salute a young lady — Miss Fanny wouldn't let the old coloured man kiss a red cheek.' "

'This staccato diction, as the malice of Wyndham Lewis did not fail to observe, makes a startling appearance in the very first novel of Charles Dickens. "Pickwick Papers" is ordinarily evoked for other qualities than psychological subtlety. There are moments, none the less, when it would be hard to tell the silent meditation of Mr. Bloom from the laconic garrulity of Alfred Jingle, Esq. The flow of Mr. Jingle's discourse is also stimulated by the sight of local landmarks, and the movement of the stage-coach is registered in his spoken reactions:

' "Terrible place — dangerous work — other day — five children — mother

— tall lady, eating sandwiches — forgot the arch — crash — knock — children look around — mother's head off — sandwich in her hand — no mouth to put it in — head of a family off — shocking, shocking! Looking at Whitehall, sir? — fine place — little window — somebody's else's head off there, eh, sir? — he didn't keep a sharp look-out enough either — eh, sir, eh?" '

You have read above 'as the malice of Wyndham Lewis did not fail to observe'. How strange it is when Mr. Levin discovers in Fanny Burney or Fenimore Cooper (very far-fetched) examples of the internal monologue it is *not* malice, apparently, but when I, in the course of my reading at that time, notice a great similarity between Mr. Jingle and Mr. Bloom, it *is* malice.[4]

There was an even more interesting precursor of Joyce (Dujardin[5] apart) namely Schnitzler, quoted by me some years later. Whether Mr. Levin had seen this or not I cannot say. But if he had he would not wish to appear to be too much beholden to so 'exasperating' a person as myself. — I do not wish to overburden this chapter with quotations, or I would add here some passages from 'Time and Western Man', to which book anyway I would like to refer the reader. In the absence of that text, I can assure him that a very serious analysis of 'Ulysses' is to be found there, although Mr. Levin would have you believe it is a lot of 'malicious' and 'exasperating' stuff.

But why is not that serious literary criticism, I wonder, like Mr. Levin's (for we know his must be that)? It helps Mr. Levin to give his lectures and to condense them into little treatises: surely that is something. — I fear, however, that nothing rational is involved. It is just that Mr. Wyndham Lewis is a bad man — *mala persona*. Even this present exposure of Mr. Levin (the author of 'Time and Western Man' protesting at the aspersions of Mr. Levin) is most awfully malicious. Mr. Wyndham Lewis is like that animal that is *méchant*, because when attacked he defends himself.

And is he not a *satirist*? — That gives them a licence to say almost anything about you. Look at the perfectly dreadful things you say about other people, if you use Satire, irony, or any of those modes of expression. And in such a genteel age, too. So all that you can say or do must be compact of malice.

Notes

[1] *Time and Western Man* (London, 1927), Bk. I, Ch. XVI (pp. 91-130), "An Analysis of the Mind of James Joyce."

[2] Feliks Topolski (1907-), Polish-born British painter and draughtsman. "He belongs to no school, but developed a vigorous personal style of swirling line and grandiose conception" — *Oxford Companion to 20th Century Art*, ed. H. Osborne (Oxford, 1981).

[3] Humbert Wolfe (1886-1940), poet and civil servant.

[4] Lewis quotes Levin here with minor inaccuracies. Lewis compares the monologues of Bloom and Jingle both in *The Art of Being Ruled* (pp. 400-2) and in *Time and Western Man* (pp. 121-22).

[5] Edouard Dujardin, author of *Les Lauriers sont coupés* (Paris, 1888). Arthur Schnitzler (1862-1931), Viennese poet, dramatist and novelist.

SECTION C
Politics

CHAPTER XI

WHAT ARE POLITICS?

THE inconveniences attendant upon the 'highbrow' state, as of that of a 'satirist', I have discussed. The recriminations and misrepresentations which the satirist must expect are as nothing to the storm of intolerant nonsense loosed at the head of any independent man writing of politics. If you attempt to avoid the pitfalls of the partisan, you may fall into the abyss awaiting the independent observer.

What are 'politics'? Let me begin by a brief and superficial enquiry. – Politics are what came into our life as soon as we departed from the purely animal condition. Man in society is an animal who is *governed*. Sometimes he is governed more, sometimes less. Some nations are naturally much-governed nations, just as some men are born to be hen-pecked. – No man, unless he has had a great deal of it, likes government; though he is apt to develop a dog-like devotion for his 'leader' or master.

But government is indispensable – whatever theories men may advance as to the origins of government they usually agree as to that. Since man is a feeble creature he is obliged to associate himself with a strong band or group of his own kind. Whether you call it a 'contract' or 'compact', or leave that out, the fact remains that he must subscribe to the rules obtaining in his particular society. Further, he can only attain to 'civilised' status – have libraries, laboratories, studios, concert-halls, and theatres, if he has the good fortune to belong to a large and complex society – subject to its laws.

Its laws, in all cases, are backed by *force*. That is indispensable too: we accept the rule of force, which is the rule of law, and hope for the best. It is the only way we can get the libraries, laboratories, etc., etc. We do not, as I have said, like getting them in this way, but there is no other. 'Government is man's badge of servitude', as I said in my book about Cosmic Man.[1] Government is the primary qualification of our liberty of course – the official representative of Otherness.

One would think there would be less incentive to be law-abiding in those belonging to that great Majority who have no use for libraries, laboratories, studios, etc. This, however, is not the case. The less government is a positive necessity to people, the less they question the rule of force. People are much more like horses than they are like camels: they accept a harness and work for their day's oats very submissively on the whole.

What 'politics' are, then, is anything to do with that burdensome machinery by means of which man maintains himself as a social being. –

There are some men who spend their entire lives in governing other people — or in working to hoist themselves into a position where they may exercise that function. Politicians as a class are not popular: this seems, on the face of it, unfair: for if they are a curse, they are a necessary one.

Politicians are neither the best nor wisest among us, any more than they are usually the worst or most foolish. Politicians could not write the wise and delightful books in the Libraries, they have not the faculties required to discover insulin or penicillin for instance — they cannot split the atom, or even make bombs: they cannot carve statues or paint pictures, or build a cathedral or a skyscraper: or design a typewriter or a bicycle: they cannot play Shakespeare, nor sing in grand opera: most of them can scarcely compose a speech — the most successful of American Presidents was not able to do that, but had a staff of 'ghosts' for his speeches. But without *something* there, where politicians are, there would be no great books, no Venus of Cyrene, no insulin, penicillin, no ether, no pasteurisation, there would be no Raphaels or Titians, no great actors, no great philosophers or musicians or mathematicians. We do not owe all this to the politicians — we owe them nothing — but *without* them it could not exist.

Their function is ill-defined, but all (except the anarchist) regretfully agree they are *necessary*. Saint-Simon and Proudhon and Jefferson among many others believed that Government should not go beyond mere police-work. All the rest could be carried on by small local committees. Today, however, as our worship of Force (or Power) increases, there is no outstanding thinker who limits the sphere of government in this way.

As our worship of Force, and Power, waxes — in proportion to the immense multiplication of power proceeding from the techniques of science — we tend to worship the politician — the wielder of a power so dread and so inclusive — as once man worshipped the thunder and the lightning, earthquakes and volcanoes. — And who can do otherwise than tremble, when he reflects upon the power that some not very intelligent little man holds in his hand? It is his mental and moral limitations that are so terrifying.

Politicians may be grouped in the same general class as soldiers, and policemen. All are men of force. The Army and Navy, we may recall, are referred to as 'the Forces'. The Police are known as 'the Police Force': or 'the Force'. Politicians are just as much *men of force* as are the other two. The only difference is that they possess no distinctive uniform, such as helmets, and belts round their waists outside their jackets, nor insignia of rank. They just dress like us. Politicians ought to wear a uniform to distinguish them from us. But they do not.

Thus, if you are the head politician — the Prime Minister, or the President — you have at times, as much as Judges, to send men to the gallows, or to the block, or the 'hot squat'. Again it is you who give the order, periodically, to 'make war'. You decree the hail of bombs, the flames of the flame-thrower, and now the pestilence of bacteriological war. You decree the extinction of millions of people like yourself with a stroke of your little pen. So no one in that position can say he is not a man of force. — He is also the leader of a nation — and a nation is referred to as 'a Power', is it not? — So Power and Force is of the very essence of the political life and function.

The man who dedicates himself, however, to a life of Force, and to the handling of Power, is a certain kind of man. Many men do not wish to be policemen; some are not attracted by the life of Arms. They have an aversion to Force. And some have no wish to rule, or to 'boss': have no appetite for power. — In this way you can sort men out. I do not think it is to speak very disrespectfully to say that it is never the most highly civilised men who have a great appetite for these things: and this fact was recognised in the ancient civilisations of India and China, by the inferior position assigned to the warrior in the caste system of the former, and by the traditionally low opinion of the soldier in the latter. The life of arms appeared to be the province of a grosser type of man.

So far so good. But there are occasions when any man is compelled to resort to force. Sometimes we must strike another man to retain our self-respect, unless exceptionally endowed by God with saintly attributes; or we may be unable to refrain from putting a bullet into a housebreaker, if he should threaten to remove something we greatly value, such as a manuscript or picture. We all sometimes might have to act the policeman, or something like it. Except where our scruples are overmastering, there are times when we may be soldiers.

I here arrive at a most critical question. Are there times when any man, whatever his aversion to force, or to the handling of power, and however unsuited he may feel himself to fulfil that function, must take to politics?

I believe that there are. But that is if anything a greater curse than being governed, which is what men have to be all the time. This is one of the most difficult questions to answer properly. Politics are nothing to do with us who are not politicians. And how, in any case, are we to take them? The moment you go over into them, from some other department of life, using the rational approach — which would be the correct one elsewhere — you get into difficulties. You are in a different medium altogether.

————

The unique character of politics — that they are something *apart from the rest of life* — is widely recognised today: or at least it is recognised as what they are to all who accept the realist position. With none, in our time, is that position uninfluential. Let me quote Benedetto Croce. 'Machiavelli discovered the necessity and autonomy of politics, of politics which is beyond, or, rather, below moral good and evil, which has its own laws against which it is useless to rebel, politics that cannot be exorcised and driven from the world with holy water. . . . (This) must be termed a profoundly philosophical concept, and it represents the true foundation of a philosophy of politics.'*

This 'represents the true foundation of a philosophy of politics': namely, that politics is a department of life *below* the more humane and virtuous levels of our nature as men; and it is 'autonomous' — a region governed by laws of its own, and distinct from all the other activities of our existence.

Machiavelli's view was that what we describe as *politics* is what man's evil nature has necessitated. 'If all men were good' there would be no

* 'Politics and Morals'. Croce [trans., S. J. Castiglione (London, 1946), p. 45].

politics: as likewise, of course — let us add — no Police Force. — Croce points out that Machiavelli's was the doctrine of a bitter pessimist — a good thing to do, perhaps, sometimes. 'In the face of such evident signs of a stern and sorrowful moral conscience, it is amazing that there has been so much idle talk about Machiavelli's immorality, but the common people term *moral* only what is moralistic unctuosity and bigoted hypocrisy.'*

If the above be the 'true foundation' for an understanding of politics — and I have always believed that it is — we must also remember that, as Croce expressed it, 'moralistic unctuosity and bigoted hypocrisy' plays a very great part, especially on the Anglo-saxon scene. And although we may accept without reserve the realistic judgement, it is never the realistic judgement which furnishes the average political pundit today with his *public* philosophy, in spite of the fact that his *private* philosophy, in most cases, would coincide with that of Machiavelli. He is nothing if not nobly ethical in public: just as our statesmen, when a big bloodletting is on, borrow the unctuous tones of the clergyman.

Another warning — in passing. You are not supposed to notice (as did Machiavelli) that your fellow men are 'ungrateful, fickle, false, cowardly, covetous' etc. etc.† Apropos let me quote from an evening newspaper‡ which is so pat an illustration from everyday life of what I wish to convey in this warning.

'Mr. Tom Braddock, Socialist M.P. for Mitcham, said recently that religious instruction in school would best be cut out if it taught that the human race was basically faulty. "I have never said a prayer in my life," said Mr. Braddock. "I resent the suggestion that we are all miserable sinners." '

You will observe that any suggestion that the human race is basically 'faulty' is apt not to be appreciated. Assimilate this truth, and it may spare you a great deal of trouble.

Politics are 'below' morals, below the reason, below even our normal impulses: and the State is below the Individual.§ If we, as individuals, behaved as the State behaves, we should all be murderers, counterfeiters, bullies, blackmailers, perjurers and should be justly regarded as arch-enemies of society.

The State (the national, sovereign, State) lives upon a far more primitive level than we do. It shows us ourselves as we ought not to be, in the process of compelling us to live as we ought to live. It seems incurably violent and morally inferior. The cause is partly to be found in Acton's often quoted observation that 'all power corrupts, and absolute power corrupts absolutely'.

* While allowing that Machiavelli was a kind of moralist, one is obliged to object that if a human scourge like Cesare Borgia is the necessary response to man's universal wickedness, the destruction which overtook Sodom and Gomorrah should immediately be meted out to him everywhere: I mean, the Borgias are not the proper answer.
† Cf. 'The Prince' [Ch. 17].
‡ 'Evening Standard', Oct. 1, 1946.
§ For many eminent thinkers the State is of course everything — in Hegel's system it is a metaphysical absolute, conditioning the individual. Plato was by far the most illustrious exponent of this barbarous doctrine. Such a type of thinking is that of men in love with Power — Hegel, the slave of the idea of the Prussian State, Plato an unusually embittered member of the Athenian aristocracy.

The human dilemma is obvious. Government, with its unrestrained force and power, is necessary (or *some* force and *some* power is): but this necessity places us in the keeping of Caliban. It exposes us to precisely that kind of violence to secure ourselves against which we have accepted human government.

———

When the man of letters turns to politics, he automatically sets himself to *study* them, like any other science. He thinks they are a subject like another. But politics are different to anything else. They are not a study you can undertake as a one-man task, of observation and methodic enquiry, as you could study, say, the organisaton of a colony of bees. — If the bees knew what you were doing, probably you could not study them either.

An American journalist, Philip Rahv, has expressed this very well. 'Objectivity, in the usual sense of that term, is unattainable in a serious political struggle: in politics knowledge is the product of participation and involvement, and the spectator, though he may retain his objectivity, is precisely the one whose ideas are the least pertinent to the matter in hand.'[2] Here Mr. Rahv is defending Trotsky's book on Stalin against the charge that, since it cannot have been objective, it therefore cannot be true. He answers that in politics the 'objective' is not the true.

Men are not interested in the objective truth about politics, any more than a Movie Star is interested in the objective truth about her personal appearance. She knows that *her* truth is subjective. It would be absurd, in any case, to choose such a subject of research as a Movie Star: either you are enslaved by her beauty, or, after a brief consultation with your senses, you decide that her beauty is a myth: there are only those two positions, nothing in between. With Politics it is just the same. Unless you are emotionally excited by a System, by a Party, or by some political Star — like Gandhi, or General de Gaulle, or Tito — and so abandon yourself to them as a red-hot political religionist, they are not for you.

To occupy yourself with research relating to sundry theories of the State, on the other hand, would be unobjectionable, if it were not for the fact that, however extinct a political theory may seem, and belonging only to the past, you can never rely upon any theory, however 'exploded', not still being in the thick of the fray. 'The fact is that political theories are endowed with the faculty possessed by the hero of the Border-ballad. When their legs are smitten off they fight upon their stumps. They produce a host of words, and of ideas associated with those words, which remain active and combatant after the parent speculation is mutilated or dead.'* Ponder Hobbes or Aristotle, or Machiavelli, Alexander Hamilton, Jeremy Bentham, Proudhon, Godwin, or any political thinker you like to name, and suddenly you may find yourself confronting a live political Star — with a smile inviting you to step into his parlour (plastered with slogans, smelling of blood). —

* Henry Maine [author of *Ancient Law* (1861), *Early History of Institutions* (1875), *Early Law and Custom* (1883) and other works].

The State is not a subject suited to a philosophic mind. It is in the same category as horse-racing or harlotry. It is much better to turn your back on the State, as a subject of speculation.

In my own case, I have not followed this rule. With candour, and with an almost criminal indifference to my personal interests, I have given myself up to the study of the State. With me the first incentive to so unattractive a study was a selfish, or at least a personal one: namely a wish to find out under what kind of system learning and the arts were likely to fare best. A craft interest, that is to say. Of course later my intellectual zeal transcended this limited and specialist enquiry. I saw that human life itself was threatened, in the frenzy of our Party games and economic lunacies. — How do we *not* think of the State, when it shakes about under our feet, and is no longer able to hold at bay the primitive chaos, man's dread of which is its most obvious, if not its only, excuse for existing?

At no time, however, have I been in the least danger of falling in love with a political Star, or becoming excited about a Party. Nevertheless, I have been reported as in love with more than one political Star of the first magnitude. — As the result of a natural confusion between my disposition and their own, busy and excited adherents of some Prophet have accused me of being under the spell of their master's rival.

Notes

[1] *America and Cosmic Man* (London, 1948).

[2] Philip Rahv, "Versions of Bolshevism," *Partisan Review* 13 (1946), 365-75; the passage quoted appears on p. 366.

CHAPTER XII

AN EXTREMIST VIEW

IT must be confessed that I did not formerly see, with the dazzling clarity with which I now do, that government and force are commutative terms, that *all* government reeks of force: and if one administration seems to consist of rather nice quiet men, and another of 'tough' people, that it comes down to the same thing in the end. I have witnessed such unlimited and universal violence that it is possible for me to appreciate what is good, without being painfully disturbed by what I regard as bad (*bad* more especially as descriptive of habits of violence). The amount and quality of the good is the main thing: of badness no State has a monopoly.

Although not politically warm-hearted, attachments of sorts I certainly have had — but they were of a far less romantic order than those sometimes attributed to me. The community to which I belong, the calling, or callings, I have followed; such — not parties — have commanded my attention. The old Ship of State of this aged country we have to take some notice of, and try to prevent the old tub from sinking — no easy matter in such weather as we lately have been experiencing. Do not let us speak of patriotism, that is much too romantic a word for the occasion. — I cannot understand the indifference of people to what happens to the inhabitants of England.

If you see a man about to step over a precipice you warn him of the danger, if there is still time. This would be all the more the case if, for some reason, you were attached to him by a rope, and would fall over too. But we do not really need the extra provocation of Self-preservation. Were you to see an absent-minded or near-sighted man stepping out into the road, where there was a high probability of his being hit by advancing cars, you would try and halt him.

England appeared to me to be in that situation midway between the Wars — wandering along in a cloud of Navycut tobacco and not very used to the accelerated Twentieth Century traffic. But I was wrong, I now see that people cannot live without excitement, and war gives them that: in the same way that they depend on stockmarket crashes, slumps, air and railway accidents, forest-fires, epidemics, street accidents, bank failures, suicides, and murders to liven things up. As Hume expressed it, 'Life, without passion, must be altogether insipid and tiresome.' I was being officious.

I am one of those persons who would put all the hotel fires out before anyone had got any fun out of them (in order to save the lives of the guests!) — and cut down would-be suicides before the rope had blackened their faces — seize the gambler's hand as he was about to stake his last hundred pounds in one wild delicious throw — leap on the murderer as he was about (to the delight of ten million newspaper readers a few days later) to perpetrate his crime. I am one of those persons who, hearing the war-drums beating in a hysterical crescendo, seeing his tribe working itself up into its customary delirium, would violently intervene, shouting *Count Your Dead*

— *they are Alive!*[1] Such a man would be very lucky not to be cut down by the frenzied warriors.

In a book called 'Left Wings Over Europe' (1936) a fairly accurate prediction is to be found of what Europe would look like a few months after the war, then in active preparation (although a few brigades of our standing army, at the time Hitler marched into the Rhineland, would have disposed of any threat from that quarter, and there would have been no war). This book was written in the interfering spirit described above. Here are the passages to which I refer.*

'Without asking, like Mr. Lloyd George, what the French have been doing in that line for the last dozen years — let me call your attention to the alternative of a successful Germany — namely a *defeated* Germany. What would Europe look like upon the *lendemain* of victory over Germany by the violent and irresponsible plutocracy of France, and the somewhat brutal masters of Moscow? Imagine Germany abolished for ever. Where the Hitlerite Totalitarian State is at present, there would be, instead, a handful of puppet dukes, or "left-wing" democracies, established in its various provinces — in Saxony, Württemberg, Bavaria and Prussia. Or, it might equally well be, a communist dictatorship would function in Berlin.

'But England's rôle would then be at an end. There would be no more courting of Great Britain, as the arbiter of the destinies of Europe. Mr. Anthony Eden's tailor would shrink into unimportance on the world-stage. The English nation is in a far stronger position now than it ever could or will be again, upon that we may depend, after such a *dénouement* as the military annihilation of Germany. . . .

Japan — or Russia — as the 'Menace'?

'If you are a pure internationalist . . . then the prospect of your frontier still being the Rhine (as Mr. Baldwin has told you it is) but finding yourself face to face, on the other side of it, with an absolutist power stretching from the Rhine to the furthest extremity of Asia (namely Russia) will be most agreeable. Otherwise not. For the most the "swaggering Prussian" could do would be to defeat you in war, in his old-fashioned *Berserk* fashion. Whereas the Russian communist would be more thorough, and incorporate you, lock, stock, and barrel, into a salvationist imperium: of which you would be a small, distant, damp, and rather tiresome colony. . . .

'Russia is busy in Sinkiang — in China, Mongolia, Afghanistan, and Tibet. Communist armies have for long overrun the interior provinces of China: the doctrines of Russian communism have obtained a firm hold in India. . . . And this is a power to whom we are proposing to throw open the gates of the West, and enable it to establish itself upon "our frontier", namely the Rhine!'

The above, written twelve years ago, is an accurate forecast. The Russians are not on the Rhine so far. But they are the masters of the greater part of Berlin, in France the largest and best organised party is communist, Poland (far behind the iron curtain) is ruled by communists, all of eastern Europe is theirs, and, when at last we boot Franco out, if Spain is not ruled by communists at least they will have great influence

* Pp. 132-134.

there. During the period of its great power England has intrigued and fought to prevent European hegemony—though in its blackest dreams it never saw a great land power extending from the Pacific to the Atlantic, like the Soviet Empire.

'A pure internationalist', as I am now, experiences mixed feelings at such a spectacle. It may not be the ideal way for it to happen: but 'sovereign states', since they will never surrender their sovereignty, must lose it in some other way: which is what is occurring.

Such is the reaction, necessarily, of the 'pure internationalist'. In 1935 I wrote 'Left Wings over Europe' almost purely from the English standpoint. I saw the issue exactly as Palmerston, or Disraeli, or Pitt would have seen it. The advice I gave was the correct advice, from that narrow standpoint. There was nothing 'fascist', or even extremely nationalist, about such an outlook. From the *purely English* standpoint or even the Western European, one could hold no other opinion as to the outcome of what was in preparation.

We are (as it is described in the American magazine, 'Time') 'throwing' ourselves out of India, and leaving Egypt: should any Spanish government except a very tame bourgeois one be there, in succession to Franco, they will (via U.N.O.) oblige us to leave Gibraltar. Our Dominions have in effect become independent nations: there is rebellion in our Western Islands, and certainly Burma will rapidly follow India in severing its connections with John Bull. As a consequence, I take it, the 1935 'pure English' standpoint—with its necessary admixture of imperialism (such as the pure American, or pure Russian standpoint of 1947 must contain since both are great imperial powers) is practically a thing of the past. There was 'Great Power' thinking in those 1935 thoughts of mine, which is entirely absent from my thinking today. To this I may add, with regard to imperial policy, that I should do exactly the same in India, or Egypt, as the present Government are doing—only I should depart with greater speed. Germany would also have to get on without me, if I were John Bull; Palestine too, and a half-dozen other places. After that, I should regard it as a matter of great urgency to empty these islands of their hopelessly swollen population, reducing it to a reasonable size. Five or six million for England, Wales, and Scotland would be my target.

———

The man who walked into the street—as described above—was not absent-minded or short-sighted. Subconsciously (for it is not conceivable that it should be consciously) *he wanted to have the accident.* You would think (to judge from all that is written and said) that this same Everyman was dismayed and disgusted at the 'Iron-curtain', the bomb called 'Gilda' at Bikini, that 'obstructionist' Vyacheslav Molotov, or Tito's 'truculent' behaviour. But you must not be deceived in that way. After all, we put Tito there—it was we fundamentally who arranged for the 'Iron-curtain'. No: my man stepping out into the road knows quite well what he is about. Cripple that he now is, *he wants another accident!*

Should this appear to you a preposterous paradox, take up any history of Europe during the past five-hundred years, and see how war follows war with the regularity of the seasons. The only difference now is that we say if we have another, 'it will mean the end of civilisation'. Dean Inge was saying that last week, and I expect he said it before 1939 and 1914.[2]

We do not need *existentialism* to acquaint us with a few patent facts. Politics is the game everyone plays now: it is a life-and-death game, with plenty of corpses. That is what makes it such fun. Jeremy Bentham, when he lifted from Beccaria his hypothetical principle of the Greatest Happiness of the Greatest Number,[3] was well pleased with the acquisition, not only philosophically valid but, he felt, almost talismanic: but he mistook the nature of human happiness. — Happiness is not so *nice* as he would have it.

Many famous cases of miscalculation are recorded in politics (though the hedonist must always be wrong, since people obviously enjoy pain). It is an error of the same kind that people are more serious and honest in politics than in poker — or in ethical politics more so than in *realpolitik*. Why should they be? Just how unserious they are, however, still astonishes me — to speak for myself. For I find it difficult to overcome a lingering belief in, for instance, the instinct of self-preservation. That instinct can hardly be said to survive today.

Nineteenth Century altruism was a child of bible-religion. No one any longer even pretends to be concerned about the 'other fellow' — or about the poor old Many. They are just *too many!* The universal nurses flourished a century ago — and if you find somebody demonstrating indignantly about the lot of the Bulgars, or the Poles, or the Germans, you know it is politics. They are not getting a kick out of feeling sublimely Christian, I mean (although of course they are availing themselves of humanitarian habits of mind, which still pays dividends, for those who know how to shed a crocodile tear or affect to be shocked).

There is, indeed, no 'other fellow' any longer: *otherness*, like *opposition*, is reactionary. We are all One Fellow. It is an extreme simplification. The subjective temper of the present age tends to solipsistic valuations: and, of course, to the blackened corpse at Gif-sur-Yvette, to Doctor Petiot's performances, as also to the Gas-ovens at Belsen (the latter the work of a 'Sleepwalker').

This extreme view of our case I have introduced into this first phase of my remarks about politics, at the risk perhaps of making any subsequent consideration of them seem academic. For if *that* is politics, it might be asked, why talk about them? But a very small number of people think of them in such radical terms. So we must momentarily put aside this extreme interpretation, and approach the subject more as it is seen by the Majority — as much intellectualists as the non-intellectual. — Also, there is a ray of hope. Had I not made quite clear how tragically necessary it is that there *should* be such a ray, when finally I produce it it would be without effect.

Notes

1 A Lewis title (London, 1937).

[2] For Dean Inge, see note one to Ch. XIV, p. 83 below.

[3] Cesare Beccaria (1738-94), Italian criminologist and economist. Coleman Phillipson, *Three Criminal Law Reformers: Beccaria, Bentham, Romilly* (London, 1923), relates the work of Bentham and Beccaria.

CHAPTER XIII

THE 'DETACHED OBSERVER'

POLITICS is for the Twentieth Century what Religion was for the Sixteenth and Seventeenth. In a time so exclusively political, to stand outside politics is to invite difficulties: or not to identify yourself, in passionate involvement, with one or other of the contending parties.

In an age so intolerant of the Individual, it is dangerous to look too like one. But the 'individual' is a verbal abstraction. A man is made up of hundreds of different compartments: some are occupied by impulses deriving from tradition; some occupied by personal experiences stored away for use; some filled with contemporaneous acquisitions; and many are empty. So the so-called Individual is not what that word means in controversy. Rather is a mixed type — not an artificially uniform one, reacting in mystic harmony with a group.

It is to that narrowness that one is obliged to object. For the so-called Individual is, in the main, not himself. He is not *all* group, that is all; not all *one* group.

I am not inclined to say that 'to stand outside' is a good thing, except for a specific purpose. Men fall naturally and contentedly into parties, sects, and groups, and find their happiness there. Automatically, indeed, they get themselves a group-personality, if their own is not a very strong one. They are unusually addicted to group-passions just now. Since the Christian religion has guttered away, deprived of that communion, Party has violently occupied the vacuum, and people often behave towards it as if it were a Church. In the case of all revolutionary Parties, that means the State. My description of the State in Chapter XI is not necessarily what the State will be: it is what it has always been up to now. So there is room for hope. But we must never lose sight of what it always has been.

Even if inclined to gregarious passions, however (which I am not) to keep the mind free of dogma is a necessity if you are a student of things, rather than to be passionately immersed in one thing.

No executive politician is an addict of his own mythologies. But must he be the only cool-headed person? Must there be *no one* with no axe to grind? Must the scientist in future incline himself humbly before the popular hypothesis of the moment, on pain of excommunication?

Writing in 1937 Mr. T. S. Eliot made some interesting observations regarding *outsideness*. This occurred in an article, contributed to a magazine running a special number on my work.[1] One of my books concerned with the politics of Shakespeare had been selected by him for debate, especially in its bearing upon the influence exerted by Machiavelli.

Mr. Eliot, in speaking of the merits of the outside position, expressed himself as follows. 'There has never been a time surely when it was more important that the thinker and the artist should endeavor to get outside of their own country and own epoch.' And as to the great objection that is taken, in our day, to a person declining partisanship, he explains: 'As for Mr. Lewis's politics, I see no reason to suppose that he is any more of a "fascist" or "nazi" than I am. People are annoyed by finding that you are not on their side; and if you are not, they prefer you to surrender yourself to the other; if you can see the merits, as well as the faults, of parties to which you do not belong, that is still worse. Anyone who is not enthusiastic about the fruits of liberalism must be unpopular with the Anglo-saxon majority. So far as I can see, Mr. Lewis is defending the detached observer. The detached observer, by the way, is likely to be anything but a dispassionate observer; he probably *suffers* more acutely than the various apostles of immediate action.'

Finally, regarding the subject of my book: 'We do not need to believe that Machiavelli was an "ideologue" of either kind. He was in some respects, I believe, rather like Mr. Lewis who writes about him: a mild, detached man, who could never be the dupe of an idea, but who would be rather inefficient in private affairs, the prey of pickpockets, and the recipient of many a leaden half-crown.'

Where Mr. Eliot says, 'could never be the dupe of an idea', I should like to improve the compliment in the following way: 'and would be most unlikely to *pretend* to be the dupe'. Pretence is of the essence of much politics in all ages: for people cannot be so simple as frequently they act.

With certain reservations I accept Mr. Eliot's description of what was my rôle (for today it is a somewhat different one). I have never been a believer in the 'impersonal' critic, and have contended on many occasions that such a person does not exist. On the other hand you simply cannot *act* and *think* at one and the same time (except in the sense that to think is to act).

Should you doubt this, engage in some violent action (make love to someone, hit someone on the nose, or stand for parliament in a hotly contested election) and see how much intellection you are capable of, apart from what is mobilised to further the act in question. It is impossible to be an observer and participant at once: logic vanishes, all judgements are impossible when your emotions are deeply engaged. And of course the 'involvement' demanded by politics means you dope your intellect and carry on with something else, variously defined.

Let me agree, then, to the word 'detached', in the limited sense of habitually reserving judgement, and not expressing oneself by action, and, in perhaps the most important things, holding to the deliverances of reason. — Impersonal detachment is another matter. For the whole virtue of accurate observation is that it is a *person* observing — stereoscopically, the product of two or more groups, never of *one*. De la Rochefoucauld, described by Voltaire as the most important writer of the Seventeenth Century, observed human nature with a detached eye. But he observed with some violence; one is always conscious of the person there. — No person, of course, is capable of perfect detachment: the effort to attain to it would damage the observation. But a group does not observe at all: it *acts*. That is how it thinks. To think is to be split up.

The surrender of your will to a group disqualifies you as an observer or as a critic. A group does not observe, or criticise, another group. It attacks it, or woos it. Valid observation demands some self-effacement: there is no self-effacement about a group. Had M. de la Rochefoucauld remained the 'honnête homme' and perfect courtier that Cardinal de Retz would have wished him to be, we should have lost a great analytic spirit, and the Court would have gained another well-drilled nobody.

If by 'detached' is meant not adhering to a group-mind (from which must of course be excepted the various natural groups of which you were born a member — a sex-group, a national group, etc.) then the word can be accepted, for the time in question.*

If the word 'detached' requires an unconscionable amount of qualification, it is not because it is my feeling (as it is of so many people) that we should repudiate the idea of those intellectual freedoms which, in retrospect, makes the last four hundred years a treasure-house for the intellect. I do not regret the invention of printing — though had the rulers of the day understood what it would be responsible for, they would have hanged its inventor, and destroyed his apparatus. I am glad Galileo stuck to the theory of the roundness of the earth: I like knowing that. I am glad Darwin was a free man, and able to proceed with his researches.

I should be sorry to appear an out-and-out partisan of *outsideness*: but here are the arguments for it, and they are not insignificant.

Under present conditions it secures to our art and critical literature the freedom from mass-contagion, mental and emotional, those particular activities require. (That does not mean aloof or cold, but merely not intoxicated.) — Make the world too ideally safe for the politician, as formerly for the religionist, and by so doing you shut out the light and air necessary for thought and the creative arts: for he is only safe in the dark. Criticism is merely the introduction of the outside light into a dark place. *Outsideness* is to be where the light is.

When all men do their best, all the time, to be in harmony with the majority opinion of their period, there is stagnation.

Whichever Party is the most right, uniformity is always *wrong* (Party itself precluding uniformity). That is the judgement of life, at least. Nature abhors uniformity as much as it abhors a vacuum. In a society where affirmation is the only language allowed, nothing is left but the subjective fug of the Absolute.

Today, in contradiction to that view of things, every agency of social change is directed to the suppression of opposition ('opposition is reaction' said the 1946 Yugoslavs), to the penalising of the critic. And this tendency it is not easy entirely to condemn, especially if you have observed at close quarters, as I have, the orgy of Opposition which accompanies the functioning of democracy in the United States. Yet the services of democracy to the arts and to critical literature, to philosophy and the sciences: and to the amenities of social life, cannot be counted. On the other hand, it has

* Now I am a doctrinaire internationalist. As there is no Party today that is any longer internationalist, I am without a Party. But, to that extent, I have surrendered my will: and if a Party appeared whose plank was *one world*, I should belong to it. As it is, there are some of us in all Parties. Were I ever to possess a Party, it would be so large a one that I should still retain a large measure of my scientific licence to observe.

never been in fact democracy, such as would be acceptable to Rousseau's strict Genevan model, or indeed to that of any fairly particular man.

My method may seem too antinomic: but I do not think this can be stated properly otherwise. — Let me next speak of the fading from our scene of a figure that has ornamented it for a number of centuries: which is so much part of the civilised landscape that this figure would be greatly missed. He is Criticism impersonified. To this significant fact, valuable as evidence in a discussion of Totalitarian tendencies in our society, I propose to devote a separate chapter.

Notes

[1] T. S. Eliot, "The Lion and the Fox," *Twentieth Century Verse* No. 6/7 (1937), 109-12.

CHAPTER XIV

SHOULD WE DISCONTINUE THE ORACLES

NUMBERS of unofficial mentors, or critics, of society, have flourished in Western countries, ever since the invention of printing, and the emergence of 'free' Western societies, no longer subject uniquely to theological guidance. In England they have been very numerous and powerful. Their rôle has not been unlike that of the sophists in Greece. Shaw and Wells have been the most outstanding examples in recent years. Is this type of man now to disappear?

The fact that of the two keepers of the public conscience mentioned above one is a nonagenarian and the other dead speaks for itself: no one has succeeded them. The 'gloomy Dean' is another whom we may cite, and he too is well on in years.[1] Of course the intellectual quality of these particular oracles is irrelevant — although Shaw has been a very creditable one, who compares favourably with the general run of former sages. It is the causes, only, of the extinction of this social type that occupy me here.

These men have been private individuals, belonging as a rule to no Party — or so small a one as not to count. They have freely commented upon the doings of their rulers, or upon powerful political Parties or personalities, often with virulence; upon the ideas, or ideologies, taking shape and finding expression, from year to year, in books, in periodical literature or newspapers, in White Papers, and on platforms or in pulpits, and even from the Throne. Usually they have been *against* the ideas in the ascendant at any given moment. They have acted as a kind of medicine for the social body.

Is it now thought too dangerous to have such 'irresponsible' critics? If so, it is a new way, in the West, of ruling: to rule in silence, with nothing but bowed heads anywhere in sight. — Contrariwise (for we cannot dispense with antinomy) there can be a great deal too much noise: too many heads bobbing self-assertively about. Too much argument leads to disorder.

Had the absolutist monarchy of France (very imperfectly absolutist according to our Twentieth Century standards of what is absolute) proscribed and suppressed the 'philosophers', or such a super 'philosophe' as Rousseau, as soon as they showed themselves, it might not have come to so early an end. It is also true that had the Tsars suppressed Count Tolstoy and all those who with considerable impunity criticised the régime and petted the serfs, that might have been better for *them*. It would have been less good for *us*: since in the one case we should not have had Voltaire, Montesquieu, Rousseau, Diderot, and the rest, or in the other case practically all the Nineteenth Century literature of Russia — seething with sedition as it was, though bursting with genius. In their place we should have had a generation of mediocrities singing the praises of absolutism.

The French Eighteenth Century and the Russian Nineteenth were, however, anarchic. The self-indulgent and weak-minded little potentates in Versailles and in the Kremlin were theoretically autocrats — and so acted as red rags to a bull: they had not the sense to go liberal (and, even when they wanted to, their wives would not let them) nor had they the will to be efficient autocrats.

In both cases their bitter critics openly flourished. In Tsarist Russia the ruling class of 'nobles' was so liberal and 'broadminded' that it tended to agree that it was wicked and parasitic (for Tolstoy was not the only aristocrat who petted his peasants): it arranged its own funeral (with a special proviso that for so corrupt and tyrannical a class there should be *no flowers*).

In Eighteenth Century France — as the reactionary American Ambassador, Gouverneur Morris [2] discovered, to his dismay — half the aristrocracy was for the overthrow of the régime — regarding themselves as almost as much 'put upon' as the Tiers. So they arranged for their liquidation, too. — Let us always remember, therefore, that with these precedents ever present to his mind, no personal ruler today, of the most moderate intelligence, would encourage criticism.

In condemning the present rulers of Russia for banning 'free speech' let us not forget that they know only too well to what 'free speech' can lead. After all, they are where they are because of 'free speech'.

With Mr. Laski[3] I myself believe that excessive strictness is unnecessary, clumsy, unintelligent: that power can be agreeably disguised; however much liberty is circumscribed, life need not appear oppressively unfree. But in neither case do you get Voltaires or Tolstoys any more — nor Shaws — if you want one or two, to give a salt to life. I am afraid you also do not get Dante or Shakespeare; the former would have been easily caught and burned alive, long before he could write his seditious 'Inferno', and Shakespeare's gallery of sovereign rulers was much too lifelike to please authority.

Let me quote, in support of this opinion, a thinker who, although archaic, is generally respected. 'Régimes of the most varied type surround themselves with men of letters, or, as they now are called, "intellectuals". As long as these "intellectuals" remain submissive and offer themselves to the service of the State, to coin theories or poems useful to the State, they cannot be anything but literary men and intellectuals of a poor quality, as is to be expected.'

Countries like Russia and Germany, it has always seemed to me, get on better with an authoritarian government. And freedom is, after all, *what people want.* . . . As to Germany: Hegel, with his omnipotent State, was doing the thinking for a majority of Germans. Today we plan to 'teach the Hun democracy'. (How reminiscent those things are of John Bull's relations with Ireland.) Had we wished to do that, we have lost our opportunity. The days of the Weimar Republic was the time to do that — with friendship and helpfulness, which is the correct technique. But if we are to try today, it is still the only technique likely to bear any fruit at all.

The English and the Americans are extremely different from Germans and Russians, and they have Democracy as their traditional theory of the

State (I mean of course what is generally meant by that term in the West). They have been anarchists for so long (more or less disciplined anarchists, which is what our 'democracy' generally amounts to) that it would be very painful for them should they find themselves abruptly under authoritarian rule. With this standpoint, I take it, most of us are in agreement, even those in favour of a maximum of controls.

It is in conformity with this belief that I am directing my argument here: with the belief, namely, that although the more intelligent among us would regard it as nonsensical to interfere with the political habits of other peoples, we ourselves accept our own political habits as a basis of action and thought: not meaning by this that those habits must not suffer change; but that the changes will be sufficiently tempered so as not to destroy the internal national mechanisms by too violent reversals, and that those changes will never lead to a type of life where we have not our decent ration of freedom.

From this it follows that we can speak of ourselves as still inhabiting a somewhat anarchic world, where my great appetite for liberty and yours may be, temporarily, and within reasonable bounds satisfied: with 'free speech', though properly and tactfully curbed, a recognised feature of our Western scene. This having been happily settled, I can proceed with what I have to say about the Critic. For we must agree, whether 'free speech' is a good thing, or a bad thing (and often it has proved the latter), if there is a ban on critics there is no longer any 'free speech'.

'Dissociating oneself from the community' is the way in which criticism is apt, rather disingenuously, to be described. But criticism of contemporary attitudes of mind, of prevalent ideas, of pastimes, of popular superstitions, of fashions, of snobberies, and so forth, does not answer to the above description. Surely such criticism should not cease in a socialist society, when that supervenes: for the community will not grow wiser overnight and will never be wise enough to dispense with criticism altogether.

Many are expressing themselves today as if the entire structure of our intellectual life must not be dismantled. They would interpret the 'sovereignty of the people' to mean that we should without demur associate ourselves with any superstitious beliefs or degrading enthusiasms of the majority (wished on it by the money-power) or join with it in any sin against taste or good sense, for which deliberately inadequate standards of popular education are responsible. — The thinker or the artist can no longer, it is affirmed, be permitted 'to dissociate himself from the community'. This may be paraphrased as follows: no *unofficial*, or private, or outside criticism (such as Mr. Shaw or Mr. Wells indulged in — or Voltaire, or Rousseau, or Tolstoy) is to be tolerated.

That is a very violent doctrine and should be combated. The 'intellectual' must enrol himself, it seems to imply, in the propaganda service of the State. And the State, in turn, would, on its thinking side, become a club of intellectual managers, headed, no doubt, by a Goebbels-like Minister.

Such type of thinking, by whatever name it may go, is merely fascism. So it is a curious fact that those disinclined for the stooge's rôle as outlined above will often find themselves abusively misnamed 'fascist' by these advocates of absolutist power-doctrines for the West, who themselves answer far better to that description.

My personal interest in the future of the public Critic is, at the most, only indirect. Not desirous myself of being a Diogenes, in or out of a tub, being much too busy in other ways to become a public oracle, it is as one of the public, not as a performer, that I would put in a word for the continuance of this institution. It is in words what David Low is graphically. He is an institution of precisely the same order: and it would be a pity to see him drawing pretty pictures of our rulers.

There is, however, a way in which I, and a number of other writers, have a stake in 'free speech'. In the composition of a novel I would prefer to have a reasonable latitude of expression. I harbour no ambition to undermine any existing government, after the manner of the philosophes or the Tsarist intelligentsia. The hereditary despots have all vanished, in any case. But to arraign M. Sartre for his nihilism—as an illustration— might lead to anything. We should claim such harmless privileges as were enjoyed, for instance, by the author of 'Bouvard et Pécuchet': our right should be recognised to express doubts as to the aptitudes and historical possibilities of our species, without the prospect of finding ourselves denounced as indulging an 'aristocratic' impulse.

That is a label, 'aristocratic', used only by the most unscrupulous, in this era of cheerless decay. In my own experience I find that those most prone to avail themselves of it for 'smear' purposes, are far richer, vainer, more high-handed, more fond of power, better housed, more pretentious than the majority. There is nothing personally I should like to be so little as an aristocrat. And I should hate to find myself hanging to a lamp-post as a sort of Sir What's-his-name, or Lord Thingumajig.

Possessing that variety of mind, I go on analysing just as the mason-bee builds its clay-walled cubicle, or as the woodpecker pecks. I am convinced that in so employing myself I am of far more use to the community than are those busy gentlemen who advocate the cancellation of the democratic licence to publish an opinion other than that ostensibly of the community. I say 'ostensibly', for what opinions has the generality, except those supplied to them by these very busybodies. The latter desire to establish a monopoly as purveyors of opinion, having appropriated the multitude. It is merely a development of censorship to say that you must blindly identify yourself with the community. It should be resisted like all manoeuvres directed to muzzle us like dogs, before we have a State that we can respect, or a Public with whose standards we can joyfully identify ourselves.

The attitude, as we have seen, of people to what is called a 'portrait' has radically altered. What Caterina Cornaro would 'take' the contemporary Caterina would angrily dismiss as a malicious caricature. A more subjective image, nearer to the heart's desire (though much farther from what the eye sees) is imperiously required. How much a time is all of one piece! In politics an alteration of the same kind has taken place. The objective is decried and disallowed: so we pass into a world of make-believe, where there are no geese left but only swans: a place of inflated values, leading to no values at all.

Tom Paine believed in the Rights of Man. To 'investigate the principles of government and to *publish'* my conclusions is by no means my wish, however (I can think these things out without publishing them) because there is something I want to do, and have always desired to do, more than this, thank heavens. Politically I stand *nowhere* any more than a fish does. I find myself in a dense medium, I swim along, consuming such small edible matter as comes my way in 1947 — I can have no more part in the government of the world than were I a fish I should have in the disposal of the tides and currents of the ocean. My mind likes penetrating the depths, where it is dark and cold, or disporting itself upon the sparkling surface, where it is warm and gay. — I do not wish to belong to a *school* of fish: that is I think the only complication.

As I am not a busybody I have not favoured one side or the other — but have only found this side or that more dangerous at a given moment. Now I have a potential Party — that of Cosmic Man. But I would not forcibly prevent people from advertising the horrible beauties of the Sovereign State. Formerly I would have said, in the language of Palmerston, that I had neither friends nor enemies, but only interests. People who live for Party find it very difficult to believe this. How difficult they find it the next chapter, I hope, will show.

Notes

[1] W. R. Inge (1860-1954), Dean of St. Paul's, theologian. He was known as "the gloomy Dean" from his criticism of popular illusions in his weekly articles in the *Evening Standard* (1921-46).

[2] Gouverneur Morris (1752-1816), appointed minister to France (1792-94) by George Washington; an anti-democrat, he supported the idea of a constitutional monarchy in France, despite his active role in the American Revolution.

[3] Harold Laski (1893-1950), political theorist and university teacher in England and America, and Labour politician with Marxist leanings.

CHAPTER XV

LIBEL AND THE GAME OF LABELLING

ON looking through 'The Partisan Review' last year (Summer Number, 1946) I read with profound astonishment the following piece of news about myself. It occurred in a 'London Letter'.[1]

'The intellectual struggle between Stalinists and anti-Stalinsts goes on and on, with frequent sensational defections from one side or the other. Wyndham Lewis, I am credibly informed, has become a Communist or at least a strong sympathiser, and is writing a book in praise of Stalin to balance his previous books in favour of Hitler.'*

I am so used to this kind of thing that it takes a good deal to surprise me. But this curious fairy-story exported to America was a record in silliness, if not in malevolence. Someone had perhaps indulged in a practical joke, Mr. George Orwell – for it was he who wrote the 'London Letter' – being the willing victim. – It would be interesting to know how this successful highbrow publicist came to regard as 'credible' a story which had no foundation in fact. The only book I have written for the last five years is one about the United States of America, its government and history. This report of my having gone communist is such utter nonsense, however, that one is put to it to see how, even in so hysterical a time as this, the above legend can have germinated and been believed.

As it happens, I have not been Mr. Orwell's only victim, in the New York magazine where his simple-hearted 'news' of London is published. It appears to me to be a kind of labelling-game that he plays – like H. G. Wells's *spotting* game, with guests in a hotel lobby. Only it is as if the identification were narrowed down to a half-a-dozen categories. All the guests that pass Mr. Orwell, in *his* hotel, are either 'stalinists' or 'anti-stalinists', 'cryptos', 'fascists', 'blimps'. His is a purely political hotel: most of his travellers travel with faked visas and postiche moustaches: all travel on political business, all live and have their being in politics. It is all very romantic and exciting.

If somebody – no matter who it may be – in order to keep poor old battered, under-nourished, poverty-stricken (indeed ruined) Great Britain out of yet another war, began to argue that Russia should not be held up to the public as the appropriate successor to Germany as Public Enemy No. 1 – said a few things calculated to calm rather than inflame (in spite of the fact that communist state capitalism was of all theories of the state the one he personally liked least) automatically Mr. Orwell would reach for his little box of labels and would select one inscribed 'stalinist'.

I do not say that he means any great harm: it is just a way of killing

---

* As to my books 'in favour of Hitler', I have written two books about Hitler, one when he first appeared on the scene, seventeen years ago (in 1930) before he came to power and revealed what a lunatic he was, and the other ('The Hitler Cult and How it will End') at the time of Munich. The first book was 'in favour': though that was not the Nazis' view of the matter; the second is very much the reverse of 'in favour'.

time with him. What I do say is that he suffers from an innate inability to imagine anyone acting from motives other than those belonging to revolutionary politics. He believes that everyone is engaged in playing a game to which he is passionately devoted.

Although I am sure that Mr. Orwell is not wanting in patriotism, yet England—the country in which forty-seven million of us live—does not enter into his calculations—it is as if it were not there: it does not exist for him except as a 'stalinist' or 'anti-stalinist' counter. If you or I for quite selfish reasons make its interests the *starting-point* for what we think about foreign affairs, he would never be able to divine that what we said about foreign policy had something to do with what would be best for the inhabitants of London (in my case of Notting Hill Gate).

'What nothing theoretic—nothing ideologic?! Go along with you!' (if I may make him use so homely an expression). 'Do you want me to believe that so contemptibly practical, utilitarian, a motive as *that* accounts for the attitude you adopt!' Something of that sort would be Mr. Orwell's genuine reaction. Or it *would* be were he not obsessed with his political game—so that probably instead of this what he would say, with a sly smile would be: 'Now don't tell me that you are not engaged in the *stalinist-antistalinist* game! I'm not going to listen to that!'

This is perhaps too kind an interpretation: Mr. Orwell may not be quite so irresponsible as this. He certainly should not be encouraged. — Again he has a theory—in which seemingly he reposes the utmost confidence —which confers upon him complete immunity to indulge his propensity to the top of his bent. Here is this strange doctrine of immunity. He believes it is perfectly in order for people to do any 'smearing' they think fit: for no honest man would object to being called a thief, no god-fearing abstainer from sexual indulgence would mind being denounced as a lecher, no statesman mind the charge that he had accepted bribes from the enemy; nor a politician take exception to a statement that he was sailing under false colours, nor a writer that he was writing a book he wasn't writing, in which he had given voice to opinions that he in fact did not hold.—If anyone resents these imputations, what is more, it is proof of his guilt.

Here are his words: 'If what I have suggested is obviously untrue, why does he (a person objecting to finding himself labelled) get so hot and bothered about it? Recently I found myself described by an American paper as a Fascist. I did not write a letter denouncing this as a "slander", because no one whose opinion mattered would pay any attention to it.' Why then, he argues, should anyone object to being described as a 'crypto' or anything else? And he would, it must be assumed, ask why I should mind it being blazoned abroad that I had become a communist, if in fact I had not.

This theory is, I feel, typical of the man. It leaves out practically everything about such attacks as his that matters—for people who have their living to make, or who are vulnerable to public opinion, or depend for their efficacy upon the confidence reposed in them by the average man.—The 'smear' factor is entirely left out of the reckoning.

The shining armour of integrity enables the honourable and upright man to curl his lip, and pass, his nose in the air, however adhesive the mud that may be aimed at him. It is a picture full of nobility. Alas, this orwellian figure does not exist in the real world. It should not be thrust into it as an argument. It would only be an argument in the Morte d'Arthur: it is not one in Westminster or Manhattan in the Twentieth Century.

Mr. Orwell is called a Fascist in America, he tells us. But this would not be attributing to him membership of some political party, only of a state of mind: indeed it could not be the former, for there are no fascist parties any longer in existence. So it is not a parallel to the assertion that someone is a communist. I have myself seen the question asked, by an American critic, whether Mr. Orwell was not a 'Blimp'. And Colonel Blimp is certainly a 'fascist' according to the vocabulary of contemporary political controversy. But I believe that intellectuals no longer know that they are saying it—they just spit 'fascist', or 'crypto', 'stalinist', 'stooge', 'Blimp', without thinking—as schoolboys emit 'swot', 'cad' or 'house-tart'. Under an anaesthetic or when at the dentist's gas is administered, in his slumber, or when he wakes up in the morning and his tongue begins drowsily to wag, the average intellectual lisps 'fascist' or 'crypto'. The life of the rank and file intellectual (who is about as *intellectual* as a sparrow) revolves about a half-dozen childish epithets, and the emotions aroused by their utterance.

But Mr. Orwell is not such a rank and file intellectual exactly. He is a prominent publicist, and is not by any means a brainless person.—I fear he has not entirely ceased to be a schoolboy: for to see him standing, boastfully undismayed, in the midst of a hail of political expletives, is discouraging—he is one of England's best highbrows. Here is a big boy behaving like a small boy, some friends should tell him that.

As to the meaning of his personal attack upon me, it was again, I suppose, the sporting instinct. The Sahib imagined himself in the jungles of Burma, doing a bit of rogue-elephant hunting!—I have not, however, proved myself a very savage animal. I have contented myself with shaking him off. I have not eaten him alive!

It is not to say because this item of misleading information in a New York magazine is frivolous, that it is harmless. To me a very alien doctrine, I should not feel 'smeared' because I was called a communist. But it is not my reactions which are in question. It is what other people feel about communism, and the importance to me—economically, socially, or otherwise—that these people should not be prejudiced against me, because of my supposed political views. The law of libel, which approaches this matter in a more practical and less lofty spirit than Mr. Orwell, takes particular note of such facts as these. And this report is not calculated to help me in New York, where I have to sell books and other things, or, for that matter, here.

———

A few words in conclusion about the subject of my imaginary book. What I am about to say would be incomprehensible to the Sahib, with whom I have been engaged up to now, since he is the Happy Warrior type. Even in 'Polemic' a few months ago I found him telling Stalin grimly what would happen to *him* one of these fine days would be that someone will drop some atom bombs on him, or words to that effect.[2]

I am no longer interested in war as a thing to talk about as if it could be isolated — I shall certainly never again take my garden hose to extinguish a volcano — but as to Russia let me say this. I hope we shall not be quite so foolish as to go to war. At least do not let us busily discover that Russian communism is *bad* — having formerly busily persuaded ourselves during a quarter of a century that it was *good* — so as to have an excuse for war. I have always regarded it as most imperfect, illiberal and autocratic, myself. But happily I am not subject to these violent reversals of opinion.

The revolutionary aggressiveness of the Russians is such as to make it difficult for us to think of otherwise than bristling with arms. However, the Russian People have always traditionally hated war; just as the Germans, more than any other nation, have been egregiously martial. That is a fact of such moment that we ought never to lose sight of it. In the case of Stalin we are not dealing with a man who will lightly go to war. He will do so only as a last resort. And Molotov, named as his successor, is no militarist, either, I should say.

What I am about to do now is to think aloud about current happenings. I shall write ahead for a while, without weighing my words. By this method I shall be demonstrating, better than by more formal exposition, how my mind works, if I ask it unexpectedly for a report — which is not often now. I do not care for dog-racing, Pools or bitter beer but I differ very little from the Majority in my growing indifference as to those events upon which I can exercise no more influence than a fly by its buzzing: so when I see 'Big Four' this, or that, at the top of a page, as a rule I turn it over. I should not be writing about 'Big' events at all were it not for the purpose of this demonstration, which I hope may prove a good way of throwing light upon the nature of my 'stalinism'.

Notes

[1] *Partisan Review* 13 (1946), 320-25. The quotation appears on p. 323.

[2] George Orwell, "Second Thoughts on James Burnham," *Polemic* No. 3 (May, 1946); rpt. in *The Collected Essays, Journalism and Letters of George Orwell*, vol. IV, ed. S. Orwell and I. Angus (London, 1968), pp. 160-81. Orwell says on p. 180:

> If I had to make a prophecy, I should say that a continuation of the policies of the last fifteen years . . . can only lead to war conducted with atomic bombs, which will make Hitler's invasion look like a tea-party.

CHAPTER XVI

THINKING ALOUD UPON CURRENT AFFAIRS

I NOW begin thinking aloud about current happenings. A number of politicians are meeting in Paris—this is the major political fact of the moment—under the name of 'the united nations'. (If when you come to read this they are no longer meeting in Paris, but in Moscow, New York, or London instead, that is immaterial. Exactly the same thing will be going on. Just substitute for Paris 'Moscow'—'New York' or wherever the place at the moment happens to be and carry on.) These assembled statesmen are supposed to be arranging a peace settlement. All the indications are, however, that another war is what in fact is in preparation. They do seem a lot of *united* nations as far as that is concerned. Do not misunderstand me! they are not doing this wilfully: on both sides the statesmen involved are more intelligent and pacific than in the past has generally been the case. Neither Mr. Molotov, Mr. Bevin, nor the Americans are fire-eaters. Committed to competition, however (also deeply separated in their political beliefs) they cannot escape from the ruts worn by the war-chariots of thousands of years of human history. — Two rival groups are plainly discernible. It appears they thump the conference table at each other and brandish their fists. It is far worse than the League of Nations, it would seem. There are more of them.*

All this is described huffily by political commentators and editorial writers as 'so much power politics'—as if these representatives of the nations ought not to be having anything to do with *power*. But four of the nations in question are called 'Great Powers', and all are 'Powers' with a capital letter. So it is surely natural, when they get together, that 'power-politics' should ensue. What should a 'Power' talk about except power, in some form or other? If you wanted any other kind of politics, the Powers would have to stop being Powers. But no Power will consent to cease being a Power—until all its autonomy is removed from it, as with Germany and Japan at present. That is two 'Powers' out of the way, anyhow.

A peace in which we have *all* the power could be written now and everybody live happily ever afterwards if other people didn't worry so much about that beastly thing, *power*: and that exactly describes the Russian feeling too. Is not *one* power all that is necessary? Both sides, as you see, have the right idea: if only there were *one* Power, instead of *several*, then there would be Peace. The Russians appear to wish to demonstrate this principle by eating us up piecemeal—only since adopting communism is an integral part of the process (this does not mean what-is-mine-is-yours however, there's a bad catch in it) the Western nations object to being politically 'penetrated' and absorbed.

'Power-politics'—or what the Junkers called *Machtpolitik* and which

* This was written before the Big Four decided to isolate themselves. They get on fine now. But nothing comes of it.

we liked to allude to by their German name too as it suggested that only the Germans indulged in them — are recognised by everybody — or almost everybody — as beastly. No State should wish for power, since power has to be fought for with blood and sweat and tears, and war is a crime. Also, if there were no more fighting — all ships and planes of war, machine-guns, tanks, bombs, and rifles destroyed in all countries — we, the English, should be better off than most, seeing that our possessions are still exceptionally large. If force continues to be recognised as an instrument of policy — if blood continues to be man's argument — these possessions will in all likelihood steadily diminish. — Foreigners have their own way of looking at this, but you know what foreigners are like.

The power-problems preoccupying the Western nations are in fact, in the main, of their own making: would not be there if they had not put them there. Thus: world war ii was more than ever decided by technology rather than physiology, martial qualities of secondary consideration. Hence Russia was able to halt the Panzers, and the Germans were defeated by the irresistible torrent of armaments pouring into Russia from the American factories. In a word, the Russians depended for survival upon the U.S.A. (the U.S.A., in its turn, of course, needing Great Britain, the British armies, the English fleet, and the British Isles). *Therefore*, it was the business of the Western Powers to be very firm about what Europe should look like after the war.

Some of the Western statesmen must have heard about communism — must have known it wasn't a Face Powder or a Laxative. They must have read, here and there, how imperialist its temper was, as displayed in China, Sinkiang and so forth. Again, the aloof Moscow rulers, trained in a desperate school, were not likely recruits to play at high contracting parties in a beautiful Gentleman's Agreement — were they? When Mr. Roosevelt before going to Teheran asked Miss Perkins to find out for him what made the Russians tick she cannot, in her report the next morning, have given the correct answer.

When Mr. Churchill's plan to attack the Festung Germania through the Balkans, because objected to by Russia was scrapped by Mr. Roosevelt, Europe as we know it today, Russianised Europe, began to take shape. — Do not blame Russia, however!

Now, as a result of these strange arrangements, the Western nations, the war ended, popped a king back upon the Greek throne. This was very defiant. The Russians, to whom we had given the Balkans, were just about to take over Greece too and were naturally rather disgusted. Meanwhile half of Greece is overrun with communists, supplied from across the Russian-controlled frontiers to the north. British troops have to be garrisoned there: the U.S. sends money and food. — A strangely exposed island of democracy: when a war comes I suppose we shall have to leave, we should be too few. Those who have sided with us, tens of thousands, will be murdered. But the same thing will happen in Berlin some day.

If we see the Russians on the Schelde it will be because things like communism are usually imperialist, and with the slightest encouragement they would go to the Schelde — and to the Cape of Good Hope — in any case. And Mr. Roosevelt was certainly not discouraging. But also Soviet Russia could not quite unreasonably argue that we had denied it its natural outlet, so in consequence it was seeking 'windows' elsewhere. Russia's great rivers flow into the Black Sea: its natural window upon the outer world is there. Or the Black Sea is as it were the hall of its house, and the Dardanelles its front door. But the key to that front door is held by Turkey. But I need not go into this any further — remind you how the English have always spoken of the Mediterranean as a 'life-line', what their feelings are about the Suez Canal and what the Americans feel about the Panama Canal. It is quite possible I believe to condense the common sense of this stupid situation as follows: England should not have regarded the Mediterranean as a private lake and of course no obstacle should have been put in the way of this enormous country, Russia, getting in and out of itself by water. (Britannia rules the waves was the moronic rant of music-hall music: but sometimes it almost looked as if British statesmen *thought* like that.) On the other hand, if that huge Slav State showed any tendency to spill itself into Western Europe all Western peoples should take up arms against it.

As to Germany, here is all plain sailing, too. Since the Russians were given Berlin, Brandenburg, Silesia, and so on (the American Army held back, much to its disgust, so that this might be effected as arranged) what is all the fuss about? You cannot unscramble an egg. The most ghastly kind of war alone can unscramble *that* egg.

It's an ill-favoured Peace. Neither you nor I made, at Yalta, at Teheran, at Potsdam, the arrangements so uniquely favourable to Russia. But seeing that they *were* made, would it not be better to accept the inevitable, and get along on that basis — we with our customary tact and diplomatic finesse trying to make our lot of Germans into democrats like ourselves, and the Russians, on their side of the 'iron curtain', naturally busy stalinising their lot?

Another thing we could do is to leave Germany at once. We shall certainly never get anything out of stopping there, and are likely to be squeezed out or pushed out. If we *do* stop we should get a cast-iron undertaking from the Americans that they will stop there too: but all that is anyway very adventurous and beyond our means. (This is 'off the record' — as it is also if I say, as I do, that we should clear out of Palestine.)

We are going about our democratisation of our zone in Germany in an awfully funny way. First of all we are starving the Germans — they are living in the ruins of their cities (immeasurably more shattered than any of ours) in great misery — which as everyone knows turns people, sooner or later, into communists, not into democrats. Lord Beveridge, in two articles written for *The Times*, describes what we are doing. Especially he tells us how, with almost teutonic thoroughness, we are seeing to it that the Germans shall not take matters into their own hands, and go fishing around for food for themselves. The food they don't get must all come from us. Here is Lord Beveridge's account of one of our master-strokes — under the headline 'Slow Starvation'.

'We are committed by the Potsdam decision to a policy of destroying war potential. In Hamburg we have just blown up one of the largest shipyards in such a way as to destroy 12,500 tons of steel where steel is desperately short. The next largest shipyard is on the list for destruction.

There is yet a third shipyard, which I visited myself, which for more than 100 years has been engaged on building small craft, largely fishing boats, never anything larger than 3,000 tons; building and repair of fishing boats is the work on which it is now engaged. It had 75 bombs on it in the war, but enough survives for it still to be able to do this work. It is difficult to suggest anywhere any way of relieving Germany's shortage of fats and proteins, without taking food from other nations, more direct than reconstructing her fishing fleet; the unfished seas are full of herrings. Yet this shipyard has been declared by the Allied Committee in Berlin to be unnecessary for German economic life and . . . will be closed down at the end of this month.' — So we are blowing up the docks where fishing boats are built and repaired lest the Germans should do any fishing by way of helping us feed them, instead of remaining a vast, helpless, discontented population which has to be fed by us, thereby reducing month by month the food rations for the British people.

From these last remarks any really intelligent man will see at once that I have fallen in love with the inhabitants of Hamburg and those of the rest of our little continental domain. — But, no: he would in fact be altogether too precipitate. For the German people take to the military life far too easily for one to feel over-sorry for them when they suffer as the result of one of their typical military gambles. — As a fact, I was just thinking of the English — those who stand in the queues, not those in the night clubs and other centres of abundance. I think of Dr. Isaac Harris's 'calcium bread scandal' — of my own stomach, among other things: which does not like chalk and bran, insufficient meat for a carnivore, inadequate fats and citrus fruits, two pints of inferior milk a week. All this being no fault of the government of the day: it has twenty million extra people to feed, besides lots of others all over the world. It is just the White Man's Burden — so sore a burden that he is now become a 'poor White'.

There is an issue of a different kind, to which I now will turn. Some terrible discoveries have been made about our ex-ally. No one knew anything about it — it has all been very sudden. I have already let slip a remark or two. Anyway, here it is, Russia, it seems, is not like other countries. It is not really a democracy, as we had always understood it was — up to, as a matter of fact, about twelve months ago. This came as a great shock. Stalin, it appears, is a dictator! That was the first blow. His régime, if you please, is totalitarian. It is only 'socialist' in name: a 'police-state', as was that of the Tsars. — Thank God for the 'iron-curtain' is all I can say, or the illusions of the starry-eyed 'liberals' would just have gone puff had it not been for that curtain! Eastern Germany, Poland, Hungary, Lithuania, Rumania, etc. etc. etc. etc. etc. etc. etc. etc., say those who have had a scandalised peep, have lost their *sovereignty* (comparable this, in the case of a State, to a woman's loss of her virtue).

Even so staunch a supporter of the Soviet as the *New Statesman* has got decidedly wobbly. Ex-U.S.-ambassador Bullitt sees the red light — is writing books advocating use of the atom bomb at once. He knew Russia quite well (where he had been a popular ambassador), and was a great propagandist for the Soviet, so it must have come as a shock to him to learn that it is not a democracy. Everything in the brief space of something under a year has been transformed; all the swans have become geese as if by magic. Hans Andersen would feel at home in the Atomic Age, where potentates ride naked through streets, the scandalous exhibition unremarked, when up pipes the voice of some little publicist and a twenty-year long spell is broken — where sucking doves turn into vultures, and vice versa, with baffling suddenness. — I have my personal surprise too: a well-known left wing publicist is writing articles which, when first I read them, I thought were mine, of fifteen years ago (when I began my battle against the drift to war) but these of Mr. Orwell are most warmly received. Today I hardly know if I am standing on my head or my heels: my sense of being in a society where all the labels have been changed overnight produces inevitable vertigo. For *good* now read *bad*, for *black* read *white*.

I listen to Messrs. Koestler and Eastman (and of course Saint George for England) about this vile tyrant, who holds 20 million persons in permanent captivity in Siberia under conditions of unparalleled barbarity. The *New Statesman* listens too, to the growing chorus; it appeals to Russia, as an old friend, to stop these inhuman practices. The people who respond indignantly to these atrocity stories are the same who a few years back, as Friends of Russia, raised their huzzas for our allies against despotism and savagery.

These tales of atrocities are indeed calculated to chill: but to flop from one hysterical extreme to another is a symptom that must give grounds for anxiety. The national health has clearly been overstrained.

As to this 'new' view of Russia, a long time — oh twenty years ago, I had heard something of this kind, I gathered that personal liberty was not the strong point of the Russian régime, that the Tsarist Secret Police, taken over by Lenin almost intact (since this huge country could not be ruled without it, and there was the machine to his hand) were distinctly tough, that Stalin's rule was on the absolutist side. Very naturally — or so it seemed to me — I was not attracted by so illiberal a theory of the State. I was told by everybody, however, that I had been misinformed — and that it was most malicious of me, too, to listen to tainted tittle-tattle of that order, and not to join in the rejoicing of all other intellectuals about 'the great socialist experiment'.

Russia proper is harder to hear about. But with regard to the broad belt of States which have now come under Russian control, a typical account of present conditions is as follows. My quotations are from an article in the 'Tribune' on Slovenia under Tito's rule. 'The spirit of culture which was evident before the war has been eliminated, and replaced by party hatreds and barbarous militarism', we learn. As examples of the 'barbarous militarism' the new School Readers, prepared for Slovenian children, are cited: the first book a child has in its hands while learning to read and write, so fixing its view of human life for good. 'Of 60 pages . . . 42 have subjects of political or military significance . . . the letter M is taught by showing gallows in the shape of an M, and children's mothers being led off to them, handcuffed by Italians . . . P is taught by "Pushka", Slovene word for rifle, and B by "Bomba" (hand-grenade)'. — Since teaching in English Public Schools is so emphatically military, and from the Boys' Brigade onwards we indoctrinate the poor child also in warlike ideals, that particular type of 'barbarity' is too familiar at home to arouse the indignation it otherwise might. As to the *Italians* who seemingly play so sinister a part as national enemy No. 1 in infant pedagogy in Slovenia, one recalls how, with us, 'The Hun' has played a similar rôle. We are not so thorough-going as Tito, but we have, in a milder form, the same idea.

Something of a quite different order comes later in this article. Let me quote. 'One evening before last Christmas about 200 children were collected and, together with adults who had been bribed to play their part with a permit to buy stockings, were marched to a nursery school in a suburb. This school was run by nuns in their own house and grounds, and for threepence a week children could be looked after all day and provided with their dinner. When they arrived outside the nursery the children "demonstrated", that is to say, they shouted such slogans as "Out with the reactionary whores", "Hang the bitches", and warned the nuns that if they were not out within 24 hours they would be hanged. The nuns, knowing the threats came from people far more dangerous than the children who had shouted them, had no option but to comply with the orders given to them by their late pupils. The authorities hastened to approve of this "spontaneous and democratic demonstration of the will of the children".'

That is a very horrible story. It was, however, things of that order that estranged many people, myself among them, from the Government side in Spain — when in that ghastly civil war the Russians seemed to be moving in as they have now moved in in Eastern Europe. 'Tribune' (in the same number) says of this moving-in process: Russia 'has pushed her influence as hard as she was able, sometimes by an overt display of force, and at other times by political intrigue . . . Communist stooges like to pretend that this extended influence is due to spontaneous social revolutions in the countries brought within the Soviet sphere, but it is not worth delaying to debate such rubbish. In several cases the methods employed have been brutal, totalitarian, and an affront to every principle for which the name of Socialism ought to stand'.

That they would be 'totalitarian' I should expect, for, as I said above, in the mid-twenties I kind of got wind of something of the sort — that Russian methods were awfully unlike those of Western democracy or the socialism of Keir Hardie, say, or Lansbury.[1] For the rest, 'Tribune' being an unusually honest paper, points out that the Russians are not the *only* imperialists on the scene just now. After all MacArthur seems to be doing a good imperialist job in Japan (the ex-Son of Heaven has a large picture of Abraham Lincoln on the wall behind his writing desk, playing the same rôle as Stalin, Tito, or Hitler portraits elsewhere, or in the old days the Virgin Mary, John Wesley, or Brigham Young). China seemingly is becoming an American economic sphere or protectorate — although the American press and radio have never ceased self-righteously to clamour against 'White empire in Asia' and the British Raj. Again, a last quotation: 'We (England) are not engaged in a policy of expansion.' No, our expanding days are over, happily. A 'second-rate power' can hardly take on more commitments. But this is the first time we haven't expanded after a war. When we contemplate, I suppose, Palestine, Egypt, India, and so on, we feel we have expanded enough. Part of Germany, it is true, is an accretion of sorts, for how long we do not know.

The paper from which I have drawn my quotation is social-democratic. With the communists and social democrats it is a case of cat and dog. The latter accuse Russian communism of having taken all the humanity out of Socialism, and the Russians assert that social-democratic régimes are not yet free of bourgeois attributes and associations. — It might be said that the social democrats stand for the old humanist socialism, the communists for the streamlined intellectualist Twentieth Century variety. But communism is split. Stalinists of twenty years' standing are running around, rubbing their eyes as if awakening from a dream, and pointing denunciatory fingers in the direction of the Kremlin.

It is completely absurd to pretend that all these people have not been aware all along of things they are affecting now, with a sanctimonious start of surprise, to discover: namely that Russia is not a democracy after the Western pattern: that Stalin is an absolute ruler, or the Politburo a body like the Council of Six: and that socialism in Russia is not what Keir Hardie or William Morris would have recognised as such: as I have heard H. G. Wells protesting, 'not *my* idea of liberty'. All this they knew perfectly well. And some of them were impudent enough to vilify me for saying what now they say themselves. I am resentful, how could I be otherwise? There was no little pink who did not shout 'fascist' at me, because I wished to spare this country another fearful war — or pick up that cute little counter 'appeaser', and aim it at my head.

———

That is the end of the demonstration. I have not quite been thinking aloud, for otherwise I should have given a picture of such wild irrationality that beside it what I have *written* would appear very judicious and restrained. There is enough, however, in my above musings upon current events to enable anyone to decide what in fact is my present position. I submit that what I am is what I was, but with a different accent on most things. In the next chapter but one I shall be outlining what these changes of accent are.

Notes

[1] James Keir Hardie (1856-1915), first organizer of Scottish miners' unions and first Chairman of the Independent Labour Party. George Lansbury (1859-1940), prominent socialist, pacifist and Labour M.P.

CHAPTER XVII

GROUP-TECHNIQUES AND REAL POLITICS

THE last chapter, colloquial as it was, like a reflex almost, should have achieved its purpose, if anything could. It is obvious enough that had I been under the obligation to make my reactions conform to this or that Party dogma, I should have been obliged, in the course of even so short a piece of thinking, to do violence to my thoughts – to push them this way or that, constrict them, in many cases suppress them, in others exaggerate and inflate them. I was thinking things that would not fit into any national-ist, or liberal, or marxist, or conservative pattern. Some items would have fitted in: others would not. – So it is with practically all real and valuable political thinking.

Of course there have to be group techniques, or ideologies, otherwise men would stagnate. The more violent of them are rules for the engineering of artificial storms: others specialise in mass-hypnosis. As doctrine they are too entangled with propaganda to be considered apart from their functional character. The kind of political free-thinking I crave the right occasionally to practise can have no undesirable effect upon the operation of a spell-binder. For one man who wants to do a little political, or other, free-thinking there are a thousand who much prefer to be entranced, to give themselves up to deceptive images, of, for instance, freedom or equality.

'What is a perfectly free person? . . . Well, there is no such person', Mr. Bernard Shaw would tell them – if they had any appetite for such truths – and enumerate for them all the things which most palpably con-dition our personal freedom.* As to equality, Prof. Harold Laski would say 'Equality does not mean identity of treatment. There can be no ultimate identity of treatment. . . . The purpose of society would be frustrated at the outset if the nature of a mathematician met an identical response with that to the nature of a bricklayer. Equality does not even imply identity of reward for effort.'†

Both Mr. Shaw and Prof. Laski are of the apostolate of socialism: and they know that socialism, no more than any other doctrine, could win the support of great numbers of men with common sense of the type quoted above. Sifting the rational from the irrational is an operation possessed of no publicity value. It sets no hearts on fire.

To go no further than 'freedom' and 'equality': these are not ideas, they are sentiments – terms with a big vague core of popular emotion. What they say is: 'Oh to be free and without restraint!' or 'Oh to be as big a man as the boss!' As more logical entities, they would excite no one, except an intellectual.

But thinkers like Laski and Shaw are precisely the teachers of the intel-lectuals, who naturally want everything to be made rational and orderly.

* 'Freedom (Talks)', pub. Allen and Unwin.
† 'Grammar of Politics'. Prof. Harold Laski. [See pp. 189-201 on "equality of reward."]

95

Among these intellectuals will be found the men of action — those who will administer, not these carefully analytic prescriptions (for freedom, or for equality) supplied by their intellectual masters, but the inflammatory stuff appropriate in the interests of successful action. This will not mean that they are deceiving the masses for they believe that a new social order will in the end benefit the majority of men. They certainly will have to deceive them *in detail* — for they must speak the language of the emotions, which necessarily is misleading. But they will be able to assert 'You will be free and equal!' with a clear conscience, because, although they know this is impossible, and even ridiculous (like saying — You will all have wings, and all be millionaires) a reasonable measure of both these things will be enjoyed by those who follow socialism.

From this it follows, of course, that the *techniques* of which I am speaking often respond to all rational requirements as expounded by such scrupulous thinkers as Prof. Laski. It is upon that level that one would prefer to remain. But here is where the difficulty comes in. The 'intellectual' tail belonging to every technique begins lashing at once, wherever you offer a criticism of a doctrine as propounded by one of the heads. This is peculiar to these technicians, or ideologues: or rather they share it with the religionist. Very few philosophers have had a complete bristling dragon, as it were, attached to them: you can and always could discuss the pros and cons of Creative Evolution or the Critical Philosophy of Kant quietly.

How much of the most scrupulously exact social teaching of men like Laski reaches the lower levels intact, and how far down it is effective, it is difficult to decide. Certainly an appetite for reality in men in general does not increase, but diminish. Let me recall my remarks regarding the great change that has taken place, in the past four centuries, in the average sitter for a portrait. Tolerance of the truth shown formerly by Queens and other exalted persons, is, in the present age, very rarely met with. Even the charlady would exact 'Glamour'. — But with other forms of truth a similar tendency is apparent.

The political doctrine, as much as the portrait of their face, must be prettified and diluted until it departs so far from what is in any way probable that our harder-minded ancestors would have rejected it with angry laughter.

As in the cultural field, so in Politics, there are Two Publics — and indeed that is what I have outlined above: one vast in size, very shy of the reality, indolent and consequently ignorant, with a very sweet tooth indeed — the other the small groups of people of severer habits of mind, a certain number of scholars, a handful of professional men or writers or journalists, the occasional workmen.

————

Without condemning Parties or revolutionary techniques in however small a degree — for men to have to divide themselves up into smaller segments, the whole being too big — it is as well to mention here that political terms and Party names age very quickly. The names borne by the Parties in the French Chamber is a veritable cemetery of revolt. If for instance you asked a Frenchman of today what his politics were, and he replied 'I am a

Radical-socialist', he would be informing you to what group he belonged (the Radical-socialist) and he would be telling you something else about himself, namely that he was neither in any way radical, nor at all socialist. Once his Party occupied the position where now we find the communists. But today they are not even revolutionary has-beens.

The history of the democrats in the U.S.A. offers another example of these transformations. The word 'democrat' in Jefferson's day meant what 'red' does now. Yet the Southern Democrats are generally regarded as the nearest thing to a tory in American politics.

These techniques for group action grow obsolete as quickly as a washing-machine or a refrigerator. They decline in strength as quickly as a bottle of smelling-salts left with the stopper off. So what is the moral, for the young man on the look-out for a suitable Party in which to enrol? Obviously to join the most extreme one he can find. Otherwise by the time he is forty-five or so he will perhaps find himself attached to a political body nine-tenths dead, which has drifted far among the Right groups but still with some misleadingly ardent name.

But I have not been writing this chapter that I might offer advice to young men. Functional philosophies do not interest me a great deal, as you are probably aware. A dragon with a pin's head of good sense, again, is a paradoxical monster. All techniques for making people do things — verbal formulas for making the figure work, words so arranged as to produce the maximum response (irrespective of what the words mean, and they may make complete nonsense) bore me, naturally. The publicity man becomes intoxicated with his own idiotic slogans. And my trouble is with a political friend of intelligence (but still part of the vibrant body of the dragon) that I will find, as we are talking, what is in fact propaganda lifting its ugly head, and to my horror accepted by him on equal terms with the factual or the intelligent.

The question, 'What are your politics?' cannot be answered by saying 'I am a Labour Man', or, as our Frenchman did, 'I am a Radical-socialist'. There is no answer really, except by observing the man's behaviour. Every conceivable way in which he expresses his personality is relevant. His *politics* are the tone in which he calls his dog (the size of the dog too, and the breed): his epistolary style and handwriting: the 'classiness' or otherwise of his voice: his attitude to property or to money: his tolerance of hereditary potentates: his eagerness for honours: open-handedness: social snobbishness: how often he has his front-door painted: (what colour). But the list of things pertinent to such an enquiry would be endless.

There would by this method be no verbal answer to the question as to what Mr. X's politics were. The result, I mean, would not be a Party-name. From the data obtained you would have got to know a lot about Mr. X. It might be of so simple a nature that the word 'Tory' would be all the answer needed. Mostly the answer has no *netteté* of that kind. — What I mean may reduce itself really to this. Politics is more real than Party, and politics exist outside of Party. Party has tended to absorb all politics into itself. All politics come to be thought of as group-politics. However, and finally, this is not a 'Party of Mr. X' I am proposing. It is politics, not Mr. X, that interests me. Politics are something flexible, vivid, various, not cut and dried.

CHAPTER XVIII

NATURE OF CHANGE IN MY POLITICAL POSITION

HAVING here and there, since politics has been my subject, referred to a change in my political position, I will now define the nature of that change. You know, from what I have already said, that I am one of those in favour of an international order. Let me start from that.

A nationalist I have never been. But I believed, say twelve years ago, that the doctrine of national sovereignty was an indispensable guarantee of freedom. At present I believe the opposite: I regard that as archaic thinking. Such group freedom is no longer possible nor is it desirable.

But in this chapter I will outline my present approach to some of the main issues of contemporary politics. Throughout they differ radically from what I believed before the war: you can take it everything I say represents a change of view.

Freedom of the kind I formerly advocated is not possible, then, because scientific techniques have so diminished distance, and telescoped time, that the earth, which once was for man an immense, mysterious, and seemingly limitless universe, is no longer that, but a relatively diminutive ball, which, if we want to, we can dart around in a few days. The people living on it are rapidly being standardised — are no longer 'mysterious', any more than is their habitat. And tomorrow television will enable us, by the mere pressing of a button, to be in the West Indies, among sugar canes and Fife bananas, or in Greenland enjoying the solitary life of the Eskimo, in an icebound landscape.

As to the desirability of the doctrine of national sovereignty, group-freedom connotes group-exclusiveness. That is not desirable for the best of reasons: so long as 'national sovereignty' is retained, by large and small groups — from one the size of the British group to so small a State as Ecuador, there will be wars. Group exclusiveness, or competitive propaganda favouring emotional attachment to soil or race consciousness, with an internationally sanctioned mystical autonomy or 'sovereignty', means, as in the past, wars all the time, against 'foreign devils'. We first work ourselves up into a suitable rage with this or that foreign devil, at the end of which period of emotional preparation we 'declare war'.

————

Group-consciousness of the familiar kind depended — or depends — upon ignorance of other groups. And however much the rulers of the various nations seek to preserve the ignorance of those they rule, by every means at their command — by the discouragement or prevention of foreign travel, by sealing their frontiers more carefully every day — deep ignorance of the old type is unattainable.*

* It is worthy of note that the present British Government is attempting to obtain the consent of other governments to the abolition of visas: this would be a great liberal innnovation.

By group-freedom we imply a competitive independence systematically sharpened by xenophobia injected into the nation's veins by the respective ruling classes. Class-consciousness is the best antidote to xenophobia. Men should not, in sum, wish for group-freedom, in the sense of national sovereignty, but for freedom of another kind, seeing that it is an unreal freedom. It has always been freedom at the expense of somebody else: it has duplicated externally the class of inequalities existing within the nation in question. It has taken the form of a collective incitement to injustice in relations with men of other races, of the same order as that obtaining at home as between the classes. In other words, it was a top-dog freedom that it proposed.

There are many who argue that national, and even tribal, differences should be retained — or even be revived and intensified. Universal standardisation, they protest, would be boring, 'abstract', and colourless. Taking the short view, there is something to be said for regionalist, or separatist, principles. If you examine them carefully, they look less inviting.

Standardisation takes something out of life — variety namely. This has to be put back into it again some day, but in a quite different form. For the variety the regionalist recommends is an archaic variety, which has no relevance any longer in the general life of the world. There is a little Scotchman in my neighbourhood (in London) who does his shopping in a kilt, a dagger thrust into the top of his stocking, and a feather stuck in his bonnet. It amuses him to imagine that he lives in the days of the Bruce or the '45. — That dagger had a meaning once: but today it is like the lance of Don Quixote.

Physical and mental diversity is a stimulus. It is obvious that when people pass out of the United States, say (where diversity is strictly rationed) into Mexico, they enjoy the strange and 'colourful' spectacle. To hear Spanish spoken, to see the peons in their large shapely hats in the market-places, is a welcome change. Or Spain with its bull-fights provides a great contrast to our northern industrial scene: it takes us back to the Roman circus. The *souks* of Morocco magically transport us to the Mediterranean world of the ancients, almost to Carthage. This is time-travel, the best of tourism.[1]

But whether it is in China or India, or in Western Europe, the Machine Age has won the day. What it has defeated I, for one, find depressing, like all that is in that situation. Local colour — which is involved with the consciousness of the people, since the man who wears the costume must mentally belong to it — survives intact in patches, or in an uninteresting decay in considerable regions. — People have died to keep their tarboosh, under Ataturk, or 'for the wearing of the green', in fenian days. Symbols of ancient rivalries, but fustian for us. So it seems a foolish death to have died. There have always been better things to die for than regional badges and regional superstitions.

As against the threadbare relics of the tribal past, I am on the side of the Machine Age.

The medievalism of William Morris, or of G. K. Chesterton and Eric Gill (although I certainly respect these men, and even share with them *other* beliefs) awakes no echoes in me. Diversity will be put back into life in due course; meanwhile the transition, as in politics so in this, is wanting in many things from which earlier men derived a healthy satisfaction.

To conclude, we should be thankful we are having our roots loosened, or, better, pulled up. We are not vegetables or trees, although we often rant about our *roots* as if we were.

––––

The idea of a World State has no open enemies, that I know of. But it has the quietest set of friends and supporters of any doctrine in history. It is one of those things that are inevitable, perfectly feasible, immeasurably to be preferred to the present chaos – but never mentioned. – This is perhaps because everybody knows in his heart that our chaos has to get worse before it will get better. Everybody prefers that the good, or the sensible, should *come to them*, rather than *they move to it*.

In the United States of America there are 48 originally Sovereign States. These 48 States do not each raise little armies (as do the nations of South America or of Europe) and make war upon each other. The American Civil War put a stop to that for good. They live peaceably under a central federal government and a common flag.

Each is a complete miniature State – apart from the war business and the diplomatic business which is its corollary, and apart from sovereignty, which has been almost completely surrendered. Each has its own bi-cameral parliament, like France or England – its own quite distinct constitution, its own laws. It could go into business tomorrow as a 'sovereign state', by calling its Governor a President, if it so wanted.

The distinct character of all these minor States, of which the United States is made up, can be gauged by the discrepancies in their laws. In some for instance virtual Prohibition obtains, in others there are no restrictions at all upon the manufacture and sale of alcohol. When the Thirteenth Amendment to the Federal Constitution was repealed by Franklin Roosevelt that did not mean that liquor was then automatically on public sale in all the States. In the 'dry' States it made very little difference.

I mention the United States because I feel sure that we have in that colossal federation an advance copy of what one day the world will be like – not culturally, of course, but as far as its political structure and racial promiscuity are concerned. These large populations of still German, Polish, Italian, or Greek-speaking people live side by side as peacefully as Englishmen, and Welshmen, while their relatives in Europe are blowing each other to pieces. This is simply because they have one central government, controlling their individual governments.

Formerly I was not merely a supporter of the doctrine of the sovereign state, but, more generally, a believer in all forms of political decentralisation. But an opportunity to study at close quarters the American federal system, and especially the methods of that arch-centraliser Franklin Roosevelt, brought me to an understanding of the vanity of regional isolationism, under the changed conditions of human life. Radio, and telephones, are two inventions which alone thoroughly disintegrate the old seclusion and exclusiveness.

––––

Next let me outline what must lie before us, in the normal course of events. Almost with the certitude belonging to predestination, or the

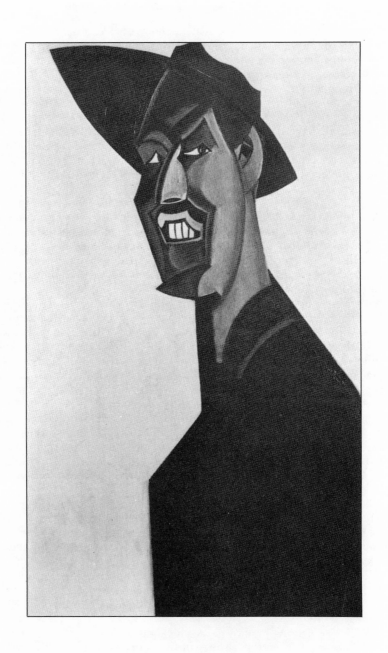

ease with which tomorrow's visit to the dentist can be visualised, it is possible to say what will happen next. Man's painful progress to full world-government normally must be something like this. Our present more radical approach to war-making — namely that wars should be 'wars of domination and annihilation',* as Lippmann expressed it — must result, as we have seen during the past year or two, in the reduction of the number of State-sovereignties. Poland and Bulgaria, to take only those two formerly impor-tant states, have gone to swell the immense bulk of Russia. The United States, somewhat more discreetly, is extending its imperial domain eastward. — The new type of 'total war' not only tends to diminish the number of small States. It at the same time produces monster States.

There are three monsters in the world today, namely the U.S.S.R., the U.S.A. and us. — We are a rather weak and disjointed monster (some think on its last legs). For all practical purposes we have to lean on one or the other of our fellow monsters, who are 'young' monsters and full of fight.

These sovereign monsters must in due course, and according to all precedent, fall on each other tooth and nail. In conformity with our new methods (no 'wars of limited objectives' but a war of 'domination' and 'annihilation') one of these colossal abstractions would attempt to swallow the other. (For when it comes to the State, we are back among the pre-historic mammals, and can get a very good idea of what life among the dinosaurs must have been like.) Were it not for one thing, this would probably prove impossible. They would bloodily disentangle, lie back drained of more wealth and more blood, and hold the regulation 'peace con-ference'. Then, after a short period of recuperation (full of sabotage, assassina-tions, riots, insurrections, and guerrilla warfare) they would begin again.

A third monster, it might be, would take shape. (There is not room for more than three.) These universal attempts at 'annihilation' and 'domina-tion' might continue (barring internal upheavals in one or other of the monstrous protagonists) for quite a long while. But, *in the end*, one monster would devour the only other one that was left. And then there would only be ONE monster. That would be the consummation wished for by all sane men. The ONE monster would be Cosmopolis.

Just now I interpolated, 'but for one thing'. And I have deliberately left out of this brief account of what *normally* must be expected to occur all question of new and revolutionary methods of destroying other people. I have not mentioned nuclear energy, and the atomic bomb and the other revolutionary developments.

That — and apparently further discoveries — means that one nation, and very soon all nations, will possess weapons of such fabulous potency that the 'war of annihilation' may leave very little there to 'dominate' after-wards.

Will the nations — annoyed at this unforeseen atomic contretemps, and foreseeing an end of all their little sports — decide to go ahead with improved blockbusters and not-too-advanced rockets — so as not to have to discontinue wars? Most people are inclined to believe that this will be the solution. It turns upon psychology. — For my part I do not see how the nations can fail to make use of their trump cards, once the game heats up.

* I quote from memory from a wartime article of Mr. Walter Lippmann.

We shall be very lucky if the Americans are strong-minded enough to refrain from slapping down theirs, in this brief interval in which they alone possess so stupendous an advantage: it is against human nature that they should show this restraint. Certainly for six months or so in the next war it might be rockets and blockbusters. Then will come the atom bomb. At the first threat of defeat, at the first serious reverse, out it will come — Gilda, the Queen of Battles!

Could an atomic war on the grand scale be survived? That I think is a shallow question. If you destroy fifty per cent of a wolf pack, a herd of cattle, or a flock of birds, does the remaining half go on much as if nothing had happened? If we lost fifty per cent of our friends at one blow, should we be inconsolable — should we be even inconvenienced? When they die in the normal course of events there is scarcely a ripple. If we lose our husband or wife, what do we do? Look around for a new mate. If we lose both our legs and arms, what do we do? We set up as limbless men, and may be better off as curiosities. We could lose eighty per cent of the population of the world tomorrow and not notice it much.

But Culture (let us bow our heads at that sacred word, which means so much to all of us, from the elevator girl in Unesco to the picture-restorer of our national treasure): what of that? An atomic war might completely obliterate some of the great national libraries, for instance, as it would start with extreme suddenness. But there are great numbers of books in the world: some think far too many.

There would be plenty of books left: no fear for Culture there! — A good many Old Masters might become radioactive. That would do them no harm. Many might be destroyed. Let me say, in confidence, that a few living masters might have a chance, in that case. There is not the slightest danger of 'the end of Culture' with which people like to scare us (and we are very easily frightened when Culture is in question)! So long as there is one man and one woman left on earth there will be what we generally know as Culture, never fear. The man will be the curator (with a noble salary) of all the 'art treasures' and she will be his secretary (substantial salary likewise). There need be no artists — this is *Culture*.

The death-roll would make all former wars seem ladylike little catastrophes, unquestionably. But Professor Einstein's estimate that not more than half the population of the earth would be killed is doubtless correct.

Quiet people, like myself, cannot be expected to look forward to such an event. But an atomic world war — if it is *necessary* — will do no great harm. — All the corpses whose arms and legs had shed their skins like discarded gloves (and other anatomical novelties for which our new toy is responsible) would be disposed of, the insane be put under restraint, the hospitals jammed with the cancerous wrecks, the ruined towns tidied up. Things would start up again, the human scene just as civilised as it was before.

But here is what interests *me*. In spite of the hearty 'business as usual' attitude — and a very firm hand with those who suggest that there is anything odd or screwy about it all: for all the 'I can-take-it' bursting gamely from blue and swollen lips, and the 'brave smiles' fading only upon mortification on the faces of the cheerful radioactive dead — for all the well-known capacity to 'keep smiling' long after there was any conceivable thing to smile about — a miracle would happen. An *idea* would steal apologetically into the minds of a number of those still sound in wind and limb whose intellective apparatus (though sluggish and clogged with slogans and soggy uplift) still functioned. The idea would take the form of a leading question: 'Are we all right in the upper storey'?

But the deciding factor will be that men have entered upon the era of super-states: then, under the eliminatory impact of this new device for wiping out life — this monstrous blast, like the breath of an outraged god — the time must rapidly come when only *one* battered entity, calling itself a 'nation', will be there. and that will be that.

My restrained optimism is, then, a by-product of atomic energy. One or two more wars it seems necessary to allow for — alas. Then the great climacteric in life on earth should come: the day on which man will resign himself to Peace. Time will then be available to attend to the fundamental problems of social justice, sidetracked continually by war.

Probably, before I proceed, I should say a few words about pacifism. Although a paraphrase of a statement to be found elsewhere in my recent writings, such repetition is imposed on me, where war is my theme. A careless reader cannot be allowed to say to himself — 'Of course, this is pacifism', and to think that, having found the valid label for it, he can dismiss it, and turn to something else. He cannot turn to something else. This is one of those matters that cannot be settled by the affixing of a label.

I have never been a 'pacifist': I have been a soldier, and have been quite ready to play my part in the battles of the Pen and Brush. My backgrounds are blamelessly unpacific — rather unnecessarily full of aggressive bustle. But what we are talking about here is not war. It is a question of the most blackguardly kind of murder, from five miles up or five hundred miles away. 'Pacifism' is a meaningless term when it comes to dropping atom bombs indiscriminately upon millions of people. To be 'warlike' at this moment is to be certifiable.

We recognise it as the act of a lunatic to destroy people by the million in the gas ovens of Belsen, Auschwitz etc. But do not let us deceive ourselves: attacking the same people with atomic bombs is criminal lunacy of precisely the same order.

Where are we to draw the line between acts of war and acts that are plainly those of brutal madmen? I drew that line myself in the year 1918, for world war i was already too abstract and mechanical: and the Christian nations had allowed themselves to engage upon a path of mutual destruction which could only end in demoralisation, bankruptcy, and chaos. World war ii was of the same type as world war i, so let us fix the line at 1945. For anything after that the familiar word 'war' is not only much too mild, but plainly inapplicable. Our good old Christian wars were bad enough: but this 'total war' is something so much worse that no confusion is possible. Mars would indignantly repudiate what is shortly to occur, and a lot of what has already occurred.

There comes a point when fun ceases to be fun: and the jolliest little ruffian (boys will be boys!) ceases to be endearing: and there is nothing funny about 'Gilda'. The arguments as to all war being barbarous (as of course it is) and that the little more, or little less, is not a valid distinction, must remain unanswered here. This is a brief note only relative to the word 'pacifist'. – Call a man a 'pacifist' if it amuses you to who objects to shooting, to order, another with a bullet through the heart. But to make a sadistic orgy of killing the man in question is another matter. Do not call that person a 'pacifist' who declines to take part in roasting him alive. I should be a pretty poor kind of *clerc* if I said otherwise. The clerks who betray mankind are the incendiaries, not those who try to stamp out the fire.

———

My political outlook has been influenced by the prospects opened up by the atomic discoveries. I can recall nothing that has given me so much pleasure: I mean, of course, political pleasure. War has ceased to be a *problem*. It used to push everything else out of the way. I am suddenly free of the senseless call to immediate action. I have transferred what would otherwise be reactions of the same kind to something else: I have gone behind war to what causes it, and past war, since its end is in sight. I exert myself in favour of a world government, the birth of which no man can hasten, nor can any man alter the volcanic violence of its throes.

But as I now so to speak have more time, and as I worry about 'keeping the old tub afloat' no more (seeing that what is best for the world is ultimately best for the English Ship of State and Englishmen must become Cosmic Men) I can think of the State more comprehensively. A World-State – all romantic loyalties, regional bias, *esprit de corps* etc. out of the way – would almost necessarily be to start with a Socialist State. Strip any nation of its purely national political trappings, mystical prerogatives, class hypnotisms, and machinery of competitive emotionalism – strip it of everything that implies 'nation' and you would get that, a socialist community, in the present age.

Then it has been borne in on me how war cannot be thought of in isolation. We as individuals make war on each other all the time – in every country, in every town, and in every street. 'Business' is the nastiest of wars – the profit-motive, as the marxists call it, is an economic war as pervasive as a virus in our blood. Every razorblade or shoe-lace that you buy you are defrauded: and proportionately the poor are robbed more than the rich. Take war away, and in any nation, by our stupidity and cruelty we will annually kill and disable as many people as would any ordinary war. Blitzes and Blockbusters are outrageous crimes: but they are only an extreme and open expression after all of the sort of men we are in everyday life. So the stupidity and the cruelty should always be the first target, not war, except in so far as it is an expression of those.

There is an important factor which is insufficiently recognised. The statesmen of the principal countries are genuinely pacific without exception. No one believes that Stalin or Molotov like or want war: their military preparations are purely defensive. Mr. Truman has spoken with great sincerity in favour of a World Government (meanwhile naturally acting as a good American). The British Government has expressed itself as supporting the idea of a World Government. Both Truman and Attlee are the oppposite of fire-eaters: of course, if they had their way, they would sit down to a council table tomorrow, and take their countries with them into a Federal System embracing all the States of the earth.

Is not this a legitimate cause for hope? These men, thinking as they do, aware of their immense responsibilities, will surely make the attempt to circumvent human nature? I wish I could entertain that hope. But when I think of Mr. Truman I see a greatly harassed man squeezed on all sides by rich and influential pressure-groups, both of the Left and the Right. There is the coming election, which rivets his attention. I am afraid the decision does not rest with him. As to the British Government, it is engaged in a life and death struggle with insolvency, inflation, unemployment and nationalisation — these are pressure-groups on its back too. Its relations with neither America nor Rusia are exactly cordial. The States capable of action would insist that world-government should be on their terms, that is the insuperable obstacle. So the toxic power of national rivalries of the credit-system, and the rest, leaves little room for sincere hope.

———

In this chapter I have been endeavouring to show, by a discursive summary of my views upon a few controversial topics, in what ways my outlook has changed (or as to the attractiveness of war, not changed). No one holds to one opinion without modification, naturally, an opinion being in the nature of a rough working hypothesis, a logical product of experience.

With people capable of sincerity, no revolutionary change is possible. Thus, if I am found advocating today a maximum of centralisation, whereas twelve years ago I was all for the doctrine of the sovereign state, these diametrically opposite principles both have been adopted — as *opinion* — with the same end in view. (Be it noted that the same principle is adhered to by various people for very dissimilar motives.) Again, if at one time I oppose in every way in my power the threat of war, and if at another time am almost complaisant about a worse threat, the incentive is the same: tremendous aversion to war. If I *knew* that war could drive out war, I should be all for war — though I do think we are approaching the time when war may become terrible enough to teach the unteachable.

This book necessarily deals much with politics — because politics has been used as a lever for attacks upon me, so, although it is not the real issue, the gravamen of the charges it is my business to refute belongs to politics, or is semi-political. Nevertheless this is not a book in which arguments can be developed at any great length. I think I have made myself suffici-ently clear in this section devoted to political questions: but I propose to add a further short chapter — by way of afterthought or appendix — which will take the process of enlightenment a step further.

Notes

1 See *Journey Into Barbary: Moroccan Writings and Drawings of Wyndham Lewis*, ed. C. J. Fox (Santa Barbara: Black Sparrow Press, 1983).

CHAPTER XIX

'MISTER IVORY TOWER'

'YOU, of course,' said a woman acquaintance in St. Louis once, 'are Mister Ivory Tower.' Probably I shrugged off that silly remark. But because it is a charge generally brought against anybody suspected as a sceptic regarding human institutions, or thought to love his work too well – if that work is 'intellectual' – I will answer it now.

I am not 'Mister Ivory Tower': that is not my name. Had you read no more from my pen than the last half-dozen or so chapters on the political issue you would know that I am the reverse of uninterested in the fate of other men. I do not shut myself up in an 'ivory tower' to dream life away. If anything too great a proportion of my life has been taken up with public matters.

On the other hand I do not belong to the 'starry-eyed' brigade: nor do I enter with sufficient zest into popular sports – like killing, persecuting, witchhunting, starving or regimenting others. I prefer not to 'push around' other people. But that, surely, is a diagnostic of respect for others, not of indifference or disdain. And if I am not found where some poor creature is being bullied or killed it is not because I am up in an 'ivory tower'.

Of the origin of the term Ivory Tower I am ignorant. But there is a well-known instance where it was used by Gustave Flaubert, when he was proffering advice to a friend – and Flaubert is generally regarded as Mister Ivory Tower No. 1. Let me quote it (without translating): it is a classic statement of the extreme attitude of intellectual aloofness.

'Ne t'occupe de rien que de toi. Laissons l'Empire marcher, fermons notre porte, montons au plus haut de notre tour d'ivoire, sur la dernière marche, la plus près du ciel. . . . On voit les étoiles briller clair et l'on n'entend plus les dindons.'[1]

This most irascible of literary mandarins was undeniably an example of intellectual pride. Yet I should never select him myself as standing for aloofness from the common life of men. His starlit 'Tower' was in the first place full of a deafening noise, since he was always in a state of blusterous stentorian soliloquy. He may have left the philistine world outside *physically*, when he slammed the door behind him and ascended into his Ivory Tower: but the philistine and the bourgeois filled his thoughts to such an extent that he cannot be said ever to have been alone. He never turned his back upon humanity. He was its greatest intellectual scourge: but he could not have lived without it.

If I were asked to choose my perfect Mister Ivory Tower I should not go to look for him among the French. They are apt to be too earthy. The necessary temperamental ingredients for such a figure are in far greater abundance among us, or in New England.

I should review our aesthetes. And the author of 'Marius the Epicurean' would furnish a more authentic specimen, I think, than would be the creator of Salammbo'. Then Henry James, puritan and incorrigible snob, writing in an exquisite private dialect, would not be forgotten. Even Mr. Lytton Strachey, who whispered faintly in his lank unmanly beard, exhibiting a gazelle-like shyness of the human herd — patently exclusive and aloof: with him we should have a likely candidate for the Ivory retreat.

But these few names, mentioned at random, show how people differing considerably in detail may find a place upon the Ivory roster. What is the sine qua non for inclusion? Self isolationism is the first prerequisite — or, to borrow another term from politics, a mood of 'splendid isolation'. An aloofness from what is regarded as the squalor of average life. Then 'aristocratic' impulses; irresponsibility; indifference to public good; contempt for 'uneducated'; pride in intellectual power; incivility to the moronic, or intolerance of the vulgar: such are a few of the distinguishing marks. It is a type seldom found, in the nature of things, except among intellectuals.

In England it is rarely found dissociated from social snobbery. The refinement and aloofness of the sensitive aesthete may be accentuated by a snobbishness: or social self-glorification may issue from intellectual pride — as with Yeats, who asserted that all poets and artists should automatically have the status of nobles. — With Pater (the Mr. Rose of Mallock's 'New Republic')[2] another factor was introduced — that of sexual perversion. The 'daintiness' — earning the vulgar sobriquet of 'pansy' — of the homosexual tends to the cultivation of a refined social aura. This is calculated to attract, upon the same principle as any young woman in the marriage market tends to suggest backgrounds of far greater social refinement than the equivalent young man.

Only the hypocrite would pretend that the mind or the ways of the average man appealed to him at all times. But there should be no breaking of the human bond at any time. Spiritually as much as physically there is no one who does not depend upon the average. There is no exception. Flaubert, to return for a moment to him, never detached himself radically: his was a pedagogic tantrum. For him the average-philistine and bourgeois-man was like a very backward child, whom he loaded with intolerant abuse and reproaches, yes, but was of the same flesh and blood as it: a large noisy French bourgeois, who was bound to all other Frenchmen as are all members of that expansive, vociferating, mass. Coldly and contemptuously to separate yourself from that huge animal body 'the people', is easier at all times for the Anglo-saxon.

In the pages of 'War and Peace' Pierre's relations with Kotelenko are the approved Christian relationship. The brotherly association of Tolstoy himself with many people outside the class-pen would serve me as an illustration. Such relationships would be completely impossible for Mr. Ivory Tower, who would certainly avail himself of every possible barrier, social or otherwise, isolating him from the Many.

So, to conclude, no letters addressed 'Mr. Ivory Tower' will reach me, because I do not inhabit an abode of that type. It has been my experience that people who affect to believe I do are usually anything but sufferers of fools gladly themselves, wipers of the noses of the underfed and polite pickers-up of the ration-tickets of the frost-bitten, nor marriers of wives less backgrounded than themselves, or marriers of their daughters to young labourers, nor spitters in the presence of ladies, nor communists with their cash, or givers of *poor devils* their dues—having generally a strange predilection for *rich devils*: I hope I do them no injustice in saying, very poor socialists: and even were I by ill chance the secluded aesthete they fain would suggest, let me remind them that those who live in glass towers should not throw stones.

Notes

[1] "Think of nothing but yourself. Let us leave the empire to go as it will, close our door, climb to the highest point in our ivory tower, onto the top step, the one closest the sky. . . . Stars are seen shining brightly and fools are no longer heard."

[2] Pater was portrayed in the character Mr. Rose in W. H. Mallock's *The New Republic* (London, 1897), in which other figures such as Ruskin, Arnold, Huxley and Jowett were satirized.

PART II
PERSONAL BACKGROUND
OF CAREER

CHAPTER XX

FREEDOM OF SPEECH AT ITS ZENITH

IN this second part of my book I turn to more intimate autobiography. I tell you how I came to write and paint: when I first experienced the satiric impulses: when politics, the last to present itself, first made its unlovely presence felt. The same end is still in view as outlined in my introductory pages: namely to spoil the sport of the irresponsible detractor, to improve my chances of some day not being too much lied about, to clear the path immediately ahead – a simple domestic operation, but long overdue.

In Part I I have shown, more in the abstract, what the hideous difficulties are: how they assist each other – can coalesce in one implacable load. Now I shall endeavour to describe by means of personal narrative, how one qualifies for so disagreeable, lonely, and uneasy a position.

All the way along the road, from the first step you take, there are alternatives. You can, for instance, pocket your pride and join a coterie. The only coterie I knew of I did not much fancy. Or again you can abdicate from your full programme, and take a job. With luck you then go through with *half* your programme. You can marry a rich woman (as did Shaw or Yeats). The danger with that is that it might assume the dimensions of a *job*.

Seeing what is before you, and feeling not unnaturally defeatist, you can, like Rimbaud, throw up the sponge at once and try and grow rich in some illicit traffic in a suitably remote spot. There are all these and many other alternatives: but if you remain obstinately on your course (engaging in such difficult country as I have been led into) then you belong in the class of the Dr. Livingstones (but with no Stanley to come to your rescue), or of Captain Amundsen (but with no Pole to reach, after which you can go home). The machine-age of the mercantile classes is a polar wilderness, or a 'dark continent', for the authentic 'intellectual'. It would, however, be incorrect to assume that he does not enjoy himself, in his frightful fashion.

In this chapter I shall call upon a few of the ideas developed in the course of the foregoing sections, but here revealing the actual incubation of an 'intellectual', of a satirist, and of a political thinker. The personal narrative of the artist, storyteller and polemical writer in the making ensues.

I could have wished that we had developed a decent circumlocution, like the Japanese, when referring to ourselves. Some derive great satisfac-

tion from writing about themselves: but the incessant reiteration of his own
personal pronouns jars somewhat upon the ear of this unworthy person.
He will, however, do all the me-ing and the I-ing demanded of him to call up
that mysterious being that was himself in his unformed days, and who
may be able to assist in the present enterprise.

In my career up-to-date (1947) as a writer, or artist, I have enjoyed great
freedom. Historically I represent freedom of speech at its zenith.
I have said almost what I liked in my books (short of the limits set
by the antiquated libel laws). If I wished, in the interests of design, to
distort limbs in a picture, I have distorted them; if I felt impelled to simplify
perspective, no naturalist law has stood in my way.

These freedoms, however, have demanded for their continuance so heavy
an effort as to have ceased to resemble liberty. All are freedoms for which
one has to pay so heavily that we as a society have about reached their
term. That is the point at which the price can no longer be found, and that
they must be regarded henceforth as illicit — legally in the same category
as poteen.

I have explained how great is the handicap of the 'highbrow': how the
writing of satire is so violently discouraged in England (where it has always
been more peevishly received than in France, 'humour' being far preferred):
that great satire is about the rarest commodity: and how, lastly, the growing
fanaticism in political life (so that now the witch-hunt is as much a recognised sport as formerly it was when sectarian passion had religion instead
of politics for its sanction) has practically made an end of free expression in
that field.

We are still, it is true, free to say or write to hell with anything, from
the Pope to the Purchase Tax, but there is really nothing to protect us
from the consequences of our rash words. No law conferring a specific
verbal liberty has been anywhere repealed, and all men are supposed to
form their own opinions: but the fact is that only a small circle of high
political dignitaries are permitted to *have* an opinion. That basic democratic
information upon which alone sound opinion can be formed is withheld, in
any case: for I should like to know what picture of the world can be obtained
from reading an English newspaper, shrunken and censor-ridden as it is?
No more protection for free speech remains to a man than to a talking
parrot. But the parrot, of course, repeats only the views of his master, so
he is safe enough. The trouble about a man is that he is liable to *think* —
a highly unpopular endowment. (Better, on the whole to be a parrot, in a
'free' society.)

To return to my three major categories of discomfort: to be a *sham*
highbrow is all right: people like to feel they are getting somewhat intellectual fare. Again, to be a *gentle* satirist (which boils down to being a
humourist) is not only safe, but advantageous. To administer 'sly digs',
to flatter by an affectation of criticism, to be 'whimsical', these sedative
practices as a substitute for genuine satire are the English way: and, as for
politics, to be a revolutionary upon perfectly orthodox lines is the *beau
rôle* — indeed it is about the safest thing to be.

Measured by the number of people affected, Politics are the big demi-
urgic reality of everyday life: it is with them that the decision rests whether

whole populations shall go hungry or enjoy plenty, languish in poverty or be prosperous – live, just exist, or die. They outweigh, in any average human scale, all other matters – like the practical pros and cons of social Satire, or the being an intellectual. You only have to place the latter side by side with politics in this way to realise their insignificance by comparison. You might modestly thrive as a popular 'highbrow', or relatively flourish as a lucky satirist: yet, were you unpopular in politics, the pleasurable equilibrium in the other two departments would be fatally disturbed.

From the start I have behaved *as if I were free*. This is the kind of thing we do not notice about ourselves: it is only by forcibly abstracting myself that I can see it. Automatically I became an artist and an 'intellectual': yet that should only be done today if you have private means, or of course after you have taken a job.

Should you, however, take a job, it occupies too much of your time. As an 'intellectual' you deteriorate. So it resolves itself, as a rule, into money, or no intellectuality.

This statement must be qualified to except the poet. A poem is usually a small short piece of work. It doesn't take long to write 'My love is like a red red rose'. For the rest of the day you can be a clerk, or an immigration official like the late Humbert Wolfe, or, for that matter a milk-roundsman or window-cleaner.

Mr. T. S. Eliot worked originally in a city bank. – He took a job almost at once. A more agreeable and lucrative one was speedily found for him than bank-clerking. He became a working partner in what was at that time a new firm of publishers. That – if the job is not a very exacting one – is about the best thing a poet can do, who has no fortune.

For a novelist, like Henry James or Flaubert, much time is required: it is not like verse. The two best novelists I know – outside the Russians – came first to my mind, and both possessed considerable private means. This is not an accident, as it might seem to the casual observer. No poor man could have written Henry James's books. Among the Russians, the novelist who accomplished most was Count Tolstoy, a rich landowner. Perhaps the best craftsman among them was Turgenev: he was a rich landowner too. Dostoevsky, in some respects the greatest Russian novelist, had no money: in order to get it he wrote with feverish haste. We are told by Russians that the writing at times is almost unbearably bad, and the *longeurs* and absurdities almost everywhere in his novels must have had something to do with these conditions.

Had Flaubert, James, and Tolstoy, been poor men, taken a job early (as schoolmaster or petty official) or struggled along to keep the wolf from the door, we should certainly have had no 'Salammbo', 'Bouvard et Pécu-chet', 'The Wings of the Dove', 'The Ambassadors', or 'War and Peace'. It is a great pity people do not understand this.

All kinds of novelists, born poor, will, I am quite aware, be mentioned in refutation of what I have said: and some would have to be allowed. But I am sure that the most searching statistics would confirm my view. There is always *something*.

James Joyce, for instance. To that penniless language-teacher a strange accident happened. A Quaker lady, Miss Harriet Weaver, at the psychological moment, made him the present of an adequate income, putting down a capital sum to be used in that way, so that he could live thereafter in peace and do his work. It was therefore as a *rentier* that he wrote 'Ulysses' and 'Finnegans Wake'. With emotion Joyce told me, while engaged upon 'Ulysses', that he, his wife, and his children would have been on the streets had it not been for this benefactress, unknown personally to him.

Again, there is D. H. Lawrence. But that novelist of genius was born the son of a coal-miner, which has tremendous romantic appeal in England – or had. It made all the difference when he was a struggling young writer, as being a Lord helped Byron. In spite of that marked advantage over other 'poor boys', his posthumously published correspondence resounds with the howls of the wolf at the door.

Much of Lawrence's work is ill-written – he who could write so beautifully, as 'Sea and Sardinia', or 'Mornings in Mexico' testify. Too often he caricatured himself and put his name to much second-rate novelettish padding. The explanation? – in large part, *money*! I am sorry. It is most squalid. But lack of money, for the creative mind, is like a raging disease. – If you have epilepsy like Dostoevsky, or tuberculosis like Lawrence, the toxins of the physical ailment neutralise to some small extent the toxins of the economic complaint. But still distortion and deterioration result.

Under present circumstances, therefore – or I should say prior to the socialist era, which is just setting in, and in which there will be no *rentiers* – to be a serious novelist you must have money of your own. This is the rule. If you have not, you compromise, you begin thinking constantly of the larger of the Two Publics – which is far too big. You take to writing 'mystery' fiction (all kinds of highbrow lore getting mixed up with the processes of criminal investigation, until you find it puts people off if you quote St. John of the Cross): or you write for the Films, or you do far too much journalism. As much 'mystery' and film writing as journalism is just as bad as taking a job. The best part of your time is devoured.

This reasoning is rooted in an understanding of the new Machine-age conditions in the book-market, which as I have shown in earlier chapters, push the good book into a small, unremunerative, 'precious' or 'highbrow', back-water: and in an appreciation of the progressive effect of the industrial age in undermining intellectual values. The same industrial age will, *in the end*, I am ready to believe, produce a new and more intellectual civilisation than that of the wigged wits who took snuff and pointed their toes, or that of the bewhiskered clubmen, who drawled about Thackeray or Darwin through their 'roman noses'. It is of the meanwhile that I write. The only Public the writer can live on, just will not 'take' anything above the mental standard of the Hollywood soap-opera plot, or lush sex matter.

It is these conditions, furthermore, which are responsible for the large-scale and well-organised coterie, like the 'Bloomsburies'. Most of the contemporary politico-literary periodicals being to all intents and purposes closed, coterie-manned, enterprises, is traceable to the same pressures. Wherever you look in art-world or literary circles, you see little congeries of people huddled together and scratching each other's backs. It is unfriendly conditions that produce this depressing spectacle.

These preliminary observations upon the economics of art were in preparation for what I shall have to say of my own situation, and to that I now will turn. — It is true that we do not want to learn how much an opera cost to write, or to produce, only to see it performed. But in any account of the work of the composer the circumstances under which the work came to be done play a determining part.

Wagner's correspondence, as an instance, is over-full of money-matters: but it cost him among other things an immense practical effort to bring into being those smoky palaces of sound we call 'The Ring'. My own reason for making economics more than a discreet incidental in this account of my career, is on account of the function of money as a weapon — often a very disgusting one — in the hands of those with whom the writer or artist is apt to find himself at odds. It does also provide distinct enlightenment regarding the terms on which the arts exist and thrive.

It would be inaccurate to say that I have produced about thirty books and pamphlets because I had money. On the contrary I had none while I was engaged in writing all but two or three of them. — This may suggest that I am presenting myself as an example of the small minority not conforming to my economic law for novelists. But in the first place I have written hasty books (not fiction, but books of a journalistic character). More important, I had what is called an 'allowance' as a student: and I was a student for a long time. I should, I feel sure, never have started — or arrived, in my roundabout way, at the point at which I started — had much money not been spent to launch me.

I do not regard this as something to be accompanied by shamefaced apology. It happens — in addition to everything else — that I am one of those vessels that need to be a long time on the stocks. Once I put out into the wintry sea I have generally succeeded under my own steam in reaching port; but like those other vessels I have used as illustrations for my economic exordium, I cannot claim always to have done so without adventitious aid. Then had it not been for the extreme kindness of friends, notably Sir Nicholas and Lady Waterhouse, there is much I could not have done at all.[1]

You only have to consider that a long and difficult book, which will take at least a year to write — doing no other work to speak of, grinding away all day with as few breaks as a popular dentist — is a problem of rent, food, heating, and lighting. With the *rentier*, all that is provided for. All he has to think about is writing the book. But what can the equally gifted man without income do? He can save up, retire to an inexpensive spot, budget for what is usually an inadequate period, with one packet of cigarettes a week and two pints of bitter beer on Saturday evenings.

The results have seldom been satisfactory. How could it be otherwise? Just as you cannot be a week-end Michelangelo, so these little areas of uncomfortable freedom, hijacked from an inexorable commercialism, are too near, at their extremities, to what you have escaped from, and their middles too uneasily conscious of their extremities.

Finally, I will gladly concede that it is *disgusting* and *degrading* that Money should play so important a part in the lives of poets, novelists, musicians, and other artists: but this is only because of the destructive power of this engine of coercion, not because money is inherently in a less poetic category than many other things which pertain to the intimate life of the poet or other artist. In the epoch out of which we are passing into something else it was regarded as vulgar to talk about money. A strange prudery — but no doubt utilitarian. Today I always make a point of asking a man of 'private means' how much money he has got. If an Englishman, even now he still flushes angrily, stammers, and decides I am a cad. Put that question to an American, and all that happens is an outburst of boasting ('blowing' as they call it in the States) and an array of highly unreliable figures.

The connection of *economics* and of *freedom* is obvious (Epictetus being a type of man so rarely met with that his contribution may be neglected).[2] Before beginning the autobiographical preliminaries to the story of my career up-to-date — which is an epic of freedom — let me speak for a moment of freedom again.

The history of freedom is well-known, but seldom remembered. The majority take it for granted, as they take the water supply. Such widespread freedom as we have enjoyed spread down from the top, very rapidly, during the 'liberal' epoch, until, at the time my student days began, great numbers of people were in possession of freedom only enjoyed formerly by princes of the blood.

Originating in the period of which Disraeli and Arnold are perhaps the most symbolic names, a strange merger of privilege and of democracy occurred. This amounted to a popularisation and great expansion of privilege (but an ultimate decline in and cheapening of authority). The Public School system mass-produced the 'gentleman': some were gentlemen already, others became so by training and propinquity. Upon all was conferred without distinction something like Roman citizenship in the shape of the Old School Tie.

There were, too, the greatly increased facilities of travel: 'Cook's' and other Tours which would supply a party of twenty or thirty people with the Grand Tour at a ridiculously low rate. Again, there was the rapid growth of great centres of luxury, like Paris, London, or Vienna. These, and many factors of a like nature, produced a capitalist elysium for really substantial numbers of people — not only for the magnate-class. It was very widespread: and the great industrial machine poured out inexpensive luxury articles in profusion, so that, in the end, the little doctor's son, who had been a day boy at Dulwich College, in his orthodox tweeds, was almost indistinguishable from the duke (greatly to the duke's disgust): and the *mademoiselle de magasin* could collect one costume at least in which she bore a striking resemblance to a socialite.

Only the working mass remained much as it was. This, at least in England, was part of the plan: for the new class was a watered-down and swollen aristocracy that had been evolved (for purposes of empire) and only the snobbery was not diluted. It was therefore a freedom based upon selfish, as well as theatrical, principles.

The freedom, however, was wonderful: and the duke joined in — threw away his strawberry leaves, stopped only speaking to other dukes, and married the chorus-girl with the fattest legs: the clergyman got broader and broader, revealed himself as a freethinker, teaching his thunderstruck flock that the 'pale Galilean' was an awfully brainy and good-hearted fellow but no more, all the rest being Hebrew mythology (but still drawing his stipend): wholesale caterers became masters of impoverished hunts — most of the London clubs left their doors ajar, and the Stock Exchange tumbled in: but snobbery comically kept pace, to gild and polish the select meretricious democracy.

The arts did their gilding too — the Nineties, with its brilliant groups, corruscated in this sunset of English power. For is long-enjoyed advantage as the first and major industrial nation was a diminishing asset, and this over-expanded ruling-class would soon be left up in the air. The Nineties was a genuine decadence: that was the first, the second came after world war i. (To compare carefully these two decadences is to understand what had happened to England in the interval.)

Emerging from my schooldays, I found myself in the debilitating post-Nineties world of the first decade of the century. My views regarding politics were those of a young alligator. I had money in my pocket: not a great deal, but enough to live. I was given to understand I should always have money in my pocket — so I thought no more about economics, my own or other people's. I drifted into this relaxed and relaxing atmosphere and there was nothing at first to prick me into wakefulness. I tasted what people call perfect freedom therefore. There were no obstacles. Everything was easy: I was healthy: the mind slept like a healthy infant, in the sunlit smithy in which world war i was being hammered into shape.

Notes

[1] Sir Nicholas (d. 1964) and Lady (Audrey Lewin, d. 1945) Waterhouse were helpful to Lewis over many years. See Jeffrey Meyers, *The Enemy: A Biography of Wyndham Lewis* (London, 1980), pp. 152-53. Lewis had to appeal to Sir Nicholas several times during the years after the Second World War when *Rude Assignment* was in process, as revealed in the unpublished correspondence at Cornell.

[2] Epictetus (c. 50–c. 130), Stoic philosopher, the son of a slave woman, was himself a slave until 68; he taught submissiveness to the inexorable, but, within that, personal moral freedom.

CHAPTER XXI

HOW ONE BEGINS

MY career began about the age of eight. I stitched together pieces of paper and wrote the first of many books of this order. They were no stupider than the Volsungensaga but in range even narrower, being confined altogether to war, instead of practically altogether to war.

In these booklets my first art-work appeared: stiff and hieratic friezes of heavily accoutred manikins. These long chains of matchstick-men — Klee-men — each trailing a musket or grasping, in a hand like a bomb, a hatchet, went right across the double page. Half of the personae obviously are Redskins, with plumed war-bonnets, and an assortment of weapons appropriate to the Indian brave: the other half must be Palefaces. These lines of lifeless foemen converge, where they meet gesticulation is sometimes indicated. There is much action in the text, but practically none in its visual accompaniment.

I was a denizen of the 'Leatherstocking' world. I started life at eight as a war-chronicler therefore. It never ceases for me to be unpleasant that the tiny mind of a little animal like myself at eight and earlier should be filled by its elders with such pasteboard violence, initiating it into this old game of murder. Born into a military aristocracy life begins full of excited little bangs and falsetto war-cries.

When I look at a photograph I have here, among many others in a portfolio, I see the same self that was responsible for the booklets: but this time he is not a child, he is in uniform among belted, pouched, tin-hatted, fellow-soldiers of world war i. I perceive a sort of repetition — it is the same pattern, only the bangs and cries of battle had become real, for the figure in the photograph, not academic. — And I am ashamed to say that even then I still saw these things as a child does.

The next landmark in my career — and it was an event which had a decisive influence upon the subsequent course of it — was the discovery by my house-master at Rugby that my study (which I shared with a boy called Middleton) had become an 'artist's studio'. In it I had set up an easel, procured oil-paints, a mahl-stick, and a palette. At the time these unorthodox happenings were brought to the attention of the house-master I was engaged in copying the head of a large dog.

I remember a very big boy opening the door of the study, putting his big red astonished face inside, gazing at me for a while — digesting what he saw, the palette on my thumb, the brush loaded with pigment in the act of dabbing — and then, laconically and contemptuously, remarking, 'You frightful artist!' closed the study door: and I could hear his big slouching lazy steps going away down the passage to find some more normal company. The English, I am afraid, are mostly of that stamp.

At length someone apprised the house-master, at all events, of what was going on in his house. What Public Schools were for was to turn out a stupid but well-behaved executive class to run the Empire Kipling crowed and crooned about. Nothing so anomalous as a fourteen-year-old fag painting in oils at a giant easel had ever been recorded. My presence before this had not gone unremarked: but it was something of a different kind, in that case, that had stimulated interest, and concern. For four terms I had not changed my form (I was still in the Lower Middle School) and showed no tendency to do so. The house-master put two and two together: two such unusual things must be connected. They in fact hardly had any connection: but it was all for the best that he was a man content with the obvious.

He concluded (quite rightly) that I had got into the wrong school. He thought that an art-school was where I really ought to be; and he wrote my mother to this effect. Meanwhile he arranged for me to have special instruction in drawing several times a week. An old Scot, a beautiful silver moustache shading his red lips, gargled away at me in a Glasgow accent, but gave me much practice in the portrayal of plaster casts, and provided me with reports of unrestrained enthusiasm. I was a much needed advertisement for him, of course, and his function, in that birthplace of Football.

The effect of the house-master's letter upon my parent was mixed. She of course deplored my slackness and indifference to algebra and Latin (forgetful of the fact that these schools specialised in instilling a contempt for learning in the 'flannelled fool' liable for the rest of his life to live with such metaphors in his mouth as 'sticky wicket', and the 'muddied oaf', content for the remainder of his days to feel that he is 'playing the game', oblivious of what the particular game happens to be).[1]

But she was predisposed to favour the idea of my becoming an artist: and my unexpected prowess as an oil-painter enabled her to forget the ignominy of the dunce's cap. She herself had always painted — used to go to an art-school in that Bloomsbury Square at the end of Great Ormond Street before her marriage and was not displeased to think that I evinced this unconquerable desire to do what she herself had always done in a desultory way. There was perhaps vanity in this.

When a schoolboy, I passed some weeks every year in Paris with my mother. These visits were not calculated to cure me of my interest in the arts. It was then I first frequented the galleries, the Louvre and the Luxembourg. The innumerable oil paintings of all the schools, in one big lazy blur of cupids, shipwrecks, madonnas, and obese women, exercised a pleasurable mesmerism upon a schoolboy whose responses were far below a phlegmatic surface: whose instincts far outran his consciousness. — However, the outcome of the whole matter was that after a stay of about two years and a half I left Rugby, and became a student at the Slade School, University College, London.

The latter institution was at that period presided over by Professor Brown, with Tonks as the guiding spirit and policy-maker. All the emphasis was on drawing. Wilson Steer and Russell made up the full professorial cast. A training was provided of a type so uncraftsmanlike that it surprises me it remained uncriticised. The model of draughtsmanship insisted upon by Tonks was cinquecento: but the painting that of an academic, inexact, impressionism, such as is now to be met with at Burlington House. Steer knew more than the others, but was a strangely somnolent bovine individual, of little use as a teacher. He moved around the life-class with a heavy, cautious step, as if avoiding puddles, and no one could call him a chatterbox. Sometimes he never spoke at all. But I did not remain very long at the Slade and then went to Paris, renting a studio in the Quartier. At this point my life as an artist in fact began.

It may perhaps have been remarked that in the last chapter I made no mention of anything but the literary side of my history—which was in the main because this book is concerned, more than anything else, with that side, or with matters arising out of the fact that I am a writer, and of a kind (as in the case of satire) exciting people to retributory action. In the present chapter, except for the booklets manufactured as a child, for the unfolding of sagas, I have spoken only of beginnings as a painter. Already I was writing at the Slade (and to that presently I shall return), but it had no bearing as yet upon my movements or mode of life.

Further, there is nothing of economic relevance, those questions do not exact attention until later. As to the Fine Arts, it is not difficult for even mechanics or a labourer's son to get as far as an art-school. The trouble is — once there — the urgency of the position, so that he is compelled to go in for training in commercial techniques, and can never keep his head above water long enough to become a straight artist, rather than a man working for his living by doing commercial designs. — If you go to see an exhibition of a young painter's work at a West End Gallery, in nine cases out of ten you may be sure he did not start economically from scratch. But hundreds who have so begun are passing every year through municipal or State Schools. It is they who produce the pictorial advertisements for vacuum cleaners, face creams, bile beans, or cigarettes you see in the papers or on the walls of the Underground.

———

About Paris I cannot write with a suitable restraint. It was the great humanist creation of the French, on a par with their cathedrals: indeed there is the same space, and lift, in the one as in the other. But, above all, the human being was never forgotten in its rambling growth: the same thing that made the French so graceful and polite, or the world's best dancing-masters and pastry-cooks, made this place supremely pleasant. To make a perfect place to live in — no other people has done that with their capital city, which has either been too formal, too tidy, too snobbish, too squalid, too tall, too much a Business Babylon, or too much like a museum.

For centuries Paris had dominated Europe socially and intellectually, no European could say his mind had delivered itself of a thought until Paris had recognised its existence, no woman was dressed until Paris had dressed her; and even up to world war i, it was intact. It was just the hectic ruin that people lived in after that. In its heyday the rest of Europe — from which Vienna must be excepted — crouched in their over-cold, or over-hot, capitals, culturally provincial. But Paris was expansive and civilised, temperate in climate, beautiful and free.

I went there in its late sunset: its multitude of café-terraces swarmed with people from every corner of the earth: it was still *la nouvelle Athènes,* divinely disputatious, with an immense student population for whom the publishers poured out 'libraries' of masterpieces, all the sciences and the arts most daring and up-to-date, priced at a few francs. For it was the impecunious in great numbers who bought them: there may have been a luxury business in books but it did not obtrude itself upon the student, and would have been of no interest to him. It was not a city of the rich, like New York — the poorest student could sit all day long (and often did) for the cost of one cup of coffee without being interfered with and observe the crowds, or be entertained by his neighbours, or by the *soulard* who drifted from café to café, extracting a few sous by his imitation of the courtship of two canaries, or the ululations of owls, with his wizened mustachioed lips.

It is dangerous to go to heaven when you are too young. You do not understand it and I did not learn to work in Paris. Many things, however, found their way into my mind as I moved about. — First of all, I altered my appearance. Driven, by a vocational ferment, out of the British rut of snobbish sloth, I now became transformed, in contact with the Latin life, into something so different that had I a few years later encountered someone I had been to school with he would not have recognised me. I still went to a tailor in Brook Street for my clothes, but persuaded him to cut them into what must have seemed to his insular eye outrageous shapes.

Gradually the bad effects of English education wore off, or were deliberately discarded. Being with 'foreigners' all the time who never 'played the game', I rapidly came to see that there was always a game — to whose rules, good or bad, you must conform. However, I need not detail the phases of this metamorphosis: I became a European, which years in Paris and elsewhere (Spain, Germany, Holland) entailed; hastening the process however, with a picturesque zeal. There are in England many invisible assets, to do mostly with character; they are not tangible and make no show of a kind to appeal to the barbaric eye of youth. All that was apparent to me, at that time, was the complacent and unimaginative snob of the system I had escaped from, the spoiled countryside, sacrificed in order to manufacture Brummagem, long ago when it was discovered that England was really a coal mine; and I noted with distaste the drab effects of Victorian mediocrity. I may add that the defects of the French were as hidden from me as those invisible assets I have spoken of belonging to the English.

My literary career began in France, in the sense that my first published writings originated in notes made in Brittany. Indeed, this period in retrospect, responsible for much, is a blank with regard to painting. There was for instance the beginning of my interest in philosophy (attendance at Bergson's lectures at the Collège de France one evidence of that). But what I started to do in Brittany I have been developing ever since. Out of Bestre and Brotcotnaz grew, in that sense — if in no other — the aged 'Gossip Star' at her toilet, and Percy Hardcaster.[2] Classifiable I suppose as

'satire', fruits of much visceral and intellectual travail and indolent brood-
ing, a number of pieces were eventually collected under the title of 'The
Wild Body'. To those primordial literary backgrounds, among the meadows
and rocks and stone hamlets of Finisterre, thundered at by the Atlantic,
in a life punctuated with Pardons, I will now make my way back, and
try and remember how my first rational writings came to assume the shape
they did.[3]

Notes

[1] Lewis is here alluding to the following lines from Kipling's "The Islanders":

> Then ye returned to your trinkets; then ye contented your souls
> With the flannelled fools at the wicket or the muddied oafs
>   at the goals.

[2] The "Gossip Star" is Lady Fredigonde in *The Apes of God* (1930); Percy Hardcaster
is the main character in *The Revenge for Love* (1937).

[3] See Appendix I for an interesting variant draft of this chapter.

CHAPTER XXII

EARLY LIFE AND SHAKESPEARE

IT has been my experience of my few very eminent contemporaries that, after their various fashions, they have been the possessors of abnormally aggressive egos (and I daresay they may have discovered the same symptoms in myself). But what are these unhealthily large egos but one of the byproducts of the situation which isolates the so-called 'intellectual' from the common life, and demands of him much more domestic morale than is good for him?

When I saw Joyce described, as I did not long ago, as suffering from 'elephantiasis of the ego', I felt the usual contempt certain critics always succeed in provoking; for even their truths are so crude as to be invalid as they stand, having all the appearance of ill-favoured errors. But *of course* Joyce had 'elephantiasis of the ego'. Had he not suffered from something which lends itself to such an offensive description, you, Mr. Critic, would have no 'Ulysses' or 'Finnegans Wake' to gabble about: to blow hot and blow cold about — inflate your little reputation by puffing, and then reinflate it by a confession of disillusionment.

The only people of eminence I was in touch with as a beginner were painters, who enjoyed the usual robust self-esteem of their kind — painting being a much healthier occupation than writing. They overlooked in me the budding artist but accorded a generous recognition to something else. The first literary form I had used was verse, which I was writing while at the Slade. And to these elders I was known as a 'poet'. The Fine Arts they imagined were already in good hands, namely their own. Verse, as a form of literary composition, preceded my 'Wild Body' stories. I wrote a great deal, including a five-act play in blank verse. As early as my schooldays I had formed this habit, but what I wrote then was of a pietistic order.

About the time I went to the Slade I began to write Petrarchan sonnets, but soon changed to Shakespearean. They were easier to do. Some were so like Shakespeare's that as I recall lines in them I am never quite certain whether they were Shakespeare's or mine. It remains for me a mystery how so dumb a youth as I was can have produced them. It is nothing short of planchette, or automatic writing. Since the publication of Shakespeare's famous sequence many people have, it is true, written sonnets that could at first glance be mistaken for his. But they were usually experienced craftsmen.

My sonnet sequence contained no dark lady, all that side was appropriately absent, but if anything they exaggerated the Shakespearean pessimism. These pastiches, at all events, attracted attention among a small number of people. Here is a sonnetlike composition of that period, which I remember a luminary of those days singling out for commendation.

123

'Doubt is the sole tonic that sustains the mind,
The keynote of this universe entire.
Self-conscious certainty is Doubt, and blind
God-worship but Doubt's sanctified attire.
God fashioned us in Doubt: for Eden-trees
Were planted there in God's initial Doubt:
. . . hope doth but tease
Us into . . . where certainty could not.'[1]

One of my earliest friends was an architect, the author of a book called
'The Canon', who became my friend because of these sonnets. Sterling
was his name. I was so young then that everything is misty: what we
can have conversed about heaven knows. Certainly not Shakespeare. I had
no idea until William Rothenstein told me, at a later date, that Sterling
had written a book of great interest. Nor, being backward and obtuse,
had I the least idea that this poor man, when he took me out to tea and fed
me on Meringue Chantilly (for I was inordinately greedy and probably did
not have to be pressed very much to eat three or four) had in all likelihood to fast himself afterwards to cover this expense. We used to go to
Buzzard's in Oxford Street where he spent as much, I expect, for a tea as
would buy him a week's breakfasts. He supported out of his slender reserves
an aged mother and sister — my informant again Rothenstein — and lived
in a small dark flat in the Adelphi. For two or three weeks no one saw
him around. At last they broke in: he was lying just inside the front door
with his throat cut. The rats, infesting the London sewers, had chewed
away some of his flesh. It seems that he had appointed William Rothenstein
his literary executor, who, in due course, discovered a sheaf of my sonnets.
These he at first believed must be Sterling's, until he identified their only
true begetter. Very much later he told me about this, and what has happened to them I do not know. They are, I suppose, my property, for they
were only lent to Sterling to read.

It was therefore an innovation for me to take to prose, when I began
preparing material for stories in Brittany — at the time I felt a little of a
come-down, or at least a condescension. My first attempts naturally were
far less successful than the verse. The coastal villages of Finisterre in
which I spent long summers (one of them with the artist, Henry Lamb)
introduced one to a more primitive society. These fishermen went up to
Iceland in quite small boats, they were as much at home in the huge and
heaving Atlantic as the torero in the bull-ring: their speech was still
Celtic and they were highly distrustful of the stranger. They brawled
about money over their fierce apple-juice: when somebody was stabbed,
which was a not infrequent occurrence, they would not call in a doctor,
but come to the small inn where I stayed, for a piece of ice. A great part
of their time was spent, when not at sea, jogging up and down between
'Pardons', all the women provided with large umbrellas. Their miniature
bagpipe is a fine screaming little object, to the music of which star dancers
would leap up into the air, as if playing in a feudal ballet. On the whole,
however, the dancing was sedate and mournful, compared with Rubens'
peasants.

Long vague periods of an indolence now charged with some creative purpose were spent in digesting what I saw, smelt and heard. For indolent I remained. The Atlantic air, the raw rich visual food of the barbaric environment, the squealing of the pipes, the crashing of the ocean, induced a creative torpor. Mine was now a drowsy sun-baked ferment, watching with delight the great comic effigies which erupted beneath my rather saturnine but astonished gaze: Brotcotnaz, Bestre, and the rest.

During those days, I began to get a philosophy: but not a very good one, I am afraid. Like all philosophies, it was built up around the will — as primitive houses are built against a hill, or propped up upon a bog. As a timely expression of personal impulses it took the form of a reaction against civilised values. It was militantly vitalist.[2] Only much later was I attracted to J.-J. Rousseau, or it might have had something to do with his anti-social dreaming.

The snobbishness (religion of the domestic) of the English middleclass, their cold philistinism, perpetual silly sports, all violently repudiated by me were the constant object of comparison with anything that stimulated and amused, as did these scenes. I overlooked the fact that I was observing them as a privileged spectator, having as it were purchased my front-row stall with money which I derived from that other life I despised. In spite of this flaw the contrast involved was a valid one: of the two types of life I was comparing, the one was essentially contemptible, the other at least rich in surface quality: in the clubhouse on an English golf-links I should not have found such exciting animals as I encountered here — undeniably the golfers' values are wanting in a noble animal zest. This is, however, a quandary that cannot be resolved so simply as I proposed — namely, the having-the-cake-and-eating-it way.

The epigraph at the begining of my first novel, 'Tarr', is an expression of the same mood, which took a long time to evaporate altogether. It is a quotation from Montaigne. 'Que c'est un mol chevet que l'ignorance et l'incuriosité!'[3] Even books, theoretically, were a bad thing, one was much better without them. Every time men borrowed something from outside they gave away something of themselves, for these acquisitions were artificial aggrandisement of the self, but soon there would be no core left. And it was the core that mattered. Books only muddied the mind: men's minds were much stronger when they only read the Bible.

The human personality, I thought, should be left alone, just as it is, in its pristine freshness: something like a wild garden — full, naturally, of starlight and nightingales, of sunflowers and the sun. The 'Wild Body' I envisaged as a piece of the wilderness. The characters I chose to celebrate — Bestre, the Cornac and his wife, Brotcotnaz, le père François — were all primitive creatures, immersed in life, as much as birds, or big, obsessed, sun-drunk insects.

The body was wild: one was attached to something wild, like a big cat that sunned itself and purred. The bums, alcoholic fishermen, penniless students (generally Russians) who might have come out of the pages of 'The Possessed', for long my favourite company, were an anarchist material. And as ringmaster of this circus I appointed my 'Soldier of Humour',[4] who stalked imbecility with a militancy and appetite worthy of a much more light-hearted and younger Flaubert, who had somehow got into the universe of Gorky.

There is a psychological factor which may have contributed to what I have been describing. — I remained, beyond the usual period, congealed in a kind of cryptic immaturity. In my social relations the contacts remained, for long, primitive. I recognised dimly this obstruction: was conscious of gaucherie, of wooden responses — all fairly common symptoms of course. It resulted in experience with no natural outlet in conversation collecting in a molten column within. This *trop-plein* would erupt: that was my way of expressing myself — with intensity, and with the density of what had been undiluted with ordinary intercourse: a thinning-out which is, of course, essential for protection.

Observing introspectively this paradoxical flowering, this surface obtuseness, on the one hand, and unexpected fruit which it miraculously bore: observing this masterly inactivity, almost saurianly-basking sloth, and what that condition produced, something within me may quite reasonably have argued that this inspired *Dummheit* was an excellent idea. *Let us leave well alone!* may have been the mental verdict. I know everything already: why add irrelevant material to this miraculous source? Why acquire spectacles for an eye that sees so well without them? So there was superstition, and, I suspect, arrogance.

But I am gazing back into what is a very dark cavern indeed. An ungregarious childhood may have counted for something. A feature of perhaps greater importance was that after my schooldays, even with my intimates, I was much younger than those with whom I associated, since I had left school so early. And, finally, at school itself, developing habits as I did which appeared odd to the young empire-builders by whom I was surrounded, may have stiffened the defence natural to that age.

The rough set of principles arrived at was not, I have said, a very good philosophy. Deliberately to spend so much time in contact with the crudest life is, I believe, wasteful of life. It seems to involve the error that raw material is alone authentic life. I mistook for 'the civilised' the tweed-draped barbaric clown of the golf-links. But, as a philosophy of life, it principally failed in limiting life in a sensational sense. After two or three intermediate stages I reached ultimately an outlook that might be described as almost as formal as this earliest one was the reverse.

———

'Wildness' of some kind or other — often more personally picturesque and romantic than mine — has been by no means an infrequent thing with the Anglo-saxon. As a reaction no doubt against the respectability of English life, many, like George Borrow, have gone to live in 'dingles', wandered about the earth with gypsies, taken service with the wild Corsairs like Trelawney, or become Bedouins, like Doughty. France, too, has produced a not insignificant crop of such men: Paul Gauguin, for instance, who worked Brittany before going to Tahiti: actually dying at a fishing-port in Finisterre after a scuffle with a fisherman in which he hurt his leg. His Breton idylls I think are the best of his work.

Augustus John — whom I knew at a very early age — has been the most notorious nonconformist England has known for a long time. Following in the footsteps of Borrow, he was one of those people who always set out to do the thing that 'is not done', according to the British canon. He swept aside the social conventions, which was a great success, and he became a public lion practically on the spot. There was another reason for this lionisation (which is why he has remained a lion): he happened to be an unusually fine artist.

Such a combination was rare. The fashionable public found as a rule that it had been leo-hunting some pretentious jackal. Here was one who had gigantic ear-rings, a ferocious red beard, a large angry eye, and who barked beautifully at you from his proud six foot, and, marvellously, was a great artist too. He was reported to like women and wine and song and to be by birth a gypsy.

When I first saw this extraordinary individual was while I was a student at the Slade School. I learned that Augustus John was an art master in Liverpool. He had had the scholarship at the Slade, and the walls bore witness to the triumphs of this 'Michelangelo'. He was a legendary 'Slade School *ingenious*', to use Campion the doorkeeper's word. A large charcoal drawing in the centre of the wall of the life-class of a hairy male nude, arms defiantly folded and a bristling moustache, commemorated his powers with almost a Gascon assertiveness: and fronting the stairs that lead upwards where the ladies were learning to be Michelangelos, hung a big painting of Moses and the Brazen Serpent.

Everything in the place was in the 'grand manner': for Professor Tonks, as I have already remarked, had one great canon of draughtsmanship, and that was the giants of the Renaissance. Everyone was attempting to be a giant and please Tonks. None pleased Tonks – none, in their work, bore the least resemblance to Michelangelo. The ladies upstairs wept when he sneered at their efforts to become Giantesses.

Now undoubtedly John had come nearer to the Michelangelo ideal than anybody else. One day the door of the life-class opened and a tall bearded figure, with an enormous black Paris hat, large gold ear-rings decorating his ears, with a carriage of the utmost arrogance, strode in and the whisper 'John' went round the class. He sat down on a donkey – the wooden-chargers astride which we sat to draw – tore a page of banknote paper out of a sketch book, pinned it upon a drawing board, and with a ferocious glare at the model (a female) began to draw with an indelible pencil. I joined the group behind this redoubtable personage. To my great surprise, a squat little figure began to emerge upon the paper. He had forsaken the 'grand manner' entirely, it seemed. A modern Saskia was taking shape upon the banknote paper: drawings that followed all came out of the workshop of Rembrandt Van Rhyn. Needless to say everyone was tickled to death. They felt that the squalor of the Dutch, rather than the noble rhetoric of the cinquecento, was, and always had been, the thing. John left as abruptly as he had arrived. We watched in silence this mythological figure depart.

For weeks afterwards Professor Tonks's life was a hell on earth. I am sure he had no inkling of the cause. However tall and graceful the model might be, displaying her young English charms before our hardened eyes, Tonks was presented, as he went his rounds, upon the students' drawing boards, with nothing but dumpy little images. I tried my hand at it, but found they did not come out very well, so I went back to a version of my own of Signorelli.[5]

The exact date of my first visit to John's studio I do not remember, but it was shortly after I left the Slade, I think. William Rothenstein (to whom I had been introduced by his young brother, who was at the Slade) was taking me there. We approached the top-floor flat in Charlotte Street: there was the noise of children, for this patriarch had already started upon his Biblical courses.

I was with John a great deal in those early days, in London, later in Paris, and on one long vacation on the coast of Normandy. At St. Honorine des Perthes (the latter occasion) I wrote verse, when not asleep in the sun. Unlike most painters, John was very intelligent. He read much and was of a remarkable maturity. I cast this all in the past tense, for I am speaking of a time long past: but I may add that I never see Augustus John today but he speaks of some book he has been reading, generally one of the few at the moment worth attention.

Nietzsche was, I believe, the paramount influence, as was the case with so many people prior to world war i. The other day I was interested, in listening to a broadcast by Herbert Read (in a 'Crisis of My Life' series) to find he had selected Nietzsche as the decisive influence, overshadowing the rest of his early reading. Germans of whom I saw a good deal in Paris as a student were very contemptuous: they called Nietzsche 'a salon-philosopher'.

But for me Nietzsche was, with Schopenhauer, a thinker more immediately accessible to a Western mind than the other Germans, whose barbarous jargon was a great barrier — Hegel, for instance, I could never read. A majority of people, I daresay, found in the author of 'Zarathustra' a sort of titanic nourishment for the ego: treating in fact this great hysteric as a power-house. At present that is what I like least about Nietzsche: and I was reasonably immune then to Superman. The impulse to titanism and supernatural afflatus pervading German romanticism has never had any interest for me. On the other hand that side of his genius which expressed itself in 'La Gaya Scienza', or those admirable maxims, rather resembling Butler's 'Notebooks', which he wrote after the breakdown in his health, were among my favourite reading in those years.

———

Since I published nothing, nor did I exhibit, while a student in Paris — though I had begun work on something eventually to appear in print — as a narrative of a career the matter of these last three chapters is strictly speaking extraneous: and, at all events, there is no more I need say here about those very early years. These chapters, however, provide me with something I shall find useful in the discussions ahead. The Russian influence I have not mentioned even, since I am bringing that out — indeed starring it — in subsequent chapters.[6] It was already very strong in Brittany. Sympathy for the outcast, which is so characteristic a feature in the Russian literature of the Nineteenth Century, did not direct me to my hoboes, but it may have intensified the latent humanism.

Notes

[1] The full text of the poem reads as follows:

To Doubt

Death's incorruptible minister is Doubt,
Whose very name of Hope is eloquent:
And so the interest in this changeful plot
Is kept at whiteheat till the curtain drop:
Doubt is the sole tonic that sustains the mind,
The key note of this universe entire, —
Self-conscious certainty is Doubt, — and blind
God-worship is Doubt's sanctified attire.

God fashioned us in Doubt, — for Eden trees
Were planted there in God's initial doubt:
This brief respite Fate grants us doth but tease
Us into hope, where Certainty could not.

Doubt's Universal empire doth but show
God fears a certain Anarchy of Woe.

This is taken from a sheaf of poems in the Lewis Collection at Cornell, with the following note on the envelope:

> These poems were mainly written in about 18th year: all before 20th certainly. Of no value, but better be kept. *W.L.*

> It is certainly not my desire ever to have these not very interesting early efforts *published.* I should be very sorry to think that after my death they might be dragged out and published by some literary promoter, for mercenary reasons. — On the other hand, I do not destroy them because Sir William Rothenstein has a duplicate of them. . . . — Very improperly Sir William Rothenstein did *not* return them to me but stuck to them. There the matter still stands. If I succeed in getting them back I will destroy all of them. Anyhow, I hope they will never see the light. *signed Wyndham Lewis. Toronto. Oct. 1942.*

[2] Vitalism is an idealist doctrine committed to the independence of organic from inorganic life, resisting the attempts of biological science to explain life with reference solely to the treatment of inorganic life through physics and chemistry.

[3] "O que c'est un doux et mol chevet, et sain, que l'ignorance et l'incuriosité, à reposer une teste bien faicte!" *Essais*, Livre III, Ch. III, ed. M. Rat (Paris, 1962), p. 526. "O what a soft and easy and wholesome pillow is ignorance and freedom from care to rest a well-screwed-on headpiece!" *The Essays of Montaigne*, trans. E. J. Trechmann (Oxford, 1927), vol. II, p. 550.

[4] Kerr-Orr, Lewis's main character/narrator in *The Wild Body.*

[5] Signorelli (1441?-1523), Italian painter whose drawing influenced Michelangelo.

[6] See Ch. XXVII, "The Puritans of the Steppes," adapted from Lewis's own contribution to the "Crisis of My Life" series.

CHAPTER XXIII

FIRST PUBLISHED WORK

IT is unlikely that I should ever have uprooted myself from Paris had it not been for warnings that the economic position for me had suffered an alteration: that my father, who had gone to America, showed every sign of stopping there: finally, that the time might not be very distant when I should have to begin to make money. It was understood that it would be by painting that this would be accomplished, and indeed writing was never mentioned in that connection. At that period the image of Grub Street was uppermost in people's minds, whenever the subject of writing as a calling was mooted.

So, although visiting Paris every year, I now returned to London. It was little more than a gesture for some time, as I took no immediate steps towards professionalising myself. At last, however, I exhibited a largish canvas in the Ryder Street Gallery, St. James, run by Robert Ross. It represented two sprawling figures of Normandy fishermen, in mustard yellows and browns, which was purchased by Augustus John — a circumstance which gave me unusual pleasure.

Except for this painting, and perhaps a drawing or two, I sold nothing to start with: I think my next sale of work occurred during my brief association with 'Bloomsbury'. I refer to an over-lifesize gouache of three smiling women, which reminded Mr. Clive Bell, I recall, of Giotto. It was purchased through Bloomsbury influence, if not by Mr. Clive Bell, for the Contemporary Art Society. It found its way to the Tate Gallery, where it remained secluded in the cellar until one day the Thames overflowed, invaded the cellar, and the last seen of it was that of a reddish expanse floating about on the surface of the muddy water.

Actually quite my first success of a practical nature was literary. The 'English Review' had just started publication, founded and edited by Ford Madox Hueffer (later known as Ford Madox Ford). I went to its office in Holland Park and Hueffer has described (and I myself I think elsewhere) 'the moujik' who unexpectedly mounted his stairs, silently left a bundle of manuscript — but with no address, only the author's name.[1] 'The moujik' referred to my hirsute and unconventional appearance. The outcome was that the 'English Review' published successively 'The Pole', 'Some Innkeepers and Bestre', and 'Les Saltimbanques'. Some weeks later when I went to enquire about the manuscript they gave me a copy of the proofs of the first story, which they had corrected and returned to the printer, as they did not know where I lived. This was a great and pleasurable surprise.

Through Hueffer I became acquainted with Ezra Pound, through whom in due course I became acquainted with T. S. Eliot, Gaudier-Brzeska, Dolmetsch,[2] H. D., Aldington, and many others.

When Hueffer married Violet Hunt, the novelist, that expanded still further the orbit of his somnolent but systematic sociability. It was at dinner at Mrs. Hueffer's for instance that I first met Rebecca West. She was a dark young maenad then, who burst through the dining-room door (for she was late) like a thunderbolt.

These intellectual Hosts were of that valuable kind of human, who shuns solitude as the dread symbol of unsuccess, is happiest when his rooms are jammed with people (for preference of note). I was commissioned by Violet Hueffer to do a mural to go over the mantelpiece of her study. This was a concession to 'les jeunes', but her spirit dwelt with the pre-Raphaelites, as did half of her husband's.

Hueffer was a flabby lemon and pink giant, who hung his mouth open as though he were an animal at the Zoo inviting buns – especially when ladies were present. Over the gaping mouth damply depended the ragged ends of a pale lemon moustache. This ex-collaborator with Joseph Conrad was himself, it always occurred to me, a typical figure out of a Conrad book – a caterer, or corn-factor, coming on board – blowing like a porpoise with the exertion – at some Eastern port.

What he *thought* he was, was one of those military *sahibs* who used to sit on the balcony of a club in Hindustan with two or three other *sahibs, stingahs* at their sides, and who, between meditative puffs at a cheroot, begins to tell one of Conrad's tales. He possessed a vivid and theatrical imagination: he jacked himself up, character as he was in a nautical story, from one of the white business gents in the small tropic port into – I am not quite sure it was not into a *Maugham* story – among the more swagger representatives of white empire in Asia.

Those were his failings, irritating to me (though Ezra Pound, who referred to him as 'Fatty', appeared to accept him – amused but impressed – as the *sahib* of the officers' quarters). But on the asset side there was a good deal too. Hueffer was probably as good an editor as could be found for an English literary review. – He had by birth artistic associations and could write himself much better than most editors. His literary standards were too exacting for latter-day England. Such productions as he was peculiarly fitted to edit are expensive to run and the circulation insignificant today. He was denied in his milieu the possibility of exerting an influence which would have been productive of more vigorous literary standards. Then his vanity never interfered in the least with his appreciation of books by other writers.

Of Ezra Pound I will say nothing except to remark that, to the best of my belief, he was by way of discovering, or of bringing forward, James Joyce; that he 'sold the idea' of Joyce as a writer of great parts to Miss Harriet Weaver (for Joyce the all-important 'contact'): that he nursed Eliot's style along until it could stand on its own feet: that by his criticism of the English Nineteenth Century poets (Shelley, Keats and their followers) and substitution of older severer models, he reorientated along with T. S. Eliot the whole of English and American criticism; he imported into England and America, the satirico-romantic standards of the French as also their use of conversational, as opposed to 'poetic', diction – this in association with Eliot. Thus he and Eliot displaced what up to then had still remained the largely Victorian approach to the appropriate subject matter of poetry.*

It was the result of Pound's busy promotion that 'The Portrait of the Artist', and 'Tarr', were serialised by 'The Egoist', and that T. S. Eliot's verse appeared there. Finally, 'Cathay' – described by Hueffer as 'the most beautiful book in the world' – was the first, as it remains the most magically beautiful, of versions of the Chinese poets, initiating the technique since used by many other – and inferior – hands.

——

If I did not exhibit pictures it did not mean that I was unproductive. I was now developing a mode of pictorial expression which was more 'advanced' than that of other people at that time. *Avantgardism* in itself, at any time, is not a merit or a demerit. Some people are the changers and some the conservers. What conferred a kind of sanction upon my violent movement away from more orthodox practice was the fact that this was favourable to the development of something that no other method would have brought out so well. As far as England is concerned there is no one else I can think of whose pigeon this was quite so much as it was mine. But of course dear old Great Britain is no place to be an artist in – at least not an artist of that sort. Severity of any kind repels her – as she always smiles good-naturedly about the 'logical' French (meaning, it is better to be easy-going, and keep the intellect in its place). You will always find that England will get back to the romantic at the first opportunity. Severity, like Satire, will only in the end be tolerated in the foreigner.

By the time I joined the Omega Workshops – Roger Fry's abortive venture – my position was that of an extremist, I suppose: much further to the left, that is, than any of the others. That was in 1913. About this scheme I first heard some time before that. I have a letter from Roger Fry dated 21 Feb. 1912, in which he says: 'Will you come to a meeting to settle the nature of the group of artists which D. Grant, Etchells and I propose to start.' There is another of 7 Dec. 1912 from Fry saying: 'I'm working very hard trying to raise capital for our decoration scheme. So far the only help promised comes from Bernard Shaw.' At last here is a letter dated 5 April 1913, which I will quote in full, for though much of it is extraneous to the matter in hand, it is best to have it intact.

'MY DEAR LEWIS. I have just finished Léon Bloy's "Mendiant Ingrat" which you recommended to me. I am simply overwhelmed by the satanic beauty of it. The man is an astounding artist and it shows that devil worship must be added to the many strange and inexplicable causes of good art.

It is fascinatingly interesting to me because I have often thought that Christianity was made to fit the peculiar arrogance and egomania of certain Western people in whom the illusion of self-importance is

* In the Nineties tentatives in these directions are discernible, but most are imitational. It was not the principle itself that was taken over.

so colossal that they have never had the faintest possibility of understanding what the universe is like. The miracle is that it is the West
which has discovered science, the only possible antidote, no doubt, to
a Western mind, for this unendurable obsession of the ego as the
centre of all things. And naturally a man like Bloy must reject it.
Eastern people who alone have had enough humility to see more or
less what *things* were like have never needed it and of course accept it
the moment it is presented to them.

Is Bloy alive still? I hope for his sake he isn't. Have you read
the other things "La Femme Pauvre" etc. I expect they are splendid
and one ought to get them.

He is the greatest warning against Absolutism (except in art) that
I know. I suppose in fact that part of the explanation of him is that he
translated an absolutism which is of the very nature of art into intellectual truth when it becomes the supreme denial of faith.

I'm very much interested by what you said about the need of
some big beliefs outside of art. I must talk it over with you. The situation of the artist becomes more and more hopelessly paradoxical the
more we get to some idea of what art is.

We must talk it over. I've taken 33 Fitzroy Sq. will meet there
soon.

Yrs. vr. sincerely,
ROGER FRY.'[3]

The house had been rented or bought: so this scheme materialised,
and will serve as a kind of milestone. I worked there with several
of my friends and future associates. Frederick Etchells was I think
the most technologically minded of us: but with no preliminary workshop
training it was idle to suppose that half a dozen artists could cope with all
– or indeed any – of the problems of waxing, lacquering, polishing,
painting and varnishing of furniture – chairs, tables, cabinets and so
forth – or the hand-painting of textiles which the plan involved. Naturally
the chairs we sold stuck to the seats of people's trousers; when they
took up an Omega candlestick they could not put it down again, they held
it in an involuntary vice-like grip. It was glued to them and they to it.
Later I believe these drolleries ceased to enliven what was otherwise an
arty-crafty conception, with a 'post-impressionist' veneer. However, certain
transactions of a disagreeable nature caused me to sever my connection
with the Omega, and as there is no purpose in returning to such matters
here I will pass on to my next milestone, namely 'The Cave of the Golden
Calf'. I believe I am going backwards, but I have not to hand any record
of the actual date.[4]

Strindberg, the Swedish dramatist, had a number of wives, one being
a Viennese. This very adventurous woman (whose favourite remark, I
recall, was 'Je suis au bout de forces!', although, often as I heard her say
it, I never saw her in that condition, her 'forces' being at all times
triumphantly intact) rented an enormous basement. Hence the term 'Cave'.
She had it suitably decorated with murals by myself, and numbers of
columns by Jacob Epstein: hired an orchestra – with a frenzied Hungarian

gypsy fiddler to lead it – a smart corps of Austrian waiters and an Austrian cook: then with a considerable amount of press-promotion she opened as a night-club.

With the Epstein figures appearing to hold up the threateningly low ceiling, the somewhat abstract hieroglyphics I had painted round the walls, the impassioned orchestra, it must have provided a kick or two for the young man about town of the moment. It was about my first job: and if I had acquired the taste for alcohol (as I had not) I might have got a kick or two myself. As it was I had to try, and as best I could, to cope with a patroness forever *au bout de forces*.

Already I had begun to make a little money, here and there, as you will have observed. I did not receive a great deal for my night-club murals (actually £60). I was quite unknown, however, and would have done them for nothing. I only went for one or two days a week to the Omega – where for such a part-time attendance what was paid was a nominal fee only: my fisherman picture was modestly priced. Until world war i I was in receipt of an allowance of some sort, though as I made rather more I progressively dispensed with it. Without this backing I do not see (as already stated) how I should have negotiated the difficulties attendant on new courses. For there is no passion here for artistic expression. It is generally on the basis of parlour games – or children's games – that experimenting in an art exists. So artificial floating is essential. I could not have lived, only paid for hair-cuts and cigarettes, with any money I made up to autumn 1913: on the other hand, in the tired intervals of hack-work (had I obtained it) I might have evolved something superficially resembling the abstract pictures to which I shall be referring next. But they would have been perfunctory: I should have been obliged to leave them like indecisive experiments. Such questions resemble problems of cooking: it is a case where time is all-important.

It was, after all, a new civilisation that I – and a few other people – was making the blueprints for: these things never being more than that. A rough design for a way of seeing for men who as yet were not there. At the time I was unaware of the full implications of my work, but that was what I was doing. I, like all the other people in Europe so engaged, felt it to be an important task. It was more than just picture-making: one was manufacturing fresh eyes for people, and fresh souls to go with the eyes. That was the feeling. A necessary part of this work was of course propaganda: without that the public would merely conclude that a few young artists had gone mad, and take no further notice of what they did.

It was at this point (circa autumn 1913) that I began again to do a great deal of writing, most of it merely the journalism entailed by propaganda. (Some had to be rather silly.) My friends and myself began holding exhibitions of pictures: with Miss Kate Lechmere I opened 'The Rebel Art Centre' in Great Ormonde Street, involving prospectuses – for lectures that were never delivered, and classes that were never held, as the war supervened – and a good deal of press controversy. Finally I planned and launched that hugest and pinkest of all magazines, 'Blast' – whose portentous dimensions, and violent tint did more than would a score of exhibitions to make the public feel that something was happening. A great deal of editorial work, and again much writing, went into that. Then the war came, and that ended chapter i of my career as a writer and artist with an unceremonious abruptness; if it can be called a chapter, for it had not got very far.

Off and on, however, I was confined to my bed now for a number of months, having contracted a troublesome infection. I began working on a novel, planned earlier, namely 'Tarr'. I had decided to join the army and wanted to leave this token book, lest the worst should happen (although as then written in its first uncouth form, it would not have been a very satisfactory testament). Also, not wishing 'Blast' to stand as a solitary explosion, I began to collect material for a second number.

The outbreak of war, although naturally quite different to the coming of 'total' war, with its black-out, flight to the country and so on, did on the instant reorient people's lives. As I was shut up so much of the time I now had very few contacts, after so over-social a life a most pleasant change. This period of sickness I spent mostly in the company of Capt. Guy Baker. It was he who made a collection of my drawings and gouaches which later he bequeathed to some museum.[5]

Baker had been a 'young captain', in the army in India, but had resigned, I think, because of a breakdown in health. Tears came to his eyes readily, like the Iron Duke whom he resembled. His health got so bad — a little in sympathy with me, I believe — that at last he was obliged to go to his home in Gloucestershire for a while. When he returned, he looked a new man. But soon — at the sight of me, still with my legs upon a chair — he relapsed into invalidism. He would limp round in the morning and we would discuss our respective symptoms. When subsequently, much later, I joined the army, *he* joined it too, though how they ever came to accept him I never understood: about the time I reached the Front, he had hobbled off there too with his regiment. — I felt about him just as if I had picked up a lost dog — a nice friendly but not very healthy looking animal, he even had a wriggle of the haunches which resembled a dog's wriggle of bashful sociability. Evidently when his military life came to an end, everything shut up and went out for this poor chap. The other officers of his regiment he had expected to go through life with — he was lost and missing from that small corps of tanned and snobbish men. He had money: but he had no interest. He found himself among a lot of complex individuals who had read a lot of books, of whom he was mortally afraid. But we got on famously, it was like having a woman around. The epidemic which immediately succeeded the war, with its millions of victims, found in poor Baker an easy prey.

'Tarr', which had appeared in serial form in 'The Egoist', was published in 1918 and was entirely rewritten for an edition ten years later, was finished during my convalescence. In Part III I am writing in some detail about it, so I need say no more now: except, a little prematurely perhaps, I will quote in full a letter written me by W. B. Yeats. I had sent him a copy of the 1928 edition.

'DEAR WYNDHAM LEWIS. This is a belated letter of thanks but I am a slow and capricious reader. I read nothing as a rule but poetry and philosophy (and of course detective stories) and when "Tarr" came I laid it aside, till I had finished a course of those I had set out upon. Then about a month ago I took up "Tarr". It does not excite me as "Childermass" did yet it is a sincere and wonderful work, and its curious, almost unconscious presentation of sex, those mechanical images and images of food—there also is mechanicism, unites itself in my mind with so much in contemporary painting and sculpture. There is the feeling, almost Buddhist, that we are caught in a kind of steel trap. My only objection to your book is that you have isolated an element for study, as if in a laboratory, which cannot be isolated unless we take the elements out of the actual world as in romantic art (or in "Childermass"). This is not a defect of treatment, but of the contemporary form you have chosen. How interested Balzac would have been in Anastasya's business dealings with Soltyk—and in her character as a whole. The art politics of all these people! Is it not the prerogative of science to isolate its deductions? If sex and their love-life is a steel-trap then I want to set up against it the religion of Buddha and so restore the unity of my thoughts—of Buddha or, let us say, "Seraphita".

I shall be in London at the Savile from Tuesday next for ten days or so and hope to see you.

Yrs
W. B. YEATS.'[6]

As this is a history of a career, not a person, I now move on to February 1919. At the Goupil Gallery I was holding my first one-man show. It had the simple but expressive title 'GUNS' because throughout it represented pictures of the war, with special reference to the artillery. These were practically all drawings: some compositions, others individual figures drawn from life or studies of guns.

The catalogue contains such titles as 'Pill-Box'—'Battery Shelled'—'Walking Wounded'—'Battery Salvo'. These were the titles of pictures which in every case, though decidedly angular, were naturalistic. What did this mean? Let me quote from the Foreword I had written to my catalogue.

'The public, surprised at finding eyes and noses in this exhibition, will begin by the reflection that the artist has conceded nature, and abandoned those vexing diagrams by which he puzzled and annoyed. The case is really not quite that. All that has happened is that in these things the artist has set himself a different task. . . . I never associated myself with the jejune folly that would assert one week that a Polynesian totem was the only formula by which the mind of man—Modern Man, heaven help him!—might be expressed: the next, that only in some compromise between Ingres and the Chinese the golden rule of self-expression might be found. . . .

'I have attempted here only one thing: namely, in a direct ready formula to offer an interpretation of what I took part in in France. I set out to do a series dealing with the gunner's life from his arrival in the depot to his life in the Line.'

I add that 'experimentation has been waived': that 'I have tried to do with the pencil and brush' what the storyteller does with his pen. And where I am saying that in the midst of war 'serious interpretation' is not possible, I have a good saying — expressing something that is echoed everywhere in what I have written, at all periods. It is: 'Truth has no place in action.'[7]

Later on I assert that the Man of Action has his counterpart in the works of the mind. 'Another comes to pictorial expression with one or other of the attendant genii of passion at his elbow.' These 'genii of passion' may lead him to the truth: that of passion. But in the moment of passion, or the moment of action, there is no truth. — And even the truth of passion, it seems to follow — although I do not say this here — is an inferior truth: just as the man of action is an inferior man to the man of mind.

My main reason, however, for quoting passages from the *Foreword*, relates to that part of it which was written to anticipate the bewilderment of the public who would come to the gallery expecting to find abstractions, outrageous conundrums in paint, and instead would discover relatively life-like war-scenes and traditionally drawn figures of soldiers. It will be remarked that I repudiate a fanaticism in the past for the 'abstract'. It is open to the same artist, I suggest, to undertake, on the one hand, any experiment, however far it may lead him from the accepted canons of visual expression, or, on the other hand, to 'tell a story' which the simplest could understand. This he has as much right to do as the literary man, a Dickens, or a Tchekov, or a Stendhal — or, for that matter, as earlier artists, who without exception showed no squeamishness about 'literary' subject-matter.

From this position I never departed. It is as much my position today as it was then. Had it not been for the war I should not have arrived at it so quickly. War, and especially those miles of hideous desert known as 'the Line' in Flanders and France, presented me with a subject-matter so consonant with the austerity of that 'abstract' vision I had developed, that it was an easy transition. Had you at that time asked me to paint a milkmaid in a landscape of buttercups and daisies I should probably have knocked you down. But when Mars with his mailed finger showed me a shell-crater and a skeleton, with a couple of shivered tree-stumps behind it, I was still in my 'abstract' element. And before I knew quite what I was doing I was drawing with loving care a signaller corporal to plant upon the lip of the shell-crater.

There was another factor. I had begun writing, on a larger scale than before: with 'Tarr', more seriously. When in the *Foreword* just quoted I claimed never to have been any fanatic, in one sense that was true enough, in another not. An illustration or two will help. Gaudier-Brzeska, the sculptor, I regarded as a good man on the soft side, essentially a man of tradition — not 'one of Us'. To turn to literature (for theoretically my narrow criterion included that) I looked upon the Imagists (Pound, H. D., Aldington, Flint) as *pompier*. About all that my first impulse would have been to shout, 'à la gare'!

At this distance it is difficult to believe, but I thought of the inclusion of poems by Pound etc. in 'Blast' as compromising. I wanted a battering ram that was all of one metal. A good deal of what got in seemed to me soft and highly impure. Had it been France, there would have been plenty to choose from. Now this was certainly what might be called a fanatical way of going about the promotion of an idea. To place against this, I never denied myself the pleasure of drawing a human face naturalistically. A great deal of *avant-garde* propaganda appeared to me pretentious and silly; and I heartily detested, and had violently combated, Marinetti's *anti-passéisme*, and dynamism.

So much for my attitude in the 'Blast' days. My literary contemporaries I looked upon as too bookish and not keeping pace with the visual revolution. A kind of play, 'The Enemy of the Stars' (greatly changed later and published in book form) was my attempt to show them the way.[8] It became evident to me at once, however, when I started to write a novel, that words and syntax were not susceptible of transformation into abstract terms, to which process the visual arts lent themselves quite readily. The coming of war and the writing — at top-speed — of a full-length novel ('Tarr') was the turning-point. Writing — literature — dragged me out of the abstractist cul-de-sac.

The writing of 'Tarr' was approached with austerity. I clipped the text to the bone of all fleshly verbiage. Rhetoric was under an interdict. Even so, it soon became obvious that in order to show the reader character in action, with its attendant passion, there was no way of reducing your text to anything more skeletal than that produced by an otherwise normal statement, even if abnormally abrupt and harsh.

In the course of the writing, again, I grew more interested with every page in the life of my characters. In the end — apart from the fact that I abstained from the use of any clichés (even the inoffensive mates of more gregarious words) eschewed sentimental archaisms, and all *pretty language* as it might be called — 'Tarr' turned out a straightforward novel.

So my great interest in this first novel — essentially so different a type of expression from more or less abstract compositions in pure form and colour — so humanist and remote from implications of the machine, turned me into other paths: one form of expression must affect the other if they co-exist within the confines of one brain. Then so sudden and dramatic a break in one's life as the 'great war' played its part.

The war was a sleep, deep and animal, in which I was visited by images of an order very new to me. Upon waking I found an altered world: and I had changed, too, very much. The geometrics which had interested me so exclusively before, I now felt were bleak and empty. They wanted *filling*. They were still as much present to my mind as ever, but submerged in the coloured vegetation, the flesh and blood, that is life. I can never feel any respect for a picture that cannot be reduced, at will, to a fine formal abstraction. But I now busied myself for some years acquiring a maximum of skill in work from nature — still of course subject to the disciplines I had acquired and which controlled my approach to everything. The considerable collection of my drawings in the Rutherston Collection in the Manchester Museum, and the painting of Edith Sitwell in the Tate Gallery, London (the latter completed at a later date) represented the work of this period.

Thenceforth in the matter of the visual arts I have done two things concurrently: this has held up to the present moment. I have never departed from a dual visual activity. It can really be reduced to what I did when I had nature in front of me, and what I did when I ws not making use of nature. In the first case I have done work in the main strictly representative or naturalist — that is to say a faithful imitation of nature, within the limits prescribed by any art work. Of this type of work the portrait of T. S. Eliot (Durban City Gallery, S. Africa), painted in 1938, is a good example, as is my presentation portrait (School of Medicine, St. Louis, U.S.A.) of Dr. Joseph Erlanger, 1944.* 'Froanna' (Glasgow City Gallery) or the meditative bust in the City Gallery, Carlisle: the pastel of Mrs. O'Brien of Montreal, 1945, or the portrait head of Rebecca West, 1932, are other examples.

Side by side with this nature work I have done numbers of things varying in the degree in which they departed from nature. In a large and fairly homogeneous group produced in 1941-2 and in the paintings and drawings done between 1934 and 1938 (the major part seen in a one-man show at the Leicester Galleries, London) I have varied between realist fantasies and semi-abstraction. The satiric realism of 'Beach Babies', and the semi-abstract 'Stations of the Dead',† or 'Stage Scene', both appeared in the same exhibition.

In the 'Surrender of Barcelona' (which was in the English Pavilion at the New York World's Fair) I set out to paint a Fourteenth Century scene as I should do it could I be transported there, without too great a change in the time adjustment involved. So that is a little outside the natural-non-natural categories dominating controversy today. — There is not a great deal more to say upon this subject, without entering upon disquisitions of a more technical order. I have now, I think, given an account of how becoming-an-artist occurred in my case. From 1924 onwards writing became so much a major interest that I have tended to work at my painting or drawing in prolonged bursts, rather than fit them into the intervals of the writing or planning of books. Writing and picture-making are not activities, I have found, which mix very well, unless one becomes the servant of the other, as was the case with Blake, or with Rossetti.

* Dr. Erlanger was awarded the Nobel Prize in that year.
† Collection Naomi Mitchison.

Notes

1 See *The Bodley Head Ford Madox Ford*, vol. 5, *Memories and Impressions* (London, 1971), pp. 232-33.

2 Arnold Dolmetsch (1858-1940), musician and musical craftsman, was a pioneer in the revival of early English music and instruments and correct technique of play.

3 This letter appears, with minor variations, in *Letters of Roger Fry* (New York, 1972), p. 367.

4 Lewis was involved with the Omega Workshops from July to October, 1913 (see Jeffrey Meyers, *The Enemy: A Biography of Wyndham Lewis* [London, 1980],

pp. 41-50). Lewis's contact with the Cave was in the Spring of 1912; the Cave was the creation of Frida, second wife of August Strindberg.

5 The Victoria and Albert Museum.

6 Allan Wade prints Yeats's letter in a more plausible text "from a typed copy belonging to Mrs. Yeats" in his edition of Yeats's *Letters* (London, 1954), pp. 762-63. The main variants occur in the fourth sentence, which Wade prints as follows:

> It does not excite me as *Childermass* did yet is sincere and wonderful work, and its curious, almost unconscious, presentation of sex through mechanical images and images of food — there also its mechanism unites itself in my mind with so much in contemporary painting and sculpture.

Later, where Lewis gives "the religion of Buddha," Wade prints "the realization of Buddha."

7 Lewis's "Foreword" to *Guns*, along with a list of the works appearing in the exhibition, is given in Walter Michel, *Wyndham Lewis: Paintings and Drawings* (Berkeley & Los Angeles, 1971), p. 433.

8 "Enemy of the Stars" appeared in *Blast 1* and in book form in 1932. Both versions are reprinted in *Wyndham Lewis: Collected Poems and Plays*, ed. A. Munton (Manchester, 1979).

CHAPTER XXIV

PRIVATE MEANS AND PUBLIC MEANS

THE 'hopelessly paradoxical situation' of the artist, to which you have seen Mr. Fry alluding in the letter I quoted in the last chapter — and for which his remedies would differ greatly from mine — consists in his isolation in an age where he no longer has any function to perform. (I here am referring of course to the visual artist.) Among the French, still mainly agricultural and 'backward', the craftsman tradition survived, and with it the fine arts, as something in the nature of a national necessity. In England it had been dead some time. But also in France it had firmer roots.

As to the narrower question of the artist's position in English society, we cannot, I am afraid, say that industrialism or Victorian philistinism are responsible for everything. A great Eighteenth Century painter, Gainsborough, as his letters show, experienced the most violent discontent when he meditated upon the taste of his aristocratic clients. The sporting aristocracy of England were far inferior to the burgesses of Antwerp, Bruges, Delft, or Amsterdam when it came to supporting an art: and the recent exhibition of the King's pictures has revealed what astonishingly little interest in pictures the English Kings have had, Charles I being apparently the last intelligent collector. I shall not make the mistake of taking the want of taste and intelligence of a class and attributing it to the entire people. There may come a day when the miners and seamen of England will manifest great taste. In the meantime the middle-class has inherited a habit of indifferent taste and a dishearteningly platitudinous approach — philistine was Arnold's name for it. That mental climate will not change for the artist until society changes completely; and as to what will be there, culturally, when it does, it is idle to speculate.

If it seems offensive to the national sentiment to refer to what has been (possibly by accident) and has continued to be the low average of response to artistic stimulus in Britain, it seems, on the other hand, very necessary for the artist to know where he stands, and not to create for him (as so many are inclined to do) a fool's paradise. — But so much for the purely national aspect of a situation which is, in one degree or another, present everywhere. The artist is a craftsman who has been largely superseded by the machine. Yet his final exit from the scene — if it must come — it is our duty to postpone.

Mr. Roger Fry's solution for the desperate situation of the artist was, I will say that for it, free of uplift. As the world at large, in his estimate, had become impossible for the artist to survive in, without destructive compromises, it was necessary to create, at least for those he favoured, an artificial atmosphere (in the case of the Omega to re-create the workshop of the past, to compete, in a small way, with the factory). By confining themselves to the special economic atmosphere in this way created, a favoured few could survive.

All kinds of private activities, like 'The Contemporary Art Society', should be fostered by a group of well-to-do friends: and a certain proportion of all their incomes should be put aside, and as much support among their more intelligent acquaintances mustered, for the furthering of this art, in which all were interested. — I never heard such a plan enunciated; I am merely supposing that this was the kind of idea guiding these people.

The impulse to contrive an asylum of some kind for what you decide are the most deserving members of a distressed calling is praiseworthy. What actually happens, as a rule, however, in such cases, is that the sheltered climate results in preciosity. A delicate organism, what tends to be this precious microcosm, vomits forth the robust, as a silkworm would a tin-tack.

Speaking for myself, I would never exchange the public world, with all its harshness and imperfections, for the stuffiness of a private world. Consequently if I were asked my opinion upon a matter of this kind I should probably say: In spite of all the damage done to artistic talent in the world of everyday, better to let it take its chance. — Here I should like to add that, not today but long ago, the State should have stepped in. It is not our place to organise private relief: that is the function of the State — especially if it is as a result of the action of the State that such relief has become necessary. Indeed, by the mere organisation of private relief we are postponing action by the State: affording it the best of excuses for taking no action.

I have said that such private planning for the artist as I have been discussing, laudable as it is in principle, is apt to lead to preciosity. It need not of course do this: it is just a tendency (perhaps, again, peculiar to social life in England) by which in my experience such planning has been marked. — But there is another issue of a somewhat different nature: namely, this is one of the ways in which the *coterie* comes into being: and the coterie is never a good thing — at least in the view of those outside the coterie. It generally happens that the most original people are, in the nature of things, outside (though naturally it does not follow that everybody outside is original).

The coterie is — like the sovereign state — exclusive and competitive. It claims for its protégés often a position they do not merit: if economically and socially influential, it would even be able to impose them upon the public by means of benevolent reviews, write-ups, a book dealing with their work, this being the source in some cases of false and confusing values. (The Futurists were an example of this, their patron and mouthpiece being a millionaire.) In the world of literature and art such social organisms, whatever form they take, are an infallible sign of great unsettlement, social disorder, and stress, as much as are secret societies, the Vehm,[1] the 'democratic clubs', etc.

Just how severe the social climate has become for those attempting to practise the arts, more especially the visual arts, is not generally recognised: one reason being precisely this artificial stimulus administered compassionately to a small number of artists, by a small circle of friends or clients; or the joyous fanfares of semi-official and official propaganda, heralding picture-circuses. This is a misleading façade: not deliberately misleading, of course, except in so far as those backing an artist of serious, and therefore unpopular, type, always seek to convey the impression that collectors are tumbling over each other to buy his pictures. — There is a very hollow little shadow of a once great craft behind the façade and the 'cultural' ballyhoo.

That it is a necessary first-step to hammer away at the economic side of this question is undeniable. Access to it by that road is easier for the practical mind. But *that* is not the problem: and, by itself, an economic solution is of little use. It is a sine qua non, no more, no less. Money does not supply you with an assignment, unless it is given to you to that end.[2] It buys you materials, it buys you time: it does not *buy* a function in a society. A Henry James would not have much appetite, you see, for writing his novels, nor Van Gogh for painting his pictures, even if by some miraculous agency he were enabled to do so, were his lot cast among a race of people who were deaf and blind and dumb, though he had himself escaped this calamitous racial absence of all means of admiring the beauty of the visual world, listening to and communicating with other men. And very soon, except for a small sensitive spot (the area of which diminishes daily) the entire human consciousness will be unresponsive to all stimuli except the coarsest and stupidest. This at least will be so unless the process is arrested.

If economics, then, are not a cure for this disease (a kind of spiritual and intellectual anaemia) — if relied on too implicitly they produce dilettantism — they are yet the first step to an understanding of the impending breakdown in all the serious arts.

If people persist in what is almost a doctrine, namely that the writer or the artist is all the better for having no money (I have even heard them say 'keep him poor'! about an eminent contemporary, on the grounds that that was a guarantee of good work) — and as in this way incidentally they ease their cultural conscience — one day they will have no good art, only such art as can be produced by supplying a widespread vulgar demand. To keep the wolf from the door with one hand, and write a book or paint a picture with the other, is *not* the way successfully to perform that particular operation.

Throughout I have been speaking, where my theme was economics, of people engaged in a lifetime of creative endeavour. Let me say at once that there are all kinds of circumstances, independent of inherited wealth or specific subsidies, or a life of uninterrupted devotion to writing, which have proved favourable to the writing of a good, or of a great, book. The seclusion of the university may supply the place of the seclusion of the medieval monastery; public service benefiting by an early retirement and adequate pension, the leisure of a clergyman, are only a few.

But the visual arts are occupations that require all of your time, as much as playing a violin or being a doctor. There the difficulties are of another order altogether, more complex and infinitely harder to circumvent. The Industrial Age alone — leaving out of count all the other circumstances — loads the dice very heavily against the creative impulse. Even where an artist may appear triumphantly to have 'arrived' a closer scrutiny might cause one to modify one's opinion. There are for instance two great arts, sculpture and architecture, and there are a number of famous sculptors and architects who presumably should have little cause for complaint. Yet both these great arts are practically extinct, or function in an academic void. Lloyd Wright, the most famous architect not only in America but probably in the world, far from being a busy builder of houses has for years had comparatively little to do, except instruct others in his school, who can scarcely expect to be busier than he has been. In general, the jobbing builder has usurped the rôle of the architect. Today there are working in England two particularly fine sculptors: Jacob Epstein and Henry Moore. But have they been publicly employed — or privately, to any great extent? You are aware what sculpture is supposed to be for. Not to be put in museums, at least, or to be seen once and for the last time in the Leicester Galleries. It is common knowledge that architecture has greatly declined from its former position as a prosperous profession.*

In the matter of sculpture there are facts which speak for themselves. For instance: the great numbers of drawings specially done for exhibition by Moore — the relative sparseness of the sculpture. Then why are Epstein's biblical titans allowed to get into the hands of showmen? Had he been commissioned, after all, by some religious body to sculpt a St. Michael or St. John for them he would not have occupied himself with Lucifer.

Oil-painting, unlike architecture and sculpture, is an art of relatively recent origin: there is no reason to suppose it is destined to survive for very long. The easel-picture was intended to hang on the wall of a rich man's house. Those were very carefully executed pictures, that an artist would labour over for a very long time. Since the Impressionist revolution all that has changed. Today quickly painted, cheaply priced, oil-paintings of which great numbers are produced, can be possessed by anybody with from twenty to sixty pounds to spare for this luxury. On very few of these can anything like the same amount be realised, should the owner wish to dispose of it. So it remains an expensive luxury. — When the State steps in, as it must as our society becomes considerably socialised, the mural rather than the easel-picture will, I think, be preferred. The latter is essentially an adjunct of private life.

Meanwhile the painter, more nimble — more 'limber' — than the sculptor or architect, is in a better case. A contemporary oil-painting need not take longer than a drawing: in fact a Modigliani, to take a typical example, is little more than a coloured drawing. He would paint one in an afternoon so that he might obtain the cash for further potations.

The art of writing is not quite in the same parlous situation as are those other arts.† The written or the printed word is in no danger of extinction. But that is not the same thing as the art of writing, or as creative literature. Literature has suffered fearfully (as described in the 'Two Publics') as a result of mass-production of books and the decay of values

---

* A new society when it comes may want a new type of house to match, but that is not what Corbusier found in Russia: according to him, the newer the society, the more archaic the taste. I merely repeat this generalisation as a pointer, not perhaps to be taken too seriously.

† It is greatly to my regret that I am unable to include music in this summary survey. But I am not conversant enough with conditions in the world of music to do so.

attendant upon modern publicity techniques. That there are other dangers too, connected with the relation between political freedom and the creative faculty, peculiar to socialised man, threatening the writer, is brought out very well by Mr. V. S. Pritchett in an article.*

'The disappointing spectacle of State endowment and publishing in Russia,' he writes, 'and our own contacts with government offices during the war discouraged us. State censorship is a danger, but not the greatest danger: the modern State does not censor, it directs. And State direction, like paid publicity, is fatal.' – Mr. Pritchett answers those people who – having done their best to bring this about – 'complain that there are no "great writers" left. I foresee that there will soon be no lesser writers either. – Within the next few years we may see not merely "cuts" but a final switch-off in serious imaginative literature.' These last terms refer to the events of the fuel crisis of February 1947, when among other things the weekly periodical press was 'switched off'.

It is my belief that 'great writers' have no great time of it anyway: and private agencies are as liable to combine to switch them off, if they can, as the State would be at its worst. But I see very well – and indeed have recognised for a far longer time than most people – the dangers inherent in too despotic a form of state-capitalism, which does not censor but *direct*.

––––

Such, in rough outline, is the immensely unsatisfactory situation of the arts: and such were the unpleasant truths which one by one unveiled themselves for my inspection as soon as all extraneous economic props were removed (1923-24). Many, it is true, were already familiar to my partly disillusioned eye.

The bleak economic aspects of being a writer, or of being an artist, could find their place under the more general heading – according to the scheme of this book – of being an 'intellectual' but not as illustrated in my own particular history and, upon a less personal level, was the subject with which I began in Part I.

I attribute my ability partially to overcome the obstacles I have been discussing in this chapter to the fact that I had got well into my career before having to attempt the impossible – namely to write books which only a rich man can write, as a rule; and to paint the sort of pictures which only in the last few years have been accepted as the 'modern' standard of vision. Even so, had I been possessed of a small fortune the 'Childermass' would not still remain unfinished; in place of some hasty work and wasteful journalism there would be valuable work.

I am here writing about myself: but it has been granted me to realise that there are other people in the world, and that anything that happens to me under similar circumstances afflicts them too: I like good writing far too well not to understand that a great deal of it is lost, all the time, simply because our society is so arranged that it can only be produced by a man with 'private means'. There is *no public means* available to assure its production. – If a tax of say ten per cent were to be levied upon all

* *New Statesman*, 27 Feb. 1947.

best-selling and potboiling work and the proceeds devoted to the promotion of good literature, so that a small number of those known to be good writers could be given incomes freeing them from hack-work, what a different appearance the bookshops would shortly present! Articles would be written headed 'Literary Renaissance in England'. It all could be done simply by making a dozen or so men and women of 'independent means' overnight, by a state-credit for life.

It must not be lost sight of that if the scene was uninviting before, now it is doubly so: indeed the period when Miss Weaver's 'Egoist' was publishing 'The Portrait of the Artist', verse by Pound and Eliot, 'Tarr' and much besides, must look, by contrast, like a golden age. Unfavourable in many ways as it in fact was, can it be said that any beginner today has as good a chance, in this time of universal unrest, disproportionate taxation, inflated prices? — And do not let anyone say that these are just the kind of austere conditions to bring out the best that is in a man either! It is not poverty, grit, and moral rectitude that ensure the writing of a good book, but a golden bullet with which to shoot the wolf at the door; and leisure that no 'leisured class' has ever known how to use, but that a fine writer does, and without which he is lost.

Notes

1 The Vehm (or *Vehmgerichte* or Fehmic courts) was a German medieval quasi-legal secret society empowered to pass and carry out sentence of death.

2 This gives the sense of Lewis's use of "assignment" in the title, *Rude Assignment*.

CHAPTER XXV

THE BIRTH OF A POLITICAL SENSE

IN order to keep an orderly correspondence between this Part and the last I announced my intention successively to describe how literature, art, satire, and politics in turn became things with which I wholly occupied myself. To implement this promise I have disinterred a child, scribbling sagas of the Frontier, traversed with friezes of matchstick men. Satire appeared — if that is the name for it — in a setting of the barbarically simple, as fishermen and vagabonds. The pieces so produced were to be entitled 'Inferior Religions'. Inferior Religion is, however, a term the application of which could be extended to almost everything. All except the great religions are material for laughter. Worship of the State, like worship of a fishing-boat by a fisherman, is imbecilic — though hardly a laughing-matter.

The political I have not spoken of in this part. Politics manifested itself first as reactions to being a soldier and to the war generally. That also was something barbaric; but I saw it was not only absurd, but criminal. People for whom *war* means world war ii only, think of world war i in terms of the former. This is natural, but misleading. Without I hope appearing to make these two abominable catastrophes compete, let me indicate a few ways in which they differed, of moment to this narrative. In the first place, I knew many people personally (other soldiers apart) who died in world war i, or in the terrible epidemic immediately following it, which accounted for quite a dozen people known to me. In world war ii this has not been the case; in fact no one I know personally was hurt, much less killed, and no epidemic has so far succeeded it. This was not merely, I think, because I was much older, and in wars it is usually young people who die — though 'total' war distributes casualties more evenly. It was rather because world war ii had no 'lost generation'. The 'intellectuals' did not this time go to the wars: they as far as possible — and very properly — kept the fires of culture burning at home.

If we take a single smallish circle of 'intellectuals', who were accustomed to meet before world war i at Mrs. Kibblewhite's in Frith Street, Soho Square, this difference can be illustrated. Practically all became soldiers. T. E. Hulme, who acted as host at those excellent parties, was killed in action. Gaudier-Brzeska, too, was killed in action. Aldington with his 'Death of a Hero' wrote one of the best war books, the material for which was obtained — and only could be obtained — on active service. The youngest of this group, Herbert Read — who subsequently edited T. E. Hulme's philosophical papers — was so gallant and enthusiastic a soldier that he was decorated with the M.C. and the D.S.O. and mentioned in dispatches.

Without overlooking, or repudiating, the patriotic impulse, world war i was an event of a totally new kind for Englishmen, whereas in world war ii there was no surprise. However, my reason for enlarging upon these differences was to show how this first world war might be — as it was — more than war. It put up a partition in one's mind: it blocked off the past literally as if a huge wall had been set up there. World war ii has left a country that, before it, was still one of the most prosperous and firm-looking, miserably poor, even bankrupt. It is altering its social and economic structure entirely. A great change, but the intellectual life has not altered greatly. I should say world war i was a deeper, thicker, higher wall—with the Russian Revolution, the passing of the German and Austrian Empires, the bankrupt vacuum at the centre of Europe, the 'bleeding white' of England—than was world war ii. But, as I said just now, do not let us promote a spirit of competition between these two odious Events—Event One and Event Two!

————

What more fitting time and place could be conceived than wars for the birth of the political sense, seeing that of all the politicians' crimes, war utterly outclasses any other—even the creation of the slum, or the holding of the ring while the rich strangle to death the poor, or the cheating of the public by false prospectuses, or the torturing of the old and infirm by a pension ensuring slow starvation (even despatching of them in infirmaries, so that they dread to enter them), or the brutal property laws: but I need not extend this catalogue of crime, its items are notorious.—As the time and place of a person's birth is in some sort a spell, so my politics bear signs everywhere of their origin in war.

Most socialist doctrine in the case of the older men is rooted in christian teaching: with the young it is rooted in power impulses. There is very little trace here, today, in England at least, of the christian basis of feeling about things: and it is difficult to see what a socialist doctrine can base itself on, if you eliminate christianity, except some impulse to power. So it may have been the vigour of the christian past that gave the particular colour to this birth-in-the-war of a political sense I am describing. For undoubtedly war has less effect upon people now, which is not only because they become desensitised, but there is no kick left in the moral nature. It is so flabby you can murder in front of it, and it responds no more than to the death of a fly—which is the point at which 'crime' ends, and there is no longer any right or wrong, which notions depend for their validity entirely upon a privileged isolation of the human spirit from the rest of the universe.

On the battlefields of France and Flanders I became curious, too, about how and why these bloodbaths occurred—the political mechanics of war. I acquired a knowledge of some of the intricacies of the power-game, and the usurious economics associated with war-making. None of the troops I came in contact with—excepting the Anzacs, whom I found myself in the midst of in the Salient for a while—would, left to themselves, have treated war otherwise than as a major nuisance. The officers in the battery were humorous about it, treating it as they would a licensed clown who sometimes 'went a little too far'.

In spite of this, I found, then and afterwards, a good deal rooted in the psychology of everybody of 'British stock' a tolerance of war as something they could not imagine not being there. Soon after the war's end I became acquainted, for instance, with Col. Lawrence. I tried to talk to him about war: but apart from agreeing that it of course was 'beastly', I did not get very far. He was, it is true, an unlikely subject: too big a profiteer — in reputation, not money. The conservatism of the English must make it difficult for their minds to give hospitality to the idea of anything *ending*, especially anything which had continued for so long, under such august patronage, as war. In England, or the European continent generally — in contrast to the New World, where it is quite a different picture — I met few people who regarded mass-killing as a crime. If you kill enough people, that is somehow all right, they seemed to think, and quite normal.

So from the start these were not popular politics I began to have. Now that I have indicated, however, when and under what circumstances they made their entrance in my case, this Part may be brought to a close. As to what form they subsequently took the chapters devoted to politics in Part I, as well as much of the new material in Part III, are sufficient evidence. But I must not take my leave of this Part in too unceremonious a manner. I have conducted the reader more or less autobiographically, up to the year 1925: and there, autobiographically, I propose to leave him. This is because in that year I was writing 'The Art of Being Ruled', and my personal life has no further relevance. Thenceforth my history is strictly that of my books.

Three of those books were suppressed — one was even smothered during its birth, before it actually saw the light, although printed and bound and already a book.[1] The true story of those suppressions would be worth telling, I agree, circumstantially: a fully documented account. But that would be a legal operation. One cannot speak of such things without a lawyer at one's elbow, and without quite likely in the end finding oneself surrounded by lawyers. Apart from being unlitigious, I have neither the money nor the time for that. There is indeed a mass of facts and figures which ought to be made available. Unless, or until, they are, I remain somewhat in the position of a fool. But I am far too busy making up for a new set of lost war-years. Other people have an interest in those facts and figures beside myself, you see: and their resources are far greater than mine. Meanwhile, the *atmosphere* propitious to such violence, is as subject-matter precisely what this book was begun to provide a museum for. Among its specimens the suppressors, too, surely should be found. I have explained the nature of the legal impediments to free speech. All I can say is this: if fifty years hence you like to drop up to the Library of Congress on the hill of the Capitol, or into the British Museum (if London, or indeed these islands, are still here then) I will arrange for you to see my uncensored indictment.

It had been my intention to continue the personal record, as an accompaniment to the career-narrative, up to the outbreak of world war ii. But apart from purely autobiographical matter, which has no place here really — such as comparisons of the strip-tease shows in the cabarets on the Rambla with the East Side 'burlesque' in New York; why I prefer Biarritz to Bournemouth; why my wife and I always went to the Pyrenees rather than the Alps for a holiday (why the Mediterranean end rather than the Atlantic); how I have always preferred the West or the North-west districts of London to S.W.; how I used always to smoke *Richmond Gems* (white packet) but now prefer *Du Maurier*—apart from matter of that kind, I found in surveying the landscape from 1925 onwards, that book after book occupied ninety per cent of the area, and all that was important in it—all except perhaps an oyster cocktail I used to get at Gatti's, above the six small Whitstables sunk in chilled tomato ketchup, a layer of horseradish ground in cream two inches thick.

There are a number of controversies, in which I found myself engaged, in the trough between the two wars to which I might have alluded. But there are generally books or pamphlets commemorating those. At all events, after a little thought it seemed to me obvious that to take those books, one by one, which had been, directly or indirectly, storm-centres— expound the principle involved, and answer the critic by its text, or by a reinterpretation of the text—would be the better course.

Notes

[1] *The Doom of Youth* and *Filibusters in Barbary*, both of 1932, were withdrawn some time after publication under threat of action for libel. *The Roaring Queen*, completed in 1930, was finally accepted for publication in 1936 and got as far as bound proofs before it too was suppressed on legal advice; it was eventually published in 1973. (For details see Bradford Morrow and Bernard Lafourcade, *A Bibliography of the Writings of Wyndham Lewis* [Santa Barbara: Black Sparrow Press, 1978].)

PART III
THE BOOKS – A PATTERN OF THINKING

CHAPTER XXVI

FOREWORD

AS everywhere else in the present work I have, in this Part, one engrossing object: namely to meet and to destroy unjust, prejudiced, and tendentious criticism – past, present, and future. It is my object to dispel misconceptions (about myself, or about my work) whether they derive from ill-natured and tendentious criticism, or some other cause.

A secondary aim is to elicit a pattern of thinking: to show how any one of my books is connected with every other: that they are a litter of books, not really discrete: how the critical books carry forward what is, in fact, a type of thinking, belonging to a certain type of mind.

It of course follows from this that responsibility is shared by all of these writings: further, that accusations levelled at this or that book can often be disproved by reference to some other book. My writings possess this unity because they are functional and because the impulse to action faithfully corresponds, without affectation, to the dictates of the will. No deviation has occurred, the central stimulus has remained throughout the same, although I have made use of various methods. Because of this unvarying character of the stimulus, it can easily be shown that, wanting in many things as they may be, and at times misdirected, my writings have not been wanting in humanity.

I am not usually accused of being stupid. The sort of accusation I have generally had to meet is that I think like Machiavelli. Like him I favour despots. That I am brutal (as satirist) to sweet kind nice people in whose mouths butter would not melt: a bad man in the nursery, wanting in love for children; and that (like Mrs. Sidney Webb) I do not feel warmly towards the poor and lowly.

Since a mildewed residue of christian morality – the only part of the religion of Christendom that appealed to the contemporary ideological politician as useful – has been employed to bait, or to camouflage, contemporary power-doctrines, it is consequently the *moral* issue that is the background of all contemporary controversy. The critical attack upon the views of Mr. X is on the basis of *goodness*, not on any other. For it is his *badness* alone (if that can be brought home to him) with which opinion can be inflamed against him. And, needless to say, all those who do not agree with the *ideologue* are *bad*: for he possesses a monopoly of the virtuous – the humane and the social – attributes.

The form the indictment takes is not: 'Mr. X does not subscribe to our doctrine, so he is lacking in judgement and intelligence, is politically unenlightened.' That would leave people cold; they would not get bloodshot about Mr. X's *intelligence*. Also, it would leave the matter open to argument. So the form the indictment takes is as follows: 'Mr. X does not subscribe to our doctrine, therefore he is an immoral and inhumane man.'

The fellow-travelling intellectuals, comprising a solid majority, who put me under a curse — because I spoke of communism as practised by the bolsheviks as inhumane and too like the jesuit or ottoman disciplines — these partisans who have controlled the literary world for a quarter of a century would not have gained acceptance for their crypto-communism in the West without a liberal flavouring of christian morality.

It will be evident how it comes to pass that such discouragingly silly accusations have to be answered as you find catalogued above. It is no use saying: 'Oh, but surely there is no occasion to take such stuff seriously.' Our politics share with the Hollywood cinema industry a cynical mass-technique: they cater for the extra-silly. Politics, in *their* thrillers (even far more full of blood and guts) give the foulest sadism a good solid sanction out of the decalogue. Where the Soviet have the advantage over our lot is that their firing squads do not wear canonicals.

Seeing that ours has been in the West a generation of hypocrites — and of persecutory hypocrites excessively partial to blood-sports, at that: who, in changing from empire-builders into fellow-travellers, retain the old sanctimonious pretexts that it is *for the good of others* they practise violence, and clothe themselves in power, and in discarding the Bible tear out all they need of the sanctions of the Mosaic law: seeing that it is a generation that has shown less care for men in the mass than any for a great many centuries, combining this demonstrable indifference to the welfare of the generality with never-ceasing hosannas to the Common Man: a generation of power-addicts who put a red tie on with a smirk, climb upon the back of the Working Class and propose to ride it to a new type of double-faced dominion: seeing all this, that any one should have to defend himself from charges of *insufficient regard for the Many* is imbecile of course.

But there it is: my interests, in the first place, have been those of the civilised intelligence — 'the politics of the intellect' as I called it. At a time when everybody was for a fanatical *étatisme* I was not. It seemed to me to promise no good to anybody — to kick out kings and queens and put masters in their place with a hundred times their power. That would be a strange kind of socialism! So I have to thrash this out — for my scepticism of course was proof of a very bad disposition. Is not *the good* the will of the majority?

Since, however, it is no longer in Western democratic countries so good a bet to be a fellow-traveller, and the intellectuals have ceased to go on pilgrimages to Moscow; since, fearing a witch-hunt this time against *themselves*, they are repainting themselves some other colour than the old sentimental pink: since they have suddenly altered so much (all but the political professionals) it might well be argued that there was no occasion any longer to answer charges based upon precepts which have today so diminished in popularity.

I of course have thought of this: but the argument I fear is unsound for the following reasons. First of all, the harm has been done, and a change of fashion will not undo it. I have been pushed into a position where I should remain, even if the pretext for driving me there could no longer today be resorted to. Secondly, these people are all too deeply committed ever to change anything but their labels. They are not interested, it must be remembered, in an objective truth: they inhabit a verbal world, of labels and slogans. However they may modify the terms of their political ritual, or I may in the future modify my views in detail, the antagonism must remain, even if for the moment our policies happened to be identical.

It is the type of mind, not the doctrine, that is important. Their fundamental insincerity — because of the pragmatism and subjectivism which is natural to them — would still call *wrong* anything that was not of their way of feeling. So I am not so much obliged to answer charges, really, as *to defend the right to be sincere;* and — from my standpoint — the necessity to be sincere.

Taking into consideration the scorn with which they repudiate the rational, or the logical, it would make no difference whatever that they were now advocating themselves what formerly they ostracised *me* for saying. They would still attack me for having given utterence to it at a time when they were saying something opposed to it. For *time* for them is still and always the reality: and a thing that is true today was not necessarily true yesterday. There are fashions in politics as there are in hats.

As a fine example of chronological thinking let me cite André Malraux. When questioned as to his recent change from communism to Gaullism, he observed: 'It is not I who have evolved, but events.' Communism and the communists have not changed, nor has fascism (de Gaulle's much resembling Franco's). *Events* have changed!

———

A 'pattern of thinking', I have explained, is what I shall seek to educe in this Part. A tour of a number of my books is the method I shall employ to compass it; by going from one to another and seeing how they fit into and complement one another. I shall not only discuss but as it were re-think the work in question as I come to it. As I read and write I shall, naturally, get interested in what I am revisiting, and rediscovering; in some cases I shall offer a new statement of the argument to which I return, a development of it — in order to bring out certain characteristic elements of that particular approach to things.

The amount of space I devote to a book is no criterion of what I regard as its significance, as literature or as criticism. Its controversial character is mainly what interests me here, since this is a book of counter-polemics; or the presence in it of some idea, which, in association with what is extracted from some other book, composes a logical pattern. — Thus it is that 'Time and Western Man', generally regarded as the most representative of my critical books so far, is given little attention. The criticism of chronological thinking — its central subject — is present everywhere in the present work: which — once more — is not a survey of what I have written. Rather than that it is a statement of what I have *not* said, but often been accused of saying.

CHAPTER XXVII

THE PURITANS OF THE STEPPES

ASKED to describe what influences were decisive in my life as a writer*
— indeed in the question addressed to me the somewhat alarming word
crisis was used, what, I was asked, had constituted for me the crisis as a
result of which I became what I am — I was at first at a loss to know what
to say. It had to be a book, too, which raised a further obstacle: for no book
I could think of had mastered my mind in the way required by the question.
There had been nothing violent about the birth of my mind. There
was no dramatic and sudden enlightenment, but a long series of enlightening
experiences — with the steady accretion of the technical means for the
communication of the burden of experience. It seemed at first quite impossible to point to any one influence responsible for my development; though
no doubt I could sort out the sources of enlightenment into weaker and
stronger impressions. — However, for the purposes of the talk I had agreed
to give it would be better if I could identify something that could be said, as
an impression, to exceed all the others, and to have left a permanent mark.
So I went on a search, backwards into my young life, keeping my eyes
open for the intellectual *coup de foudre*. For guidance I divided my activity
into the creative and the critical: and since — as I believe I have already
remarked — the critical with me grew out of the creative, it must be to
the source of the latter that I must give especial attention. — And at last,
stepping warily as I moved about in the misty youthful scene (everything
before world war i has become almost an alien land) I came up against
a solid mass of books — not *one* book, as I had thought I might — which
supplied the answer. This was something that revolutionised my technique
of approach to experience — that did not merely give me a great kick at
the moment, and then quickly fade, as most things do. — The mass of
books to which I have referred is the creative literature of Russia. And
when I took down some of these half-forgotten volumes — went again with
Pierre in his incongruous white hat and green coat on to the field of
Borodino, and with Raskolnikov lifted the axe to strike down the aged usurer[1]
— I very nearly had *another* crisis, hardened as I am now to such influences.
For the purposes of my broadcast the search was ended. I had no
occasion to go any farther, and I started at once to write out what I proposed to say. But for anyone who has read 'The Apes of God' or 'Childermass', it will be obvious that those influences however strong, were not
the last: on the surface, at least, all trace of them had vanished in the
twenties. But in my earliest essay in the writing of fiction, 'Tarr', it is
another matter: and it is to that story this chapter and the next are devoted.
Dostoevsky, on the European continent, continues to exert a magical
influence; as an instance of which I may cite the Swiss theologian, Barth,
who acknowledges two main sources of inspiration, namely Dostoevsky

* It is by kind permission of the British Broadcasting Corporation that I use material from
a talk in the 'Crisis' series, March 1947.

and Kierkegaard. I have noted several instances, by the way, in which these two names have been bracketed in this manner. In England there has been a decline in sympathy with the Nineteenth Century Russian novelists, which partly is fashion, and in part to do with the long infatuation of British intellectuals for everything Russian of a much more recent date. This raised an ideologic barrier to enjoyment. But these great novelists of Tsarist days should not be looked upon as a sort of rival of the contemporary Russian. A careful reading of their books assists, on the contrary, to an understanding of the Russians of today. Stalin dancing upon the table at a victory banquet is a page from Gogol. The unexpectedly able Russian generals, beating off the Panzers, at Smolensk, or before the capital itself, one recognises as one reads of Kutuzov at Borodino, more than a match for Bonaparte.[2]

As a student in Paris, in French translations, I first read all these Russian books, and I lived for some time wholly in that Russian world – of 'Poor Folk': in the tragic family circle of the Karamazovs; with Verhovensky, Shigalev, and the nihilists; with Rudin, losing interest and departing when he saw the spell he had cast had collapsed; listening to the Kreutzer Sonata and noting the big hips of the lady's-man; or submissively assisting at all the exclamatory archness of those Varvaras and Natalies.[3]

So my 'crisis' – if we wish to retain that over-forcible expression – was even more than a collection of books: it was a world. As I have described myself as doing, tracing my steps back, I was not suddenly stopped by a wall of books. Rather I passed imperceptibly into a warmer, richer, atmosphere – as crossing the Atlantic one enters the area of the Gulf Stream; I heard again the raucous voice of La Baboulenka crying: 'You do not know *what*? By heavens, are you *never* going to drop that roulette of yours? Are you going to whistle *all* your property away?'[4]

And I saw the ruined General wilt before the glare of his aged mother, borne aloft like a carnival figure in an armchair.

Paris was full of Russian students (this of course was before the Russian Revolution), who walked about in pairs, in tight black semi-military jackets. They conversed with no one – they were contemptuous of Western levity, stern and self-absorbed. It has been said that when Dostoevsky wrote 'The Possessed' there were in Russia no Stavrogins or Verhovenskys, that they came much later and this was a divination of the future. In that case these characters, now become flesh and blood, were met by me every day on the Boulevards, and they decidedly looked the part.

These were the new Puritans, who were to dominate Europe: a generation with many points of resemblance with the black-coated sectaries who began to swarm in England in the first days of the Seventeenth Century, and who subsequently transmitted their passionate disciplines to, and became the genius of, the North American continent, the 'New World'.

The world of imagination I inhabited at that time, however, was anything but puritan, taken as a whole. For this great volume of creation produced in the Nineteenth Century by a group of men over a space of fifty or sixty years there is no parallel since the Renaissance – to which the Tudor stage, of course, was the greatest English contribution. The impression conveyed is of a release on the grand scale of prodigal energies.

All the writers, it seems to me, responsible for this new world of the spirit are of the same half-Western, half-Eastern, ethos; which, among other things, gives them a peculiar value — like everything about Russia. They must, in consequence, for the Western European, remain a great universalising influence. And all the Russians, Tolstoy almost as much as Dostoevsky, were conscious of their curious relationship to the West — of it, and yet not of it: conscious also of something like a mission with regard to it, namely as the purveyors of sincerity to the over-institutionalised European. We find this missionary spirit, itself institutionalised, its ethical passion dimmed in the process, in the contemporary Russian.

A cultural see-saw, of westernising and anti-westernising, proceeded among the intellectual leaders: but to hold themselves apart from the West — a little contemptuously apart — was by far the more popular attitude. — From 'The Gambler' and elsewhere in the pages of Dostoevsky a very shrewd analysis of the Western European could be compiled. There is for instance the Junker: 'he had legs which seemed to begin almost at his chest — or rather, at his chin! Yet, for all his air of peacock-like conceit . . . his face wore a sheepish air'. Then there is the Frenchman: 'He was a true Frenchman in so far as, though he could be lively and engaging when it suited him, he became insufferably dull and wearisome as soon as ever the need for being lively and engaging had passed. Seldom is a Frenchman naturally civil: he is civil only as to order and of set purpose. Also, if he thinks it incumbent upon him to be fanciful and original, his fancy always assumes a foolish, unnatural vein, compounded of trite, hackneyed forms. In short, the natural Frenchman is a conglomeration of commonplace, petty, everyday positiveness.' — No more today than yesterday, I think, do we appreciate how genuine sincerity can take even a self-righteous form, and how insincere and untrustworthy, in many respects, the West must seem to these Puritans of the Steppes, whose lineaments already are visible in the dramatis personae of the Nineteenth Century Russian classics. When however, self-righteousness grows so extreme that it violently liquidates all whom it regards as sinful, it is natural it should awaken hatred and alarm.

A great deal of what I read as a student I either did not understand, or took no interest in. I knew, for instance, what I was witnessing everywhere in Dostoevsky; namely the almost muscular struggle of the human will to repulse evil and cleave to the good — or to embrace evil with a convulsive violence, and then to repent, with more convulsions. It was the unrelievedly gloomy epic of spiritual freedom — which the further you went, got to look more and more like predestination. — But in the first place I was not myself of a gloomy temperament: also since I was not interested in problems of good and evil, I did not read these books so much as sinister homilies as monstrous character patterns, often of miraculous insight.

I am inclined, I find, to attribute to myself less understanding, when I first read all these books, than I in fact had. But what is quite certain is that the politics in Dostoevsky — almost as distinctive a feature of his work as the mysticism, and, I now am of opinion, far too much influenced by it — these very unusual politics were entirely lost upon me at that time. Three years ago I read again 'The Possessed'. There were all the names and scenes, just as in the past, when first I read it. But it was a very different book.

Evidently as a student I had read it somewhat as a child reads 'Through the Looking Glass'. That is the only possible explanation.

Dostoevsky was an arch counter-revolutionary, and it is not only in 'The Possessed' – which is the highwater-mark, almost a counter-revolutionary tract – that this passionate reaction is to be found. But when in his letters one reads that he thought of postponing a journey owing to the news, which had greatly upset him, of the death of the Tsar's aunt, that makes one feel that when he refers to himself in his diary as a 'conservative', in this one particular he was right. Yet what an extraordinary work 'The Possessed' is! Stavrogin, Tihon, Verhovensky, Shatov – what a prodigious company.

Allowing for a great deal that was unintelligible, the impact of such books was due to much more than their vitality. Perhaps Ivan Karamazov supplies the correct answer, where he is speaking of the young men who sat drinking and talking in the corners of the Russian taverns. 'They've never met before, and when they go out of here they won't see each other again for the next forty years. But what do they talk about for the moment that they're here? Nothing but universal problems: Is there a God? Does the immortal soul exist? Those who don't believe in God discuss socialism and anarchism, and the reorganisation of mankind on a new pattern; which are the same questions, only tackled from the other way up.'

That was what 'Russian boys' had their minds filled with apparently, and what these books showed them ardently discussing in taverns as they drank, as if the fate of the universe hung upon their words. Well, what do young Englishmen discuss under similar circumstances? Probably 'the Dogs', or football. What do young Frenchmen discuss? Undoubtedly women, and their smartness in handling same. – So it was in everything. Here was a more serious world altogether, thought I. Then what consummate realists these people were! – with their slovenly old gentlemen with a great reputation for sanctity – the 'saintly fools' of the monasteries, with their embarrassed 'bashful' smiles, smelling slightly of vodka; the police commissioners who behaved like a Marx Brother; Napoleon Bonaparte persuaded that he was directing a battle, while in fact everyone had forgotten his existence and fought it in their own way: the Chagall-like figures skimming along the surface of the water in pursuit of the river-steamer; or the celebrated cloak of Gogol, or his walking Nose.

I too 'came out of that mantle of Gogol': a lot of things have happened to me since, but there was a time when I did not follow my own nose, but *his*. Paris for me is partly the creation of these books. I now realise that if I had not had Tchekov in my pocket I should not have enjoyed my Dubonnet at the 'Lilas' so much or the beautiful dusty trees and beyond them the Bal Bullier. It was really as a character in Tolstoy – I remember now – that I visited a *bal musette*. And the hero of the first novel I wrote reminded a very perceptive critic of Stavrogin.

In view of all this I think we may really say that the first time, moving down the rue des Ecoles, I arrived at my particular bookshop, opposite the 'Montagne', to find a book by Faguet, and took away 'Tales from the Underworld'[5] as well, *crisis* was at hand.

Notes

¹ Tolstoy's *War and Peace* (1869) and Dostoievsky's *Crime and Punishment* (1866).

² In *War and Peace*.

³ Dostoievsky: *Poor Folk* (1846); *The Brothers Karamazov* (1880); *The Possessed* (1871-72). Turgenev: *Rudin* (1856). Tolstoy: *The Kreutzer Sonata* (1889).

⁴ Dostoievsky, *The Gambler* (1867).

⁵ Dostoievsky, *Notes from the Underground* (1864).

CHAPTER XXVIII

THE SCHICKSAL – THE GERMAN
IN MY FICTION

SO I was for some years spiritually a Russian – a character in some Russian novel. As such I made my bow in London – to the deeply astonished Ford Madox Hueffer – which lemonish pink giant, it is true, in his quilted dressing-gown, with his mouth hanging open like a big silly fish, surprised *me*. Though the muscovite spell had lost much of its primitive strength, it was partly, still, as a *Russian* that I wrote my first novel 'Tarr'. – But it was not about Russians: it was almost entirely about Germans.

The hero – Otto Kreisler – was a German student. Just now I said how this first of my fictional figures provoked a comparison with Stavrogin. Rebecca West, in the 'Nation', wrote at the time in the most generous way.[1] 'A beautiful and serious work of art that reminds one of Dostoevsky only because it too is inquisitive about the soul, and because it contains one figure of vast moral significance which is worthy to stand beside Stavrogin.' Rebecca West was by far the best book-critic at that time, this was a notice that afforded me great pleasure and encouragement: but I have quoted it for its bearing upon what I have to say here. Among the old press-notices where I discovered it I came across these other observations in a paper called 'The New Witness' long since extinct. 'A book of great importance . . . because here we have the forerunner of the prose and probably of the manner that is to come.'

In form 'Tarr' does resemble somewhat a Dostoevsky novel. Not only is this the case in the nature of the subject, but to some extent in the treatment. Its dynamism is psychological, of the boa-constrictor type – a steady enveloping compression. Although there is much action, it is the mind not the senses that provide it.

The parallel to Dostoevsky must not be exaggerated however, as Miss West pointed out. The writing, with its abruptness and for that time a new directness, its strong visual notation, is as unlike as possible the Dostoevsky diffuseness.

The character of the German protagonist aside, however, 'Tarr' – neither in order to repel new attacks nor put old ones in their proper perspective – would call in fact for especial exegesis. It has not to be defended, because it was never assailed. Some pundits in the 'twenties said it was ill-written: this referred to the first edition, and was perfectly true. It was a very carelessly written book indeed. That criticism does not apply to the revised version (1928).*

At the time of the first publication of 'Tarr' it was extremely favourably reviewed – and the era of puff and blurb in place of criticism had not then begun. *That* started with Mr. Arnold Bennett, when he turned reviewer and star-salesman for the publishers, and was the godfather of as fine a brood of third-rate 'masterpieces' as you could hope to find anywhere.

* Phoenix Library. Chatto and Windus. 1928.

But there was no reason why 'Tarr' should be received otherwise than well in 1918 since at that period I had offended no one by the analysis of the world of bestsellers and of fashionable rackets, nor had I given utterance to any political judgements liable to excite contemporary fanaticism.

A better novel than 'Tarr', namely 'The Revenge for Love' (1936), just cannot be mentioned, or considered by the average critic at all, and in my lifetime will never be republished (it is out of print) because its theme is political and its intentions have apparently been misread.[2] It is not a book of political edification but one of political realism. I am quite content that people should read it much later on, when all the dust of these present conflicts has settled. They will, I think, perceive that it is not quite what contemporaneously it has been supposed to be. I say this, not at all to arouse an interest in it: merely to put on record the extent to which the literary world of this time is as intolerant as the worst religionism — it does not burn but it boycotts. How by this malevolent suppression I am injured I need hardly point out, as much in my reputation as in my pocket.

Retrospectively, then, the principal figure in 'Tarr', the German Otto Kreisler, has its importance in such a survey as this. Seeing what was occurring when I actually was writing this book (1914-15), seeing what the history of the last thirty years has been like — and still is — it has great political relevance. It was not written, I need hardly say, for any jingo reason, for the writing of it had been started considerably before the outbreak of war. But the first edition was disfigured, I am sorry to say, by a 'patriotic' preface: the main figure was a *German* — he was *a bad man* — the Germans are our *enemies* — all our enemies are bad men naturally — the Germans are all bad men. That sort of thing. I blush.

As some slight excuse I must repeat that at that time a great war was a great novelty for English people and everyone I knew was mentally squaring up to 'the Hun'. Myself I was annoyed with the Germans for being so militaristic (did not realise how our *own* wealth, power, and dominion also rested upon force and in our slyly camouflaged way what militarists we were too) and disturbing my life as they were doing, with their infernal *Machtpolitik.* — But I will not prolong my apologies: it was a moment of great popular excitement, and I had been infected by it.

Not only is the most substantial male figure in the book a German, the heroine, Bertha, is likewise German — is in fact, as someone pointed out, the complete expression of the kind of Germanic culture encountered in Hauptmann and Sudermann. Otto Kreisler represents the melodramatic nihilism of the generations succeeding to the great era of philosophical pessimism. Whether national socialism is the ultimate term of that malady it is impossible to say. Nietzsche was another and more immediate source of infection: and to his admonition 'When you go to consort with the *Weib*, take your whip with you', Kreisler had been attentive. 'He (Kreisler) approached a love-affair as the *Korpsstudent* engaged in a students' duel — no vital part exposed, but where something spiritually of about the importance of an ear might be lost — at least stoically certain that blood would be drawn.'

As a student in Munich I became very familiar with the German student and his habits. Later in Paris I had many German friends — most of them 'bourgeois-bohemians'. There was no original for the figure in the book:

but there was a great abundance of images and other impressions out of which material my figure could be put together. Paris was the scene selected: and it was no imaginative feat to see this rigid, scarred, and frowning figure of a typical ex-student, brushing upwards his moustaches as he fixed his eye coldly upon some specimen of the opposite sex.

Kreisler was a man still, after a number of years, in receipt of a modest allowance from his father. For a prolonged period of training as an artist he has nothing to show. He is not an artist, is devoid of talent: but it is not that. He likes sitting at café tables watching impassibly the movements of the gregarious habitués, his eye resting sometimes in painful contemplation upon the women haunting this spot. But he never moves: he enjoys drifting silently with time, until they should reach the brink of the cataract. — The brink is not far off: he is expecting his allowance to discontinue at any moment: all the more so as his father is married to his late fiancée. When that happened he began sitting with greater immobility than ever in front of his *chopines*.

There is no escape from the machinery of the *Schicksal:* he stares bleakly at the café clock, as though it were a timepiece in a Poe story, ticking stolidly along until the predestined moment is reached when it releases the chopper suspended over him and it thunders down upon his neck. Too old at thirty-six to make a fresh start, when the allowance stops life for him must stop too. 'Doomed evidently' is the title of the chapter where he comes upon the scene. And the subject of this book is in fact the elaborate and violent form of suicide selected by Herr Kreisler, involving a number of other people. He is revenging himself upon society for the fate that has overtaken him. Since the jig is up, he decides to have some *macabre* fun: to make a rumbustious exit. Finally he kills someone in a duel, and arrested as a vagrant, hangs himself in a rustic jail.

The ponderous Germanic machinery of the mental processes of the leading characters thuds forward to its climax. Kreisler had developed a myth peculiar to himself on the subject of Woman. Casually observing the progress of this individual's life from year to year, you would probably decide that its main events were love affairs. This, however, in the light of a careful analysis, would be an inversion of the truth.

When the events of his life became too unwieldy 'he converted them into love: as he might otherwise, had he possessed a specialised talent, have transformed them into art. He was a sculptor — a German sculptor of a mock-realistic and degenerate school — in the strange sweethearting of the "free life". — The two or three women he had left in this way about the world — although perhaps those symbolic statues had grown rather . . . lumpish — were monuments of his perplexities'. — Or in another place: 'Womankind were Kreisler's Theatre. They were for him art and expression: the tragedies played there purged you periodically of the too violent accumulations of desperate life.'

He possessed something like an astrological technique for interpreting the significance of his encounters with these creatures, who seemingly composed a fateful pattern in his life. His sexual superstitions supplied the motif in his ritual of self-destruction. The *Weib* now in his father's bed cuts off the thin stream of vitalising gold, like a *couchant* Fate.

These are a few facts or descriptive details about the main figure, samples of the treatment, specimen parts of the ponderous mechanism set in motion, like a demonstration in predestination. But from the first this romantic German is a man as good as dead already. He has accepted violence as the natural end to a violent Berserk nature. The part of the book in which we first see him has for title 'Doomed Evidently' — the fatality, far from being masked, is advertised. The 'Schicksal' or Fate presides throughout, in playful mood.

This condemned man hero, or rather protagonist, is expected to awaken neither sympathy nor repulsion in the reader — for it is not a moral tale: he is a *machine* (a 'puppet', not a 'nature'), aloof and violent. His death is a tragic game. In these respects the analogy with his countryman of two decades farther on, in the 'thirties — still under the same influences as himself — is obvious. Herr Hitler and Herr Goebbels were 'Doomed evidently'. That too was an empty mechanical tragedy, their death a foregone conclusion.

The book should have been called 'Otto Kreisler', rather than 'Tarr', who is a secondary figure. Incidentally, Tarr was the name of a well-known cricketer: and the character is, of course, not German, but English. In the first sixty pages Tarr is to be observed disentangling his sex-life — a very different one from that of Kreisler, though momentarily he is involved with a German Schatz belonging rather to the universe of Kreisler than his own. The involvement is in the sharpest contrast with the Kreisler type of involvement, which is always melodramatic and rooted in a stormy pessimism and painful wonder. Tarr's is sceptical and humorous, full of the English understatement of passion, and antagonism to animal mysticism.

Tarr at the start is found stolidly rushing from one person to another to discuss his sexual conflict. Finally he gets round to the object of his passion in person. With her he discusses it too. Bertha, emotionally constructed to deal with *Kreislers*, not with *Tarrs*, adapts herself as best she can.

The warming-up process, indulged in by Tarr, with the first chance-met acquaintance, proceeds as follows: a typically English scene. 'So they sat (in the café) with this absurd travesty of a Quaker's Meeting, shyness appearing to emanate masterfully from Tarr . . . Tarr had a gauche puritanic ritual of self, the result of solitary habits. — Certain observances were demanded of those approaching him, and were quite gratuitously observed in return. The fetish within — soul-dweller that is strikingly like a wood-dweller, and who was not often enough disturbed to have had the sylvan shyness mitigated — would still cling to these forms. Sometimes Tarr's crafty daimon, aghast at its nakedness, would manage to snatch or purloin some shape of covering from elegantly draped visitor. . . . Tarr possessed no deft hand or economy of force: his muscles rose unnecessarily on his arm to lift a wine glass to his lips. He had no social machinery . . . was compelled to get along as well as he could with the cumbrous one of the intellect.'

In the physical description of the young Englishman, Tarr, may be seen a caricatural self-portrait of sorts, though not of course in his character or behaviour. The glasses worn by Tarr did not occur in my own case at that age; but I sat for some of the merely visual attributes — 'Tarr had wings to his hips. He wore a dark morning coat whose tails flowed behind him as he walked strongly and quickly along, and curled on either side of his lap as he sat. It was buttoned half-way down the body. He was taller than Butcher, wore glasses, had a dark skin, and a steady, unamiable, impatient expression. He was clean-shaven with a shallow jaw and straight thick mouth. His hands were square and unusually hot — all these characteristics he inherited from his mother, except his height.'³

The daguerrotype coat with curling tails and heavy side-pockets — a garment I had seen Central Europeans wearing — was the type of garment which in an earlier chapter I described the scandalised Brook Street tailor as furnishing me with, after my own design.

These descriptions, supplemented by quotations, should answer the same purpose as a 'trailer'. As it is possible from those brief glimpses of next week's movie to obtain a fairly accurate idea of it, so you should now know enough about this novel to understand me when I say that no Russian actually *could* have written it. This is the conclusion I came to when I began examining it again.

It is probably Dostoevskian only in the intricacy of the analysis of character and motive, and a comprehension of that never failing paradox, *the real*, in contrast with the monotonous self-consistency of what man invents without reference to nature, in pursuit of the ideal.

Though this book would never have been written quite as it is without my having been a hallucinated inmate of that Russian world as a student: though when I read the 'Gambler' and cry with laughter as a *new* set of Poles replaces those who have been thrown out of the Casino and solemnly take up the plundering of La Baboulenka where their compatriots had been forced to leave off, I feel I might very well have written that myself, that that is how I see life: nevertheless the fatality — to go no farther — depicted in the case of my German is of an entirely different quality from that in the Dostoevskian universe. The 'signifying *nothing!*' of Shakespeare is nearer to it than the nihilism of Shigalev.

Notes

¹ R. West, *The Nation* 23, No. 19 (August 10, 1918), 506-8; reprinted in *Agenda* (Wyndham Lewis Special Issue) VII, No. 3-VIII, No. 1 (1969).

² *The Revenge for Love* actually appeared in 1937 (Cassell) and was issued in a new edition by Methuen in 1952.

³ Lewis's quotations from *Tarr* (1928 version) show many minor inaccuracies of transcription, only one of which ("soul-dwellers" erroneously in the plural) has been corrected here to restore intelligibility.

CHAPTER XXIX

A PERFECTIONIST

MY other field of activity, Painting, for the reasons specified, does not occupy a very prominent place, in the present volume. In that neighbouring field one is as much immersed in distracting controversy as elsewhere: but it is of a more technical and 'shoppy' order. Above all, there are no politics.

The Paris surrealists, certainly, are great politicians. But there it is the literary men, the propagandists of surrealism, who are the politicians, not the painters. Dali, and Chirico, the two main exponents of surrealism, are reactionaries. As between headquarters in Paris and Chirico at least there have been mutual repudiatons. Delvaux, the Belgian, on the other hand, refuses to allow himself to be called a 'surrealist' (though he is one, if anybody is).[1] So, though there is a core of communist politics to surrealism, its principal pictorial exponents have either repudiated it, or have never recognised it.

Then it is quite true that all the more violent forms of visual expression have generally been regarded as 'left-wing' or revolutionary. As such they must be classed, it seems to me. The pictorial habits of the Royal Academy point in the opposite direction: they are stamped as products of (to use the communists' language) 'bourgeois' civilisation more plainly than anything else I can think of on earth. But these comfortingly distinct groupings are unfortunately unattainable for the following reasons, or only imperfectly so.

Picasso, the great iconoclast, has most appropriately joined the Communist Party. No complications there, one would think. He would not, as a citizen, have at any time voted the ticket of the Comité des Forges. He is, if anyone, a man of the Left. But the Russian Government, disregarding his politics is most inclusively hostile to all the supposedly 'left-wing' art of Western Europe. I have, I believe, already had occasion to refer to this. It strongly discourages its artists from emulating the so-called 'avant-garde' which it describes as the expression of a decadent bourgeoisie. Consequently most Soviet painting is what is described here as reactionary.

The meaning of this is really simple enough. In the destruction of Western civilisation – the undermining and disintegration of standards and traditions – the various arts have played an important part. But the pickaxe or the dynamite that would be so useful where there was demolition to be done, would be entirely out of place in the Soviet, where all that was over. The work of revolution, of preliminary unpicking, has been carried on in the West by a host of people – as was pointed out by me in the days when the affairs of Western Man were all my care.

As further evidence of how, although politics are today ubiquitous, they do not really enter into the painting of pictures: a critic writing about a picture by Mr. Russell Flint, R.A., for instance, does not condemn it as subversive, or as politically reactionary, but as reprehensible *as art*.

Similarly, he does not praise – or blame – a Salvador Dali, a Léger[2] or a Chirico, on account of its sturdy – or detestable – left-wing politics, but solely on its merits, or demerits, as a work of art. That is why I say there is no 'politics' in the fine arts.

When all this has been said, there is one factor which remains: namely, there are, in the arts (under whatever label, or no label) revolutionary minds. Such would have no necessary relation to current revolutionary politics. Since I am obliged to talk about myself, among these I should say that my own had to be reckoned: of the somewhat uncommon variety we may describe as 'perfectionist'.

The revolutionary is often not very particular about what he conceives as the truth, provided his activity bears fruit. If a politician, he rapidly discovers that compromise is indispensable for *action*. What I call a 'perfectionist' (making use of the popular expression) whether in art or politics, is an apriorist, working in the void, and with a propensity to ignore the conditioning factors. – I am speaking here, of course, of my earlier rôle as artist: though I am paying some attention to this because of the light it may throw upon other orders of things.

The character a person displays in playing bridge will undoubtedly reveal itself in his behaviour as a negotiator, motorist, or husband. So let us turn to my first book dealing with the fine arts.

———

'The Caliph's Design, or Architects, where is your Vortex?' is a painter's notebook. These are mostly rough notes; not planned, but written down hastily, from time to time, as some problem presented itself. It is therefore anything but a literary feat. I had not then the necessary experience, in any case, to marshal my arguments in the most effective way.

There are some things that the art critic, or art historian, however astute, does not think of: I mean there are perceptions that the artist alone can compass, as a result of first-hand experience: for it is one thing to wait upon, and to interpret, as a literary man, the deliverances of the performer in the visual arts, quite another matter, as a performer, to interpret nature in terms of the philosophy of the moment, or of some more personal impulse. So when Reynolds, for instance, asserted that you cannot compose a picture with nothing but cold colours, probably it would have occurred to no critic to challenge Gainsborough as did his rival – since he would not have painfully weighed, as had Reynolds, the *colds* and the *hots* against each other.

Certainly the critic would never have realised, as did Gainsborough – turning over in his mind the best method of confuting his rival – that colours are not merely *hot* and *cold*, for this is what it amounted to: that an all-blue is not just a *cold* picture – that one dominant colour is a different thing to several colours, and the problem of contrast and balance does not arise, any more than in a monochrome – as in fact it is. Further, that blue, especially, can make a universe of its own (as we see in Picasso's 'blue-period', or other blue monochromes) compensating by much of one colour – its intense blueness – for what is lost by the banishment of yellows and reds.

In questions quite distinct from those of colour, or from such matters as the use of a broken, or 'weak' line, in place of a 'strong' line, of thick pigment, glaze or *alla prima*, the artist knows things not generally spotted by the critic. And there is, I think, something in this small book – 'The Caliph's Design' – which bears out what I have just said.

The subtitle is *Architects! Where is your Vortex?* And the position of primary importance given in it to architecture – to which should be added the secondary arts of utility – in visual culture, above all in deciding what kind of mind the majority shall have, and what sort of 'public' the painter or sculptor gets, is not even now generally alluded to or taken into account.

It is necessary, before I expound what I venture to regard as the insights displayed in this early pamphlet, to speak of my state of mind at the period. First, I was, as I have said, a perfectionist. No political planner could be more fanatical a planner than I, but the disciplines involved were formal and cultural. The biggest visual fact, *the City*, was my starting point. The haphazard manner in which everything struggles and drifts into existence filled me with impatience. I would have had a city born by fiat, as if out of the brain of a god, or someone with a god-like power; in my parable of the Caliph's Design issuing from the decree of a despot.

Possessed of no historical sense – being doctrinally a man of the Present – the stagnant mass of our smoke-blackened metropolis did not endear itself to me: its chaotic agglomeration, whether of nasty slum or Victorian clubland, did not speak to me of Stuart or of Hanoverian kings, or anything of that kind. Those impulses which we choose to call 'creative' had so perfectly the upper hand of the conservative (which I suppose is 'creation's' opposite) that the Past was blotted out altogether.

Vaguely I was conscious, no doubt, that it could not be done: but had I possessed the power I should certainly have torn down the whole of London – or at least all the centre of the city. Upon its ruins would have risen a bright, a new, and an enchanting capital. I am as convinced as ever today that it is a great pity I had not the power.

In the first place it would have been white, and would have looked like sets for a movie about Babylon (designed, perhaps, by le Corbusier). I had blueprints for hanging gardens between Blackfriars Bridge and Westminster. Bank clerks and shopgirls in glittering crowds would have danced the shimmie-shake in snow-white palaces, to the thunder of black bands, upon the present site of Scotland Yard. The Houses of Parliament would, needless to say, have been razed to the ground. A very elegant white-and-blue balconied structure – with the balcony-terraces five hundred yards in length standing over our muddy little river – would take the place of what is unfortunately there. The parliaments would sit in vast circular theatres underground. All above ground would be given over to the festive side of law-making. Old Ben might have his being, out of sentiment, in a wireless tower of aluminium girders rising at the extremity of the building.[3]

My argument starts thus. 'No one denies the hideous foolishness of our buildings, our statues, our interiors.' I may say that at the time of writing I did not appreciate how this was matched by the 'hideous foolishness' of our social and economic life: nor how impossible it is, until that core of bottomless foolishness is altered for the better, to acquire the kind of gay intellectual shell that I wished (that I still would wish, if I did not know it was impossible).

Divergence of opinion, I next asserted, centred around this point: namely, 'Is it not preferable to have the outward expression of the vulgar and the stupid forever there before us, in an appetising and delicious idiocy — reminiscent of the "highness" of game, only in this case a visual degeneracy or necrosis — and to have all this at the disposal of our superiority and wit.' Some hold this view: others would like to improve our scene and get rid of whatever is offensive to taste and to intelligence. — And I do think that in politics there is some contrasting attitude of this kind — towards mankind as it is (with its wars, slumps, and the rest of it) and mankind as it should, and could very easily, be made. A parallel specially to note.

'A stupid form,' I wrote, 'is for the painter nourishment for his talent just as is a stupid person for a Gogol, for a Flaubert, or for a Dickens. There is this obvious *stimulation* in what is stupid and inferior. Should, under these circumstances, every ill-made or tasteless object, such as abounds in contemporary life, be got rid of, or should it rather be joyously accepted?

'There would today, in "modernist" circles in the art world, be as great an outcry if some philistine proposed that our preposterous statues, advertisements of ale, whisky, or of dentrifice — cheaply ornamented crockery, neon lights, bewitchingly tiled Tube stations and tea shops — that all these should be done away with', just as there is from the 'beauty-loving' public when a 'beauty-spot' is threatened with commercial defilement.

Now how much 'modernist' art — in this term we can include the French Impressionist school — has battened upon what is silly and ugly, upon the commonplaces and vulgarities of modern everyday existence, is forgotten or not realised. And Picasso, who started as an impressionist, and his fellow artists, made a fetish almost of a box of matches, a bottle of beer, an ugly vase or kitchen chair. The one thing that never intrudes into their deliberately plain, or squalid, universe is a traditionally 'beautiful' object, or even anything *in its own right* intelligent. — They regarded it as their function to transform it, by technical magic, into something intelligent. Never, however, into anything 'beautiful'. All European art, or almost all, for a century past, would be classed by a fastidious Chinese or Japanese as rough popular art, of the same kind as the realistic Ukiyo-e polychrome prints.

This, with the impressionists, called itself 'realism'. So it was called by Zola, the friend of Cézanne. And there were no doubt politics in it somewhere. It was the painting of the Common Man, and of the common objects which belong to him. This is its merit, as it is its definition. But it is an ethical, and not an artistic, virtue.

There was something else. I have mentioned (not for the first time) Flaubert, that great Frenchman who was deeply influenced by German Nineteenth Century pessimism. In these successive schools of painting, culminating in the plunge into abstraction, or the romantic twilight of the Unconscious (and Freud is the more recent, clinical, form of German pessimism) there is a defeatist isolationism, as it were. Prior to our epoch men have not left their scene as they found it. They were great builders. In the visual department of their lives, not content with creating an imaginary life upon small areas of paper or of canvas, to record their responses to life, they have collectively set about constructing a new shell for their society, expressing its religious beliefs or their novel sensibility and passion for form. They wished to escape from the formless and the accidental. We are the first men to accept the formless and accidental – a visual chaos. Our scene is composed of a disorderly wilderness of brick and concrete, springing up fungus-like in response to some commercial urge. As a result, the profession of architect is practically extinct, both here and in America (compare Chapter XXIV), one does not need *architects* for what happens so simply without them: hence their occupation is gone. Similarly all the objects that we use have ceased to have any relevant form.

This decay of all form and elegance is the expression of our defeatism, of our pessimism. We no longer feel able to cope with our world, much less to give it a beautiful order. We eschew 'beauty' therefore. But it is not merely that the effort to create it is too great. We no longer desire it.

A great vogue exists for what is in fact the *grotesque:* the reverse of the beauty and order upon which we have turned our backs. Mr. Alfred Barr,[4] formerly director of the Modern Museum in New York, possesses a great talent for classification. To the intense disgust of those commercially or otherwise interested in the matter, he classified much of Picasso's work as 'comic'. It is, I believe, the correct pigeon-hole. Much of his output consists of highbrow jokes. 'Comic' is in no sense a derogatory term: but it might interfere with cultural uplift, or militate against a meaty sale, to an uplifted 'sucker'.

———

Painters of the impressionist, or post-impressionist, schools, I have observed, never admitted any object *in its own right* beautiful or intelligent into their compositions. Their task, they considered, was to photograph (after their sketchy, spotty, manner) what was there, irrespective of its quality. What the Zeitgeist handed them was there: and Time was infallible. Their attitude was one of fatalism. They even developed a superstition about the factual, or accidental, as if all these objects – chairs, tables, coffee cups, trees, people – had been dice, which had fallen after that fashion and so must be accepted. If a farmer had painted a gate green, although the rest of the scene seemed to demand that it should be *white,* no matter, green it must remain. It was green 'in nature'.

Visual form played a very different part in the culture of China or Japan, or with the Egyptians, and even Greeks of antiquity. All these peoples thought of human life as of one piece: they attempted to banish from it, as far as was possible, mean, clumsy, ill-proportioned, unintelligent things, whether as that concerned their temples, domestic architecture, objects of common use, garments or what not. Whereas those of whom I have been speaking – of the modern age – were content to galvanise a tiny area, where intelligence and taste could subsist and survive, as if in an Ark intact upon the surface of the deluge.

Needless to say, they experienced none of the sensations of people physically isolated – only of those mentally cut off from others. They lived in Paris, still a charming city, full of good talk and food and pretty girls. But

the 'bourgeois' for them was anathema, as was the English Philistine for
Matthew Arnold. The blight of modern monopoly-capital, with its imbecile
standards — the ultimate expression of which is Hollywood — was closing in
on them. The date at which artists ceased to think of creating outside a
small semi-private world of their own I do not know. But monopoly-capital
dates from the first decades of the Nineteenth Century, and the world-
development of the great banking fortunes.

At this point a paradox obtrudes, complicating the issue. First of all, one
can imagine a society where the artist and indeed the cultivated man as
well, had developed so exclusive a sensibility that any unsightly object
would offend him. And compared with the Chinese or Japanese of a few
centuries ago, we, as a race, are no doubt coarse and insensitive. It was the
he-man in the Western European that denounced Whistler's Japanese-
taught 'perfectionism' as revealing the aesthete.

In this immature tract I pointed out how, paradoxically, painters
themselves suffered in no way in the most hideous surroundings. What
was, if I may say so without rank immodesty, original in this criticism was
what was implied, rather than stated: namely that it would be better if
they were not so brutally complacent. For indirectly these repulsive backgrounds are of the greatest moment to them through the consequent
shrivelling of their public (see my description of the 'Two Publics').

Myself I greatly relished, and still do, a really hideous city like Birming-
ham or Pittsburg: so I can speak from personal experience. But I really think
that this should be classed as a confession. — If a man were married to a
grotesquely hideous woman, he would, I suppose, have to get to like that
type of face. That, however, would be anti-natural, which is as bad as to
be anti-social.

I will quote two passages from 'The Caliph's Design' proving how
clearly already this great central difficulty of contemporary art was understood by me. 'So when I say that I should like to see a completely trans-
figured world,' I write, 'it is not because I want to *look* at it. It would be a
great mistake to suppose that. It would be *you* who would look at it. It would
be you who would benefit by this exhilarating spectacle. I should
merely benefit — I and other painters like me — by no longer finding myself
in the position of a freak: the queer wild men of cubes, the terrible *fauves*
or wild beasts. . . .'

Even more enlightening is this second passage. ' — This is worse for the
crowd than for the more fortunate few. The life of the Crowd, of the Plain
Man, is external. He can live only through others and outside himself.
Then he, in a sense, *is* the houses, the railings, the public statues, the
churches, the roadhouses. His beauty and justification is in the superficial
life of all that he *sees*. He dwindles, grows restless and sick, when not
given the opportunities to live in this communal manner.'

———

It was natural just after world war i for people to pause and re-orientate
themselves. The upshot of these criticisms of mine was not conclusive, it
did not result in a dramatic reversal on my part. I no longer accepted

unreservedly 'L'école de Paris', as it is at present called. My own work prior to this came under review. I abandoned abstraction but was still well content with the disciplines I had acquired (as explained apropos the 'Guns' exhibition).

In my criticism of 'L'école de Paris' I have never gone so far as to get out of sympathy. But from that time as a philosophy it has seemed to me uncreative. It makes the best of a bad job, perhaps: and we all do that, after all. It is only when people insist too much that it is a *good* job – that it is not a *pis-aller* with foundations that are unreal and highly unsatisfactory – that I grow restless. Wildly to acclaim disaster is the worst type of defeatism. There is nothing so bad as lyrical enthusiasm about defeat.

This chapter will, I hope, make its contribution to the overall pattern. Treating as it does in some detail of my 'perfectionist' tendencies, as artist or critic of art, it should serve to enlighten the reader as to the meaning of other perfectionisms, not connected with visual art, which I analyse elsewhere in this record.

Notes

[1] Giorgio de Chirico (1888-1978), Italian painter; originator of Metaphysical Painting. Paul Delvaux (1897-), French painter; influenced by Chirico and Magritte.

[2] Fernand Léger (1881-1955), French painter; first of Cubist, then of proletarian leanings.

[3] Old Ben, i.e., Big Ben, the bell of the clock tower at the Houses of Parliament in Westminster.

[4] See Alfred H. Barr, Jnr., *Picasso: Forty Years of His Art* (New York, 1939).

CHAPTER XXX

A RENAISSANCE PROPHET OF ACTION

'THE Lion and the Fox' is my first political book. It is something else, too, of course: but here I am going to consider only the political implications of Shakespearean tragedy, which I attempted to lay bare — not any of its other aspects, psychological, literary, or historical. I should add that its publication was unavoidably postponed: its true date is before, not after 'The Art of Being Ruled' (1926).

It would be difficult to have a better press than 'The Lion and the Fox'. There was nothing in this book to annoy anybody. The seed of many of my subsequent books, however, was in the political thinking to be found there: and it has been, of course, the political thinking in my writings that has (1) given my routine enemies an opportunity to get at me; and (2) has genuinely enraged or puzzled, or both, a number of people.

There is little or no political theory in 'The Lion and the Fox': it is a study, more than anything else, of the handling of the hero or titan by Shakespeare in his great group of tragedies. As, however, most of these were public figures, some views on the subject of government could not fail to emerge. There is a profusion of evidence in, for instance, 'Coriolanus' of Shakespeare's private reactions. To this key political play I will presently return.

Shakespeare was entirely emancipated from the emotional legacies of feudalism. I even refer to him as a 'bolshevist', and he possessed, it seems to me, a very radical mind. As much as Machiavelli, he lived in a revolutionary time, shortly to witness the execution of the reigning king; with then an interlude of very modern Caesarism. The crowned head, for him, was like any other, of course: he knew a great deal about kings.

In Machiavelli's case the 'Prince' was, it is important to recall, a *new* self-made ruler, a martial adventurer: one, that is to say, who did not inherit power, but seized it. This Italian was only interested in the founding of States, and he thought uniquely of power. — The attention paid by Shakespeare to his doctrines would certainly not be that of one sharing this nasty obsession. What would attract him in Machiavelli would be the latter's exposure of the manner in which the thirst for power maddens men, and how ruling is in fact a disease.

I will begin what I have to say by turning to the chapter headed 'Coriolanus and Aristocratism'. Let me quote p. 238 practically intact. 'Coriolanus, as a figure, is of course the super-snob. Of all Shakespeare's heroes he is the coldest, and the one that Shakespeare himself seems to have felt most coldly towards. He was the child of Volumnia, not of Shakespeare, and one that never became anything but a schoolboy, crazed with notions of privilege and social distinction, incapable of thinking (not differing in that from the rest of Shakespeare's nursery of colossi), but also congealed into a kind of machine of unintelligent pride. He is like a Nietzschean, artificial "aristocrat," with little nobility in the sense that Don

Quixote caricaturally embodies the noble, but possessing only a maniacal intolerance and stiffness. . . .'

The following description, for instance, of the behaviour of the little son of Coriolanus by a friend of the family is 'true to life', but too true not to have been observed with a mind detached from any infatuation with the speakers. It is impossible that this picture of little Coriolanus growing up 'just like his father' is not meant to illuminate Coriolanus for us:

'*Valeria.* O' my word, the father's son; I'll swear, 'tis a very pretty boy. O' my troth, I looked upon him o' Wednesday half an hour together; has such a confirmed countenance. I saw him run after a gilded butterfly; and when he caught it, he let it go again; and after it again; and over and over he comes, and up again; catched it again: or whether his fall enraged him, or how 'twas, he did so set his teeth; and tear it. O, I warrant, how he mammocked it!

Volumnia. One on's father's moods.

Valeria. Indeed, la, 'tis a noble child.

Virgilia. A crack, madam.'

'Indeed, la, 'tis a noble child' is a remark that would certainly not pass the censorship in a despotic super-feudal state, or recommend its author to a Nietzschean autocrat. And had Shakespeare wished to engage the sympathy of almost any audience with this fine little fellow he certainly would not have chosen such a pretty and also flimsy thing as a butterfly to show him wreaking one of his 'father's moods' on.[1]

A performance of 'Coriolanus' at the Comédie Française, in the feverish 'thirties, at which I assisted, was productive of the next thing to a riot. At that moment in the play when Coriolanus passionately denounces, in the presence of the Tribunes of the People, the populace, the French Theatre audience, unable to contain itself any longer, leaped to its feet. Men shouted defiance at one another, fists were brandished: in some instances hot partisans of the aristocratic principle seized vociferous proletarians by the throat, bellowing 'communard!' (Where I sat the 'aristos' were in far greater force than 'le populaire'. There were some brisk exchanges.)

Although Shakespeare had no fondness for the Coriolanuses of this world his distaste was not doctrinaire. 'It was human nature about which Shakespeare wrote, and he did not write on a tone of morals, nor on one of class-prejudice or class-illusion.' This play is an excellent place in which to study the functioning of an inductive mind, recording all impressions upon equal terms, with the absence of *parti-pris* of a chemist or cartographer. He knew a number of very tiresome aristocrats of course – they sat on his stage and got in his way. But he liked the mob just as little. Whenever Coriolanus, or some other of his characters, is heaping abuse upon the multitude, he only had to think of the Pit at the Bankside and he could load their tongues with vitriol. He was if anything too little a man of doctrine or of principle. He saw that there was some bad in everybody. He made no ideological exception.

––––

Machiavelli was a prophet of action of existentialist type. Action he regarded as the only reality. It would be impossible to find a more single-minded advocate of the agent-principle. 'Shakespeare,' as I wrote, again, 'differed profoundly from such a theorist of "action" as Machiavelli . . . he was without that mechanical appetite for what he would regard as a useless and degrading performance of a series of (however logically perfect) tricks.' And this would apply also to the Machiavellian obsession regarding power: for with him power was the highest end of action.

Machiavelli's political philosophy took the form of the glorification of an heroic man—a 'Prince'—a model for other 'Princes', a paragon.

To that extent there is a certain licence for comparison. Both the political philosopher and the philosopher-dramatist were interested in the pathos of the One—solitary, charged with responsibility. Their interests, however, are traceable to quite different stimuli. All Shakespeare's heroes die violent deaths. Machiavelli's, theoretically, never die. They are replete with Roman *virtu:* but this they combine with the most consummate craft (hence the metaphor of The Lion and the Fox'). They never die if they can possibly help it, and the whole idea is that they should *not.* His whole doctrine is a prescription for the most triumphant success: the avoidance of death by assassination through the violent forestalling of all potential assassins.

Shakespeare associated Machiavelli with Montaigne as one of his two main sources of philosophic inspiration. But the doctrine of personal power so dear to the former played, as I have said, no part in this. It was not necessary that it should. Here, after all, was the first scientific hard-boiled theory of the State. It would be the brutal, matter-of-fact exposure of the criminal callousness underlying all government that would appeal to the Renaissance mind, whether English or continental. Some regarded it as a caricature of statecraft. But all felt they understood the State better after reading Machiavelli.

The literate in Tudor England would know Machiavelli, it is probable, indirectly, through a translation from the French (1577) of the 'Contre-Machiavel' of Gentillet, in which Machiavelli was represented as Anti-Christ No. 1. Some were more shocked than others: all were delighted.

Thereafter none failed to interpret the struggle for power—which is what politics are—rather more in its nakedness, than 'clothed and in its right mind'. In other words, the insanity at the root of that ferocious struggle was made plain to them. As dramatists, they saw that all these 'great people' it was their task to write about were, for the most part, mad.

The 'sad stories of the death of kings . . . all *murdered*' were told, if anything, with more savagery and fatalism on account of the bleak doctrine of this extraordinary Florentine—three hundred and ninety-five references to whom were once catalogued as occurring in the literature of that period. His influence is comparable to that of Darwin in the present age.

Darwin was more inclusive. He revealed what was then called 'Mother nature' as 'red in tooth and claw'. A dear kindly old motherly body became overnight a homicidal old hag. Life was seen as a mad fight for survival—the 'unfit' were trampled under foot by the 'fit'.—On the other hand Machiavelli was mainly responsible for tearing the mask off those who seek and exercise power over others. As I express it in 'The Lion and the Fox', he 'gave away the position of the ruler . . . revealing even the very nature of all authority'. – 'Every organised duplicity felt itself unmasked by one of its own servants and satellites.'

Frederick the Great of Prussia, a scarcely less perfect specimen of a power-addict than Cesare Borgia, read Machiavelli to good purpose. As a young man he (as a good Machiavellian) wrote a refutation of 'the Prince' entitled 'Anti-Machiavel'. The enemy of the human race', he called his master: to which Machiavelli would have smiled his sardonic approval. No Prince could afford to underwrite so indiscreet an advocate.

It was Niccolò Machiavelli's great merit that in the act of worshipping his detestable god he betrayed him. Here is another negative merit: he was not a hypocrite. He will speak complacently of a batch of murders perpetrated by his favourite politican (crimes of State, of course) as we would speak of a 'bomber's moon' – promising big lovely piles of dead women and masses of Bosche brats. For we have our innocent moments too. Earlier, the Germans were very proud of the job they did on Warsaw: and the German camp-Ghouls of Auschwitz and Belsen sniffing the gas from their charnel-houses would no doubt smile naïvely in one another's eyes, their blue-eyed simple peasant-smile. These were their 'enemies' they were exterminating, *nicht wahr?* When – returning the ball, so to speak – we hanged our defeated enemies at Nuremberg we were awfully clumsy. They took fifteen minutes to die of slow strangulation, and, because the opening was so narrow, when they fell through the trap their noses, in some cases, were torn off. That was extremely clumsy. – But once you start that sort of thing you may end up anywhere. Belsen after all may only be a start. In 1947 a Borgia is a small-time killer. And 1954 may put 1944 in the shade.

Personal rule was of the first importance, Machiavelli thought (on the homely principle of too many cooks spoil the broth). Consequently it was politically sound for Romulus, at the founding of Rome, to dispatch his brother. *Two* brothers would not found as good a State as *one:* no other course was open to him.

Again, when you get that *ruling feeling* and seize a city-state, setting yourself up as its master, to be tolerant is fatal. People would take advantage. They would have bumped you off before you could say knife – for they are incorrigibly violent. So you must wipe out a few dozen straight away. Then there will be no discontent or treachery. You know what people are like – always grumbling and plotting!

Is this extreme frankness of Machiavelli's really a virtue, however? For it is his only one. People in general are almost as unpleasant as he declares them to be. But by what right do you go and plant yourself on them as a ruler? And are you not asking for what you get if you do so? This never seems to occur to our Niccolò. And no one said at that time that they felt impelled to rule over other people *for their own good* and out of a keen sense of duty. People were not so Machiavellian as that in those days. They just said they liked power.

I should be very sorry to be responsible for this little Florentine doctrinaire (the Crocean view of whom I queried in an earlier chapter). Because he was not a hypocrite, that is not everything. Several books have appeared of late in praise of machiavellianism, and friends have said to me more than once that I was responsible. This was, however, an absurd mistake. It signified that the friends in question had not read 'The Lion and the Fox' with great understanding, I am afraid.

There is no tendency to make a hero of Machiavelli in 'The Lion and the Fox'. When I am showing how close Georges Sorel and Machiavelli are to each other, I write as follows.

'The agent principle for both was the only one. Both have no room in their minds for anything but their arid roman doctrine of "power" and force. . . . "Even in his histories," Villari writes, "Machiavelli's men appear incapable of any ambition or passion save the political; there is hardly any mention of letters, art, culture, or religion." It is where Villari is comparing Machiavelli with the Greeks that he says this, showing how the author of "The Prince" was a true child of Rome, his nature alive only to the suggestions of power and mechanical control . . . "political ideas alone seem to have existence." '[2]

It would be false to say, as I hope the above extracts will have shown, that Machiavelli was for me a thinker to be admired in his rôle of enthusiast for power. Those who today are extolling Machiavelli's principles are themselves power-addicts. But men for whom 'political ideas alone seem to have existence' are today very numerous. They are not the kind of men I am disposed to admire. Those 'alive only to the suggestions of power and mechanical control' or an 'arid Roman doctrine of power and force', or a doctrine of power and force not Roman, it is not in my nature to applaud.

Machiavelli was a propagandist for Action. For him, as for M. Sartre today, or for Marinetti ('the father of Italian Fascism') yesterday, we only exist when we act. And action in this context means action of a material and mechanistic type. Those 'political ideas' which 'alone seem to have existence' are adumbrations of action.

But such principles as these I have combated, since the first days of my public life, when I led a band of hecklers into the Doré Gallery in Bond Street where Marinetti was lecturing.

The vitalism with which Futurism was drenched, or with which Surrealism is charged, has no attractions for me. And when those philosophies emerge in politics, they produce in me the same sensations as they do in the arts or in literature.

Machiavelli, however, *did* 'give away the position of the ruler'. It was he who 'revealed even the very nature of all authority', to quote again what originally I said about him. As such the student will always turn to him with such respect as one feels for a clear-minded, as it were austere, impeccably truthful, criminal.

There remains the personal question — not as that affected Shakespeare in his grandiose single figures (either kings or great captains) but in its application to theories of the State. Ever since the English cut off the head of Charles I personal rule has been invested for them with many of the attributes of Satan. Yet there is much to be said, in theory, for personal rule. And much was said in favour of rule by the One in 'The Lion and the Fox'. Even, as you may recall, a famous Englishman expressed the view that 'a *benevolent* tyrant would be the best type of ruler'. It is the benevolence that is the trouble.

The three main types of rule (and at all times we would do well not to depart from this Aristotelian rule of thumb) are rule by the One, rule by the Few, and rule by the Many. It is one of the central problems of politics, of course: all I need say here is this. In the last few years we have had many instances of rule by the One of an authoritarian type.

It has been the general tendency to suggest – if not actually to state this – that the arch and only exponent of personal rule of an autocratic, or authoritarian type, has been Herr Hitler. This is natural, since he was the arch-enemy of the Western democracies (not – as again it is the tendency to suggest, – because he was an extreme example of personal rule – as was certainly the case – but for other reasons). Before Hitler made his ill-fated appearance there were heads of governments in Europe at least as despotic as he ever succeeded in becoming. The autocratic rulers of Russia, the Tsars, had been succeeded by even more autocratic personal rulers: namely the communist dictators.

Lenin and Stalin, like the Tsars before them, were merciless rulers; indeed outdoing their predecessors. Their personal rule has been marked (as today is often pointed out) by the greatest savagery. But mockery of socialism as unquestionably that has been, Russian poverty is probably now better organised, corruption made more dangerous, religious impostors have disappeared. – Hitler revealed himself as a homicidal lunatic: but even he in the first years of his power effected changes for the better which it is very difficult for a government without such great powers to attempt.

In the interest of truth these facts must be allowed. Personally I would rather muddle along with the democratic rulers of the West.

To pursue this line of thought – by which I hope to lead the reader to a realisation of the fact that personal rule is not something confined to the dark ages and is not, in itself, without advantages – all government of late has approximated more and more to personal rule: Franklin Roosevelt was a demagogic autocrat, and Mr. Churchill, as war-leader, exemplified personal rule – though abruptly dismissed when the war ended.

Personal rule has the great disadvantage of its effect upon the person exercising it. Also for one benevolent ruler you might get nine who were bad. And even one who starts harmlessly enough is apt to become unspeakably bad. – In 'The Lion and the Fox' what I was looking upon with a not unfavourable eye was in fact the Patriot King. His interests are identified with those of the People – he stands between them and the rapacity and pride of the oligarchy, the *ottimati*. And so it may be: may be *if* the king is not a blackguard or a fool, and is really a patriot.

Notes

[1] This paragraph, the passage from *Coriolanus* (I.3), and the paragraph preceding it all come, like the paragraph in quotation marks, from *The Lion and the Fox* (London, 1927), pp. 238-39. In transcribing, Lewis introduces some minor errors, here corrected. (See List of Emendations.)

[2] *The Lion and the Fox*, p. 94 (with some insignificant changes).

ADVICE TO THE INMATES OF THE
POWER HOUSE

Foreword to Chapter XXXI

IT is a Power House — we might call it that — in which we live. It is given up to the generating of *power*, the atmosphere is heavy with power. Men stalk or strut about, frowning with importance, because they have access to *power*. Some are heavy with power, as a woman is with child. At the microphone some are almost dripping with power — their words are like bullets or drops of blood, so that the timorous shiver slightly, and the bravest feel none too comfortable.

Socially life in the modern age is like being in an immense building, full of a radioactive something we call 'power'. It is 'malignant', this kind of power, and we are all slightly cancered (just as the inhabitants of Didcot are said to be many of them slightly unwell).*

This disease we name *power* is most unfortunately *power over us*. If we were not there, there would be none of this type of *power* at all: without any Germans there could have been no Hitler. What is really terrifying is that it is all something derived from *us*. A fraction of what makes any prominent statesman so prominent is *us* — you and I. All these Somebodies would be nobodies if it were not for us. The man who walks with the heavy pomp of the *enceinte* is heavy with us, we are responsible. We all are laid under contribution — our toiling hands, our skills, our intelligence.

All are potential blood-donors to swell the veins and magnify the bulk of a Moloch called 'the State'. (For this Power House goes by the name of 'the State'). Its Bank is a 'Blood-Bank'. We are forcibly bled to feed it. Its Capital is drawn from our veins.

Not a pleasant situation, of course. Not particularly comfortable. But what is the alternative? Where I spoke of Politics, in my first part, I made it perfectly clear, you may remember, that there is no escape from this Power House.

Although the power, the presence of unbridled power, causes (in really bad periods) endless suffering, yet *without* Government — that fat spider that feeds on us, upon whose prodigious web we are convulsed like helpless flies — without all that, there would be no libraries, laboratories, universities, theatres, publishers, great buildings: the Power is, in its origins, for those purposes, and (oh irony!) to assure us safety and peace.

Like our mortality and the death-sentence tactfully deposited upon our cradle, which for the rest of our days we carry about in our pocket — we take it out and look at it sometimes and think for a moment what a funny document it is: like that, just as we are born to die, so are we *born to be governed*. Sometimes we are left alone for a while — nothing reminds us of our situation. As in Kafka's 'Der Prozess', at any moment, however, there may

---

* Didcot is a centre of atomic research in Great Britain.

be heard the *knock*. They are there at the door. We, the governee, must always anticipate that domiciliary visit. Moloch wants more blood – his myrmidons are there! For we are born blood-donors: and when food has for long been scarce, it is a serious matter being asked for *blood*.

In some periods it is just so bad that life is not worth living, and the libraries, the laboratories, and the theatres lose their meaning for us. But there is no doubt whatever that without a centralised life you get nothing of that kind, which – if the Government at the moment is not *too* impossibly brutal – does give value to life: and (whether in fact one is or not) makes one feel a little better than a cockroach or an ephemeron. Without centralised life you just have innumerable little islands of people – no great society, but infinite itemisation and insularity, a prospect which nothing but the insular mind would contemplate with any degree of complacency.*

Now in this Power House of ours there is roughly (1) the staff, and (2) the rest of the inmates, – or the governors and administrators and the governees. – You might be inclined to say that with any gumption at all a man must aspire to belong to the staff – to govern rather than be governed. This is not at all the case, however.

Your duties as one of the staff (who handle the Power) take up all your time. It is dull work: only congenial if you are a dull man or a very violent and disagreeable one. No good musician, to take instances, wants to leave his music for politics, nor does a doctor interested in his work, nor a man of science, a poet, or historian, or a novelist. The much-photographed, well-housed, well-fed politician, the object of much deference and flattery, is rather like the much-photographed Hollywood Star – he is only envied by the very simple and untalented people, or by the power-addict. On the other hand he has something the glamorous Star has none of – namely *power*. This means licence to interfere with, direct, and control other people. But you may be a very gifted man, like Einstein or Bernard Shaw, and not desire to order people about – arrange what they shall eat for breakfast and where they shall work.

Now I am not one of the staff, I have never had anything to do with Management, have no taste for bossing. I have almost ostentatiously been a *governee*. I have had an active preference for the governed in contrast to the governing.

What I am about to say in this chapter relates exclusively to this subject. Whether I am temperamentally managerial or the reverse: whether

* Though this is not the place to discuss Mr. Aldous Huxley's latest book, 'Science, Liberty, and Peace' [New York, 1946], where a radical decentralisation is advocated, I should like to interpolate a brief note. His proposals are humane and sensible, but, as he must know, have no chance of being realised. It is like proposing to build a stone house where no stone is available. Architects who kept on publishing plans of beautiful stone houses in such a country would be wasting their time. – Human nature is a very unmanageable and unsatisfactory material: but it is essential to start from that and have it always in mind, with all its shortcomings, in drawing up plans of the kind of society at which men now should aim. Major Douglas's *social credits* again would be an excellent thing: but where is the use of talking about them? Our currency systems are antediluvian yes: but Power thrives upon what is hopelessly out-of-date.

These remarks do not mean that Mr. Huxley is not worth reading: the more people that read him the better. He is a good and sensible man, and he does help to chart the horrors.

my philosophy of life is a boss philosophy — in other words, a power-doctrine — or some other kind, I shall make it my first business to show that it decidedly is not a power-doctrine.

If we come to see the nature of the problem of civilisation with exactness that is a great advance, though we can *do* nothing. Action just implies more power, not more civilisation or happiness. A defensive technique can be developed, no more. You will find I have compared it elsewhere with jujitsu.

To conclude, I have an axe to grind, no man alive has not, whatever he may say. But it is as it were an innocent axe. No claim to an impossible benevolence towards the human average disfigures these pages. But I am their great friend compared with the smart alecks who flatter them and use them as pawns in the power-game. And now, brother governee, I will proceed with the business of this chapter. I have been accused of being in favour of the Management — also complimented on it. Let us talk about that for a while.

This longish chapter is a thorough re-discussion, as the result of a re-thinking, of one or two of the main arguments of a book called 'The Art of Being Ruled'. I do not think quite the same now as then. But that will not affect the validity of this re-discussion as a means of answering my critics. Anyone desiring to do so may check up on the text of 'The Art of Being Ruled', which is still in print.

In this reconsideration much new material will find its way into the argument: so that this essay will be a useful adjunct to the original text. I shall endorse all, or almost all, the arguments I am re-interpreting. It is obvious that I could not take up these arguments again, forcibly advancing them in a new form, did I not, in the main, still regard them as valid. — But today I certainly should not write this particular book, or think of treating of these particular subjects.

'The Art of Being Ruled' is what its title proclaims it to be, namely a treatise expounding the art, or science, *of being governed*, or *ruled*. Yet so sincere a discussion lends itself to misinterpretation: numbers of people have thus believed, or affected to believe, that this is a manual of *how to rule* — not a study of the best method to cope with the ruler. — Had it been written for the benefit of the would-be autocrat or power-thirsty politician, I should be a sort of Machiavelli. This impression I shall do my best to dispel.

In detail what I wrote then referred, in some instances, to transient social symptoms. Homosexuality, for example, on the increase during world war i was a protest against the mass sacrifice of the male youth of the country (women 'bravely' consenting), attained epidemic proportions afterwards. That passed. In world war ii there was less emphasis upon the male youth — suffering was more equal. Yet since the termination of world war ii homosexuality has again become epidemic in England. Newspapers have raised the question of cleaning up the cities, since this time even in provincial centres it appears there is a swarming of pathics.

My argument, however, did not depend upon such details as these. From the more general features of apathy and decay there was only a partial recovery: and today the natural enthusiasm which would be felt by many people at the advent of a genuinely popular government — at last

— cannot but be damped by post-war conditions. The socialists have been handed a bankrupt society to socialise, in a ruined world; the only nation capable of helping them is a capitalist nation. Hence 'austerity'. And so the symptoms of degeneration remain.

It is not an easy book to write about, because its argument bursts out into manifold byways. There is a further complication. It was my idea at the outset — inspired by the Hegelian dialectic, with its thesis and anti-thesis — to state, here and there, both sides of the question to be debated, and allow these opposites to struggle in the reader's mind for the ascendancy and there to find their synthesis. I did not take this very far: vestiges of it nevertheless exist, a source of occasional embarrassment.

'The Art of Being Ruled' might be described from some points of view as an infernal Utopia. For epigraph it has a quotation from Chapman's 'Duke of Byron' as follows:

> and they make
> A doctrinal and witty hieroglyphic
> Of a blessed kingdom.

The Utopia, or the 'blessed kingdom', emerging from the picturesque analytical labyrinth of this book, is one of quiescence, obedience, receptivity.

An account, comprising many chapters, of the decadence occupying the trough between the two world-wars introduces us to a moronic inferno of insipidity and decay (which is likewise the inferno of 'The Apes of God'). That was, as it were, Utopia-gone-wrong. For the *abdication* left nothing to be desired.

The loss of appetite for power, and heroism, was for the European — was then and is now — the beginning of bliss: or, to speak more accurately, the beginning of the end of evil. The European has for so long suffered from an excess of Will, that what must ensue from the extinguishing of this would, by contrast, be so wonderfully agreeable as to deserve the name utopian.

This is the reverse of a philosophy of action, as you see. In this tendency, amounting to anti-action, it continues, or makes explicit, what was the indirect teaching of 'The Lion and the Fox'. The advantages of the rôle of the spectator, for instance, rather than that of the performer or man-of-action, I expatiate upon — the 'greater mental satisfactions' of the spectator: seeing that the performer is too busy playing his part for indulgence in the delights of the intellect. To avail themselves of the spectator's privileges, 'detachment' and 'passivity' (wherever the choice is open to them): such is the advice offered to men in general. In a word, something like the *apathy** of the Stoics is what you will find as the central doctrine of this book. In that consists the true 'art of being ruled'. It might be described as a manner of jujitsu for the governed — who are so much the weaker party in their encounters with government.

The art of ruling, on the other hand, consists of course of the extraction of the maximum amount of power from the human material, to be used for the inflation of the ego of the ruler. This is only achieved at great personal risk: it involves continual disappointments and fatigues, hardships of every descripton. The game is decidedly not worth the candle. A very nasty,

---

* Not to be confused with the current use of the term. [The Stoic use involved a notion of spiritual peace and well-being achieved through virtue.]

dark and unattractive picture I draw, in my book, of the ruler's lot, or of the life of those enjoying great positions.

The method employed by me, in this instance, I am now satisfied was mistaken. That was a Utilitarian mistake. If you prove conclusively to people that a certain course of action will entail infinite hardship and discomfort, and quite likely ruin and death, but that it will show that they are 'white men' — or gentlemen, or any pretty verbal bauble of that sort — *that* is the approach which assures success. The more horrid and dismal you propose to make their life the more chance you have of being listened to. I did not know that, however, in 1925.

The date of writing of 'The Art of Being Ruled' is, in effect, 1925, six years after the termination of world war i. I had recognised that a great revolution was under way; that an entirely new epoch had begun, for England and for the world. It had its roots in those ferments of which Cubism, Futurism, and Vorticism were intellectual expressions.

How many people there are at any time — in years of decay and defeat — who understand what is happening to the society of which they are members is not easy to determine. There must be an appreciable number: but they keep it to themselves, I suppose. In 1925 I was not yet emancipated from tribal, or national, superstition. 'Western civilisation' had still an exclusive meaning for me: not so much as Prussia meant to Hegel, or France to Barrès (or to Flaubert): but that Western culture which was responsible for my mind's particular configuration, for its rational bent, I could not see disintegrating without emotion.

Such were the backgrounds of my thinking, as I wrote 'Man and Shaman', 'Sub Persona Infantis', 'Natures and Puppets', 'Vulgarisation and Political Decay'. It is out of what I observed happening around me that I built up the 'doctrinal hieroglyphic' to be found between pages 47 and 313, which is the kernel of this book, and the part of wide application, outside its temporal context. I was fascinated and amused by the spectacle, as well as extremely depressed. This mingled depression and exhilaration is, I believe, a not unusual state of mind, in times like these.

Some of the implications of what was going on were of a paradoxical nature. That was apparent to me: and it was to that perception that the main value of that essay was due. I saw the advantages to be obtained from this demise of a society, of an ethos, and I traced the road out of the disgusting maze. But for some time I was very sore and that soreness increased, if anything, during the immediately ensuing years. The sentimental side of me suffered (I think now) more deeply than it should. — All that is to be found in those books will never be seen again, naturally, with that sharpness or excitement (it was the 'peak in Darien', so to say), or with so much distress. Habit soon anaesthetises; it dulls and blunts.

Everybody had loved the war. London had never been so gay — the newsvendors' eternal cry — 'great British victory!': glamour, death, champagne, syphilis. Financially there was delirium, the bloodbath was a

Lucky Dip. The 'merchants of death' wallowed in profits: the shoeblack even was in the dough. Harlots lit rose-tipped cigarettes with Bradburys. The war was wonderful. Soldiers enjoyed getting a wound – it meant another wound stripe. It meant being 'in blues', back in gay, rich, wicked old Blighty.

But suddenly it *stopped*. It only went on for a paltry four years. Why can't wars go on for ever?

After six years of peace even the biggest fool was dimly aware he had become a debtor – also a citizen of a different kind of State. Here I do not refer to the small wage-earner, however. Nothing political registers in the minds of the poor, the majority of workers. They could not eat much less without being dead. All bosses, of whatever political complexion, think they ought to work harder and get less for it. 'Western civilisation', for instance, means about as much to them as entropy or the second law of thermo-dynamics. Nothing ever happens to them. They have no history. They have no 'stake' in any country. They have no race except the human race. (It is only the sahibs who are 'white men'.) Talking of sahibs, they say that in India millions of peasants mix up the English with the Moguls. Millions of Englishmen, though they may be more *au courant*, are 'political illiterates' just as much as 'Untouchables' or Fellahin.

In the educated class it is different. They are stupid, but things *do* happen to them. If somebody is recording what happened in such and such a period – 'what men felt or thought' – it is of them the historian is speaking. To that first of the new kind of wars a deep and violent reaction occurred among the moderately privileged, as in what was left of the landed society. (Afterwards, of course.) They saw they had burnt up their wealth in that big Guy Fawkes bonfire of world-war. ('Hang the Kaiser!' howled the Yellow Press. It had made much money. The blood of that old moustachioed mountebank would bring them in another shower of gold.) A society has premonitions of its end. This one began burning up the rest of its money, before 'they' took it away from them. Mortification already set in at the edges. They began to stink. I have recorded that stink.

It was not merely a class or a nation that was there inviting observation: the British Isles did not stand alone in obvious climacteric. The very nature of our human stock it was impossible not to regard as calling for an enquiry of some kind. To ask what human beings *are*: of what value is their life, if any. It was necessary to ask whether human life does not have to change radically, or altogether to disappear. 'The slowness, sloth, and commonness of the stock of *Homo Stultus*' came under review for more eyes than mine.

Contemplating in retrospect the recent spectacle of senseless violence, brutal whoopee, 'blood-money', criminal rapacity, blasphemous hypocrisy of propaganda, gullibility, what 'man can do to man'; contemplating both the intellectual and moral nullity of the immense majority, observers in various countries came to the same conclusions. It was agreed that there were certain ineradicable faults of character in man; perhaps of structure. Often he is skilful and quick. But you cannot leave him alone with a keg of gunpowder: he will immediately set a match to it. – Today after world war ii we feel that the German nation should be kept away from anything sharp or pointed – even penknives and pitchforks are somewhat risky in their hands. After world war i it was widely felt that the entire human race required supervision. This signalises a further degeneration.

World war ii, its causes and its after-effects, differs in every respect from its predecessor. Number Two was not a money-war but ideological. Nationally it has been even more disastrous. But nationality in England is largely a Tory cult, and national calamity is not taken *personally* by the population. The war moreover has provided England with the best – or at least to start with the most promising – government it has ever known. No great compliment, but relatively, a mighty fact.

The old type of national adventurer has been blasted off the scene, in every corner of Europe. So this time there will be no 'Im Westen Nicht Neues' or 'The Death of a Hero'.[1] These were novels against Junker and against Tory war. Not even the Tory, however, today would encourage such criticism of the violence that has just ended. Though he has been finally ruined by it, has he not destroyed his old antagonist, the Junker?

An obvious danger is to be discerned in this changed mood. In England it is as if no one dared listen to anything against war *itself*. That is out of bounds, as a subject: it is as if the war were still in progress, with its censorships and disciplines. Sentiment of the 'We can take it' type has made war taboo. Worst symptom of all is to be found in reactions to the Atomic Bomb. Or, rather, there is no reaction. Its mention is resented, as if it were a rival to the doodlebug and blockbuster, but an unfair and unsportsmanlike one (as might be expected, seeing that it is American, the Briton would growl). It arouses no interest, and is disliked.

If war as a subject is interdicted, those in the last analysis responsible for war, namely the human species, are not fair game either. Of Germans, to whatever party they may belong, you can say what you please: recommend their wholesale extermination, or propose their piecemeal enslavement. But to speak disrespectfully of the human species, drags *us* in. If you assert that such serious defects in our species should be attended to, with a view to neutralising them, that would be treated as an *attack*. Yet if a doctor informed you that you were ill and would die unless you agreed to a certain treatment, you might reject the diagnosis, but you would not call it an *attack*, or exclaim that it indicated *contempt* for your body.

After world war i there was no such coyness, or disinclination to think things out to the bitter end; to ask all the tragic questions that a great human blunder provokes. This time there is no admission of tragedy – the habit of covering tragedy up and hiding it away, or 'putting a brave face' on it, during the war is still strong. There is nothing but a dreary silence. A much-censored people become self-censored: the English have become a colony of clams. The Press apparently censors itself automatically into what is as good as silence, too. – So now when the need for free debate, and for concerted action, is more urgent than ever, there is only stagnation, and a great aversion to action. In a word, people are less anxious than ever for responsibility. Apathy (the word used colloquially) is unrelieved: the long patient queues are as it were worms. There is none of the baby frolicsomeness of the nurseryland of the 'twenties. Every decade it is more thoroughly understood by everybody that they have no freedom, and progressively they desire it less.

I have been speaking exclusively of the English scene, where the intellectuals, the writers, and pundits are dismally absorbed in beating the economic Blitz. They appear to be utterly paralysed: the most they do is to mumble about their childhood on the microphone. What they *think* one does not know, since they write nothing – and indeed say nothing either. They are too afraid that they might say the wrong, or the unpopular, thing.

It must be remembered that the great number of intellectuals were before the war flirtatiously communist or fellow-travellers. It was quasi obligatory. Almost as much as in the United States, however, the same petty calculation that led the average intellectual to hoist himself on to the marxist bandwagon now prompts him discreetly to drop off it and to walk away. But where to? Generally he just goes on, but unostentatiously, walking in the same direction. Some walk in the *opposite* direction. Some lie down upon the nearest patch of grass and go to sleep and dream of horse buses and hansom cabs.

The years immediately ahead are so overwhelmingly dark and unpromising that only the precarious present has any reality at all for them, and the taverns of course are fuller than ever. Pouring daily through their bladders is a torrent of flat beer (hard liquor cannot be bought by any but the rich). Thus in a bleary dreamland the Britannic intelligentsia old and young kill time and fish for scribbling jobs, or assignments to which no work to speak of is attached.

In France the situation is very different. The ultimate value of existentialism, for instance, is a matter we are not called upon to decide. But such people as Sartre or Camus – with books such as 'Être et Néant', 'Huis Clos', or 'Miramolin' – at least keep the place alive and keep the 'Néant' at bay. They do reply, whether well or ill, to the spectacle of social ruin in which they find themselves, and invent a doctrine of hideous pessimism to match the challenge of the diabolical Zeitgeist.

———

But now back to the problem of my past sins, allegedly so heinous. Admittedly I approach the human problem with no heroical nor sentimental design. But the cheapjack political journalist, or *salonard*, with his little stock of coarsely-coloured political ideas, that come in the mail to him from the 'Avantgardiste' mail order house, must not be allowed to get away with the charge that I preach a power-doctrine. It is not, has never been, *I* who traffic in power! I must rebut the charge that I offer to the would-be tyrant a tempting prospect of man's helplessness: that I have been responsible for something akin to the introduction of a ravening wolf into a nursery.

One of the first questions dealt with in 'The Art of Being Ruled' was that of inherited, or artificially generated, martial ferocity. This is of course the central problem of Europe and its wars. Mr. Bertrand Russell's solution after world war i was 'kindliness'. Failing that, he considered the solution adopted by the Houyhnhnms towards the Yahoos, 'namely extermination', is the only one. He added that 'apparently the Yahoos are bent on applying it to each other'.

But who are the Yahoos? My grocer and my postman, the teller at

my bank, the Smith's bookstall man from whom I buy magazines – they
are the kind of men who get 'wiped out'. But are *they* the Yahoos? I do
not think so: for they are quiet, good-natured people. From the 'ferocious'
solution of the Houyhnhnms I for my part turn away. Nature, I suggest,
will step in: has already done so.

Nature, I mean, will whisper in the ear of the little overtaxed male:
'Why be so big and tough and take all the knocks? No one believes in you
any more. Stand down, reduce your chest measurement to the C.3 mark.
That is the way to survive. The survival of the fittest is out of date. The
C.3 man will be there while you are pushing up the daisies!'

The feminisation, or neutralisation, of the White European, some
change affected by the glands of internal secretion perhaps, will produce
the desired result. All this, in 1925, seemed indicated by everything with
which the social scene was charged. In many directions, even, could be
seen what looked like the emergence of a third, or neuter, sex.

That was a uniquely favourable moment to observe the first violent
symptoms of disintegration. A little later and they go under the surface
and are more difficult to study. The feminist had been followed by the
feminising male – a compensatory movement – and these developments took
a spectacular form. New York was far less affected than London; the
American he-man is a redoubtable conservative obstacle. But I remember
in 1931 in New York a journalist relating some violent incidents in a
nightspot, and his subsequent reflections ran like this. 'You see how things
have changed,' he said. 'A few years ago if you were rude to a fairy he
would go away into a corner and cry. *Now* he gives you a sock on the
jaw that knocks you cold and telephones for an ambulance.'

The change from the traditional social pattern, dominated by sex, into
an asexual pattern, with maleness shorn of all but its merely organic
distinctness, will come about in many ways. One of the most obvious, is
via class-war. Man constitutes as it were a *class*. Among the many class-
wars by which European society is being very effectually disintegrated, the
sex-war occupied a position of great importance.

Though no longer a 'war', the effects of that civil war of the sexes are
everywhere evident: in the form of pressures tending to dissolve the
Family (which is the stronghold of the 'masculine' as much as of the
'eternal feminine') is revealed the same great design as was, in the first
place, responsible for setting in motion the 'sex-war', and its Press-slogans
injurious to the man as husband.

I have spoken of these 'wars' in an earlier section, but now I must
refer to them again. The 'class-war' is the prototype – the war of the poor
against the rich. Organised upon the same principle are the sex-war (man
against woman); the age-war (old against young); the war of urban-man
versus agricultural-man; of the highbrow against the lowbrow. In all
societies there have been these divisions, and many others. These are the
seams where the various patches of which our society is composed are
sewn together. Unpick these patches – of which *every* society is made up,
of necessity – and chaos comes again.

As to urban versus agricultural man, all Marxist parties favour the
proletariat as against the peasant: agricultural man is traditionally the

great conservative, the factory worker (or formerly the urban populace) the potential revolutionary. By the age-war I refer to the tendency to incite the young against their elders. The same motive is again operative here. The revolutionary of course regards the young as his natural allies: the old (with caution and scepticism that years generally bring) his natural enemies.

In most primitive or patriarchal societies the Elders are the leaders: and this tradition is always very strong. Also, the old are the repositories of tribal or national tradition: but it is precisely those traditions that it is the purpose of the revolutionary to undermine. All advertisement of the 'young idea', 'youth at the helm' slogans, and so on, is encouraged, if not promoted, by Big Business or the revolutionary mind of contemporary politics.

Regarding these 'wars' I have always been in two minds. First, as much wars of this sort, as armed conflict, are techniques I cannot applaud, even if I recognise that they are means to ends of which I approve. As I stand for fundamental change, I am for the *end*, at least, in all these instances. Alas that the good so frequently lies at the end of a sewer, or cleverly concealed in a lunatic asylum.

However, the aim throughout is definitely to reduce the 'high' to the level of the 'low' (as if we were all primitive christians): to dissolve privilege in any shape or form, wherever encountered. And has not the European world been a 'man's world'? Its laws the reporter on the sex-war front was wont to refer to as 'man-made laws'. Man, that classic example of privilege, secured his many advantages by *force*. So he stands condemned – in an age committed (theoretically) to the discouragement of physical force – as enjoying power resting ultimately upon physical violence.

As a symbol of the bully and violator of elementary human rights, men often are ironically situated. A weedy and insignificant specimen of the male sex-class hardly looks the part. There are a group of functions which involve him in this class struggle. 'Apart from *man as father*, or *man as husband* or *man as leader* (in the tribe or State), there is an even more irreducible way in which man is a symbol of power and domination. Man as man, *tout court*, is an anachronism.' Such is the situation I have just indicated.

The discrediting and dethroning of this feeblest and smallest of sovereigns, the little father of the family, in his squalid domestic 'castle', is one of the main features of the demasculinising process.* Many of the specifically masculine attributes would disappear at the same time as the loss of status.

Such is the political aspect of the transaction. But Big Business, as well as the politician, has for many years had the male principle under observation; both have their plans for its elimination. To think of the housewife, for instance, puts the modern economic planner in a rage. The entire horsepower of this good woman, all the year round, consumed in attending to one man and perhaps a couple of children – washing, cooking, scrubbing, sewing, shopping! That must without delay, he insists, be

---

* 'We do not want an Englishman's home to be his "castle", we want a community to get the best out of every human being.' Mr. Silkin, May 17, 1947.

superseded by some kind of barrack-life for working people, the male and female segregated, with communal meals, crèches etc. The housewife must go!

There is something besides this: there is the simple question of man's *economic* prerogative. Great numbers of men are engaged in unskilled work which a woman or a child is equally capable of carrying out: on account of the sex prerogative, male privilege, some inefficient little man demands a wage superior to what a woman or child would receive, for doing the same thing.

These operations are obscured just now by the great social changes which have marked the first two years of post-war ii. But those changes will finish what the 'suffragette' and the post-war i 'sex-war' etc. began. The abolition of the Family as we have known it up to now is more than ever on the agenda of those who have the power to change what they want to change. It is not an idle or ill-founded prophecy to say that a third sex ultimately will emerge. The way in which the more intelligent promoter of these social readjustments envisaged the matter was that something like the sterile female workers of the beehive should be, not perhaps *aimed at*, so much as anticipated, in the ordinary course of things.

All this of course is hardly more than a speeding-up and deliberate organisation of tendencies inherent in the Machine Age. Wasp-waists, corsetry and crinolines (aside from the question of their absurdity) could not have survived. The economic injustice imposed on women by barbarous laws must, in a period obsessed by problems of social justice, be ended. It is a something superadded about which I have been speaking.

A few words before leaving the subject of the Family, and of the Third Sex respectively. It would be absurd to suppose that the working man would be the loser as a result of the dismantling and dispersion of the Family. To live cooped up with a snarling woman, or a lazy slatternly one (I am speaking realistically) who adds child after child to the household until there are so many there is scarcely room to move in their little dwelling, is not a thing to look back on with regret for an uprooted landlord. A family group that he is unable to feed and clothe, half of them adopting the habits of scavenger dogs—to have to relinquish *that* male privilege should be easy.

This man would be far happier, who can doubt it, in a monastery: happier still in a men's communal dwelling, collective farm, barracks, bunk-house, club: anywhere liberated from the crushing responsibilities of sex, of fatherhood and the upkeep of a dirty little 'castle'. As to the woman, is there any question that *she* would be far better off as a member of a 'third sex'—with her pin-up boy over her spinster's cot, no children tugging at her like a rag-doll, with some such healthy work as a 'clippie'* or (a little grander) a confidential secretary? This postscript should suffice to dispose of any feeling that I have been betraying an inhuman streak.

———

Sex, too, in one of its most obsessive forms, played its part in the early

* Woman omnibus conductress: post-war ii.

stages of the disintegrating process: the 'nineties led the way with a great literary martyr.

World war i produced socially more shock symptoms, as I have already observed, than has world war ii. Whether male inversion must count as one of them depends upon whether post-war ii can show as severe an epidemic as its predecessor or not. In the Universities of post-war i the Proust-reading, Wilde-worshipping, undergraduate turned daintily to Sodom, while the female student repaired to Lesbos. The building up of the species was suddenly out of favour:* the stocks of the species did not stand very high. Young men wanted to be women. The man's rôle was patently unprofitable: too much had recently been asked of him. In the decade of 'What Price Glory' he reacted violently. If you think this analysis is fanciful, what other cause would you assign to such epidemics? Although only world war can account for the violence of this fashion, however, it may not occur (in the 'forties as in the 'twenties) as a result of war alone. War is only part of a larger pattern.

How male-inversion correlates with other sex-movements is explained by me in chapter iv of Part viii, 'A. of B. R.'† 'It (male inversion) is as an integral part of feminism proper that it should be considered a phase of the sex-war. The "homo" is the legitimate child of the "suffragette".'

What is quite certain is that socially the conjunction of the women and one of these ubiquitous perverts boded no good for the normal male. There was an affinity between the rouged boy and a violent type of young middle-aged woman, of the kind Lawrence wrote about and describes as 'sitting on a volcano'. Intrigues hatched themselves where Jockey Club mingled with the odour of Ninetyish carnations blooming in buttonholes upon male bosoms. – The male-invert fashion shared many antagonisms with the average woman. An embittered, and no longer young, woman is able to revenge herself upon the he-man, for whom she would no longer be attractive. Often it has been alleged that the 'pansy' shelters behind the woman, but, as I pointed out somewhere, it is equally true to say that women act through these militant anti-he-man perverts.

———

Now to give more careful attention to the purely *class* aspect of these movements. Once 'war' between classes began to spread, as a result of Marx's teaching, naturally it did not stop at *economic* class. Wars are fought with armies, and 'class-wars' similarly are contested by disciplined groups possessed of a high esprit de corps.

What Sorel called an 'artificial' bond has to be created, to cement people to each other. And this bond has to be of an *exclusive* nature. They have to cease to be conscious of all the other things they are, outside that particular category. Thus the 'proletarian' should forget that he is *also* a Catholic, or vice versa – a Catholic that he is a member of the working class. In the making of a Christian, in patristic times, the same care was taken (cf. St. Augustine) to make the convert banish from his spirit all

* The attitude of the ancient Hebrews to this aberrant sexuality was severely practical. They condemned it as *unpatriotic*. So undoubtedly it is, in so far as it spells sterility.

† Abbreviation to be used for 'Art of Being Ruled'.

emotional ties, of family, or of sex, attachment to his home town or nation.

Power here is what is involved. 'Actually . . . the more you specialise people, the more power you can obtain over them, the more helpless and in consequence the more obedient they are. To shut people up in a water-tight . . . occupational unit is like shutting them up on an island.'

In this sense a class is a corral: it is a confining something, limiting a person to a certain pattern, giving to his character a restrictive definition, to his personality a strong and exclusive group colour. — 'Class' of course is here being used in the wider sense, as found in such expressions as 'account-ants, as a class, are very circumspect', or 'clergymen, as a class, are very self-indulgent'. I perhaps should have said this before.

A typical American, for instance, of the Babbitt-order, is classifiable in a number of ways as a rule. About each of these departments of his being, by which his original ego is conditioned, he develops a good deal of fanaticism. First, he is a U.S. Citizen. That compels him from birth to a variety of conventional attitudes. Next he is, for instance, from the 'Deep South', or a Westerner, or a Hoosier. Then a member of the 'Grand Old Party', let us say: perhaps a Veteran of some kind. Add to that his religion — Catholic, or Jehovah's Witness, or Christian Scientist, and you have a man composed of intensely coloured segments, as it were: classifiable as probably is no other national.

All of these sects, or clubs, or societies, or communions to which he belongs take each its toll of his independence; seeing that in each of these capacities he becomes terribly *typical*. That rather unreal thing (unless you have something to *do* with it) freedom, he has traded for something he likes better. — I have chosen the American rather than the Englishman because the latter is, in that sense, freer, and therefore less suitable. He has not gone so far along the path of social mechanisation.

Men find their greatest happiness in type-life. Some strongly marked occupational type — the helmeted 'Bobbie', the barrister with his wig, the schoolmaster with his mortarboard and cane; or pronounced national type — such as the strong silent Englishman, the 'mad Irishman', the tough hustling American: out of being these types men derive infinite satisfaction. It is on account of this type-hypnotism that it is so difficult to persuade anyone of the great disadvantage of competitive nationalist emotions, and of the desirability of cosmopolis. Engaged as I am almost daily in desultory propaganda for world government, I find myself in collision all the time with the type-spirit. — Were one able suddenly to remove all the obsessive archetypes, conferring upon men's lives their mechanical patterns, everybody would be as miserable as are primitive peoples when White civilisation interferes with their ritualistic practices.

———

All the problems of Freedom are intimately connected with the *class* and *type* questions, as interpreted above. — The great majority of men have no desire to be *free*, if by that we agree to mean *individuals*. To be free of another person, or of a group, is to be distinct from, not identical with, that person or that group. *Free* is a word that would have little or no meaning did no other people except ourselves exist. 'Free' means not obstructed by other men. For no one complains that his freedom is encroached upon by the sharks, where he wishes to bathe. In that case he speaks of his *safety*, not his *freedom*.

The free man and the individual appear to be commutative. In order to break down a personality, to cause it to lose its integration, the obvious step to take is to turn it back into its component parts. Thus a fully integrated personality has fewer 'class' symptoms than lesser personalities. 'The more highly developed an individual is, or the more civilised a race, discontinuities tend to disappear. The "personality" is born. Continuity, in the individual, or in the race, is the diagnostic of a civilised condition.'

This refers to the kind of segregation of the 'selves' composing the personality met with in a Pirandello play. The schizophrenic or 'split-pipe', is the psychiatric dual man. But you can have ten or more men in one. None of these selves individually can be a civilised creature, so long as there is one or more others there.

A popular illustration of this destructive use of segregation would be Mr. Low's cartoons of Ramsay MacDonald showing two warring figures, his 'earlier self' and his 'later self'.[2] The two halves of a severed earwig become estranged and do battle when they meet. So with a 'self', once it is thoroughly dissociated from the other segments of the individual.

Now to press home this important phase of the case for the defence: no dispassionate reader of 'The Art of Being Ruled' would detect in it an enthusiasm for the herdesque phenomena I describe. I mean that I am not to be seen in its pages gleefully *herding* people. What I am doing is carefully – exhaustively – analysing their tendency to herd, and to fly from the rigours of the individual state. If I note that this renders them more defenceless, and easier to rule, I do not announce this gleefully: for I myself take no interest in ruling, and both dislike and despise the appetite for power. Their centripetal urge is something as powerful as gravitation. They coalesce. To rule you must be an individual, of some kind: one who is without this irresistible urge to coalesce – one who stands outside, controlling the coalescence.

My main contention, as I describe it, is that people cannot have too much of class: that it is not generally understood the extent to which they have a passion for merging their personalities in a network of conventional classifications. They are, in short, so *clubbable*. – Throughout the book I am discussing, that is, there is no tendency to *incite* people to fuse into conveniently controllable congeries or congregations – for human society is rather too insect-like already to suit my taste. Rather I am apt a little to deride them for being so shy of differentiation, so lost without their bellwether.

Above I have equated freedom and individuality. But in 'The Art of Being Ruled' you will find this stated differently. There it stands: 'Freedom and irresponsibility are commutative terms.' This, however, is regarding the matter from the standpoint of the Majority. It is of course not my view of freedom. It is, in fact, the same as saying, *to be free is not-to-be-free.* What I call in 'A. of B. R.' 'the dance of the Puppets' is to my way of thinking the reverse of freedom.

In page 142, where I find this part of my book epitomised, is the following passage. 'Absence of responsibility and automatic and stereotyped rhythm, is what men most desire for themselves. All struggle has for its end relief or repose. A rhythmic movement is restful: but consciousness and possession of the self is not compatible with a set rhythm.' The libertarian slogans of the closing decades of the Eighteenth Century were based, I assert, upon unreal premises. They ascribed to man impulses that are not normally his. They deal in aspirations which, if realised, would be disagreeable to the majority.

Not one, but several men I know, who were soldiers in world war ii expressed themselves as greatly soothed by having all responsibility taken from them: by being told where to go and what to do. In other words, they were saying how pleasant it is to be an automaton: to move to the rhythm of a great machine, like the Army, to obey a will alien to one's own. In every case, I should add, they were people who in civilian life were subject to no fixed routine. But I must also remember to say that only one of them was in action: though that is not important, because people would rather be told to go to their death than not to be told to go *somewhere* and to do *something.*

It is fashionable to speak of consciousness as of something quite unimportant. And certainly without consciousness there would be great uniformity, which currently is a main objective. In surrendering awareness — in a blissful drowning of the ego — substituting reflexes for acts of consciousness and will, one is moving backwards into the primitive. Many highly organised movements have blazed the way *back.* The great influence of the psychoanalytic doctrines of the Unconscious, for instance (the 'desire to return back into the womb' type of suggestion) has had the effect of leading an entire generation back to the frontiers of primitive existence.

A life submerged, in a state analogous to that of dreaming, has the advantage of being easy: and the stresses of our times have been severe and continuous. So the reverse of effort is what the sick mind of the age needs, and these are the kind of doctors it has acquired.

There is nothing distinguishes the European from a primitive people so much as their respective standards of consciousness. Primitive man has not sorted himself out from nature as has the former. The Oriental — the Indian or the Japanese — suffers (as I feel it to be) from so acute a subjectivity as to approximate in some respects to more primitive mentalities.

They have seemed to me (when I have come in contact with them, mainly in business transactions) to believe that they could *wish* things true. They will ignore everything that they do not like being there (it really *is* not there for them) and concentrate upon what is agreeable to them: they would seem to think that by *willing* they can spirit things away, imposing upon reality what they wish to be there. It is as if reality appeared to them malleable. If you put back something they have spirited away — something which, unlike them, *you* want there, and whose reality you insist upon upholding – they are impatient, but indulgent. Their attitude is that *you* are playing a highly subjective game, and putting things there which were never there before. But the thing, whatever it is, will vanish again as soon as your back is turned. They are shameless, and they are tireless. As a consequence, these people possess a very different standard of truth from that of the European, who, however untruthful he may be recognises an objective status to the world outside himself.

In politics the facts are the same. It is not a contrast in ethics. The European statesman is faced with a dreamer – who wrestles with him fiercely from the heart of an exotic nightmare. Think for instance of Cripps or Churchill: matter-of-fact negotiators. They would approach reality gingerly and sceptically, as a thing to be laboriously and painfully bent (if possible) to their will. Whereas their opposite numbers in India, or Burma, or anywhere east of Suez, would approach the same reality with shining eyes and the utmost disrespect for its pretensions to solidity.

Now a subjectivism of such proportions as I have been describing, verging sometimes on solipsism, must, in its exclusion of awareness of the external world, imply that consciousness, even if present, is feeble and dreamy, like the cloudy awareness of a person awakening from a deep sleep.

Consciousness is privileged. The fashionable denigration of it is, like so much else of that order, insincere – I mean, of course, tendentious. The denigration is a discouragement, which, in its turn, in the last analysis, is a *command:* a denial of that privilege to Twentieth Century man. Much of what is provided for him is in the nature of an anaesthetic. In that anaesthetised condition he should pass his life: that, as I understand it, is the idea.

Never exposed to the rational disciplines inherited by the European from the classic world, the cultures we have been discussing promote the woolly and dreamy or the imperfectly co-ordinated with what is external to the subject. For us the world has presented itself to our senses sharp and hard of outline. It is stamped with the objectivity of the rational. This is a privilege: that is all I have been saying.

Even the characteristic theory of the State of Western Europe and more especially of the Anglo-saxons, stinks of privilege: I mean *of privilege widely spread* – not confined, as in the Oriental cultures, to the small immediate circle of the ruler. We inherit the ideas of freedom of the Achaian Greeks, which gave great independence to a quantity of people. It is a doctrine of 'free men', namely free in contrast to the slaves, of Pelasgian origin, who were as essential a feature of Greek life as was – as is – the Negro in the United States, or the 'Nig' as they call their house-serfs in South Africa.

Our democracy is a flower – if a wilted and shrivelled one – of that distant Hellenic servitude. And since there was no alien population in the early days of democracy in England, at the end of the feudal age, to provide the servile bed so necessary to 'freedom' of that variety, we were obliged naturally to keep a substantial section of our own people in a servile condition.

In this connection it must not be lost light of that the famous 'free-

doms' that were fought for by Pym and Eliot and the other Seventeenth
Century gentlemen were not freedoms for the prentices of London or for
the labourer on their estates, but for a privileged class.

The battle for power in which the would-be despotic kings—and the
kingly power altogether—were worsted, left a relatively large number of
people enjoying almost incredible personal freedom. But for one man in
that position, there have always been a score who were tied down to a
hard and servile life.—Probably more people than deserved freedom had
it.—Those two or three centuries of widely dispersed freedom have not
been the rule, historically, but the exception. It is unlikely that so many
people will ever be so free again.

That was a period of great vigour. More people wanted freedom then
than is generally the case. Afterwards the Nineteenth Century—the
'English century'—was one of amazing freedom too, in England, for those
who *were* free.—But even in those free ages *true* freedom was desired by
few people. More beer, more tobacco, more public entertainments, good
juicy executions, better-paid work—which is desired by everyone—is of
course only an irresponsible type of freedom.

In the form of an interrogatory I will now summarise those matters
treated of so far in this chapter. My answers will throughout have a personal bearing. I wish to make clear how personal interests have not guided
me to my conclusions.

My first question is this:—Do men desire freedom in the way it is
generally supposed that they do?

Evidently no, seems to be the correct answer. But let it be noted that
I do not ask this question, and make this answer to it, in order to smooth
the way for despotism. It depresses me that that has to be the answer.
I would like men to desire freedom much more than they do.

Question. Do men attach great importance to being that privileged
and responsible being, Man: the petty 'lord and master' of the domestic
hearth, the breadwinner, the crusader, the responsible citizen—valuing
his vote and ever ready to cast it?

Answer. It seems they are not so crazy as all that about being the above
responsible being as you might suppose. This is especially true as the bread
gets harder every day to win: as that famous castle, 'the Englishman's
home', has grown too expensive; as the wife and children do not grow less
unruly; and as the wars do not grow shorter or less bloody or less ruinous.

Question. Is the Family, as an institution, destined to disappear?

Answer. Of course. It is a rival to the State. In it the State finds itself
confronted with millions of small rivals. The Family is an institution of
the same kind as the sovereign State. 'States' rights' and the Family are
doomed under the same law of centralisation and monopoly.

Question. Is the average man a self-reliant individualist?

Answer. It would seem not. In fact he would rather rely upon somebody else: and has very little use for individuality. He prefers to be a *type.*

Question. Is he unhappy if obstructed in his desire to create?

Answer. No, for he has none.

Question. Does he chafe at restrictions upon his 'spirit of enterprise'?

Answer. Oh no. He has no *enterprise.* Only one man in a thousand has even the slightest trace of it.

Question. Is it really as bad as that?

Answer. As *bad?* Are you really so anxious for competition? — Initiative is obviously not the average man's strong point. One cannot but admit that he is, in the main, devoid of inventiveness: he automatically makes use of other men's inventions. His will is feeble. He is always in search of a Leader (a Führer, a 'Strong Man') to do the willing for him: to tell him to do such and such a thing — to believe such and such a thing. (For *belief* is *will.*) — When initiative is entirely removed from him, and all his actions are mapped out for him — all responsibility lifted from his shoulders — he is well satisfied.

Imaginary Heckler. A pretty account of your fellow men, Mr. Lewis, that you have just given us! Does it afford you great satisfaction to describe them as sheep, and a dull flock at that?

Answer. No satisfaction. It is depressing to live in a sheepfold: especially if you have no vocation for the job of shepherd. You thought, it is evident, that as I describe them as sheep I *must* want to be a shepherd. That is poor logic. The would-be shepherd never describes his prospective flock as *sheep.*

Imaginary Heckler. Why are you so interested in mankind then?

Answer. Not because of any desire to carry them about, wipe their noses, tuck in their bibs, select their food, map out their days. You have mistaken me for a politician.

(The Questions are resumed.)

Question. Are men dismayed at the thought of returning to more primitive conditions?

Answer. By no means. When the tree-dwelling phase of evolution was ending, to get them up on their hind-legs, to stop them from dropping back on all fours, must have been hard work for those anxious to say good-bye to their tails. As it is, we go upright, yes. But that is a discipline easy to break down.

Imaginary Heckler (back again). You get a kick, Mr. Lewis, out of despising us?

Answer. No. I do not get a kick out of those kind of things. The majority flops back all the time. We all, teachers, writers, scientists, politicians are propping it up. Half of life goes into that unceasing effort. It is the big dull problem called 'survival'. There are no *kicks* to be got out of that. — The teacher exhausts himself on the unwilling scholar; the creative writer has to waste all but a fraction of his life in wresting from society the physical means to create; the man of science sees his discoveries misused by that violent moron monopolising wealth and power, whose unintelligence is only matched by his destructiveness. Lastly, the exceptional politician, a Lenin or a Jefferson, has the most difficult material to work in of any creative mind. — Yet as between man and creative man, there is no difference of *kind.* Their destinies are not separable. There can be no super-men. Separation could only be of a much more limited order.

A reader to whom the views expressed in my Interrogatory have proved unacceptable, will find what I next have to say even more so.

I spoke above of a *separation*, limited in kind, between creative man and his backward fellow. This should be our aim. Not a divorce, but a separation, between these incompatibles is all I suggest. The backward mass drag down and stifle intelligence. What is socially valuable in human life should be put out of reach of the elemental inanity in man, just as we place the national treasures in a place of safety when expecting bombardment from the air. (No place has apparently yet been devised where we can preserve them from the picture-restorer!)

It is the fact that the backward and the enlightened live cheek by jowl, in such promiscuity as calls imperiously for some action. Formerly under aristocratic governments there was obstruction, too, but it was of a different order. Aristocracies experienced less temptation to interfere in civilised activities, even if not very civilised themselves. Their consciousness of social superiority and power gave envy no foothold. The arts and sciences or learning occupying a place of social inferiority, were left alone, more or less. People enjoy patronising, and the arts and sciences found 'protectors'. Then the more savage and retrograde sections of the community were held in check at a respectful distance. Not that it was otherwise a desirable system, for usually it was savage and retrograde too. But the problems that arise, more particularly cultural ones, in an age of multitudinous government were absent.

On the whole the sciences fare better today than other civilising agencies. Nevertheless the very inventions which are of immense benefit to everybody meet with far more resistance than those periodic proposals for wholesale massacre we call 'war'. Insulin had a stormy career before it was made available for public use. The employment of ether put an end to a nightmare of pain, it made possible great advances in surgery. Yet the first to advocate its use had to contend with the kind of opposition an inhuman murderer might reasonably anticipate from his victim.

How to effect a recognition of an irreconcilable human dichotomy of the civilisable and the uncivilisable; proceeding upon that recognition to classify people accordingly, confining the unteachable residue to a situation in which they had not the power to obstruct, is not at all easy. But it makes it very much easier the moment you reflect that these unteachables have no desire to be taught: and, what is more, are quite content as they are. It is in fact through pretending that they are longing to be taught, to improve themselves, to enjoy civilised advantages, that we have arrived at the present confusing situation.

There is nothing illiberal in these observations and suggestions. They are mere commonsense. The majority want to be fed, clothed, and housed properly, to be provided with plenty of coarse entertainment—bread and circuses, in a word—and *that is all*. They do not, and never will, wish to acquire, or allow you to impose on them, 'culture'.

We know this, for it has been proved in innumerable ways. I have, in many different places, set forth the evidence. Out of any hundred business magnates, for instance, here or in America, what proportion acquire, or evince any desire to acquire, 'culture'? Not more than one or two per cent is the answer. Yet their wealth enables them to safisfy those tastes, if they existed. As we know, big cars, palatial homes, coarse or silly amusements is what they want and what they get. But these are average men: theoretically, according to the politician, they should, as soon as wealth makes that possible, have flown open-armed to the Muses.

It is not a crime to be backward, any more than it is for a monkey to stay simian. If, in a position of power and authority, you do not treat your backward brother-men properly, you are a criminal. If you dishonestly make use of them, confusing their minds with chimeras, in order to climb to power, that is criminal too.

But many public men are, by this time, themselves genuinely confused. The good statesman thinks that 'the humblest' should have the same opportunities as himself to go to a show of German Primitives or Chilean Surrealists — go to a concert of classical music or of modernist music — to have the run of the London Library, and access to all ballets and operas. This amiable public man quite forgets how little interest he takes *himself* in all that type of thing: how he never reads a serious book — only detective fiction: how he hates going to a picture gallery, disliking the childish Primitive almost as much as the deliberately hideous Surrealist; and how he dozes at a concert, until the kettledrum gives a nasty bang, and only keeps awake at the ballet to watch the girls' legs. Should he examine *himself*, as an average human specimen, this benevolent statesman would be at once enlightened. One sentimental illusion, at least, would be dispelled.*

The number of people who are, under favourable circumstances, cultivable, civilisable, is very large; but is small beside those who are not amenable to civilising influences. It is in the proportion, perhaps, of non-commissioned ranks to the rank and file in an Army. Among the latter are many individuals of great steadfastness — good-hearted, trust-worthy, likeable. And no social stabilisation according to type should be over-rigid or exclusive. The most unresponsive mass can throw up pianists, biochemists, scholars, painters; it must be the business of the State to catch them, conferring upon them those privileges they require in order to work. But the social structure remains hierarchised, in the interests of everybody.

Once again: no hardship or indignity is implied in such proposals. A ratcatcher likes catching rats: he does not want to play the piano. He despises the piano. The ploughboy does not want to think, but to plough. Burdensome and unpopular occupations (mining or stoking) should be spendidly paid.

Those who thrive upon flattery of the plain man — who would describe these proposals as wanting sympathy for their client — are high-pressure political salesmen: but they are not selling anything solid. — There is at least one charge that I need not anticipate: that of being a flatterer.

* What has been said above may seem not to be borne out at the present moment. Is not art booming? — the reader may query. There is Unesco, after all! There is official publicity, about 'great public interest in art' — of use mainly to gallery officials, not to art. It must suffice here to say that a careful scrutiny would reveal no facts that would contradict the above statement of the case.

It might be thought that no time could be so unpropitious as the present for proposals of this character. That is, as a matter of fact, not at all the case. It is true that in most nations one type or other of socialism (state capitalism is generally favoured) is displacing liberalism or conservatism, or in some cases is already in control. But all socialism today is hard-boiled.

The distance separating us from William Morris is not computable except in light-years. It is true that no man is good enough to be another man's master. But it is a truth of equal validity (and one which has the added advantage of not being valid only in the sphere of ethics) that there will always be masters. The Kelmscott Press nestled in the ivyclad Elysium of the Victorian sunset. Social justice as understood by the ecclesiastical legislator in the Middle Ages bloomed again in the mind of the burly, bearded, prosperous, Victorian craftsman.

Twentieth Century socialism has another social justice from that. It has no more illusions than a matron of an Infirmary. A world of prefabricated houses is *not* where the rainbow ends.

Liberty means for contemporary socialism the austere reverse of License: *Equality* no longer means a mechanical uniformity. It amounts, I think, to a declaration of the equality of the duke and the dustman. It is worth no more than old bus tickets to the dustman. What is *not* implied, however, is any change in the fundamental intellectual inequality of Prof. Einstein and Sir Waldron Smithers, for instance; or the physical inequality of Joe Louis and Professor Laski.

In the more general sense, the inequality of those richly endowed by nature is not threatened. Genuine inequalities are quite intact. All that is said is that the old *boss* is no longer there. That defines Equality.

Liberty has no florid connotations. There is no tendency to open wide all doors, shouting, 'This is Liberty Hall'! It is not like that. In truth the latter-day socialism is apt to be very fussy about people keeping where they belong. The miner is not encouraged to wander off and get a job as a ship's cook or a lion-tamer, as in the days of laissez-faire, nor are boys upon leaving school invited to exercise their fancy as to the ideal calling. They are to be 'directed'. No, the heyday for the small man who wanted to act big is rapidly passing, or of the man who claimed for himself a higher wage for being lazy than for hard work; or for the dumb who were rewarded for being so stupid. The last few decades of Liberalism were the golden age for all that.

This is therefore a particularly favourable moment for considering proposals for the elimination of friction between the backward and the enlightened, seeing that there is no sentimental obstruction, of a kind that would always favour the stupid as against the intelligent, the idle and irresponsible as against the diligent and conscientious, the destructive as against the creative. A tough public mind is taking the place of a soft one.

This new socialism bleakly recognises that there are rough and dirty and dangerous trades that cannot be made into anything else: that society will always, somehow, be divided into people who boss (or 'manage' or direct) and those who do the dull, inconspicuous, uninteresting work. The dream of everybody working two hours a day in a post-office or shoe-factory, and for the rest of the time attending an art-school or a dramatic academy, is archaic.

In view of this changed outlook a genuine Utopia of work is possible — not a spurious arty and crafty one: one in which everybody does exactly what nature — not man — indicates. So, instead of a tawdry pipe-dream, a rational ordering of life according to fundamental aptitude becomes the aim: the actor will act; the politician govern and inflate himself; the research-worker, the profit-motive banished, work with more profit to science; the butcher will dissect his carcases, without cutting out all the best bits for the richest customers; the lawyer will pettifog, as is his nature; the dentist gas people for the extraction; the detective shadow his man; the money-lender practise (in a small way) his usury; the etcher etch; the sculptor sculpt; the fiddler saw at his sobbing and shrieking instrument.

The changes I am anticipating are a happy recognition of structural unchangeability. The life-pattern of the miner or butcher will be identical, except for the different destination of the butcher's best pieces of meat, and the better equipment for the pits (though coal will still be dirty and heavy). — It is the illusion of change in respect to something that is in the nature of things fixed, which creates a sentimental instability, and obstructs authentic change.

Change can occur at the top alone. Because of the new fixity greater freedom will be possible at the top. But the top will be the real summit: and I do not mean 'Guardians' or any kind of *political* apex. (I am not thinking on philosopher-king lines.) I refer to a summit consisting of the departments of the social body which are fundamentally the most complex, conscious, and highly individualised.

———

All *élite* theories — to which this does not belong — suffer from a priggish taint, even a crème de la crèmishness. The very world *élite* holds up its nose in the air and emits a fastidious sniff. The more intellectual minority proposed here as the occupational nucleus of a partitioned-off *area of creative development* as it were, at the apex of a massive human group, takes with it no effluvium of éliteness, at least not as conceived by me.

Here is something throwing light upon this way of thinking, 'What's in a name, if a workman is allowed to work? All any true scientist or true artist asks is to be given the opportunity, without interference, indifferent to glory, to *work*.'* If what I at present propose were not more fundamental than, and quite different from, the traditional social division into a 'higher' and 'lower' class, it would not be worth considering.

The plan under discussion is strictly practical in aim; calling, or occupation, is the sole principle involved in the establishment of the frontier between (1) the changeless Many, and (2) the changeable Few: the unfree and the free. What it says is that an astronomer's, a mathematician's, a composer's, an historian's, or a philosopher's is a high and severe occupation. It immensely extends the horizons of the individual so engaged, it involves

* 'A. of B. R.' p. 117.

creation, daily a new and free effort; whereas what a butcher, watchmaker, excise clerk, operative on an assembly line, lighthouse keeper, or railway porter does is mechanical, requiring no conscious intelligence or imagination. – In 'The Art of Being Ruled' I gravitated to a more idealistic division. But whichever way we approach it, I do not think that man will ever cease to turn, in more optimistic moments, to this solution.

Élite theories, from Plato to Nietzsche, are in every case theories of government. The élite, because of its innate superiority, rules over the servile mass. It enjoys ruling, and its time is mainly occupied in that way.

In Nietzsche's case the matter was complicated by Darwinian backgrounds. He saw a past of mankind evolving into some super-human form, just as man had left behind his simian phase. The melodramatic disdain this Prussian professor developed for the *canaille* he was leaving behind upon the evolutionary ladder was remarkable. A sort of feudalism was the result.

It is most necessary to make it very clear that there is not the least taint of *Uebermenschlichkeit* anywhere in my mind. I hope I have been successful in doing this. – A plumber, while I write, is working in my bathroom. I am working here. He is putting in a new waste pipe for my bath. What I am doing is more ambitious than repair work. I am as it were proposing a new bath – a new house. But *not* a new mankind. Just a stricter separation of the different functions.

Harry the plumber (who has a head like a Fifteenth Century French king) is impenetrable. So no doubt am I. Out of our two impenetrabilities we greet each other in brotherly style. He tells me of his day-long diarrhoea earlier in the week: I am a casualty of the bottleneck at Notting Hill Gate, hence – I tell him – my recumbent position. We talk of wounds, and the blue ring of healing flesh, of house drains, of diarrhoea.

Our outlook on life is wholly different but our two jobs are both earthbound, connected with the problems arising from the faulty character of our human workmanship. There is no difference *in kind*. However, Harry would not enjoy taking my place – he would far prefer to be under my bath, looking for a leak. I was not taught to plumb when young, so I should not like to be him. – On a strictly human footing we are friends. It is only if Harry and I sat together on a committee to decide what kind of statue should be erected to commemorate President Roosevelt that things would cease to go smoothly. I should say, perhaps, that I have not formed part of such a committee. But had I done so I feel quite sure that most of my fellow members would have been Harrys.

———

The practical occupational cleavage I have proposed would of course have to be prevented from degenerating into a vulgar top-dog one. In 'The A. of B. R.' a tincture of intolerance here and there regarding the backward, slothful, obstructive majority – 'homo stultus' – is present. That I will – regretfully – allow. But in a mixed society, the sciences and the arts have to be protected against Caliban: against Matthew Arnold's *Philistine*, Flaubert's *Bourgeois*, or Swift's *Yahoo*. Or rather to protect them adequately is an impossible task: the sciences are misdirected and misused, the Arts scorned—debased, diluted, vulgarised, brought to the level of an unintelligent pastime. Bitter impatience with the philistine or the bourgeois it is natural to experience: but that is an emotion very different in origin from a snobbish disdain. That is a distinction upon which I continue to insist.

I speak, in 'The Art of Being Ruled', of a division as profound as that between one species and another. But let me quote a little from Part V of that book. 'Goethe had a jargon of his own for referring to these two species whose existence he perfectly recognised. He divided people into *Puppets* and *Natures*. He said the majority of people were machines, playing a part. When he wished to express admiration for a man, he would say about him, "He is a *nature*." This division into natural men and mechanical men . . . answers to the solution advocated in this essay. And today there is an absurd war between the "puppets" and the "natures", the machines and the men.'

But having said that, I recognised how these mechanical men are the natural allies of technology, of machinery. '. . . owing to the great development of machinery, the pressure on the "natures" increases. We are *all* slipping back into machinery.' In a Machine Age, however, the problem is always present of whether the machine will not reduce the man to its own automatical level. Goethe's human 'machines' or 'Puppets' would be the active abettors of such a decline to automatism.

My earlier references to the Unconscious, and the manner in which an entire generation has been encouraged to withdraw into those labyrinths, may at this point be recalled. Goethe's 'machines' would exist upon a much lower level of consciousness, obviously, than his 'natures'.

The new social pattern I advocate is, as I have remarked, not a theory of the State. It is not concerned with the art of ruling. Yet the success of any social system depends upon effective government. As it happens this new hierarchic-occupational pagoda has inherent in it a technique of government. All that is necessary is a recognition of the character of the 'Puppets'.

To recognise that the 'mechanical' type of men do not aspire to be agents: that they are happiest when weighed down with a minimum of responsibility — that for them to be free is *not to be free* (or that subservience is freedom — freedom from responsibility): this is essential. To enjoy freedom in any significant sense is the last thing they desire. A setter, a pointer, a retriever wish to fulfil those functions their names indicate. They like to hear 'their master's voice', which it is their joy to obey. The majority of men want as little authority themselves as that. As I put it in 'The A. of B. R.' (to re-quote) 'absence of responsibility, an automatic and stereotyped rhythm, is what men most desire'. And further: 'consciousness and possession of the self is not compatible with a set rhythm'.

I went so far as to cite the ideal of obedience of the early Jesuits, quoting that 'a member of their order should regard himself as a corpse, to be moved here or there at will' and I comment that to describe this as 'inhuman' (as is so often done) is a shallow sentimentalism. For do not most people desire to be dolls; 'to be looked after, disciplined into insensitiveness, spared from suffering by insensibility and blind dependence on a will superior to their own'. And those words of mine have cost me dear – ridiculous as that even today may seem.

The Jesuits, however, were fanatics. I took that exaggerated illustration to capture the reader's fancy. The quiet jog-trot of everyday repels such violent images. The people we are talking about are quite unpicturesque and usually stolid. Summon to your mind the khaki-clad citizen army, and sufficient evidence is furnished by that of how readily men merge themselves in an iron pattern. The toes on our two feet could not respond to others more blindly: these infatuated men include their death among the things they would not dream of denying to authority.

The sole aim of this elaborate re-discussion has been not to answer criticism so much as to counter misinterpretations. I was congratulated a short while ago by a man known to you all by name, upon this particular book. In discussing it with him I was embarrassed to find that he regarded it – approvingly – as teaching something 'managerial', of great interest to prospective 'leaders of men' or those managerially minded.

That the power-technician might learn something from it I suppose is true, as the poisoner can learn something from a treatise on narcotics. But it was certainly not in the interests of power in any shape or form that I wrote it. This re-discussion will I hope have cleared this up. My difficulty is, and was, that the stark unvarnished truth has to compete with flattering, even adulatory, versions of the same thing. One is always in a weak position if one is speaking the truth. I should be very sorry if it were thought that I *enjoyed* what is revealed of human feebleness, or lack of independence. Then there is the added enfeeblement and apathy for which the European decadence is responsible. No reader of 'Time and Western Man' or 'Paleface' can suppose that I am *enthusiastic* about that. But I do see that it is no doubt forced upon us by circumstances: like most things, it has a useful side. This decay of the will and apathy can be made use of. So in a sense I make a virtue of necessity.

I have just said that one is always in a weak position if one is speaking the truth. Anything that can lay claim to be the truth is necessarily of extreme complexity. If you simplify, it is no longer the truth. Too relentless a search for what *is* has often obtained for a man an evil reputation. Also, there must be nothing ill-favoured about what at length you exhibit as the result of your search. 'Beauty is truth, truth beauty' – you have to remember that. They demand, in other words, a pretty picture (vide my earlier chapters).

A primitive peasantry will never believe that an entomologist or ornithologist engaged in field work among them is doing what he is doing. They think he is searching for hidden treasure, or is mentally deranged. Men are like that about any activity that does not, if unorthodox, conform to a routine aberration.

This has been a kind of key chapter. Elsewhere in this book I reply to attacks made upon me by individuals, as was the case in Chapter XV. Here I have not been doing that: it is not an individual attack I have been concerned with, but what is apparently a widespread misapprehension, regarding what is implied in my text. Stating, in other words but in even more uncompromising terms, my position — as to the best technique for the governee to avoid getting crushed or losing a limb in the power-house of which we are the unhappy inmates — I have struck at the root, I think, of this misunderstanding.

Misapprehension we take for granted. It inheres in this time of ours — hyper-sensitive, averse to candour, suspicious, persecutory, and above all one-track. For many decades flattery of the 'sovereign people' has been so much *de rigueur* as to make it impossible to speak plainly without inviting the accusation of being *anti-people:* anti-people and therefore *pro* their traditional rulers, either royal, or aristocratic, or capitalistic. I believe I may have succeeded in conveying that I am not pro *any* ruler. I am — after my fashion — all the time upon the side of the *ruled.* I identify myself with humanity, and regard Government as the most deadly machine of all those invented by men. But it is quite indispensable.

Notes

[1] War novels by Erich Maria Remarque (*All Quiet on the Western Front*) and Richard Aldington.

[2] There is a series of Low cartoons of MacDonald (but not including the one Lewis mentions) in *The Tragedy of Ramsay MacDonald* by L. MacNeill Weir (London, n.d.).

CHAPTER XXXII

DEFENCE OF WESTERN CULTURE

ARRIVING as I do now at 'Time and Western Man' I feel that I am standing before a substantial fortress, once full of vigorous defenders, but now silent, probably a place where bats hang upside down and jackals find a musty bedchamber. To be frank, I have no desire to re-enter it. — What was it set there to defend? Obviously the Western World, which in less than two decades has fallen to pieces.

A society, or a group of societies, which were so feebly led, so easy a prey to faction, so defenceless against claptrap and emotional slogans, so unable to distinguish the spurious from the genuine, so demoralised and given over to feuds, had little survival value; I am glad the *coup de grâce* has been delivered — by itself, to itself. Western Europe, bankrupt, if possible more confused than ever, broken and apathetic, awaits the coming of the next phase, whatever that may be — still feebly wrangling about frontiers that no longer mean anything; making itself new constitutions, contrived apparently to produce instantaneous deadlock; existing in an inflationary morass, the only stable thing left an outsize flourishing Black Market.

No one in 1947 would be likely to give a thought to 'Western Man'. How hollow a ring the two words have, with their ironical capitals! Yet there was such an entity. It is only necessary to mention at random a few of the beacons along the road he has travelled, since his archaic starting-point — Darwin, Voltaire, Newton, Raphael, Dante, Epictetus, Aristotle, Sophocles, Plato, Pythagoras: all shedding their light upon the same wide, well-lit graeco-roman highway, with the same kind of sane and steady ray — one need only mention these to recognise that it was at least excusable to be concerned about the threat of extinction to that tradition.

The type of mind belonging to that particular tradition is, among the other types produced so far by the various cultures, the one I happen to prefer. For it to remain intact, however, and to transmit its ways of thinking to other generations, Western Europe had to remain intact.

Any person concerned to perpetuate that kind of mind, would not be indifferent to the fate of Western Europe; and, it follows, would be greatly opposed to a continuance of its fratricidal wars — first Franco-Prussian, then Anglo-Prussian. He would know that in these terrible blood-baths Western culture would drown — as now at last it has.

Already in the days of the gunboat 'Panther', gliding into the bay at Agadir and anchoring under its crenelated Kasba — Edward the Peacemaker (what strange subtitles kings acquire!) and his theatrical nephew the German Kaiser engaging in a little game of noughts and crosses — as far back as that 'Western Man' was as good as finished. When in 1914 'the lights went out' in Europe, they went out for good. So in 1926 it was somewhat late to build a fortress against the barbarian.

Before you laugh at that, however, ask yourself if, even today, *you* are fully conscious of the fact that the Western tradition is forever passed away — as a living thing at least. As history, its phantom will be visible for many years, deceiving the inattentive eye. Suffering at present from an attack of that most unenglish complaint, nationalism, England has gone to live with its history: so here people may get along quite comfortably with the ghost — rather preferring it to the real thing.

———

For me — as much as for a man of the Fifteenth Century, say — Western Europe was what I recognised as the home of my mind. As you know, I have now extended that cultural habitat in all directions, becoming a universalist, making the world my parish. I have plunged into the cultural melting-pot, in other words: and with me a small fraction of what was Western Man has surrendered his identity to that more comprehensive synthesis. There is no occasion for me to apologise for my present indifference to Western Culture. I see a quite different road, on to which everything is moving bodily and I with it.

This more massive highway should lead to a more rational type of society. There is no repudiation here. The West has delivered its contribution, has come the full circle, from Pythagoras and his numerical universe to the likewise numerical atomic basis of the material world as adumbrated by contemporary physicists, so that the distinction of one substance from another turns out to be a matter of numerical patterns.

In another chapter I have confessed how I have not been free of vacillation. I saw a culture I was born into being dissolved or picked to shreds by an ant-like process. I have had romantic rebellions. It seems to me that I should have forgotten the Past entirely. At this time I am perhaps culturally — politically — a little where I was in 'The Caliph's Design'. I perceive as it were a white and shining city, a preposterous Bagdad, in place of the contemporary ruins, social and architectural, of 1947.

On the other hand, I am fully conscious, in the present case, of how incapable people are of rational behaviour. Atomic power (to restate in brief what I have exhaustively canvassed in another place) by reducing their normal irresponsible behaviour, in the matter of war, to an absurdity, will do what seemed yesterday the impossible. There is better than an even chance at least of that.

———

The place occupied by Western culture is being rapidly filled by something else. Is 'Time and Western Man', therefore, only of historic value — as a technique for the defence of Western culture, had that not been past help? It is, I believe, far more than that, and its techniques possess a permanent usefulness. All the arguments seem to me just as valid now as the day they were written. The group of thinkers upon which I delivered an assault — 'Time-philosophers' I named them — represent a type of thinking common to all ages. They increase in numbers and influence in such a period as this. In all times and places, however, they should be answered in the manner used in this book. It should be a permanent armoury for the reduction of their pretentions.

Miss Stein and many like her, exponents in the 'creative' field of the 'time-philosophy', will, three centuries hence, be recognised as what they are, the dark stammering voice of a social dissolution. If when I wrote my book, or now, the Western spirit were defensible, that would be the way to defend it. The second, or more purely philosophic, part – and the more valuable – attains, I venture to think, a validity distinct from the issues prompting the construction of this dialectical fortress.

The fact that I now am interested in advancing ideas of an entirely different order, would present no obstacle to my giving you an idea of the contents of that book – which represents, in a sense, the limits of my oscillation – as much as of 'The Lion and the Fox', for instance. But it would demand a great deal of space. More especially the second part has been made the widest use of – without acknowledgment – both by poets, novelists, and essayists. To such things a half-suppressed author becomes perfectly accustomed. So finally let me recommend it as an excellent place to steal from if too lazy or too stupid to think out anything of your own, or if of a naturally thievish disposition. In that bleak fortress there is still much loot.

CHAPTER XXXIII

WHAT IS AN 'ENEMY'?

THE year 1927 saw the publication of 'The Lion and the Fox', 'Time and Western Man', a book of stories called 'The Wild Body', and Vol. I of my large magazine 'The Enemy'. This was, I should think, a record volume of printed matter to be discharged at the public in a single year. Evidence of an inordinate vanity might be seen by some people in this orgy of self-expression. That is not, however, the explanation.

Let me begin with the economic angle. What I wrote was not of the kind that involves a really boisterous sale. Philosophy or literary criticism are in the same sales-category as poetry. Customarily the author of such a book as 'The Lion and the Fox' is teaching at a university, or is an official of some kind. The money he receives from the sale of a book is a pleasant little windfall, enabling him to pass a vacation in Lapland, or in Mexico; to spend a little more than he normally would – or to give his wife a dyed ermine coat, or buy a new car. I had actually to *live* on quite unmunificent advances. I did no journalism. Most journalistic channels were blocked, for me, by 'Bloomsburies', who filled, as they still do, the politico-literary press, where fairly profitable reviewing was to be had. And 'la grande presse' was of course not open to me. I was a 'highbrow' and a 'difficult' and contentious 'highbrow' at that.

It is not my meaning that this great output is wholly to be accounted for by the struggle for existence. But had I been able to secure a fair amount of journalism I should no doubt have produced fewer volumes. In lieu of journalism I was apt to write a book. Where people would have written several articles of considerable length, I would start a magazine or do a pamphlet.

The oddity of this procedure was fully recognised by me. A full-length book ought to be more than a pamphlet. Yet publishers have no fondness for pamphlets. They stand out for their seventy-five thousand words minimum of text.

Economic difficulties, with which I began, were greatly aggravated by another factor, to which I shall now refer. I knew that as a novelist I could never get past the cordon of ill-disposed Bloomsbury critics, unless I went aside continually, counter-criticised, and of course propagandised, on my own account. Every book I wrote would have to be vigorously defended by at least one pamphlet, in the way that a capital ship requires the support of one or more smaller and more active craft. Just to write novels, however good they were, was useless. I could write a hundred 'Childermasses' and they would be shot to pieces, or still worse ignored. I had offended a literary sect or coterie, which largely had control of 'highbrow' criticism, too deeply at the beginning.

Some of my lesser books, as writing, were extremely hurried; in some cases, I regret to say, slipshod. At the time I had a sort of rule, to the effect that one page of fiction should take anything from five to ten times as long as a page of non-fiction: which does not allow for a very beautiful page of prose. But I regarded the whole business as a tiresome necessity. These were not to be monuments of controversial style: I devoted just as much time to controversy – for which I have no particular liking – as the occasion demanded and no more.

The little rule to which I have just alluded, about the time to be devoted to a page of fiction or of non-fiction respectively, had of course nothing to do with the question of the greater labour involved in creative composition. I looked upon it as five or ten times as important, that is all.

These remarks do not apply to the two books I have named at the beginning of this chapter; but it certainly would to 'Paleface' or 'Hitler'. In no case, however, did I take the same great trouble with a book of criticism of any sort, at that period, as I did with 'Childermass', for instance, or 'The Revenge for Love'. – I now believe this policy to have been mistaken. But I do not know quite how I should have lived, had I suffered from crafts-manly compunctions, in the first two or three years of my literary life proper. Merely re-writing 'Tarr', I recall, took longer than it did to write a book named 'The Diabolical Principle'. The latter appeared first in 'Enemy No. III', comprising the main body of the text.

Finally, had they not been silenced or discouraged by a lively cross-fire from my hasty pamphleteering, out of magazines and books, the literary militia of Bloomsbury would have sunk all my books, one by one, as they appeared. – As it was, I suffered damage, of course. A method employed by some ill-disposed critics is to go to the office of the literary editor of a paper (known to them, of course), take away a book for review, and forget to review it, so that no notice of it appears in that particular paper. This blank is almost more valuable than a sneering review, or a damning with faint and weary praise. My enemies of that time were versed in all the stratagems of literary warfare.

I possessed friends and supporters too, however, gained for me by my books, not as a result of social contact, political eligibility, or a log-rolling compact. 'Bloomsbury' and other things notwithstanding, I had no reason to complain of the press.

———

The title of the magazine, 'The Enemy', has a sinister sound, just as 'Blast', my first magazine, had an explosive one. The selection of so menacing a title was merely on the principle of giving the sensation-loving public what it wants. – All children enjoy being startled, or delight in a loud bang. 'The Enemy' as a title, like 'Blast', was a pleasantry.

But 'The Enemy' signifies a little more than just a cute name for a new paper. It was intended to convey, first, that the criticism to be found within was uncompromising. Julien Benda is quoted on p. x of 'Enemy No. I'. And that provides as good an explanation as any of the type of 'enmity' intended. – I was not the first to notice, I wrote, 'that peculiar, debilitated, *unanimity* typical of the present period'. Benda had drawn attention to its prevalence among the French. Well, I will undertake to supply the greatly needed *discord!* That was the idea. 'Discord' would have been a more accurate title than 'Enemy'. Here, however, is what I quote from Benda.

'Our documents for determining the aesthetic tendencies of present-day French society are . . . above all, the works of those authors who obviously give – seeing their success – the greatest satisfaction to the public taste, and must most accurately represent it. One is sorry to have to remark that those authors are of second rank, and that that law enunciated in other times by a critic (Faguet) according to which *good writers, far from incarnating the prejudices of a time, are on the contrary, opposed to them,* no longer holds in our day.'

Following these words of Benda's I write: 'All other times have bred criticism and its wholesome revolts and corrections . . . by this toleration those times have shown that they possess some humility, or in other cases that they were great enough to allow censure. The names we remember in European literature are those of men who satirised and attacked, rather than petted, or fawned upon, their contemporaries. Only *this* time exacts an uncritical hypnotic sleep of all belonging to it. This . . . is the sleep of the machine.'

We had at that period (1927) entered the hush which has grown deeper every year, until today there are few people who disagree or dissent for fear of a bad mark. I took the decision to break that hush. I spoke with as much boldness as if I had been living in the Eighteenth Century – or in the Ritz. It is the last time there will be *discord* of that kind in England. This is not a boast. I am sorry to have to say it, but my forecast will prove only too correct.

———

The particular note of solitary defiance – and I find it recurring even now as I take myself back into that period and begin speaking of the 'Enemy' – what must have seemed an exaggerated individualism on my part, in 'The Tyro', as much as in 'The Enemy', is not to be traced, oddly enough, to love of the ego, but to a sense of *typicalness:* of a type out of place. I have never felt in the least alone.

From the time I first recognised it I have regarded this *typical* factor as something meriting special consideration. Certainly there were not many people who thought as I did about anything. I did not look upon myself as 'a rare type,' however. I could not understand why most of my acquaintances looked at most things as they did, and as I did not.

Before continuing I would like to lay stress on what is the essence of this paradox: namely the originality in question did not seem peculiar to me as an *individual.* (All these remarks have no bearing upon the current denigration of 'individualism', which I recognise, of course, as mere political strategy. In the collectivisation of society people make it their business to root out 'individualism' – synonymous with nonconformity – to eliminate the 'sport'.)

As they were generally senior to me at the start, the outlook of the majority of my friends I regarded as something to which I should eventually attain – just as their way of signing their names aroused my admiration: the more incomprehensible the hieroglyphic, the more I admired it. But my critical faculties slowly awakened. I began to criticise their reasoning for its worldly uniformity of outlook. That is how it began.

It was not my ambition, as it was that of my earliest friends, to be as like somebody else as possible, or everybody else. I was astonished at the eager slickness with which they picked up slang, for example. So I decided to stand outside this perpetual acting.

I am obliged to confess that in my youth I came to consider any discrepancy I detected as meaning that I was right and the majority wrong. After a time I came to see – allowing for varying degrees of intelligence or of taste, and putting that aside – that it was just an odd angle of vision of some sort. It might be of no importance but it was better, I thought, to keep it rather than force it into a conformity unnatural to it. It did not matter being rather odd; like an albino in the physiological order. – It was probably a good thing to have something so contradictory around: somebody who did not hasten to agree with everybody else. I will not say, 'Hence "Blast" and the "Enemy," ' of course. Something of these psychological backgrounds, that is all, contributed to the particular note of mock defiance: the images of the bedizened horseman, or the masked harlot swaggering across the cover of the latter of these reviews.

Naturally by the time of my 'Enemy' period, I had come to understand that I belonged to a widely diffused human group. Undoubtedly there were very few of us in England. All the more reason to insist upon the type-side of the matter, it appeared to me.

The gist of this excursion into psychology is that I felt it to be an accident – a disagreeable one – that I was straying around by myself. I was a group-animal, behaving as one of the solitary breeds by chance (I never confused myself with lions or eagles). I had all the confidence of a herd – that was not there. In England there had been numbers of us at one time. I knew that from the books I read. Many of their authors thought the way I did.

———

Let us retrospectively applaud that bold discordant voice. It did not harmonise with a time of great demoralisation. Here I must ask, however, as in the case of 'Time and Western Man' – 'Why show such concern if you detect some degenerate little Briton, or a whole litter of them, concocting knock-out drops for that poor old nitwit, once Western Man, which if he was so far gone in his dotage or degeneracy as to swallow them – well, why interfere?' – I now applaud the end, however much I might despise the means. So I criticise the 'Enemy' on certain sides, without any change in my low opinion of his enemies.

CHAPTER XXXIV

'GRANDIOSE TOYS . . . ENDOWED WITH
UNEXPECTED INTELLIGENCE'

A NOVEL—if you can call it that—'The Childermass', has no place in this survey. It is about Heaven: the politics of which, although bitter in the extreme, have no relation to those of the earth, so they do not concern us here. Its appearance in 1928 caused no controversy: there were no assailants with whom I have to settle accounts. No one said they were 'in it'—nobody claimed to be the Bailiff or Hyperides—there were no claimants to be the original of Satters or of Pulley. It was not put on the Index, as several of my books have been. It can be sold in the Dublin bookshops. Its history has been the most peaceful of any of my books. And blessed is the book without a history — or rather, without 'des histoires'! The second volume, when it appears, may change all that: I can only speak for volume one.

It has often been asserted that this is my best book. Unfortunately, it is, as I say, only half a book: its completion may, I hope, not be long delayed. But I have promised that before. A serious disagreement with the publishers obliged me to sever all connections with that firm. A new publisher would have to undertake to buy the unbound sheets, such copies as remain, and commission me to finish it. As yet I have not been able to make an arrangement of this kind. It is a great pity. But business is business.

'The Apes of God', on the other hand, fits into the pattern certainly. It produced a great deal of disturbance, I have spoken of this work once or twice already. The social decay of the insanitary trough between the two great wars is its subject, and it is accurate. However it is magnified and stylised. It is not portraiture. A new world is created out of the shoddy material of everyday, and nothing does, or could, go over into that as it appeared in nature.

Many people have asserted that they are the originals. All these claims are invalid. There is, as an illustration of this, a figure called 'Dan', who is described as a ravishingly beautiful young man: like the St. John of Leonardo, a male peach. This character suffers from nose-bleeding in the pages of my book — by no means an uncommon thing in youth. Someone who was young at that time, but whose intense physical beauty I had never, for my part, noticed, told me one day that he had recognised himself. I said how—who? He said Dan! Then he reminded me that his nose sometimes had bled. At which I sternly pointed out that Dan, in the book, was an authentic naïf—in fact a simpleton. It made no difference at all: and this man—for he is now a big hairy man—is still persuaded he is Dan.

There was another man who got five hundred pounds out of a newspaper because it had reported, in its gossip column, that he was a character in 'The Apes of God', whereas I had declared that he was not. Now since the figures are, all of them, by reason of their scale and their vitality, remote from the photographic reality of life, as I observed above: and in this satiric dimension, as we might call it, are most unlike the beings we meet with every day; even if people believed they saw a resemblance to themselves – which would be the effect of a lively fancy only, since there are no 'portraits' there – it would be very vain of them to object: unless, that is, their resentment were assumed, which is sometimes the case.

H. G. Wells and I had an 'Apes of God' lunch together at that time: he had some interesting things to say on the subject of the rage that people may *affect to feel*, and their motives. Self-advertisement is a principal one. Wells, as a satirist, spoke *en connaissance de cause*.

So much has been said already about Satire in general, in Part I, that I need say little more. The David Low type of pictorial satire, as I showed there (and the parallel is entirely valid) is much more devastating than the Vicki type. Vicki carries his victims off into another dimension: they can laugh good-naturedly at what happens to them there, because those images cannot be identified with the originals, whereas in the case of Low's naturalistic portrayals, to laugh is much more difficult for them. So with these 'Apes' of mine. They are plainly puppets. As a proof of this let me quote a letter from Mr. Augustus John. 'In your "Apes of God" you have,' he writes, 'as it were, suspended upon magical wires colossal puppets, whose enlarged and distorted features may be attributed to those of not a few contemporary figures known to fame, infamy, and myself. Some of these you, from your own superabundance, have endowed with unexpected intelligence; others, by an ingenious operation of trepanning, you have bereft of what wits they had or could lay claim to. – These grandiose toys you manipulate with a gargantuan and salutary art unexampled in our or any other time I know of. Your readers and especially, I feel, your subjects, must be compelled, before the work of criticism begins, to salute with a wide and comprehensive flourish the lofty genius of the author. – This act of homage and surrender I now myself perform.'

Following this most gratifying of tributes from a great painter in whose eyes, as you see, this was a 'gargantuan puppet-show' (and that view, as I have explained, is mine as well) I will bring forward a tribute of a different order, this time from a writer. He seems impressed rather by a dynamic quality in this book, of a kind not belonging to puppetry. The terms in which this tribute is couched are so exceedingly flattering that I almost hesitate to reproduce it here. It is evident that Mr. Richard Aldington (for it was he) looked upon me as fulfilling the time-honoured functions of the satirist – consisting of the dropping of molten metal or administering of punitive buffets to the fatuous, the overweening, or the crooked.

'I was excited to learn from "Everyman" that you are already engaged on another novel. . . . There is no one who can write like you, and you have a tremendous opportunity. . . . "The Apes of God" is the most tremendous knock-out ever made. And the most brilliantly witty piece of writing, merely as writing, which I have ever read. You needn't ever doubt that you have added something permanent to European literature.'

The extreme decay of the bourgeois era, preceding the present socialist one, was what I depicted. It was its last sickly saraband. W. B. Yeats's view was that everyone would attack 'The Apes' – or ignore it: but that it would be amusing to watch how it altered things in London. Yeats's judgement was at fault. Nothing could change the kind of people of whom I wrote — they had not the necessary vitality for that.

Finally, any reader interested in techniques, for the occultation of certain authors, and the conferring upon others of iridescent reputations, should refer to the pamphlet 'Satire and Fiction'. Roy Campbell had been asked to write a review of 'The Apes of God' for a certain London periodical: the acting literary editor returned the review with a four-page letter in which, among other things, he said:

'I'm afraid I cannot publish your review as it stands. I find you take a far more serious view of its (The Apes of God's) merits than I can, and indeed take Mr. Lewis altogether more seriously than I think is justified.'

Things of this sort happen all the time: indeed there are certain papers in London in which no reviewer would be allowed to treat a book of mine even with respect. It is a rare occasion, however, for the reviewer to endanger his own interests by divulging what is going on. To have such a flagrant example of discrimination to expose was an event of which I took full advantage. In a substantial pamphlet I published the correspondence, the Rejected Review, and many other relevant items.

It is not the only review of a book of mine returned to its author to which I shall refer. Shortly I shall give the fact about another and equally bad case of editorial dictation, the scene in that case being New York, however.

When one considers the great number of trashy books which every year are permitted to meet with an unctuous reception by complacent editors in their review columns, one sees perfectly well how natural it is for such a writer as myself to be unpopular. All the same, were that not resisted no good book in the end would ever get past, unless backed by a powerful coterie: so in defending myself I play a not unuseful part, and defend many, many, other people. I am a sort of public bodyguard.

CHAPTER XXXV

REBECCA WEST AND CARLO LINATI

LET me open this chapter with a quotation. The author of the article from which I take this passage is discussing Spengler. — 'Now, it is puzzling that Spengler should have got any sort of prestige in this country . . . he has been the subject of some brilliant criticism that should have finally discredited him by now. There was Mr. Wyndham Lewis's superb disquisition in "Time and Western Man" which cut through the stuff like cheese. Why did not that have greater effect? And that raises another question. Why does Mr. Wyndham Lewis not produce a greater effect on his time? There is no one who has had greater acumen in detecting the trends of contemporary thought that are not candid, that are merely rationalisations of a desire to flee towards death. There is no one whose dialectic style is more sparkling. There is no one who can more deeply thrill one by a vivid and novel vision (as in parts of "Childermass"). Why is it that he is not moulding the intellectual life of his time more powerfully than he does? — There is a partial explanation in his new book "Paleface" '.*

So 'Paleface' is a clue. And it is about that book I am writing in this chapter. It is one of the pamphlet-books I spoke of; not a job of which I am technically very proud. — The writer of the lines I have just quoted was, and is, one of the two or three acutest critics in England. (I have quoted her once before.) From early days she has been very generous in what she has written about my books. Here she asks a question to which the present volume is designed to supply an answer. For if that question were not asked by many people beside Miss West, and often answered in a highly unsatisfactory way, I should not be writing it.

Rebecca West could not have chosen a better illustration than 'Paleface' to explain things. 'Time and Western Man' itself, however — which she mentions too — should have afforded enlightenment. — You cannot contradict your time too flatly and be influential. That is impossible. Such men as Voltaire, or as Mr. Shaw, were very contradictory and contentious: but it was not their *time* they contradicted. It was not what was most vigorous in it they attacked. *They were perfectly in tune with the Zeitgeist.*

To quote again: 'Mr.Lewis has picked out the admiration for the Negro that has been fashionable in intellectual circles during the last few years here and in New York, as an example of the movement towards death. . . . And there, I believe, he is wrong.' According to Miss West these fashions, far from spelling weakening of Western culture, signified the opposite of that.

Events, I think, will prove that Western culture was *not* exactly on the up and up; that this and cognate fashions were not at all examples of its vigour. I was right, I believe, and Miss West, in this particular matter, wrong. Where *I* was wrong was to care what happened to Western culture; or to suppose, even if it were desirable, that it could survive in the

* Rebecca West, 'Time and Tide', 24 May 1929.

new era we were entering upon: of which world war i and the Russian Revolution were the opening blasts and nuclear energy the perfect symbol.

What I was saying in 'Paleface' would be violently disliked by nine out of ten intellectuals — not because it was unreasonable (and it is every day being endorsed by events) but because that internal and domestic imperialism of Black serfdom in the United States, was a primary emotional asset of the revolutionary, a prime target for agitation. These revolutionary interests were not paramount for Rebecca West: but she was better acquainted than I was with the circumstances, since she had lived in the States, and knew the extent to which discrimination against coloured people constituted a monstrous social injustice.

The political side of this question did not concern me at all. The cultural I thought should be independent of that in any case. My position there was very similar to that of Mr. Herbert Read today, who claims complete autonomy and independence for the artist. I cannot stop to discuss that: but I crashed head-on into a political racket. At the same time Miss West would see that the action I was taking against cultural miscegenation would react unfavourably upon the chances of Negro emancipation — and this was politics. I saw only at that time the obscene burlesque, only registered the howling and stamping of the primitive African horde. And I regretted Johann Sebastian Bach in the midst of a universal Boogiwoogie.

When all is said and done, there was, and is, a *cultural* problem there, to which our great sympathy for the Negro and horror at the conditions of semi-serfdom in which he still lives (and I was at Detroit at the time of the race-riots) should not blind us.

That I was not the only person in the world alive to that problem is evidenced by a letter from Ernest Hemingway (date 24 Oct. 1927) from which I shall quote a few lines. It is a reply to a letter of congratulation which I had sent him after reading 'Torrents of Spring'.[1] That book is a skit, and Sherwood Anderson the target of the satire.

'I am very glad you liked,' he writes, ' "The Torrents of Spring" and thought you destroyed the Red and Black Enthusiasm very finely in "Paleface". That terrible — about the nobility of any gent belonging to another race than our own (whatever it is) was worth checking. Lawrence you know was Anderson's God in the old days — and you can trace his effect all through A.'s stuff after he commenced reading him.'

I have always had a great respect for Hemingway. In quoting this I ought to say that I am quite ignorant of what today his views are upon such questions. I should suppose, like my own, very different. In what I have quoted, however, a reaction very unlike that of Rebecca West was common to both of us.

I am not setting up the author of 'For Whom the Bell Tolls' as a model. But he is the greatest writer in America and (odd coincidence) one of the most successful. Consequently, if such a book as 'Paleface' or the type of thinking displayed there greatly diminished my influence (as I am sure it did) among the intellectuals referred to by Rebecca West: then, what an original fellow Hemingway must be, for it did not prejudice him against

me at all. In fact 'Torrents of Spring' was, in fiction form, performing the
same purgative function as 'Paleface'.

Were Hemingway and I, then, a couple of eccentrics? – That of course
is not the explanation. What Rebecca West did not, I think, realise at that
date, was that there was *no one* – myself or anybody else – who could
possibly have 'influenced' in the way she meant, or 'moulded the minds of',
the intellectuals in question.

Their minds were as much shut as those of religionists, to any discourse
other than that of political edification upon marxist lines. They were as
impervious as an early Calvinist to anything but matters relating to their
political cult. Mention Kameneff or Zinovieff – Lenin, or the Communist
Manifesto – and they sprang into passionate attention. Speak of art as if it
mattered apart from the State, of common sense, of the ethics of technology,
of that very relevant subject, the politics of Machiavelli, and their lips curled,
their eyes went dead. The 'intellect' had got locked up in hysterical little
mechanisms. Any time after 1925 all that was 'merely' cultural was at an
end. There was no philosophy except the political backwash of Hegel; no
art, except violent and destructive sensationalism: no criticism except
marxist criticism, of the kind produced by Edmund Wilson.

Once a revolutionary régime is established, all is at once serene and quiet
on the art front. As explained earlier, the situation is loosening up already.
There is no serious resistance any more to the advance of State Capitalism.
The work of preliminary cultural destruction and propaganda is over. –
Peaceable little pictures of Flowerbarrows are creeping out again. Open
pats on the back are given to Royal Academicians.

How it came that Hemingway saw eye to eye with me was because he
was an unusually fine artist, so took a strong personal interest in what
happened to all the arts. His interest in politics was, I should say, very small.

––––

About the time of 'Paleface' I began, with considerable exhilaration,
to swim against the tide. The 'tide' is usually going in the wrong direction
anyway – or in the right direction in the wrong way. This particular tide
I was positive was doing so. All are now agreed, I think, that it was, and
that my diagnosis was correct.

It had at that moment the name of *Lawrence*: for 'tides' have names.
It was the floodtide of the great reputation of that sick man of genius. –
There was nothing antipathetic to the Red and the Black, of course, in 'Paleface'; it was against the exotic romanticism of Lawrence, involving 'poor-
white-trash' attitudes, not against the coloured skin.

'Paleface' attacked the visceral philosophy – 'the consciousness in the
abdomen', which (as I wrote) removes 'the vital centre into the viscera;
taking the controls out of the grasp of the "hated intellect" '.

D. H. Lawrence's abdominal raptures about the Mexican Indian
were backward-looking surely. The Mexican pantheon is not contemporary.
Send a peon to Yale or Oxford (as an experiment, not because this would be
good for him) and you will find out his abdomen was the same as anybody
else's. But he was dear to the avantgardist. I had sinned.

The wonderful job of debunking Hemingway did in 'Torrents of Spring', killed Sherwood Anderson's 'Dark Laughter' with laughter of the most dynamic quality.[2] 'Paleface' did a little laughing in the interests of that congenital topdog, the white man, lest his delusions be dispelled too brutally. It was indicated likewise that he had his points – as he has.

As evidence that no racialism disfigured this book let me quote[*]:

'The German philosophers of the beginning and middle of last century have perhaps provided us with the best example of "internationalism" of anyone in modern times: such men namely as Goethe or Schopenhauer. Schopenhauer's father gave him the name "Arthur" because Arthur is the same (he argued) in all European tongues. At least it is not exclusively German. . . . And Schopenhauer himself never ceased to criticise his countrymen for their german-ness. Nietzsche after him did the same. Goethe before him was quite as confirmed an "internationalist": he always advocated a universal language, a Volapuc, for Europe, and hoped for a confederacy of states and abolition of frontiers. – Today we are, with Fascism, with Irish, Czech, Catalan, Macedonian, Indian, Russian, Turkish, Polish, nationalism (which invariably takes the form of abolishing every local custom and becoming as like everybody else as possible) at the other pole to that goethean attitude of mind, so common a century ago, so rare today. This appears to me very regrettable indeed. I should like everybody to be imbued with the spirit of internationalism – and to keep all their local customs.

'In addition to my often expressed desire for a universal state, I have another craving, up till now unexpressed (that is publicly). I would, if I were able, suppress all out-of-date discrepancies of *tongue*, as well as of *skin* and of *pocket*. I should like to speak, and to write, Volapuc – or some tongue that would enable me to converse with everybody of whatever shade of opinion: – above all so that no shadow of an excuse should subsist for a great Chemical Magnate to come hissing in my ear: "Listen! That fellow says 'Ja' – I heard him. Here is a phial of deadly gas. Just throw it at him, will you? He won't say 'Ja' any more, once he's had a sniff of that!"

'But this is not the end of the matter . . . (nor of) the many difficulties that must confront any honest Paleface, called to the defence of his skin. Although people of a lightish complexion have overrun the globe, they have – he would be obliged to confess – taken with them – and stolidly, irresistibly, propagated – a civilisation which is exceedingly inferior to many of those they were destroying, belonging to people of dark, or "coloured" complexion.

'Confining ourselves to "skins", if this Paleface is informed that he has been inexcusably arrogant – his "superiority" at the best a very temporary, material, or technical, one – he cannot find much to answer. Further, the charge has to be met of having imposed often with great cruelty a rotten, materialist, civilisation upon all sorts of people, of having wiped out races of very high quality, such as the Indians of North America, in the name of a God who was all love and compassion. So he is convinced of hypocrisy of the ugliest – of the "civilised" – kind, on top of everything else.

'How can the White Man meet – for he cannot refute – these charges?

* 'Paleface' (pp. 67-69).

As an Anglo-Saxon he is unable to point to America and England today, and claim that the civilisation to be found in those countries is a justification of his dominion. What is he to do? If a timid man, as the Paleface often is, all those vindictive pointing fingers will put him quite out of countenance.

'Now I of course can find him arguments with which to meet his passionate critics. I am glad to do so, because his opponents are a stupid crew for the most part. All the same I recognise that my Paleface's case is dangerously open to attack.

'Worse than this, as an artist it is my conviction that all the very finest plastic and pictorial work has come out of the Orient: that Europeans have never understood the fundamental problems of art as have pre-eminently the Chinese. These hasty remarks will have served to define the nature of my disqualifications for the rôle of White deliverer.'

This typically 'hasty' passage makes it very clear that it was my design to attack the Paleface sentimentalising about the dark skin, and the mysterious dark soul within it (as if all souls were not mysterious), and *not* the Asiatic or the African. 'If the Negro community,' I pointed out elsewhere in that book, 'has not had a band of distinguished philosophers, men of science, and poets to point to, it is, I am sure, merely because the Negro has not had the opportunity.' But that was sweet reason, mere common sense. That was no good at all. And it would have irritated the Nazis, with their stupid race doctrine, just as much. My book was not accepted as a tonic for the White, but was attacked, by intellectuals, for not being in the pro-Black racket: for attaching a reactionary value to White culture.

Lawrence was a rather different issue. The red-hot partisanship aroused by poor Lawrence, who is now almost forgotten, is a curiosity of literary history. Only a few years ago (1940) in New York an English writer of my acquaintance went about for a while with an American woman-intellectual. He told me how one day 'Lady Chatterley's Lover' had been mentioned. He expressed contempt or indifference for it. Thereupon his lovely friend burst into tears. It was almost as if he had spoken disparagingly of her person; or had high-hatted the sexual impulse, while visiting the Venusberg.

This was the kind of atmosphere heavy with emotion one had to contend with from the start. When lecturing at Oxford once I ventured a few criticisms of Lawrence's 'dark unconscious'. Immediately I became aware of the presence of a 'dark unconscious'. Indeed the room was full of them. At the end of my address I was darkly heckled for half-an-hour by woman after woman.

Many people were just as sick as I was of Lawrence's invalid dreams, his arty voodooism. That was proved by the excellent reception the book received in a still largely independent press. But it added a black mark to my name. Those for whom books were either good or bad propaganda chalked it up as a *bad* book.

As I have quoted a distinguished English critic at the commencement of this chapter, let me end it with a passage showing how, about that time, my position looked to one of the most distinguished of Italian critics of the day, Carlo Linati. Surveying our scene from the other side of Europe, I appeared to him to be 'cursed'.

'Wyndham Lewis non è scrittore popolare,' he writes, 'è piuttosto un *outcast*, una specie di poeta maledetto che fa parte a sè e che pochi buoni stimano, appunto anche per questo.'

Introducing me to the Italian public: 'The name of this writer will be certainly little enough known to the student of contemporary English literature . . . the literary majority-reviews, however favourable and even enthusiastic they may be upon the appearance of one of his books, often have an air of forgetting him – wilfully.' As to anthologies, 'anthologies cite him rarely'. – It is a devastating picture.

He could, however, have gone farther than this; for, in fact, *no* anthology, to my knowledge, has ever included any work of mine. As to popular editions (Penguin, or what not) I have not 'made the grade'.

Are you not ashamed to be reading a book by such an insignificant author – whose works are thought so poorly of (whether 'Childermass', or 'The Apes of God', or 'The Revenge for Love', or 'Men Without Art') that no one has ever thought it worth while to ask his permission to use them in an anthology, or include them in an edition of 'contemporary classics' – or whatever they called their series of well-thought of contemporary authors?

To regain your confidence and self-respect, read again the quotation with which I opened, and discount what has happened to me from 'Paleface' onwards. (I could furnish you with many other tributes from the pens of the most eminent Twentieth Century writers, which would send your confidence rocketing up, did not a proper modesty and space forbid.) Remember that my occultation is a purely *political* phenomenon (taken full advantage of naturally by a hostile coterie). I will not include my 'highbrow' handicap. Many 'highbrows' have been imposed upon the general public by a coterie, or by the political intellectuals.

Well, it is pretty tough I know. But let us end on a Song.*

> 'I knew you'd like the Enemy! He's the person
> May pen in plastic fashion a new verse on
> The *Heldenleben* and collossi's lot,
> Or with his pen put penclubs on the spot.
> He knows to live comes first. No bee in his bonnet
> Outbuzzes any other that lands on it.
> His balance is astonishing when you consider
> He has never sold himself to the highest bidder,
> Never has lived a week for twenty summers
> Free of the drumfire of the camouflaged gunners,
> Never has eaten a meal that was undramatic –
> Without the next being highly problematic.
> Never succumbed to panic, *Kaltes Blut*
> His watchword, facing ahead in untroubled mood.
> He has been his own bagman, critic, cop, designer,
> Publisher, agent, char-man and shoe-shiner.
> What he has narrated of double-dealing
> Is nothing to what he could, of professional stealing,
> Of the betrayal of unpublished texts to ladies,
> *À court d'idées*, and other crimes (his fate is
> Of course to be a quarry of rich pickings,

---

* 'One-Way Song'.

He's the bulls-eye of "brain-pickers" like the dickens) –
Of unwelcome names bluepencilled in an article
Caught in the act, and not minding a particle.
(We suffer from a strange delusion – that is
That our age is "straighter" than was grand-daddy's!) –
Of that discrimination against all writers
Suspected of having eyes in their heads. Good fighters
When-driven-in-corners are common: but here's a fellow
Who does not wait to be trapped – an aggressive fellow!
I was sure you'd like him and that was why I brought him –
It was a piece of luck it happened that I caught him.'

Notes

1 *Torrents of Spring* (New York, 1926).
2 *Dark Laughter* (New York, 1925).

CHAPTER XXXVI

ANTI-WAR BOOKS

A GROUP of books have now to be considered, all of which ultimately are concerned, to the exclusion of everything else, with the thought of war. They are not — with one exception — in themselves important. They threw no fresh light upon any subject (as does for instance 'The Doom of Youth'). War has been a recurrent theme in these pages. I have explained so fully already my present ideas about it, that the words I have used above, 'to the exclusion of everything else', describe what I now regard as their essential limitations. Nevertheless they must find a place here, because of the influence they have exerted upon my career as a writer.

The books ranged from the early account of the gathering storm cloud in Germany in 1930 (to which I have already alluded in Part I), to those written shortly before the outbreak of war. All were to do with war, and were anti-war.

Nothing excuses a man, or a Party, for war-like agitation in the Machine Age, whatever reasons they may give for it. But there was this great dilemma for the war-hater, which in the end became glaringly apparent to me as to everybody else. Assuming the impossible, that one's own countrymen could have been persuaded to renounce war as an instrument of policy, there would have remained in Germany a demented military adventurer, namely Herr Hitler, whom nothing would deter from wholesale 'patriotic' bloodshed. Had we behaved with the most exemplary restrait and magnanimity, the result would have been just the same.

So this group of books against war can be written off as futile performances — ill-judged, redundant, harmful of course to me personally, and of no value to anybody else? Certainly they were in the main just that.

'Appeasement' — a natural accompaniment of all anti-war action — is equally a waste of time. 'Appeasement' is not *wicked* (that is the blarney of the warmongers): on the contrary, it is virtuous and full of common sense. But it is much too good sense to have any practical value in human affairs.

My general aim, for instance, in 'Hitler' (written 1930, published 1931) was to break the European ostracism of Germany, call in question the wisdom of the Versailles Treaty and get it revised, end the bad behaviour of the French chauvinists, attempt to establish healthy relations in Western Europe. This was undertaken in the interest of Western civilisation (the private interests of Germany had no weight with me at all: my 'spiritual home' always has been, if anything, France).

What I urged was humane and sensible, but impossible. So it was time ill-spent. I might as well have walked down Cheapside or Piccadilly with a placard which said, in heavy type, 'All nations draw together, conciliatory and forbearing, for the sake of civilised values! Call an immediate halt to all manufacture of arms and explosives! Revise all oppressive treaties!

Remove all barriers to trade, abolish all tariffs! Cancel all war-debts! Make an end of international usury! Renounce such practices as trade wars and boycotts! Let us make Europe an Asylum – an Asylum of Peace!'

The police-constable who first caught sight of me would have seen 'Let us make Europe an Asylum!' He would read no farther. I should have shortly found myself endeavouring to explain to a police doctor just what kind of Asylum I proposed that Europe should be. – However I should have wasted no more time that way than the way I did.

Until people are governed and trained – from childhood up – quite differently, until the doctrine of the 'sovereign state' is repudiated, there must be war. It does not matter when it comes, or how. It is a part of our 'way of life'. It is the way of life that must be changed – much more radically than even communism changes it. But can it be changed?

———

What I am about to say would be irrelevant, were it not for the necessity to provide an antidote to the venom of the political pundit. The only way I can think of doing that is by going into a few personal details.

The personal loss entailed, in every sense, by my stand against war was incalculable. Had it been a capitalist war it would have been otherwise: but it was a Left-wing war (though it was not because it was a Left-wing war, but because it was *war*, that I acted). I received less money – to take that first – than I should for any other type of book, and for one of the best of them practically nothing, as advances go. I did myself so much damage that at the time it diminished the value of my other books.

This is not *boasting*. One does not boast about being a fool. – But let me continue my recital of the attendant facts. From 1932-36 I was very seriously ill, so ill that it was currently reported that I was dying, and those standing to benefit in business ways by the death of a well-known person began to look at me hopefully for a short while. I underwent several operations: this cost, first and last, a great deal of money. As a consequence I was unusually hard-up and could ill afford to write unpopular books.

At length I was so pressed for money – to be thoroughly circumstantial – that I went for an operation into the general ward of a hospital. (I must have been in every nursing home in London before this). Some patients would die every twenty-four hours or so where I was: I still can hear the soft thudding rush of the night-nurses, when certain signs apprised them of the approaching end. For some reason it was preferred that death should occur in another ward, reserved for the purpose. The patient would be hurriedly wheeled out to die. Though I saw death often enough as a soldier, that was the only occasion on which I heard the authentic death-rattle.

So then, I was not only over military-age – it could not be said that the prospect of further military service was responsible for my 'pacifism' – but was sick into the bargain, and in a condition in which people generally are not engaged as I was, fighting what is most truly a scourge. Nor was I a pacifist — religious considerations did not enter into it. I had no investments, so I had no money to lose: nor any job that would be affected. I had no Party allegiance. Our prospective enemies were no special favourites of mine. It would be difficult in fact to imagine anyone with less motive, of the usual kind, for disliking war.

The only *personal* interest I had was that of any sensible person (who is neither a politician nor a business man) who recognises that war, in harming the community to which he belongs — whether it be a lost war, or a 'Great Victory' — must also harm him. But that alone would precipitate no one into action. — Mine were not personal reasons, unless a sense of the public good is personal; or a reasonable care for the interests of one's country; and an immense repulsion at the approach of what brutalises men and confirms them in the ugliest of their archaic habits.

Lastly, I was perfectly conscious of the extreme unpopularity of opposition to war — and I mean unpopularity with the intelligent too. — Such are a few of the salient facts. I would have you bear these facts in mind; not as being to my credit, except in a negative way — but just 'for the record', in the American phrase.

———

'Left Wings over Europe' and 'Count Your Dead' are much closer to the brink of the abyss, than when I first began thinking about war, from my first Hitler book onwards. 'Count Your Dead' is, if I may say so, a first-rate peace pamphlet, which would have resounded in a smaller, more instructed, society like the hammering of an alarm-gong.

'Left Wings', on the other hand, is quite unimportant. It is a violent reaction against Left-wing incitement to war. (Only the I.L.P. stood out, for the older and more humane socialist principles. All the Left had been sold the idea of war.)

Today I am in complete disagreement with much of the contents of 'Left Wings'. This is not retraction: it is contradiction. Its support for the principle of the 'sovereign state' is a good example of this: or its antagonism to all centralisation of power. Those two views are diametrically opposed to those now held by me upon this subject, as explained in an earlier chapter.

Were you, for instance, to revive states-rights in the U.S.A., and the federal authority were reduced to the point at which it stood during Jefferson's administration, you would have at once forty-eight state-militias and state-aircorps: within a few years wars would start — just as we always have them here, and for the same reason, namely, *no central authority*. It is only the powerfully centralised administration for which Abraham Lincoln was responsible — and fought the Civil War to secure, beyond the possibility of future secession — which prevents the North American continent from being a worse Balkans.

There is nothing much to salvage in 'Left Wings'. Any argument based upon the continued political identity of the European peoples must be confuted by events. Clearly it was better for these heavily armed, commercially competitive, States to destroy each other, as they have done, since such a situation is archaic and ought not to exist. All enjoyed having violent quarrels. It is perfectly fearful of course for the people *in* the States. But what can they do? It is like being passengers in an enormous ship, with a mad crew.

CHAPTER XXXVII

FALSE BOTTOMS

BETWEEN 1930 and 1939 – the period during which Europe was drifting towards world war ii – my time was not wholy occupied with writing books against war, preparing for a largish exhibition of pictures, and being ill. In 1932 the following books appeared.

'The Doom of Youth'.
'Snooty Baronet'.
'The Enemy of the Stars' (Final version).
'Filibusters in Barbary'.
The first and last of these were suppressed.
In 1933 –
'The Old Gang and the New Gang'.
(A pamphlet).
'One-way Song'.
(Verse).
In 1934 'Men Without Art'.

All these books have to be passed over although individually they are of much greater interest than those of the anti-war group. 'The Doom of Youth', because of its subject-matter, qualifies especially for inclusion in the present survey. It may be regarded as a very extensive appendix to 'The Art of Being Ruled', carrying forward the social criticism of the section bearing the title, 'Sub Persona Infantis'.

This is a study of Youth seen as a *class*: an account of the cold-blooded exploitation of that class in the Twentieth Century. 'There is no question,' I write, 'that in the technique of "youth-politics", Youth is considered simply as an abstraction – a mere natural force. For the "youth-politician", pure and simple, Youth is not a human thing at all, but something like water or wind – to drive a mill, to secure electricity.' So we must reconcile ourselves to 'a loss of romance if we are going to exploit romance'.

Hitler was, of course, one of the most notorious Youth-politicians, the 'Hitler Jugend' being one of the key institutions of the national socialists. Mussolini was an earlier example of youth-politician, with his theme-song 'Giovanezza'. Earlier yet were the Russians. I quote from an article headed 'Marxism for Babes', the following passage: 'The future Russian national character is possibly being determined in no small degree by the intensive training in communist ideas which is being imparted to children almost as soon as they have left the cradle.'

The Russian communist youth-organisations certainly preceded the Fascist, the latter sedulously imitating marxist models, in this, as in so many other things. Youth-politics, however, actually originated as the Nineteenth Century was turning into the Twentieth: and (let us avoid a patriotic inflation of the chest) it was British. I refer of course to Baden-

Powell's Boy Scout Movement. This was a juvenile militia: and all those movements that followed it possessed similarly a military character.

The 'doom of Youth' signifies the ending of the tender romance of youth, as understood by our grandfathers. Its place is being taken by Youth as a political force. 'Youth' may be bracketed with 'the Proletariat': they are the two major discoveries, or inventions, of modern power-politics. First the Poor – then the Young. 'The Proletariat' is a century old: but 'Youth' it remained for the Twentieth Century to uncover and exploit.

In the Western democracies 'Youth' as a political specific is put to other uses. The Boy Scout movement was never developed with us beyond the 'scout' stage, of a Kipling-reading late-Victorian schoolboy – recreational rather than fanatical. The exploitation of Youth with us has followed 'age-war' lines: I mean the 'young idea' has been employed – in business and in trade – to undermine the theory that the older you get, the more valuable you become, so expensive in the past for the employer. In politics it has been Youth's function to act as the natural advocate of new and revolutionary ideas – to rout the old and conservative. But in my chapter 'Advice to the Inmates of the Power House' these techniques have already been charted. In 'The Art of Being Ruled' I developed very fully what I deal with, in a new form, in 'The Doom of Youth'. This latter is to be found in the section entitled *The Dossier*. 'The sickly and dismal spirit of that terrible key-book, "Peter Pan", has sunk into every tissue of the social life of England,' is my lament. That poison did its work in between the wars. But there are no Peter Pans in 1947, just as there are no Kensington Gardens in the old sense of a middle-class dream-park.

Then 'Youth, in the old dreamy, useless-but-ornamental Western sense – that sentimental notion of Youth is dependent upon the Western conception of the Family.' Since the Family is on the way out, the traditional 'sweet-scented manuscript' version of youth passes away too – even without the politician's and propagandist's expert assistance. Little more remains to it of downy innocence than to a child-actor in Hollywood.

The title of the eleventh chapter of the 'Doom' reads: 'One of the Aims of Youth-politics is to shorten Human Life'. Practically every aspect of this particularly fascinating subject is canvassed in 'The Doom of Youth'. But already I have given more space to it than I had intended. I must move on at once, dismissing without so much as a hurried glance 'Men Without Art', or others of the list given at the opening of this chapter. They are not controversial. No choleric intellectual goes into action about them. The book I have singled out here is a novel, entitled 'The Revenge for Love'.

————

This book originally was called 'False Bottoms'. The title was altered at the request of the publisher before publication. It appeared (in England) in 1937 – the same year as 'Count Your Dead'. We all, of course, were hurrying, in the old Ship of State, towards the lip of the maelstrom. It was no time to bring out a serious book, certainly not a novel.

'The Revenge for Love' was submitted to one of the more friendly New York publishers, who returned it with a short note to the effect that he could not publish it, and that it would only be a waste of time sending it elsewhere, as no other American publisher would take it.

It is not my wish to reopen here the question of 'The Revenge for Love'. It is out of print, and will so remain in my life-time.[1] I am content as I declared when first referring to it that some day, when the passions of the present time are no more than feverish memories, people will take it up and read it as *a novel* – not glare at it with an eye inflamed by politics, which prevents proper focusing and makes the eye see something which is not there at all.

For the trouble about this book is politics. It has a communist for a hero. No great harm in that. But this is not the dewy-eyed daydream of the par-lour-pink imagination, but a tough ordinary little party-man, dialectically primed to do his stuff. It is not beautiful mushy stuff, but hard practical militant business, he goes through with like a plumber: only a plumber who has to deceive the householder sometimes: has to sabotage perhaps the bourgeois drainage system. In his activities there is a strain of Groucho Marx. All reality sooner or later has a strain of that, as much in war (as Mr. O'Flaherty has shown)[2] as in class-war.

Is this novel pro-communist? Is it anti-communist? – An inevitable question. But when the novelist sits down to write he does not listen to the harsh importunities of *Pro* and of *Anti*. The biologist looks at life dispassion-ately: if what he discovers is unpleasant, he does not prettify his report. The novelist is, in part, a biologist. But the problem of the objectivity of the artist I have discussed at length in Part I.

The difficulty in this case resides in the fact, I suppose, that the subject-matter is forbidden territory, as much as religious subjects are. Were I, for argument's sake, to describe a few months in the life of an average priest – treat of his bitter effort to master his animal nature, his troubles about belief, perhaps his antagonism to his Superior – it would probably give universal offence. This would especially be the case because I am not a Catholic. Some pages of candid realism of Mauriac I have marvelled at – or equally of Graham Greene. Both, however, are Catholics. Not being a com-munist, with my Percy Hardcaster I found myself in a similar position to a non-Catholic, at a moment of very bitter controversy, realistically portraying a priest. Clerics, the Royal Family, or agents of the Third International, are taboo. The explanation of what happened to my book is in the main covered by the above.

———

In New York I met a young man who had something of interest to impart. He enquired if I were aware that I had been 'the subject of a political storm'. This was said smilingly. It was only a literary storm: but it had annoyed his sister, who played a leading rôle in it.[3]

It appeared that she did book-reviews for a certain New York periodical. I am debarred from naming it, of course. I do not, however, recommend anyone to express the view that these incidents are imaginary – for that would be a point at which I could invoke successfully the law of libel, which unfortunately in the main is so arranged as to protect the rich and to

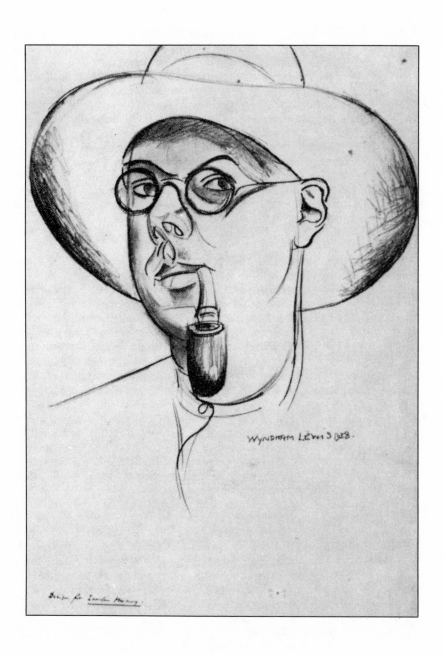

Wyndham Lewis 1928.

Design for 'London Mercury'

prevent the poor from properly defending themselves. She had sent in a review of 'The Revenge for Love' — as you will see in a moment, of a very favourable nature. That is where the 'storm' began.

By return of post the review came hurtling back. Since this was the first occasion on which a review of hers had been found unacceptable, she re-mailed it. Once more it was returned, with a note from the editor inform-ing her that this laudatory review could not be used. Realising that probably, without looking at the book, the editor would say on principle that it was bad — seeing who its author was — she for the third time despatched her review, enclosing a letter in whch she asked her editor to read the book, pointing out that her judgement as a reviewer had not been called in question before, and that the book seemed to her to be all she had said in the review. For the last time her article — and the book — were mailed back to her. All I can remember of the letter she received on this occasion was where the editor observed that if Percy Hardcaster was *her* idea of a communist it was not *his*.

Such was the 'storm'. Not much of a tornado, just a typical minor episode in a world where books — whether good, bad or indifferent as books is a minor detail — get suppressed. And these are supposedly literary reviews — where the intellectual's reputation is given its most valuable advertise-ment, or has administered to it a dose of silence damaging in the extreme. But they are in fact not *literary* reviews at all — there are no literary reviews any longer — but political reviews masquerading as such. Everything is judged as politics, not as literature. And this is one of the major disasters of this period, for the writer who wishes to remain independent.

For we are locked up with these people, in a way the writer never has been before (cf. 'The Two Publics', Part I). The deciding factor is political: but this should not be the case with a book any more than with a painting or a musical score. In the present case the well-heeled 'radical' in the editor-ial chair prevented my young — but at that time unknown — friend from drawing the attention of many thousands of intellectuals in America to 'The Revenge for Love'. For that happens to be one of the publications most generally read by the 'intelligent'.

This is an occurrence to be placed beside Mr. Campbell's rejected review of 'The Apes of God' (the outline of which I gave in Part I, where I was cataloguing the misfortunes of the satirist). This time, with 'The Revenge for Love', the motive for the suppression is political, whereas with the Campbell review politics played no part. The result, however, is the same.

It is not difficult to realise the great number of times transactions of this sort remain a 'professional secret' between editor and reviewer, for the one — and extremely rare — occasion upon which the reviewer reveals to the unfortunate author what has occurred.

Rebecca's* feeling was that this 'jeune homme de bonne famille' would not be likely to relish the denunciations — uttered by a character in my book — of the phoney socialist. Maybe she was right.

This review is of interest not only because of its fate at the hands of the politico-literary editor. It is of great interest to see these matters about which

---

* Rebecca C— was the name of the reviewer — again I am obliged to give no more than the first name.

I am writing from the viewpoint of a total stranger like Rebecca C——, living in another continent: also holding very different beliefs from my own. Accordingly I will quote here and there from her article.

Rebecca C—— is, or was, a follower of the exiled Russian leader, Leon Trotsky. I have no part, of course, in the polemical exposition of this eager young heretic. It is what is not politics alone that concerns me. I cannot banish from the text all trace of those irrelevant enthusiasms.

She herself expressly exempts me, however, for she writes: 'Wyndham Lewis's only politics are art. . . . Since this is a political age, Wyndham Lewis being completely the truthful artist has cast his searchlight on (it).* This has involved a political reprisal – complete silence surrounding the book. It was published in London in 1937. Though it is his greatest work, it has gone unread by those in London who praise him. The reception given "The Revenge for Love" is only another symbol of the system's revenge for love. "That deep grave – a book." It has been buried by a conspiracy of silence both by the right and the left. For the literati of the right he is Public Enemy No. 1 since he demolished them in that scathing satire "Apes of God". For the left, he was of course completely taboo even before the appearance of this novel.'

At this point she explains how it had come about that I was anathema to the left intelligentsia. She does not say this, but the interests of the *professional* left – like those of the professional right, or Tory – are restricted to a very narrow field, outside which nothing has much meaning. The books of Ortega y Gasset, for instance, to a leftist of that order would be of no interest at all: the good observation to be found in them, the robust Spanish wit a blank, of no relevance. By 'left' Rebecca understands, I think, her enemies, though she and her friends belong to a still farther left. The cleavage between the two factions of the left has, since that time, grown prodigiously, until today the straight stalinists are, I believe, in America, the weaker party.

My early sympathetic treatment of the national socialists she believes brought on a 'boycott' – although, she says, such a boycott 'would be as stupid as to stop reading Balzac because he once flirted with duchesses and royalism. Even the *avant-garde* magazines in the United States have been silent about Lewis's last work'. (No American *avant-garde* magazine as a fact has mentioned my name since 'Time and Western Man' – even that was too something-or-other. Kirstein's 'Hound and Horn' as far back as that, except for one review, was impeccably silent.)

'Partly ignorance, partly inertia, many assume that an artist has stopped functioning since the last time they deigned to read him, oh way back in 1929. . . . As long as an artist is safely dead like Kafka or Rilke he has a better chance of being brought up-to-date than a *live* artist, alive to the present – May the Lord have mercy upon his soul – he might as well be dead. To all pantheonisation, true artists reply with Marat: "I'd rather be alive!" '

Rebecca C——'s article begins as follows:

'This extraordinary work is the first truly modern novel to express artistically the complete absolute quintessential Nothing, the underlying

* She writes 'on Stalinism': but I cannot accept that, for the true – in contrast to the sham – stalinist I have not found indifferent to the people.

lie of this imperialist epoch. There may be writers who have felt this but so far only Wyndham Lewis has succeeded in giving it form. . . .'

She then outlines the narrative. 'This attempt,' she says, 'to graph the curve of the book is ridiculously inadequate to convey the scope, the profundity, and the art of the book. From beginning to end, the tension is unbroken. No unnecessary persons, scenes, words — no short circuits. Every part of the book carries on the electric charge until the circuit is complete. To explain the full meaning of this work where every word is full of meaning, one must do what Beethoven did when asked the meaning of a composition — play it over again — a thing impossible to do in a review. Therefore read it if the price is not prohibitive.

'What is the meaning of the title *Revenge for Love?* That daring leap from the kingdom of dehumanising necessity to the kingdom of freedom, that creative Promethean act by which a revolutionist, a friend, a woman, an artist attempt to break the cash-nexus, that creative love the crime of crimes against the system, must be crushed out by torture, must be revenged. This revenge for love is the large theme of the novel expressed variously in the outrageous punishment meted out to Hardcaster, revolutionist, Stamp the artist, and Margaret his wife, a character very much like Lear's loneliest daughter Cordelia. The tension is like that in Lear — they are flies to wanton boys who kill them for their sport. These three are trapped in an absurd wanton senseless system, a system of lies which Wyndham Lewis symbolises in the "immense *false-bottom* underlying every seemingly solid surface" upon which they tread, the "prodigious non-sequitur". Like a composer developing a motif, not by simple repetition but by a continual transforming and deepening of all the incalculable resonances latent in the original motif, Wyndham Lewis traces the "false-bottom" in faces, gestures, places, communists, lovers, friends, artists, and finally in the ex-bootleg machine turned into a gun-running machine, with yet another false-bottom — no guns! A symbol strangely prophetic of the Musica-Coster affair.

'What underlies the fiasco in Spain, none of the novelists have made clear. Malraux, Hemingway, and others smear the issues with eloquent rhetoric. Take this eloquence and "literachoor" and wring its neck for hiding the truth! Fearlessly truthful, Wyndham Lewis alone has expressed in art, what (others have) expressed in polemic. He did not take the romantic battlefield, the heroic martyrs, beat our brains with the bones of corpses or blind us with the mass bombing. He did not attempt an analysis of a whole epidemic. Like a scientist, he isolates instead some microbes during the Lerroux administration. . . .'

Finally: 'He (Mr. Lewis) shows up all the false "politics" which made such a lavish use of the poor and the unfortunate, of the "proletariat" . . . to advertise injustice to the profit of a predatory Party, of sham-underdogs athirst for power: whose doctrine was a universal Sicilian Vespers, and which yet treated the real poor, when they were encountered, with such overweening contempt, and even derision. This devastating portrait is not . . . from a reactionary viewpoint. The figure that unmasks the bourgeois fraud in the Popular Front is himself a communist. . . . In this book there is no moralising, no cant, neither sentimental Hope (Malraux) nor hysterical fear.'

The 'figure that unmasks' the bourgeois comedians of revolution, pretending to radical sentiments, is an authentic communist, Rebecca points out, one not playing with communism, but a militant professional. Hardcaster comes from the people: he is fighting for the people, as naturally as a Macedonian hillsman fights for the isolated species of man he is; with that matter-of-factness, unselfconsciousness, craft, grotesqueness war entails. I was glad that Rebecca, who hates the communists, did not omit that point, which is one of obvious weight. When I met her I need not say that the generous friendship of youth was delightful, and though I met with much friendship in New York there was none I valued quite so much as hers and her brother's. What seemed to me astonishing was something like tolerance although it was not that—what I may describe as an ability to withdraw herself *at once* from anything that repelled her and as it were from another dimension see it without passion. Her brother's playing (he is a pianist) had been described as 'Thomistic': and this young woman—physically like a youthful Virginia Woolf, but unaffected—had a Thomistic quality too, bland and severe. She would distort nothing, I am sure, to make it conform to her personal bias, nor omit something for the same purpose—not even a Stalinist!

Just as real war is not an affair of waving operatic plumes, surmounting a proudly erect figure, brandishing a sword, but the squalor of a mud-caked, or dust-steeped, perspiring creature, as often as not on his belly, or emulating the stealth of an Indian rather than the martial stance of a Sixteenth-Century copperplate of a plumed Capitan: so it is in the class-war, necessarily. That reality I attempted to convey.

Should anyone hunt for some of the books mentioned here in the popular libraries, or in cheap editions, and failing to find them, wonder why, let him turn to this chapter, or to that I have entitled 'Rebecca West and Carlo Linati'. He will in that way find the major part of the answer.

Notes

[1] As already noted, Methuen bought the rights from Cassell and brought out a new edition of *The Revenge for Love* in 1952.

[2] Liam O'Flaherty, *The Informer* (London, 1925).

[3] Rebecca Citkowitz; the journal in question was *New International*.

ENVOI

THE writing of this book has presented one obvious difficulty. I have gone back to the past in order to defend ideas of twenty years ago with a changed outlook. This, however, turned out to be less troublesome than might have been expected. Certainly in many particulars I judge the issues in question differently today. In other cases I discovered there was remarkably little change. In more serious work, where the thinking had deeper roots, the conclusions arrived at were as a rule in accord with present beliefs. In more purely topical books of political journalism it was otherwise: there the views expressed often rest on no more than expediency.

To illustrate this: were I to advocate today that England merge its economy with that of the United States, or – the reverse – that it stick to Europe, even if that meant Russia – in neither of these cases would it of necessity represent a high opinion on my part of the political system of the country indicated, only that it seemed the best course for a ruined country to take. I am neither an enthusiastic capitalist nor communist: but I *do* believe that one of those two choices has to be made. – Such judgements are in another category altogether to philosophical or literary judgements, that is my point. I would never recommend people to read a book unless I considered it worth reading. But then the happiness of millions does not depend upon any book, or one's literary judgements might be more capricious. I might be found adopting a benevolent attitude towards 'The Little Minister'. – There are no *good* politics. All nations are brutes. What is more, they brutalise *us:* we are born nice, but gradually we develop a bad character. This is largely because of the bad example set us by the State.

Let me give a few examples of the kind of criticism in past books which corresponds as much today as when it was written with what I think. In the analysis of the Western decadence there is not a word to alter. In places the writing could be improved – I accorded critical writing too much the status of informal letter-writing. Except for that (vide my analysis) – and it applies only to some critical books – I would not touch those texts. Today I should not write such books at all. People ought to be allowed to drop to pieces in any way they choose. I even disapprove of propping them up. Let nations, like men, die in peace. I rather feel as if I had been delivering pep talks to men dying of cancer, and am sometimes surprised that I was not more unpopular than I was.

The elaborate analysis of contemporary ideas which is 'Time and Western Man' expresses a judgement to which I still adhere. The 'time-philosophers' are still for me what they were then – men who presided at, and speeded, the dissolution of an ancient culture. They were not creators of a new system of ideas. The difference in my approach here is that these disagreeable vultures had their rôle to play, as agents of change. Was it sensible to shoo them away? The analysis is accurate and valuable. To the shooing part – a natural human revulsion towards the vulture species – I demur. But that is quite distinct from the historical analysis.

'The Doom of Youth' – rather a scientific undertaking, with its extensive *dossiers*, than a literary one — 'Time and Western Man', the centre part of 'The Art of Being Ruled', and parts of other critical books of that group* contain nothing which disagrees radically with my present view of things.

I linked with what I am thinking now these past debates into *a central pattern of thinking*, which is common to the past and to the present. This is the clearest refutation of and best answer to those who have never liked what I say, and, being smart you see, pretend that it is something it is not.

Now that the English intellectuals are exclusively engrossed in scraping a day-to-day living — shades of the prison-house, or Power House rather, beginning to close in upon their dim frustrations — it is unlikely that any analysis of what has happened to us, and is still happening, will be contributed from that quarter. Unless some scholar from the relative security of a university can do so, no more first-hand analytical reporting from the darkening Western continent will be forthcoming. It would sound boastful if I — knowing the time as I do, and the immense obstacles to independent literary expression — hazarded the opinion that the above group of books, written by me in the trough between the two world wars, might be the last independent utterance of that sort before the deluge. To which you can now add this.

I have not been writing this book out of vanity or to boast. I think they are probably just what I say. But I have only revisited those remarkably prophetic pages in order to extract material with which to compose a true image of my mind, to replace the false picture which has been surreptitiously circulated.

When I say the mind, that must be understood to include the character. It is character and motives rather than anything else which one has to protect and put out of reach of smearers. No one cares about the intellect — I don't have to worry about *that*, but what the domestic requires in applying for a job — a good character.

* Critical and polemical books, perhaps I should repeat, much more than others, lend themselves to misrepresentation, and so have featured, almost exclusively, in this study.

REFERENCE MATTER

APPENDIXES

AFTERWORD

INDEX

LIST OF ILLUSTRATIONS IN THIS EDITION

["Michel" refers to the descriptive catalogue in Walter Michel's *Wyndham Lewis: Paintings and Drawings* (Berkeley and Los Angeles: Univ. of California Press, 1971).]

LIST OF ILLUSTRATIONS IN THE ORIGINAL EDITION

[For the sake of completeness we print here the "List of Illustrations" found in the first edition of *Rude Assignment*. "Michel" refers to the descriptive catalogue in Walter Michel's *Wyndham Lewis: Paintings and Drawings* (Berkeley and Los Angeles: Univ. of California Press, 1971).]

Wyndham Lewis, 1928 [photograph]

Would You Oblige Me With a Light Please? [cartoon by David Low]

Wyndham Lewis, 1903, by Augustus John [drawing]

Wyndham Lewis, 1912 [photograph]

Wyndham Lewis, 1916 [photograph]

Wyndham Lewis and Jacques Maritain, 1942 [photograph]

Artist's Wife [Michel, 875]

Cover for *Enemy*, No. 3 [Michel, 633]

Design for *Enemy* [Michel, 649]

Cover for *Enemy* Prospectus [Michel, 634]

Mr. Tut [Michel, 780]

Pensive Woman [Michel, P85]

Madge Pulsford [Michel, 417]

Stephen Spender [Michel, P86]

Rebecca West [Michel, 786]

Gestation [Michel, 971]

The Sun Sets [Michel, 847]

Surrender of Barcelona [Michel, P61]

The Dream of Hamilcar [Michel, 614]

Manhattan [Michel, 637]

Cave Woman in a Chair [Michel, 433]

Woman With Hands on Table [Michel, 467]

Inca and the Birds [Michel, P49]

LIST OF EMENDATIONS

[The following emendations comprise corrections of obvious (and not-so-obvious) spelling and printer's errors; a very few changes in Lewis's informal conversational punctuation in order to improve intelligibility; corrections of minor errors of fact (e.g., 157:17/171:17); and corrections of Lewis's transcriptions from his own or others' published works. His transcriptions of letters from W. B. Yeats and Roger Fry have not been changed, although — as the Notes point out — their accuracy is doubtful. Also left unchanged is the slip whereby he has Galileo sticking to "the theory of the roundness of the earth" (p. 77 above) rather than that of heliocentric planetary motion.]

FIRST EDITION			THIS EDITION		
Page/Line			Page/Line		
25	33	Finnigans	28	33	Finnegans
27	15	that naturally	30	15	that, naturally
29	31	Intellectuels?'	32	31	Intellectuels.'
30	1	Méfaits de	34	1	Méfaits des
	3	*Clercs*, being as		3	*Clercs* being, as
30n	1	believed,	34n	1	believe,
34n	45	capitalist-socialist	38	45	capitalist-socialism
36	23	Reason without	40	23	Reason) without
37n	4	on découvre propriétés.	41n	4	en découvre propriétés. . . .
	5	principale est		5	principale comprend
29n	9	that *dream* and that *fiction*	43n	9	*that* dream and *that* fiction
40	15	'intellectual	44	15	'intellectual'
45	37	Weston	49	37	Western
49	47	Kunthistorisches	53	47	Kunsthistorisches
51	13	not territorial	55	13	not a territorial
					[*correction from MS at Cornell*]
55	17	Cossimo Tura	59	17	Cosimo Tura
56	17	Finnigans	60	17	Finnegans
57	18	"Well	61	18	' "Well
	26	Fennimore		26	'Fenimore
	33	"The		33	' "The
	36	'How		36	' " 'How
	38	This		38	'This
	46	"Terrible		46	' "Terrible
58	8	Fennimore	62	8	Fenimore
62n	7-11	[*printed in italics*]	66n	7-11	[*printed in roman*]

244

	FIRST EDITION			THIS EDITION	
Page/Line			*Page/Line*		
63n	1	'Henry Maine.	68n	1	Henry Maine.
66n	1	132-135	71n	1	132-134
67	44	Vyasheslav	72	44	Vyacheslav
68	22	*many!* the	73	22	*many!* The
78	23	Wells	84	23	Wells's
78n	4	Nazi's	84n	4	Nazis'
80	40	lofty, spirit	86	40	lofty spirit
85	26	citrous	91	26	citrus
87	40	writing desk),	93	40	writing desk,
	42	Young.		62	Young).
97	34	Ausschwitz	104	34	Auschwitz
101	18	Mallocks	108	18	Mallock's
105	44	of a Dove	113	44	of the Dove
106	6	Finnigans	114	6	Finnegans
108	41	*magazin*	116	41	*magasin*
113	46	Collége	121	46	Collège
115	14	Finnigans	123	14	Finnegans
117	31	l'incuriosité?'	125	31	l'incuriosité!'
	41	le pére		41	le père
119	46	Tonks' life	127	46	Tonks's life
121	28	Maddox	130	28	Madox
	40	Gaudier Bzeska		40	Gaudier-Brzeska
	41	H. D. Aldington		41	H. D., Aldington
124	42	Strinberg	134	42	Strindberg
128	41	Gaudier Brzeska	138	41	Gaudier-Brzeska
	46	á la gare		46	à la gare
134	37	Mogdigliani	145	37	Modigliani
137	30	Mrs. Heppelwhite's	148	30	Mrs. Kibblewhite's
					[*see Pound's Letter Three and note 85*]
	33	Gaudier Brzeska		33	Gaudier-Brzeska
141	1	in this part,	153	1	in this Part,
142	6	fellow travelling	152	6	fellow-travelling
	22	fellow travellers		22	fellow-travellers
143	17	were not advocating	155	17	were now advocating
146	29	liniaments	158	29	lineaments
148	3	Maddox	161	3	Madox
151	29	too, Bertha	165	29	too. Bertha
	37	soul-dwellers		37	soul-dweller

FIRST EDITION			THIS EDITION		
Page/Line			*Page/Line*		
156	35	Ukiyo-ye	170	35	Ukiyo-e
157	17	Mr. Robert Barr	171	17	Mr. Alfred Barr
158	28	Caliphs	172	28	Caliph's
160	43	artificial, "aristocrat,"	174	43	artificial "aristocrat,"
161	9	half an hour altogether	175	9	half an hour together
163	9	Niccoló	177	9	Niccolò
	42	Niccoló		42	Niccolò
164	14	political	178	14	"political
166	39	Kaffka	180	39	Kafka
170	11	is in effect,	184	11	is, in effect,
187	24	lines).	202	24	lines.)
	40-41	fundamental, than		40-41	fundamental than
205	31	wont	220	31	won't
207	1	fa parte a sé	222	1	fa parte a sè
217	41	Kaffka	233	41	Kafka
217n	1	'On Stalinism' . . . sham-	233n	1	'on Stalinism' . . . sham —

A LIST OF BOOKS, WITH APPROXIMATE DATES

[We print here unchanged (except for typographical corrections) the list of his works that Lewis chose to include under the above heading in the first edition of *Rude Assignment*. For a more complete and accurate listing, see the Lewis bibliographies by Bradford Morrow and Bernard Lafourcade (Santa Barbara: Black Sparrow Press, 1978) or Omar Pound and Philip Grover Folkestone, 1978). Lewis's list stopped at 1942; we continue it here with a selection of later publications.]

1914.	*Blast No.* 1 (A Magazine).
	Timon of Athens (Portfolio of Designs for play).
1915.	*Blast No.* 2.
1917.	*The Ideal Giant.* The Code of a Herdsman. – Cantleman's Spring-Mate.
1918.	*Tarr* (A novel).
1919.	*The Caliph's Design.* (Architects! Where is your Vortex!)
1921.	*The Tyro.* No. 1. (A Magazine).
1922.	*The Tyro.* No. 2.
1926.	*The Art of Being Ruled.*
1927.	(1) *The Lion and the Fox.*
	(2) *Time and the Western Man.*
	(3) *The Wild Body.* (Short Stories).
	(4) *The Enemy. No.* 1. (A Magazine).
1928.	(1) *The Childermass* (vol. i) (A novel).
	(2) *Tarr.* (A novel, – completely revised edition).
	(3) *The Enemy.* No. 2.
1929.	(1) *Paleface.*
	(2) *The Enemy.* No. 3.
1930.	(1) *The Apes of God.* (A novel).
	(2) *Satire and Fiction.*
1931.	(1) *Hitler.*
	(2) *The Diabolical Principle.*
1932.	(1) *The Doom of Youth.* (Suppressed).
	(2) *Snooty Baronet.* (A novel).
	(3) *The Enemy of the Stars.* (A play).
	(4) *Filibusters in Barbary* (Suppressed).
1933.	(1) *The Old Gang and the New.*
	(2) *One-Way Song* (Verse).
1934.	*Men Without Art.*
1936.	(1) *Left Wings over Europe.*
	(2) *The Roaring Queen.* (A novel). (Suppressed before publication, after printing and binding completed).
1937.	(1) *Count Your Dead – They are Alive.*
	(2) *The Revenge for Love* (A novel).

(1937). (3) *Blasting and Bombardiering.* (Autobiography).

1939. (1) *The Jews. Are they Human?*

(2) *The Hitler Cult. And How it will End.*

1940. *America, I Presume!*

1942. (1) *Anglosaxony* (A pamphlet).

(2) *The Vulgar Streak* (A novel).

1948. *America and Cosmic Man.*

1950. *Rude Assignment* (Autobiography).

1951. *Rotting Hill* (Short stories).

1952. *The Writer and the Absolute.*

1954. (1) *Self-Condemned* (A novel).

(2) *The Demon of Progress in the Arts.*

1955. *The Human Age: Monstre Gai* (Bk. II); *Malign Fiesta* (Bk. III)
(A continuation of *The Childermass*).

1956. *The Red Priest* (A novel).

1963. *The Letters of Wyndham Lewis,* ed. W. K. Rose.

1969. *Wyndham Lewis on Art,* ed. W. Michel and C. J. Fox.

1971. *Wyndham Lewis: Paintings and Drawings,* ed. W. Michel.

1973. (1) *Unlucky for Pringle,* ed. C. J. Fox and R. T. Chapman
(Short stories).

(2) *The Roaring Queen,* ed. W. Allen (A novel, suppressed in 1936).

1977. *Mrs. Dukes' Million* (A novel).

EARLY DRAFT OF CHAPTER XXI, "HOW ONE BEGINS"

TO go back to the beginning, I must detail the events which led up to my embracing the life of art and letters, rather than deciding upon one of the more popular callings. Though when I say 'deciding upon' my will played no part in it. It was a fiat from the unconscious.

My career began then in a Public School. I can imagine no clearer confirmation of the claim that the creative impulse of this order is biological — as much as the dam-making function of the beaver — than my own case. For as a schoolboy I was a dolt. Yet, in this most unlikely of subjects the strange instinct to interpret and to recreate declared itself.

In the 'muddied oaf' at the goal (or in the scrum, where I brutishly functioned, a good pusher and kicker, though of no use in other parts of the field where initiative and a modicum of intelligence were required) this paradoxical flowering occurred.

In those days I *was* Mr. Kipling's 'flannelled fool at the wicket' (a duck's egg my customary score — there is no *scrum* in cricket, in which one can bury one's head and push and kick). I was so stupid that these idiot sports seemed ends in themselves, as they were represented to be. It was my intention to enter the Army Class. But I had not even enough I.Q. for that. 'Woods and Forests', I think it was called, was all I could aspire to, I was informed, or the Indian Police.

I have said my career began at school, where my vocation first became apparent to myself and those about me. But I should perhaps go further back; in childhood I wrote romances upon quires of lavatory-paper, which I stitched together. These early books of mine were no more stupid than the Volsungensaga or the more savage books of the Old Testament, but were that sort of thing. No spark of reaction showed itself against these standards. Profusely illustrated, these books display stiff and hieratic friezes of heavily accoutred mannikins. These chains of matchstick-men, each trailing a musket or grasping a hatchet, went right across the double page. Half of them are obviously Redskins, with plumed warbonnets, leather stockings, and an assortment of weapons proper to the Indian brave: the other half are plainly Palefaces. I inhabited the world of Fenimore Cooper. — It is most sad that the tiny mind of a little animal like myself at six should be filled by its elders with such pasteboard violence, initiating it into this old game of murder: but being born into a military aristocracy means that life begins full of excited little bangs and falsetto war whoops. The important fact however is that I diligently converted all this into visual and verbal terms.

When I look at another photograph I have here on my table, showing the same self in uniform among belted and tin hatted companions of World War I, I perceive a repetition — it is the same pattern, only the bangs and cries of battle were then real, and not academic.

To return to the Public School. In my study at Rugby I painted in oils.

At the age of thirteen I was already equipped with an easel, paints, canvases and so forth. Instead of poring over my school books, there I would sit and copy an oil painting of a dog. I remember a very big boy opening the door of the study, putting his big red astonished face inside, gazing at me for a while (digesting what he saw — the palette on my thumb, the brush loaded with pigment in the act of dabbing) and then, laconic and contemptuous, remarking 'You frightful Artist!' closed the study door — and I could hear his big slouching lazy steps going away down the passage to find some more normal company. The English are, I am afraid, like that.

Rugby, as you are no doubt aware, was Dr. Arnold's imperial human laboratory. On top of the old 'Tom Brown's Schooldays' foundation he built an organization for incubating empire-builders. He was one of the two most influential organisers in jingo-England. Disraeli was the other. The latter made the great nineteenth century British Queen into an oriental Empress: whereas Dr. Arnold created the 'Public School Boy' and, of course, the Old School Tie. Rugby is a very old school. But the mushroom growth of new Public Schools which the latter half of the nineteenth century witnessed may, must, be regarded as Arnold-inspired. It was a novel brand of Briton. — In this unpropitious atmosphere I suddenly revealed unusual tastes. It registered in an unexpected quarter: namely, the mind of my house-master.

As a consequence of the time spent painting in oils my academic progress was phenomenally slow. Also, I was unruly at that age, and was frequently beaten by my house-master, both for idleness and breaches of the rules. He used to rush up and down his dark study, lashing at me with his whistling cane. I was one of the bad spots in his house: until one day he discovered about my secret habits. Then he would send for me every once in a while, and ask to see my pictures or drawings. More than that, he arranged for me to be sent to the drawing master several times a week — an old Scot, with a beautiful silver moustache, who gargled away in a Glasgow accent, but provided me with splendid reports. And so I received preliminary instruction in drawing.

So I drew and drew, and painted dogs' heads and sea-battles: but I did not change my form in four terms. I was still in the lower-middle school. The house-master then said to my mother that it might be better to encourage me to follow what was uncomfortably plainly my vocation, and send me to an art-school. She herself had always painted — used to go to an art-school in Bloomsbury Square at the top of Great Ormonde Street before her marriage, and was not displeased to think that I evinced this unconquerable desire to do what she herself had done in a desultory way. There was perhaps vanity in this. Every year I would go to Paris with my mother, when a schoolboy. Those visits were not calculated to cure me of my interest in the arts. It was then I first frequented the galleries, the Louvre and Luxembourg. On several occasions we stayed I recall at a pension in the rue d'Alger, which was full of books — the library of George Augustus Sala, whose widow I think ran it. The invitation of this pension-library left me indifferent: but the unnumerable oil-paintings in the museums, in one big lazy blur of cupids, shipwrecks, madonnas and fat women, exercised a pleasurable mesmerism upon a very lazy schoolboy, fated to paint, but whose instinct far outran his consciousness, which remained that of a most uninteresting specimen of English school-life.

I left Rugby after about two years of kicking balls and being beaten for neglect of work, and went to the Slade School, in Gower Street, London. There I became an artist while still a schoolboy. At once I attracted great attention: although this was not because what I did was particularly remarkable, but owing to the lack of talent exhibited by most art students. Professors Brown and Tonks were in command, Russell taught drawing and Wilson Steer was supposed to teach painting. Before long they made me a 'scholar'. This was something like a 'massier'. William Orpen and earlier Augustus John had been 'scholars'. My duties, which I shared with another student—for the scholarship was split—were to start things off in the morning by posing the model. But I was seldom there to do that; the bad habits of the Public School still clung to me. I preferred smoking and reading the paper or talking in the drying-room to painting the nude. So the same thing occurred there as had already befallen me—only this time it was more violent, since they were paying me, not I paying them. My scholarship was taken away from me and I was shown the door. Professor Brown even went so far as to order Campion, the doorkeeper (a reliable old soldier, with tatooed arms) to keep me out. One day when I went there, after my disgrace, to obtain a model's address, Campion informed me of this on the doorstep. Even Professor Brown summoned a student to his office whom he had observed the day before on top of a bus with me in the King's Road, Chelsea. He expressed regret at this, for, Brown said, I was a 'bad influence'.

I suppose I was a couple of years at that institution too—four being the rule; then, after a short spell in London, I went to Paris. There I began my education in all directions—during the years I was in Paris, or in Madrid, Munich, Haarlem, etc. gradually the devastating effect of English school-life wore off. The vocational ferments which had driven me out of the British rut of snobbish sloth—which failings I had caricatured—transformed me, in contact with the Latin life, into something so different that had I a few years later encountered a schoolfellow he would not have recognized me. I still went to a tailor in Brook Street for my clothes, but persuaded him to cut them into the oddest shapes. My hair was abundant and was now worn extremely long.

In Paris I began my education, in many directions. I acquired several languages. I attended Bergson's lectures in the Collège de France—when that little gray-faced man came out of the little door at the back and went to the lecturer's desk none of the audience of fasionable women applauded him more respectfully than myself. *Les données immediates de la conscience* produced a great effect in my just awakened mind. I became a great reader, though formerly I had never opened a book. That Paris will always remain for me— *that* Paris, for now it is a different one—the geographical source of all life and light and true happiness. It had been the greatest school of Europe for so long that merely to be there meant that the mind waked up—mine from its barbarous torpor.

My first stories and literary sketches were written in Brittany, where I spent many months at a time in a now fruitful indolence. For indolent—with a new indolence—I remained. Mine was now a drowsy sun-baked ferment, watching with delight the great comic effigies which erupted beneath my astonished gaze: BROTCOTNAZ, BESTRE, and the rest.

During these days I began to get a philosophy—and a very bad one, I am afraid. Like all philosophies, it was built up around the will. As an expression of my personality at that time it took the form of a reaction against society. But it was militantly vitalist. It was not until later that I read J.-J. Rousseau, or it might have had something to do with his anti-social dreaming.

The quotation from Montaigne — whose familiar vein and great directness pleased me greatly — which is the epigraph to be found at the beginning of *Tarr* (my first novel, published during World War I) is a key to my state of mind. 'Que c'est un mol chevet que l'ignorance et l'incuriosité.' The human personality should be left, I thought, just as it is, in its pristine freshness: somewhat like a wild garden — full, naturally, of starlight and nightingales, of sunflowers and the sun. The 'Wild Body' I envisaged as such a garden. The characters I chose to celebrate — Bestre, the Cornac and his wife, Brotcotnaz, le père Francois — were all primitive creatures, immersed in life, as much as birds, or big, obsessed, sun-drenched insects, in the wild garden of which I have spoken. The body was wild: one was attached to something wild, like a big cat that sunned itself and purred. The bums, alcoholic fishermen, penniless students, many Russian, who might have come out of the pages of *The Possessed*, who were my favourite company, were an anarchistic, no nihilistic material. And as ringmaster of this circus I appointed my 'soldier of Humour', who stalked imbecility with a militancy and appetite worthy of a Flaubert, who had somehow got into the [. . .] of Gorki.

This I said was bad philosophy. That is because deliberately to spend so much time in contact with the crudest life is wasteful of life. It seems to involve the error that only the raw material is authentic *life*. After two or three intermediate stages I developed as great an obsession for the ordered garden as at first I had professed for the wild one. — That, at all events, is how I began. And my earliest paintings were of fishermen, of the sort you find in the pages of the *Wild Body*. With pleasure I recall that my first exhibited oil-painting was purchased by Augustus John. It was exhibited at the gallery run by Robert Ross (Oscar Wilde's great friend and literary executor) in St. James's. It was a large empty yellow picture of large sprawling Normandy fishermen of various hues of mustard.

My 'wildness' had so thoroughly disinfected me of my early respectability that whenever I returned to England I came here almost as a foreigner. Once I got on an English cargo ship in Vigo, I remember, to return to London by sea. The crew would not believe I was English, until one of them came up and, after a few minutes conversation, solved the riddle. 'He's an English gentleman,' this seaman announced. And his analysis seemed to satisfy the others completely, and account for my strangeness. . . .

TWO FRAGMENTARY DRAFTS OF CHAPTERS ON
THE HITLER WRITINGS OF THE THIRTIES

I

THE BURDEN OF DULLNESS

WHY has nature provided us with no psychical insight so that when we encounter a mass-murderer we are apprised of the fact by an instantaneous repulsion? – The mass-murderer I have in mind in putting this question is Herr Hitler. I never met him, it is true, so my question strictly speaking does not apply to me. But books of photographs displayed him in every imaginable position and every mood, from the jocose to the sternly censorious.

As a portraitist I feel I should have detected the awful symptoms, even if I was wanting in the visionary power to see this little figure, only a few years hence, popping into his gas-ovens not thousands but millions of human victims – or letting loose his ghoulish doctors among the shrieking 'guinea-pigs'. Surely however such a monster never lurked beneath so homely an exterior. And his habits, apparently, matched it in disarmingness. All reports agreed that he had no vices – was a vegetarian pussyfoot who had never looked at a woman, and neither pipe nor cigarette had ever defiled his rather prim lips.

> There are warlike persons who, perhaps with the intuition of the quarrelsome in recognizing another of their kind, spotted Hitler at once as a potential Tamerlane. . . . But heavens! – what a flair a man must have to detect a Tamerlane beneath that platitudinous exterior – the plebeian protégé of the Junker Papen, with the humble cut of whose German sports-jacket, and with whose disarming toothbrush moustache, we are all now so familiar. Still I confess that in one respect I was badly taken in, in 1930. What more than anything else caused my judgement to trip was that unusual trinity of celibacy, teetotalism, and anti-nicotine.

– This is from *The Hitler Cult*. Two of my books are about Hitler – the first (called *Hitler*) I wrote in 1930, almost three years before Hitler came to power. The second (called *The Hitler Cult*) was written in 1938. This is by far the better book. It is better-written, better documented – and *later*, consequently representing a maturer view. When you come across a political movement in its infancy, as I did – an already massive infant, but unformed and untried – you can scarcely be expected to understand it so well as after five years of watching it in action, possessed of unlimited power for good or evil.

In spite of this the first book alone is mentioned by my critics and detractors – written as it is in a vein sympathetic to Hitler, it will be obvious that it is a far more useful book to refer to than the second, which is the reverse of sympathetic. So number two is conveniently forgotten. It may be a better book, but not for *their* purposes.

Anyhow, this pair of books is the main subject of this chapter. No subject, I know, is so stone cold and dead flat as Herr Hitler. Historians will spend their entire lives searching out every particle of evidence about him, because he was responsible for the death of so many people. But this excavation of the recent past is necessarily a boring task for me.

How much of one's time a dull man can occupy! All Europe for a decade and a half has had to stare fascinated at the empty features, listen to the mouthings, painfully acquire a knowledge of the foolish third-rate mind of this little soapboxer — who has vanished, and we hopefully assume is dead. — It is, however, one of our major problems how to prevent dull men from taking up all our time. The modern politician has the means — and unfortunately often the will — to stop us from thinking about anything else but *him*. Of course why I have had to spend so much time (over this particular one) is because other dull, but malicious, people have been able to attract a boycott to me. These are people who in your walk of life, if you are not an 'author', may be wholly unimportant. In mine, as they write the reviews of one's books, decide whether one shall go on the air or not, whether one shall be invited to writers' gatherings, be asked to belong to their organisations, be published and publicised or not, the thousand things that produce what we call 'reputation', they count heavily in one's working life.

These are the intellectual small-fry — not 'cryptos' necessarily at all, they may be equally cryptical anti-stalinist stooges of god-knows-what; or be idle rich playing at parlor ping-pong; or ex-idle-rich in a pink disguise earning their lives by scribbling in the weeklies; almost anything that walks on two legs in fact and has learnt how to read and write. But it is labelled 'intellectual'.

Hitler first appeared as articles in *Time and Tide.* At that period Hitler had never been heard of in England. Those journalists who were by way of being experts on Germany poohpoohed my articles, asserting that Hitler was an ephemeral figure, momentarily jumped up, who would be wiped out in the forthcoming Reichstag elections, and never be heard of again. By one man I remember I was described as 'an innocent abroad'. Yet the reverse of what they predicted happened. Instead of being politically extinquished, he rapidly climbed to absolute power.

I had no pretensions to be more than a casual visitor in Germany: was the reverse of an expert. How I came to go there at that time was as follows.

In 1930 I went to Berlin to contact German publishers. The Insel Verlag of Leipzig had made an unexpected offer for the translation rights of *Childermass.* This had fallen through: but it had drawn my attention to Germany. I spent about a month in Berlin — in that grim capital I made the acquaintance of the National Socialist German Workers Party — not with Herr Hitler (who was not there) or with any Nazis, but one could not move foot up or down the Friedrichstrasse . . . without making the acquaintance of the *movement.*

Groups of party boys, of this strange new movement, looking like oversized boyscouts, hung about at every street corner. They did not infest the cafés — they had not the money to do that. They were the party of the moneyless, financed by industrial millionaires.

'When in the winter evenings,' I quote from *Hitler*, 'along the boulevards of *Berlin im Licht*, the muffled, uniformed, hawkers take up their stations and utter their dismal cries, it is not sport, as with us, but politics, that is the dominant motif. Indeed, dismallest and loudest, the "Nacht Ausgabe" resounds above the rest; and *that* is the organ of Hugenberg . . . the cry of "Tempo" is lighter than that of the "Nacht Ausgabe".' 'Tempo' stood for the Weimar Republic, 'Nacht Ausgabe' for the Dritte Reich.

During these winter days and weeks in Berlin it was borne in upon me that something was happening here which might set Europe alight. I was not especially interested in Germany, but Europe was important to me: too important, as I have elsewhere explained.

Since World War i the French had forgotten their promise to disarm.* Indeed they had piled up costly armaments, until they were, although essentially a weak state (as a dwindling nation, of most unenthusiastic conscripts), in military and financial ascendancy in Europe. The nations to the east, ruined by World War i, were treated by them as economic colonies, and the 'deux cent familles' and the Comité des Forges grew fat upon the plunder.

These imperialists were nothing if not tactless — and our creation the Weimar Republic was given no chance of establishing itself. Had it not been Hitler it would have been some other ambitious agitator — denouncing, as he did, the Diktat of Versailles, the 'bleeding white' of Germany with impossible reparations (tribute politics, *Erfuhlungspolitik*), the insolence of the French, the iniquity of the Polish Corridor and so forth.

A nation of savers, the Germans had seen all their savings dissipated in a torrent of worthless paper-money. This happened twice, first just after world war i, then again during the '29-'30 Slump. So ten years after world war i, Germany, as now, had been converted into a dangerous vacuum of discontent and misery in the centre of Europe.

Into this vacuum now had moved, to quote a London newspaper, 'something comparable only to a national-religious upheaval.'

Action of some kind was imperative. Your attitude could be one of indignant rage: you could bluster: 'How dare those rats complain of their lot! They have jolly well deserved it!' That is the 'squeeze the pips til they squeak' attitude. Or you could take a chance, and be friendly to them — or try to be.

Really only two things could be done about such an 'upheaval' the early stages of which I was witnessing. To march in and extinguish it — a few infantry batallions would have been sufficient at that time. Thereby we would have perpetuated the angry blank in the centre of Europe. The other thing to do was to revise our policy as regards Germany — to 'give them a break', in other words. This seemed to me the better course. We could not afford to have Germany there as an impoverished slum. It was not appeasement (that warmonger's cliché) — thinking purely of England's interests, it was the latter of these alternatives that should have occurred to us first.

The next phase of the drama was when Hitler entered the Rhine. By *then* perfectly plainly only one course was open to us. Go into the Rhine, with adequate forces, and hold Germany down as we are doing at present.

As it was England did a most extraordinary thing. No action was taken

---

* In saying 'French', 'Germany', 'Italian', I always mean of course the particular gang governing those unfortunate people, *not* the people themselves.

to stop Herr Hitler building up from nothing an immense air armament. The British government did not revise its disarmament policy, acquiring an effective armament. But it *did* continue to hurl threats at the Germans every day. So 'the few', a handful of gallant young men, had to lay down their lives when war came, to save England from being overwhelmed — the French, of course, folding up at the first shock of war.

That at least is how the matter presented itself to me. Now I know — seeing what were the character and aims of Hitler as set forth in *The Hitler Cult* (which is I fear being wise after the event) — England had no alternative but to march into Germany as soon as Hitler became Reichskanzler, stamp out the Hitler Bewegung, and, faute de mieux, start the sort of business that is going on at present.

Our mistake was the Versailles Treaty itself — or, at least, the reparations, and the treatment of even the Weimar Republic Germans as a ticket-of-leave nation. Things had gone too far by the time Hitler had arrived. One thing leads to another: and by 1930 the Western Democracies were already years too late. But I dare say you have to go much further back than that — once world war i had occurred all the rest had to follow. These competitive commercial and military systems could do little else but destroy each other.

When I come upon a chapter headed 'Adolf Hitler a Man of Peace', I feel very foolish — knowing all we do, such an announcement is painfully absurd. It was I suppose, in part, wishful-thinkful.

What I based my belief on were protestations, and disciplinary actions. The soldier, this man said, was never warlike, he knew too much about war. (True — but, like everything he said, calculated humbug.) He dismissed any member of his militia indulging in provocative behavior, either towards Poles or French. He was a big warm-hearted bemedalled dove! — But the politician can take any form. I lost sight of the politician under the drab tunic of the *Frontkampfer.* I overlooked the fact that politicians, in their madness for power, can risk their skins, acquire iron crosses. An inexcusable blunder.

Actual *war* on the part of a bankrupt, totally disarmed nation, however, did not enter the picture at all. Germany could no more make war than a five year old boy could go into the ring with Joe Louis. On the other hand, great anger and determination was displayed by this big tough nation. Not *then*, but some time or other, immense difficulties were in store for everybody, unless we were more serious. These passionate demonstrations, this great popular following (already there were 107 Hitlerite deputies) could not be shrugged off — or ought not to be.

So something else began: *Hitler* was the first of a group of books occupied, to the exclusion of anything else, with the thought of *war* — with the great and futile effort to avert, in such way as lay in my power, that repetition — that encore. The well-meaning imbecility of those proceedings — doing me infinite harm and no one else any good — I have commented on in an earlier part. Let me repeat what I said then, that I am at present acutely aware that collectively people are incurably tolerant of war. In the case of England, bankruptcy and even beggardom would appear as a wonderful opportunity of displaying 'grit'. — So why I had *war* of all things on the brain passed most people's understanding. The atom bomb is so unpopular that, if by some accident it is mentioned, I pretend I've never heard of it or look quite blank and drop the subject.

But let me get back to my book. 'Everything now almost, since the war,' I wrote, p. 128, 'seems a matter of life and death.' (It did not seem that to any one except me. I quote this to demonstrate my attitude to 'emergencies'. I even say — and mean it! — that I 'have no choice'.)

'I do not write this book *from choice*, for instance — I would far rather, if it rested with me, be engaged in scientific research, or in artistic creation. Ever since in the War,* where I served on the Western Front with the Artillery . . . there are certain questions I have asked of life. . . . The war, as you know, went on and on, and these questions in the end *asked themselves* as it were. . . . A state of emergency came to appear for me, as for most soldiers, a permanent thing. Unlike, I dare say, most of my companions, I realized that something in this "storm of steel" required explaining — and the academic meterology of average public opinion, or of the Press, for these monstrous disturbances.'

Seeing that people often make up in malice for what they lack in intelligence, and only the laws of libel deter me from naming a few who are just plain liars, I will purify the air about these first impressions of the latest recrudescence of German nationalism. (My second-thought, namely *The Hitler Cult*, I shall afterwards examine.) A few quotes should help.

If there is one thing more than another that was characteristic of the nationalsocialist it was, I suppose, his idiotic hatred of the Jews. The American Civil War was ostensibly fought for Negro emancipation: our last war may one day be regarded as one fought for the emancipation of the Jews. The future historian will marvel at our immediately afterwards engaging in a little war in Palestine with the very people we had ruined ourselves in order to emancipate (having established ourselves in this ancient homeland of the Israelites for no very obvious reason). This the historian will put down to British muddleheadedness. — Here anyway are two passages about the *Judenfrage* [pp. 37-41]:

> One of the principal opponents of Hitlerism, the Austrian, Graf R. Coudenhove-Kalergi (a prominent anti-semite also) writing of the assassination of Rathenau, made the following assertion:
>
> > "Rathenau . . . wurde in erster Linie nicht darum ermordet, weil er Verständigungspolitik trieb — sondern weil er Jude war."†
>
> This is no doubt true. Whether socialist or monarchist, the German inherits this very powerful prejudice. . . . To deal with this situation anti-antisemitic societies have recently been formed. The principal one has its offices in Paris. (Mr. H. G. Wells is a member of its committee). . . . So it goes on, the battle of ideas. . . . It is perhaps only fair to the Nationalsocialist to say that the Jew has often lent colour to these accusations. But the Jew no doubt would retort that, coming as he generally does from Tartary, he cannot be expected to be much attracted by carol-singing, protestant hymn-music, or the teutonic Royal-Academicism of official painting, and that in any case he buys and sells — being a man of affairs — novelties that are good business propositions. He might

* World War i.

† [Rathenau was assassinated not primarily because he promoted a policy of understanding but because he was a Jew.]

go more deeply into it than that, of course, and protest that it was not *he* at all, but the great 'aryan' inventors and technicians, who have been responsible for all the destructive 'modernism' of the present Western World. Western Science is to blame, in short. He has made use of this (he could point out with some show of reason) but would of his own accord never have *invented* it.

I will not pursue this argument: but we will suppose that as we turn away we have heard the Nationalsocialist demanding angrily what suspension bridges, telephones, and elevators, in themselves, have necessarily to do with Jazz and Negro Art: and (to give the Jew the last word) we can imagine that we hear him in his turn pointing out, always to some effect, that as to the latter, is it not the Negro, in the Land of Elevators, who is employed to [operate same? — so the music of ex-slaves gets mixed up, not unnaturally after all, with the modernist machinery, employed to]* whisk cartloads of Babbitts up and down their megalopolitan steel and concrete towers. But we should immediately hear the Nationalsocialist insisting that this New York civilization was rather judeo-american than european-american. All the replies, and counter-replies, however, of this fierce dispute, we will allow to die away.

As to England. Some one has to govern England, it must be conceded, now that the Normans have faded out, and that the Irish have thrown up the job and decided to settle down in a well-earned obscurity, upon their own private bogs, locking themselves up politically with their local Island politics — washing their hands finally of this ungrateful anglo-saxon land. I might even agree (without prejudice) that indeed the Jews (first of all dearly bought, I think — of Mr. Bernard Shaw and myself) govern England to the complete satisfaction of everybody, and without a hitch, or so'much as a single rift in the lute! But that would not be quite true: for if indeed, wearing the trousers, the Jew is the brilliant and bossy Hausfrau of this stolid english hubby, the latter has at least, in his quiet way, succeeded in influencing her, decidedly for the good. In short, upon that hypothesis, is not the Jew here, from the Hitler standpoint, disinfected and anglicized? — just as in the States he has been transformed (that yankee Abraham or 'Abie') into a true Western product — presented, to crown everything, with a wild white Irish Rose! How, under such circumstances, could Abie 'remember Carthage'? It would be against nature to dream (too much) of Zion — with Kathleen Na Hoolan crooning away in his ear!

What an Englishman or an American friendly to Hitler should perhaps say is this. He should say to the Hitlerite that he takes the Jew too seriously: 'For *better or for worse,'* in the words of the english marriage service, there *is* the Jew! . . . and as a 'middleman' of uncanny penetration, may he not even have an important civilizing function?

The abominable massacres in which this particular phase of Jewish history culminated would retrospectively make it impossible to treat, as I have above, with patience and toleration the prospective butcher. Otherwise it shows, with I think a judicious insight, the exact relation of these two races, most unfortunately thrown together at this juncture: one, the Jewish, recently emerged from centuries of barbarous ostracism and exhibiting a natural elation; the other, the Germans, having, after two centuries of growing power, gambled for the mastery of Europe, and in one catastrophic sweep lost all their gains — relegated to a pariah position among the nations, and passionately resentful.

* [Lewis's transcription accidentally drops the lines in brackets.]

This would have been accepted as a fair account of the matter by the contemporary Jew. This was by no means the case, however, with the Nationalsocialist. This was far too big a dose of impartiality for *him* — of sweet reason and moderation — and when he came to power the German translation of this book was withdrawn from circulation and with my permission 'returned to pulp'.

Here is a further passage (pp. 137-138) on matters of the technique of art:

> Reduced to *technique* — to the mastery over matter — the 'aryan' claim does not appear so lofty as in the sweeping generalization we have read above. Are there perhaps *two* sorts of men, after all, who are the complement of one another, one is inclined to ask — men of action, and men of art, for instance? Is the present day 'Aryan', in isolation, not enough? Without him, indeed, the civilized world might well go down (by reason of the valuable starch secreted in his character in great quantities). But is this Master of Matter not so superior after all as he has believed himself to be?

What you have been reading above is the common sense of these matters: but that was not what anybody wanted. Everybody was supposed to foam at the mouth, all the time, both by the Nazis and the majority of people here, both Tories and left-wing.

The nationalism of the Hitlerites, like all nationalism, of course bored me extremely. Their 'racism' was a joke — although of course race itself is a real enough thing. The playing at soldiers (though as I show in the 'Doom of Youth' it pleases the kiddies and was the Pied Piper of Berchtesgaden led them off to the slaughter house in their millions) was both silly and — even then — mildly disturbing. But there were two things for which I felt much sympathy, in what was at that time the declared programme of those people. One was, emphasis as to the necessity to clean up the social scene. The other, a much more fundamental issue, was economic.

Here *debt* was the key word. As I wrote: 'The decade that has elapsed since the termination of the war has been blackened in every country by the shadow of the colossal loan-finances involved in that event. And the shadow grows deeper as we recede from it.' The usual thing after a war is to denounce the armament manufacturers; no one ever thinks of the financier who supplies, at crushing interest rates, the money to buy the armaments, and all the other things, more costly even than armaments, needed in war-time. — It was what I regarded as a critically important distinction between *Berufskapitalisten** and a rich working man that impressed me.

All those among us who do the independent thinking for the others have been so battered, bored, and stupified by the avalanche of events, that few any longer cast so much as a weary eye in the direction of our antediluvian credit system. But it still is *there*. We still 'pull in our belts' because of it, still find it impossible to buy books we need, support the daily nuisance of an unreal economic system, more laden every day with debts. Our country is sinking into the status of a second class population, instead of forming part of a world-vision, because of the 'Cross of Gold'. — The Nationalsocialists were not the first people to attack the unreality of conventional economics —

• [Professional capitalists.]

but they were the first considerable political party to give this issue a major place in their programme. This was, to me at least, an important fact. In my first Hitler book I quoted from Mr. T. S. Eliot's 'Criterion' commentary of 1931. I will now re-quote it.

'We need more and better Economics,' almost with rashness Mr. T. S. Eliot in the relative privacy of the columns of the *Criterion* asserts. 'We need another Ruskin. The trouble with the Science of Economics of today is that it appears in a form in which very few people, if any can understand it. And, in a democracy, it is essential that people should understand the matters upon which they are exhorted to make decisions and that they should not be called upon to decide upon matters which they do not understand. When I read, say, an economic article in the *Referee*, or any of the numerous productions of Major Douglas and his disciples, I am confirmed in my suspicion that conventional economic practice is all wrong, but I can never understand enough to form any opinion as to whether the prescription or nostrum proffered is right. I cannot but believe that there are a few simple ideas at bottom, upon which I and the rest of the unlearned are competent to decide according to our several complexions; but I cannot for the life of me ever get to the bottom. I cannot, for instance, believe in over-population so long as there is room in the world for every one to move about without suffocation; I cannot understand the concurrence of over-production with destitution, and I cannot help feeling that this has something to do with people wanting — so far as they are in a position to want anything more than food and shelter — the wrong things, and cultivating the wrong passions. . . . I am not even convinced that the accomplished economic specialists of the Harley Street of finance always know what they are about themselves. I have served my own apprenticeship in the City; endeavoured to master the "classics" of the subject: have written (or compiled) articles on Foreign Exchange which occasionally met with approval from my superiors; and I was never convinced that the authorities upon whom I drew, or the expert public which I addressed, understood the matter any better than I did myself — which is not at all.'

In this country Mr. Herbert Read, as well as Mr. Eliot, did what they could to promote an understanding of Money. But it is one of those instances where a number of people agree that a great abuse exists, but unanimously decide that, human nature being what it is, nothing can be done to change it, except by force. And where is the force to come from?

The way the primitives of the Nationalsocialist movement — not the brazen little overlords of their days of power — approached the problem, then, was to make a rigid distinction between *Das Leihkapital* or the Loan-capital of so-called high-finance, on the one hand, and, on the other, those who use money not as a commodity with which to indulge in gigantic usury, but as capital used creatively. William Jennings Bryan's celebrated rhetoric, 'You shall not crucify mankind upon a cross of gold', which electrified the United States of America in the 'nineties, found a modern echo in these not very [*MS breaks off at this point.*]

II
[*The second fragment is untitled.*]

During the past twenty years thousands of books have been written — I myself have either read, or glanced at scores — favourable to the soviet regime in Russia. Were these books written by communists? Certainly not — they were invariably the work of people described as 'liberals', or just curious travellers, who gave the public, for what it was worth, the fruit of their observations.

Seventeen years ago I wrote a book giving an account of what was at that time a completely unknown movement, called the Nationalsocialist German Workers Party. This was three years before Hitler came to power. My general aim was to break the European ostracism of Germany, call in question the wisdom of the Versailles Treaty, end the bad behaviour of the French, attempt to establish healthy relations in Western Europe. — Herr Hitler was the major obstacle to any such programme (I did not of course know that then). And this was undertaken in the interests of Western civilisation — which had been deeply shaken by World War i: not in the interest of the Germans, nor of their brand of pseudo-marxism, nor needless to say of the little politico whom the Junkers were about to put in as a proletarian figurehead. — Ever since I have been called a 'fascist'.

But if that makes me a 'fascist', then all the thousands of persons who have, at one time or another, written friendly and unbiased accounts of Russian Communism are a lot of 'reds', and ought to be recognised as such. But I have never heard one of them accused of being that.

The faulty reasoning — deliberately faulty — underlying this kind of nonsense is inherent in a political position, which, with the arrogance of a religion, demands — 'Are you one of us or are you an enemy?' This is undoubtedly communist in origin — for the communist was taught never to allow himself to be drawn into an argument, but to advance his doctrine as if it were the law.

This simplification of the natural pluralism of belief, of the multiplicity of forms of thought and of feeling present in the world at any given time, and its reduction to something like three strait-jackets, into which everything living must be thrust, is characeristic of the contemporary intellectual. One strait-jacket is marked *good*, one *no-good*, and one *nothing* — and for these sectaries there is nothing else whatever in the world.*

All intellectuals who reached maturity between the two wars are seminarists of the Russian professionals of revolutionary technique. Even when they turn against their old teachers, they still continue their stacatto dialectic — although, once they have turned (as most are doing now) it no

---

* There was no difficulty about interpreting these labels formerly. *Good* stood for Party or fellow traveller: *no-good* meant a fascist heretic, or a capitalist; *nothing* indicated those living in outer policital darkness (Eskimos, or the unenlightened masses in backward countries). Today the strait-jackets are still there, in which all thought must be confined — but one cannot with any confidence say what the labels stand for. I suspect the capitalist of having bought the *good* label. — It should be remembered, by the way, that the Russian communists were never absurd like their Western interpreters. These *jackets* were the handiwork of our parlour-pinks.

longer means anything.

I am a political freethinker: such I have always been and have knelt in no church built by a politician. — It is difficult for the political freethinker (belonging to no political communion or exclusive sect) to understand that he cannot, without gravely compromising himself, scrutinize with a certain benevolence the collective farm system, for instance, of the Soviet Republics. If someone stepped up to him, while he was so engaged and said: 'I observe, sir, that you have repudiated the doctrine of Western Democracy?' he would think that he was being accosted by a madman. Or, rather, he would have had that impression formerly. One is very used to such absurdities today. You now would know at once that this was merely an intellectual.

At present there is, as I have remarked, among intellectuals a powerful reaction against communism. Numbers of people, though still spluttering 'fascist' from time to time, are great labellers in the opposite sense. So whereas ten or fifteen years ago one was liable to intellectual excommunication if one saw so much as a scintilla of good in any of the fascist heresies, today there is the same *Verbot* regarding Russian communism.

But 'fascist', 'crypto', and such are like the cries and counter-cries of fans at a baseball or boxing match. What is behind *this* however is a sport far more barbarous and deadly than any disgracing the Roman circus, surging up into periodic orgies of bloodshed.

Or, to take a less sinister illustration — perhaps nearer to their innate silliness — these are reminiscent of the old cry of 'get your hair cut'!, or that obscene sound which is referred to as a 'raspberry'.

I believe that intellectuals no longer know they are saying it — they just spit 'fascist' or 'crypto', 'stalinist', 'stooge' without thinking — as schoolboys emit 'swot' or 'house-tart'. Under an anaesthetic or in his slumbers, or when at the dentist's gas is administered, or when he wakes up in the morning and his tongue begins drowsily to wag, the intellectual lisps 'fascist' or 'crypto'. The life of the rank and file intellectual (who is about as *intellectual* as a pack of sparrows) revolves about a half-dozen childish epithets, and the emotions aroused by their utterance.

If today I rather go out of my way to speak with respect of some of the institutions of Russian Communism, that is to be explained upon very different grounds from those that would ever occur to Mr. Orwell. Elsewhere I have mentioned how further consideration, and more varied experience, have caused me to modify my critical attitude to communism: and if I see things I like in communism — directions in which it deserves our special study — I shall continuously say so. But *today* more than ever I should be apt to do that. It is not just that I believe I can [*MS breaks off.*]

SIX LETTERS ON *RUDE ASSIGNMENT* BY EZRA POUND
EDITED AND ANNOTATED BY
BRYANT KNOX

LATE in April 1946 Wyndham Lewis read the following words from a letter addressed to T. S. Eliot:

> Now as to ole Wyndham whose address I have not, to thee and him these presents. While I yet cohere, he once sd/ a faceful. & apart from 3 dead and one aged [word?] who gave me 3 useful hints. ole W is my only critic — you have eulogized and some minors have analysis'd or dissected — all of which tell the old ruffian if you can unearth him.[1]

Pound's greeting, care of T. S. Eliot, was posted from St. Elizabeths Hospital in Washington D.C., and marked the renewal of their correspondence, which had been completely severed during the Second World War. In June, Lewis replied. His letter opened with a tongue-in-cheek jibe at Pound's predicament: "I am told that you believe yourself to be Napoleon — or is it Mussolini? What a pity you did not choose Buddha while you were about it, instead of a politician" (*Letters*, p. 394n). All in all the letter was chatty and somewhat mundane, and in subsequent letters to Pound it becomes apparent that Lewis frequently suffered from an inability to incorporate matters of substance: "I never know what to say to you when I sit down to write you as I am now doing" (*Letters*, p. 403).

Pound, nevertheless, was happy with the renewed correspondence. It afforded him the opportunity to campaign for publication of Lewis's work, to promote the kind of intelligence which Lewis represented, and to deluge him with a myriad books, pamphlets, and articles which he hoped he would read. Such men as Brooks Adams, Agassiz, Benton, Blackstone, Confucius, Del Mar, Frobenius, Kitson, and Morgenthau, to name only a few, were recommended by Pound. He also encouraged Lewis to write articles on some of these men and hoped that he would countenance this formidable array of intelligence. But by July 1946, Lewis was obliged to set Pound straight: "My dear Ezz. The writing (and reading) you would have me do is impossible. It takes me all my time to keep alive. I have none on my hands at all"

[The first three *Rude Assignment* letters from Pound to Lewis printed in this volume are held in the Contemporary Literature Collection, Special Collections, W.A.C. Bennett Library, Simon Fraser University and are reproduced with the permission of Percilla Groves, Special Collections Librarian. The second three *Rude Assignment* letters from Pound to Lewis printed herein are held in the Department of Rare Books, Cornell University Library and are reproduced with the permission of Dr. Donald Eddy. All six of these previously unpublished letters by Ezra Pound are Copyright ©1984 by the Trustees of the Ezra Pound Literary Property Trust and are used by permission of New Directions Publishing Corp., Agents.]

(*Letters*, p. 453.). By the end of 1948 Lewis was exasperated with Pound's persistence and complained to D. D. Paige, who was then editing Pound's letters: "Have no wish to read more economics — have something better to do. However many times I may say this he [Pound] returns to the charge" (*Letters*, p. 462).

The pace picked up in 1951 when Pound heard through his son, Omar, that Agnes Bedford had renewed her friendship with Lewis. Bedford was Pound's lifelong friend and musical amanuensis who arranged many of Pound's musical endeavors.[2] When Lewis was beginning to go blind, Bedford sometimes acted as his secretary, and after his death she assisted Anne Lewis in arranging his papers. D. G. Bridson, the B.B.C. writer and producer and close friend of Lewis, has spoken of the friendship with Bedford:

> [She] was seeing a lot of Lewis when we [Bridson and Lewis] became friendly. That, of course, was shortly after he had gone blind — and she was helping him with his correspondence &c. She was a very kind and loveable person, and Lewis was much indebted to her for her goodwill and devotion over the years. I gathered from him that at one time there had been talk of his marrying her (in the late twenties) but he had decided against it, and married Anne W.L. instead. I think you may presume that there was a break between him and Agnes at that time — though whether it lasted until his departure for America in 1938, I don't know. I should not be surprised if it was not his going blind in 1950-51 which brought them together again. Anyhow, from then on they worked together a lot.
>
> (Letter from D. G. Bridson, 8 March 1978)

Pound was soon writing to Bedford, regretting his lack of close contact with Lewis: "Had to leave Sodom [i.e. England and France] in the 1920s/ but possibly cd/ hv/ maintained closer connections. However, no retrospects/ its whaaar do we go frum here?"[3] By the end of March 1951 Pound began to think of Bedford as an auxiliary force not only capable of inducing Lewis to read the authors he recommended, but of convincing him to set pen to paper in defence of cultural standards. "Nacherly," he wrote Bedford, "the quicker WL starts on certain 1951 ideas, the sooner the quicker" (5 May 1951).

The six letters which follow were written by a man whose struggle for the improvement of the intellectual and cultural milieu was waged from behind the walls of St. Elizabeths Hospital, a mental institution in Washington, D.C. From here Pound conducted a voluminous correspondence; established, with the aid of various editors, "Poundian" magazines and pamphlets; published poetry and prose; and contributed many articles and reviews to international journals and newspapers. His visitors included some of the twentieth century's most prominent poets and writers — T. S. Eliot, William Carlos Williams, George Santayana, E. E. Cummings, Charles Olson, Robert Lowell, Marianne Moore, Hugh Kenner, and Conrad Aiken.[4] The letters here printed were written in March 1951 and were prompted by the arrival at St. Elizabeths of Lewis's *Rude Assignment*, probably sent to Pound by Bedford.[5] Within a month he was asking Bedord if there was "ANY sign of WL taking in Ez VOLuminous notes on Rude Ass/?" (5 May 1951). By early July Pound still had not received a response from either Lewis or Bedford regarding these letters into which he had put so much effort: "Naturally difficult to direct W.L.'s thought to useful channels, or even find if yu hv/ read him the notes on Ru/ Asst/ and got any scintillas" (8 July 1951). Lewis apparently never did reply to Pound's comments.

Nevertheless, Pound continued promoting Lewis's work. He asked Bedford: "Cd/ Hutchinson, either at W.L.'s request, or otherwise be purrsuaded to send review copies ASSIGNMENT RUDE to a few continental critics? hand picked or Ezpikt or whatso" (30 March 1951). And in another letter: "SEE that a copy of W.L. 'Rude Assignment' gets to Verlag der Arche, Zurich . . ." (27 April 1951). Pound's promotion of Lewis's writings did not stop with *Rude Assignment* but continued as a campaign for the total corpus of Lewis's work. He wrote Bedford: "AIM to git WL/ to new generation that hasn't read him. Still want 'I presume' [*America, I Presume*] back in print" (8 July 1951).

By 1953 Lewis was totally blind, a fact which Pound at times found difficult to accept. In many of his letters to Bedford he wrote snippets of verse or enclosed material for Lewis — these he would ask Bedford to read to him. But on one ocasion he caught himself writing as if to the old Lewis and in a moment of poignant anger expressed the futility of the gesture: "Vide verso fer Wyndam, but yu may as well read it, as he gawdamn it cant" (26 August 1953). Yet despite Lewis's blindness Pound's indefatigable attempts to get him to bless or blast various causes and specific ideas continued: "must be some way for W.L. to knock off an article on the birth of intelligence in murkn university system. Git it in somewhere," he urged Bedford (28 May 1953).[6]

Many of Pound's comments on and recommendations for the improvement of *Rude Assignment* were probably extremely distasteful to Lewis. Indeed, the very nature of Pound's commentary would tend to compromise Lewis's artistic and philosophical credos. The letters, for example, abound in references to Blackstone, Agassiz, Del Mar, Major C. H. Douglas, and others — men whom Pound recommends that Lewis read in order to write a "proper" autobiography. But were Lewis to accept Pound's entreaties, he would be practicing that for which he once criticized Pound — namely, the "creator-as-scholar" methodology: "This imitation method, of the *creator-as-scholar* — which may be traced ultimately to the habits of the American university, spellbound by 'culture' — and which academic *unoriginality* it was Mr. Ezra Pound's particular originality to import into the adult practice of imaginative literature — does not appeal to me extremely, I confess" (*Letters*, p. 224). Pound, Lewis argued in the same letter, is "mainly a translator — an adapter, an arranger, a *pasticheur*. . . ."

When we consider some of Pound's specific remarks in the letters we see, again, that he and Lewis were often on opposite sides of the fence. In Letter One, for example, Pound intimates that Lewis might benefit from considering Major C. H. Douglas, the Social Credit economist, as a "sound" man, one of the "positives" recommended by Pound earlier in the same letter. Pound praised Douglas because he was the "first economist to include creative art and writing in an economic scheme, and the first to give the painter or sculptor or poet a definite reason for being interested in economics."[7] But in 1939 Lewis had expressed a contrary opinion, referring to Douglas as a "credit crank."[8]

Similarly, Lewis's praise of Roosevelt as the "arch-centraliser," whose methods, he says, brought him to "an understanding of the vanity of regional isolationism" (see p. 100 above), is strongly opposed by Pound (see Letter Three, where Pound condemns centralized governments for knowing little about local needs). Pound regarded Roosevelt, with his policy of centralization, as an enemy of civilization and made him the target of some of his most scathing vituperation.

Another issue on which they disagreed was Mussolini. Although both men had praised Fascism, Lewis's initial support of Hitler and the National Socialist Party, displayed in *Hitler* (1931), did not extend to Mussolini.[9] As late as 1952 Lewis scolded Pound for his "incomprehensible intervention in World War II (when in some moment of poetic frenzy he mistook the clownish Duce for Thomas Jefferson)."[10] Lewis had always regarded Italian Fascism as "political futurism" and unworthy of serious attention.[11]

Rude Assignment is Lewis's book of counter-polemic; and as Pound remarks in Letter One, it is certainly a "good clearing of cloacae." Yet Pound really has little to say about Lewis's main thrust in *Rude Assignment*. He is often more concerned with airing his own prejudices than with responding to specific statements made by Lewis. In a sense, Pound is writing to himself — the letter as echo-chamber. The importance of the letters, then, lies more in what Pound has to say about himself than in any specific insights they provide into Lewis's life or thought. Letter One is particularly illuminating in this respect. Seventeen lines into the letter Pound begins to drift from Julien Benda, the topic at hand, into self-congratulation on his early noting of the "FLOP of froggery"; proceeds to defend the type of Fascism in which he believed; and continues with references to his own concerns: Juan Ramon Jimenez, Mussolini, and politically motivated distortion of news reports. Not until near the end of the first page does Pound cite the passage of *Rude Assignment* about which he purportedly writes — and then he gets it wrong: "All this ref / p. 54 and thaar abouts." But page 54 and thereabouts have no connection with Pound's remarks, and even when we guess he meant to type "34," the connection remains vague. What does emerge is that Pound wants Lewis to engage in the propagation of sound ideas, not merely in the destructive analysis that is all that Lewis's chapter VI offers.

Many of Pound's major statements and ideas in the letters concern matters which had preoccupied him for years: politics, economics, usury, Fascist ideology. Such subjects are typical of his concerns in the early fifties, and have been well documented by Pound scholars. The letters repeat well worn ideas, yet the particular mode of expression is stimulating, and Pound's casual remarks often illuminate little known areas of his thinking, or qualify in some way those already known. In the latter category, for example, Pound's well known admiration for Ford Madox Ford materializes as a profound respect. His praise of Nietzsche's rhetoric in *Thus Spake Zarathustra*, the value he finds in Henry Morgenthau, Sr., and his condemnation of the Italian philosopher Benedetto Croce are all casual remarks yet constitute news for Poundians.

The following letters are presented in facsimile to ensure the unique flavour of Pound's actual typescripts. The editor's transcriptions provide easier reading and in no sense are they presented as definitive. Emendations have been kept to a minimum: paragraphing and some spacing has been

266

regularized, the corrections for a few obvious typing errors have been enclosed in square brackets, and only the most unambiguous spelling errors have been silently corrected (otherwise spelling has been left as in the original). The first three of the six letters that are printed here are part of the Ezra Pound–Agnes Bedford collection held by Simon Fraser University Library, Burnaby, British Columbia. These letters, which take Pound's commentary about half way through *Rude Assignment*, first appeared in Black Sparrow's *Blast 3* (1984), with fuller introduction and notes by the editor than in the present edition. The remaining letters continuing Pound's commentary are held at Cornell University Library and are published here for the first time.

My sincerest thanks and appreciation are extended to the following people for their generous and valuable assistance: Ralph Maud, Seamus Cooney, James Laughlin, the late D. G. Bridson, Percilla Groves, Molly Simmons, Barry Maxwell, Gretchen Haas, Peggy Fox, Charles Watts, and Linda Knox. The letters herein are used under the auspices of Special Collections, Simon Fraser University Library; the Department of Rare Books, Cornell University Library; and with the permission of The Ezra Pound Literary Property Trust.

Bryant Knox
Vancouver, 1984

Notes to Introduction

1 Wyndham Lewis, *The Letters of Wyndham Lewis*, ed. W. K. Rose (Norfolk, Conn., 1963), p. 394n. Subsequent references will be parenthetically cited in the text as "*Letters*."

2 For a full treatment of Pound's musical association with Bedford see *Ezra Pound and Music: The Complete Criticism*, ed. R. Murray Schafer (New York, 1977).

3 Ezra Pound, Letter to Agnes Bedford, 5 May 1951, Simon Fraser University Library, Burnaby, B.C. Subsequent references to the Pound–Bedford correspondence at Simon Fraser are cited by date parenthetically in the text.

4 For accounts of Pound's myriad activities and intellectual excitement and frustration during the St. Elizabeths years, see the St. Elizabeths issue of *Paideuma* 3 (1974); Catherine Seeyle, ed., *Charles Olson & Ezra Pound: An Encounter at St. Elizabeths* (New York, 1975); Eustace Mullins, *This Difficult Individual, Ezra Pound* (New York, 1961); and Louis Dudeck, ed., *Dk/ Some Letters of Ezra Pound* (Montreal, 1974).

5 At Pound's request Bedford had sent other things: "Wyndham did 2 books – lively, in 1940 – V. [ulgar] Streak & 'America I presume' – I want any others" (16 April 1946). Bedford kept sending material to Pound until Lewis's death in 1957.

6 And in other letters "Whether he now haz leisure to KICK some sense into some of 'em [newspapers] I dunno / Agassiz and Blackstone need reBOOST" (7 April 1951); "Sabotage of chinese studies alZO might interest W.L." (9 December 1952); "W.L. might take up theme of danger of world governed by chipmunks and prairie dogs" (27 February 1953); "W.L. meditate that Jefferson saw ALL debt not repayable in 19 years as tax without representation/ shoved onto unborn and minorenni" (27 February 1953).

7 Ezra Pound, *Selected Prose 1909-1965*, ed. William Cookson (New York, 1973), p. 232.

[8] Wyndham Lewis, *The Hitler Cult* (London, 1939), p. 26.

[9] Geoffrey Wagner cites Lewis's constant ridiculing of Mussolini in the late twenties and early thirties in *Wyndham Lewis: A Portrait of the Artist as the Enemy* (New Haven, 1957), pp. 73-74. Lewis later renounced his support of Hitler in *The Hitler Cult* (1939).

[10] Wyndham Lewis, *The Writer and the Absolute* (London, 1952), p. 41.

[11] See Wagner, p. 74.

W.L.

ASSIGNMENT, hv/ impression it is best of yr/ theoretico-dogmatics. but not yet finished, and 'theo-dog" may apply only to first part. Cert/ good clearing of cloacae/ interim notes as I read/ too fatigued to wait, holding stuff in what's left of head/

Naow as swell az kicking them goddam punks/[1] wot about noting the few ideas Ez has occasionally set down/ as Ez never did fall for any of them punks that got a great deal too much attention BEFORE W.L. fetched out his tardy insecticide. (Incidentally can't remember having translated Benda's "La Traison," but believe am first to mention or boost the dratted little negative (Dial time) and sent first copy of La Traison to London . . . BECAUSE of the desolation and lack of anything much better in Paris/[2]

credit fer noting the FLOP of froggery at fairly early date.

*** wd/ be timely in view of PRESENT circs/ and Fascist lable to note the KIND of Fascismus Ez talked of (sticking to K'ung and Johnnie Adams, and providing a DAMsite better historic view than Toynbee/ and NEVER falling fer the Fabian concrete mixer. / / /

What about a W.L. analysis of the SOUND ideas, the positives during the past 40 years/

submerged by the crap/

and of course the crap DES CLERCS providing the Rothermeres[3] etc with the avalanche material which has damn well submerged/ most everything else. Note Jimenez title "Animal di Fondo" not exactly with this bearing, but not rotten.

la mas triste palabra: habria podido ser[4] . . . waal, wot bout picking up the IDEAS that WOULD have been useful if every time, let us say, purely fer example, Muss said he needed PEACE. fer the London Slimes to report it as "WAR Speech"

or Ian Monro[5] saying he had to watch EVERY pair of words in his news, cause IF it wuz posbl/ they wd/ take out a phrase, twist the meaning and use it as headline. (all this ref/ p. 54 and thaaar abouts.)[6]

Also the TIMEliness of certain sentences in my Studio Integrale AT the date that trans/ of K'ung was printed in chink and wop bilingual. I spose I ought to have INSISTED more on that text/ but we were not in geographic vicinage in 1927 or whenever I got the first VERY poor version into print.

Also look at the Analects/ if Hudson Rev/ hasn't sent it to you, I'll ax 'em to.[7]

O.K. yu shd/ HAVE read al that crap, and got out the bug-powder, but what about reading a few serious authors? Blackstone, Agassiz, and especially Del Mar (ask Swabe[8] for copies on loan, or see what is in the British Mouseum.) Alexander Del Mar, almost everything except the "Science of Mon"/ that was a bit off his beat . . and in the less competent part of his mind. . . bothered by mistranslation of Ari/ etc. I spose, incidentally, that Frobenius was the bloke Gaudier had been reading in the Bib/Nat/[9] anyhow, time W.L. started looking for solid stuff. another distinction: what one CAN believe, vs all this crap, the curés deguisés try to hoax people into thinking that *they* believe. W.L. having at one time EATEN a lot of wind and dust, might have edged rancour over time wasted. Even the fat man,[10] with all his fuzz, had a few right lines/ too bad he never got to Doug/ who was good diagnostician. but not sufficiently anti-bugrocrat. Hence POST-gesellite ratiocination.[11]

Might say ENG PASSANG/ that ole Santayana gave ground on proposition: no philosophy in the occident since gorNoze when, only philo-epistemology.[12] K'ung's four *tuan*, [*ideogram drawn in*] superior to Aristotl (even before the disciples castrated him, but [*i.e.* by] removing *teXne* from his list. Drop from Nic/ Ethics, to Magna Moralia (which whalo-Morely didn't want to add to Kulch, saying wd/ do me no good at Cowslip (no, that is spelled Oxford.[13]

Incidentally it took a Chinee to loop up the EXACT spot in Erigena where he plugs fer right reason as source of authority. wot we need is more COLLYboRation.

Important item in Meridiano d'Italia 11 Feb/ re Idea Luce per l'Europa.[14] dunno how to get copies of whole series. BUT sometime W.L. might reflect that woptalia was the ONLY place where one COULD print certain facts. Ole Meridiano di Roma stopped in U.S. post, for economic ideas.///[15] which is how close the MUZZLE wuz on is [*i.e.* in] Roosenpoops hellhole.

"The state is organized fear" that is anti-fascist. or at least anti M's "lo stato è lo spirito del popolo".[16] Certainly LESS fear in Rapallo over 25 years period than any where else, unless up in the Bunter's Persia.[17] or some such./ If I ever git another edtn/ of Pivot thru the press, kindly ref/ the two or three comments by the translator.[18]

esprits purs/ sorry yu missed (if yu did) Jo Adonis or Costello "whadda I wanna see iz th' guy that'ud turn down $60,000."[19] **Ez gittin ready to KICK some of them az has sposed he never THOUGHT anything of interest, merely because he refrained from emitting general statements before he had collected enough specific data to know what a general statement might mean. finger (or nose) exercise: List some of the shysters (past and recent) whom Ez never did fall for. Including Neitsch (save fer rhetoric in Zar/a) Bergson, Sorel, Pascal.

A lot of false dilemma in all this occidental crap. and Mencius met, I shd/ say, about ALL the main varieties of nit-wit, and classified 'em.

demur, re/ p. 41 Assignment/ suggest W.L. insert word "BEFORE 1914" (after 1917 at least there wd/ seem to hv/ been considerbl attention to war as product of economic stink, a designed activity.[20] Alex the Gt/ paid his soldiers debts, and died QUITE bloody dam soon after, less than six weeks if I remember rightly, from MYS(ehem)sterious causes. Try the test cui bono[21] BOTH to war and to that greatest of fakes Original sin. (the idea of org.s.) After all W.L's first sketch for first portrait of Ez/ was a Holbinian cine-star,[22] and W.L. cdn't stand it, tho he prob/ forgets the eggspesiion on his mug as he destroyed it (in fact how CD/ he hv/ knowd the eggspression as there warnt no wall mirror, and he cdn't hv/ held a pocket glass while operating on that delicate water colour.

ad interim
and strictly anonymous communique

prob/ more to follow az I procede thru deh woik.

[LETTER TWO]

W.L.

FOR the Wreck-ord (re/ p 52)[23] I recall Yeats re/ WL/ "PoWWnd'z evIL genius"/ both he and Orage trying to separate or save Ez/ FORD never (let me say NEVER) made any such etc/ and, of course, no such KIND of machination could have entered his occiput. Orage argued on point of philosophic coherence/ and our opposte directions at the time. Fact that mind better be ALIVE than dead, didn't convince him.

What is "Cakes and Ale"?[24]

Shd/ think Joyce's mind was formed in Dublin/ unlikely to hv/ been influenced by Dung when so far thru Ulyss/[25] Did J/ ever read any Whitehead/? Did yu evr hear him mention anyone but Dujardins, Vico, Svevo and Mr Dooley?[26] not that it matters a dam/ Book had to be PUT over, fer practical reason/ but cert/ I sd/ it was an END not a start/ P.S.U. after that FINISH/ period of rot, p.t.c   what he may have absorbed later, when he READ nothing gornoze/ american slang via his children.[27]

Pity de Angulo hasn't left (so far as I kno) any orderly statement re Dung (spell it wiff a Y, milorrr)[28]

WL seems to hv/ lured the J/ into serious discussion of something.[29] Can't recall that I EVER did/ tho must have approached it at times/ prob/ because I never rose to his mention of names such as Vico orn [?or] Dujardin/ etc/ One up to Humb/ Woof.[30]

been trying to get a BR/ highly respected stud/t legal "philos" to do a condensed Blackstone/[31] all the parts containing principles or necessary history/ blighter hedges/ or proGODDAMcrastinates mebbe WL could do it/ Ez simply not got physical force/

purpose of law: to prevent coercion either by force or by fraud. fer garzache start putting some of the essential concepts into circulation.

civilization NOT a one man job.

ef I cd/ purrsuade yu to give some serious attention to PIVOT. . . . not think of it as merely heathen chinoiserie.

mania for having so many laws that they cannot be executed without crushing taxation/ hiring cops to protect people from themselves.

wash up the puppytician//.That detritus Em/Ludwig at Hauptman's talking about LLard George.[32]

(parenthesis, ever read the elder Morgenthau's "Amb/ Morg's Story"?[33] very clever lubricator. also what he does NOT include. identical zones of ignorance in Leahy, MMe de Chambrun, Hull, and even Stilwell,[34]

Has WL/ ANY excuse for the existence of a smear like Croce??[35] on any grounds save that "gawd made him, having nothing else to do"? (o.k. Ez is a emotional, or dont cheat his own nose.)

NOTE/ a faculty of the olfactory sense is that it does not have to come into direct contact with a thing, in order to discern certain properties of it. Thanks for them kind words re/ Plat and Heg. p. 62 feetnut.[36]

keep down the taxes and the central govt/ cannot become a goddamned nuissance BOTH at home and abroad.

for "credit"/ ref/ Ez/ necessary both trust AND mistrust.

had never thought about Low: a great and dirty criminal, tho possibly sincere in his ignorance.[37] P. 65. pp/1. O.K. first Confucian statement so far in WL.[38] (? or hv/ I missed one?) AND nobody but Orage ever seemed to twig wot Ez/ wuz at in 'Studies in Contemporary Mentality.' even tho Flaubert had started it.[39]

p. 65 pp/ 3, as sd/ Mencius.[40]

J. Adams: "nothing more dangerous than preventing a war".[41]

GET a review copy to Eva Hesse, Munich-Schwabing, Bauerstr/ 19.iii probably most intelligent reviewer on the continent. Do yu see 'Ecrits de Paris?' Also rev/ cop. to Camillo Pellizzi 12 via di Villa Albani. Roma and why not to D.D. Paige, casella 30, Rapallo. it wd/ also reach Gabriella Mistral via DDP/ as she is in Rap/[42]

weren't both Shaw and Wells stinking fabians? and Bennett (Arnold) a better mind? at least when he wrut Old Wives (french derivative but. . .) Did either Sh/ or Wl/ criticise fabianism, with ALL its filth? Pore ole Fordie did NOT swallow it, or milk Burrns and Oats.[43]

Neither did the bgrs/ S & W crit/ the REAL rulers, tho Dizzy[44] had already pointed to them.

Partisans both/ split minds, Shaw and Bertie Rsl never having tied up to the missing halves.

mabbe Wells was split above the midriff/ horizontal not perpendic/ split??

Dont believe serfs had much or ANYthing to do with it. (p. 75)[45] Shaw and Wells-bellz merely of the rising, not of the slopping-down party. WL. might ref/ the Leopoldine Reforms mid xviii th.[46]

Yu damn well measure the times yu are right against Mencius and the other 3 of the 4 Books.[47]

no it is NOT fascism/ it may be (p. 75 bottom)[48] nazism or Berlinism, but it was neither theory nor fact in Italy. where Croce and that Cambridgified mutt Einaudi, esp/ the latter had a publishing house and nasty britified publications. just DUMB. but tolerated.[49]   fascism rising out of guild ideas, and of balances mixed economy etc/ etc/ and Farinacci very true in saying putt the 25 top gerarchs together and each one will be found with a different idea of the corporate state.[50]

and of course D. Low never disagreed with his owners. newspaper caricature per nesessita, the voice of a large herd, herded by the owners.

when a little squirt like Max DOES a caricature contra corrente[51] it stays privately on Orage's wall. which aint fer suppressin' Low but for giving someone a chance to talk back/ which they do NOT get in Shitain. (birds nest in the shrubbery on the dung-heap, or perhaps we shd/ say "once nested".)

Mr Orwell, a LOUSE. Neruda noticed this also. physically diseased (extenuation. . . .)[52]

turning backward to Fordie again. accepted him as delayed preraph/ son of bloke wot wrut on Troubs/[53] who had curious theatric letch to dress up as a tory WITH a large income. None of us ever had any mercy on the hang over from his earlier nerve brakdown or then had faintest understanding of what that meant.

Pow-wowers[54] (why didn' yu say it first?) yu can hv/ it. I aint in position to shoot it. Most of these observations are in past works, whence WL at lib/

to take 'em for any useful purpose. WITHOUT perusing sd/ scripts/ and wop-print.

The beastly Bullitt, by the bay, had, incidentally, been woke up but not disinfected by the spurloss verschwindet[55] of 5 intimates some time before 1939. The perfect pus-sack.

Hv. yu read Col Murray's "At close quarters"?[56]

Why dont yu send a copy of Rude to Alice?[57]

strictly anynonnymouse
ad interim.

not obsession, but to keep it together/ re Fordie AGAIN/ in perspective/ measured against the successful fakers? some decent ideas are THERE in his books/ NOT out of date. in fact his politica vs/ Shw/ Wel/ Bertie/ and the goddam lotuvum before, contemporary or since?

cert/ much more intelligent than Joyce/ reach excede grasp

man too weak to FINISH certain jobs, but not so swinish as to pretend they dont exist.

[LETTER THREE]

W.L.

p. 92[58] IN-NO-Vation, me foot/ return to pre 1914 when passports only needed for sloughs such as Rhoosia and Turkey. post 1919, how many Ez letters to the Paris Tribune, denouncing the first step toward universal bondage/ well, not the first but a dirty one. And COULD Ez/ get ANY highbrow support, or make people see ANY disuse in pissports, visas (at $10) and the bank-stoodge Woodie-cod-face)[59] also coin (same coins) good in Frog/ Baviere, Swiss, Ausstria and Woptalia. The eggstent to which the occident has rotted in 35 years vurry amazink.

Benda, forget in which rotten frog sheet/ must be six years ago saying: Yourup does not WANT to be united. [*Deleted:* W.L. also note enc/ printed 4 points.][60] Earl Godwin[61]/ got to seeing Am/ inkum snoopers only one step from police state/ due to ROT of police, due to laws to prevent people being themselves. and inkum. ONLy mechanism left to govt/ to get taxes WITHOUT honest money system.

what yu can do is to stimulate COMMUNICATION between intelligent men in different places/ did the O.M.[62] ever git over feeling that anything from E. of Suez is something out of a zoo?

World State no enemies?[63] nuts/ And for why/ because a son of pig at 3000 miles remove knows less of what any local need is/ and gets more and more abstract with the distance/

Si quieren un goberno di usureros, por lo menos un gobierno di usureros Bolivianos, y no un gobierno di usureros internacionales.[64] yan a l'il realism, please, re the U.S.

or specify/ world state AFTER and without. senza/ power. IF Local control of local purchasing power cd/ be guaranteed against monopoly of the press by archswine.

WL didn't notice END of U.S. consterooshun on Dec 23/ 1913.[65] almost no news of the event leaked to europe, and not much to the yankoboobs?

Oh goRRRRd/ I didn't mean to mention F/ again, 'ow cd/ yu disburbe the ghost. YU hv/ spelled Madox wiff TWO DDs.[66]

I dont mind. and he was indubitably born to suffer, that being his A.1.series A.corn.

P. 128/ pp/ 1 last line:[67] AN' thaaar'z whaar yu're [*inserted:* or were] wrong. and mebbe hook up on the other end of W.B.Y's bumbusted Bhuddism "withering into".[68]

next pp/ and pp/ 3 O.K.

ov course it AIN'T "difficult to believe", fer anyone whose memory goes back that far. Yr/ eggspression re/ Gaudier was "the Lavery of sculpture",[69] all of which purity was highly stimulating to such of yr/ contemporaries as cd/ take it. (possibly not a very heavy force at the polls.) Gaudier re my mantelpiece glass box: "Museo für orientalsiche Kunst".[70] Ever looked at Pier della Francesca's De (something or other, probably Proportione) Pingendi?[71]

132/[72] well well, here is some real fascismo/ using the term not as pejorative, but simply in ref/ historic fact as to what DID happen and happen with considerable amelioration of product. IN ITALY.

and may add that the last dhirty Biennale I was inveighled into looking at showed the damned Hun pavillion as the decent one/ all other furrin exhibits a mess/ sub Brodsky etc. really diseased.[73] And be it said the wops pampered a lot of rats but what of it, the general level of technique improved and a considerable amount of sincere effort went into it on part of qualified non-painters who worked at the selection. Damn sight better than Bun-Pips and Omega am'mosphere.[74] The favoured did NOT appreciate, having had no eggsperience fuori d'ITalia,[75] and the omitted nacherly squealed, or mumbled. And a few efficient blokes with a market suffered not at all from the competition (stimulus). Results cert/ much better than in Frogland de nos jours/[76] crit/ shd/ observe chronology/ i.e. when one place rots and another sprouts.

Good deal in Vlaminck's: intelligence is internat/, stupidity, national and art is LOCAL.[77]

did I say that Marinetti[78] asked my op/ re/ something on his wall about 5 ft by 7. Pointed out that yu cd/ shift various chunks from here to there, in short introduced subject of COMposition. His Eccellenza quite suprised, a new view of the subject not previously in his etc.

Yet he was useful. [added: &] Went, at advanced age, off to combat like various other big pots. Got no credit, as his "friends" sd/ it was just fer advertisment. all'o'wich relates to the Kulchurl level.

coterie/state. QT': a membership card in this party does NOT confer literary and artistic genius on the holder. Doubt if Marinetti was millionaire. Shd/ think Picabia must hv/ had nearly as much.[79] Yus, yus, a vurry useful work, or shd/ be if some of the points can be rammed into the bleating booblik.

133/[80] might NAME whom they wanted to keep poor.

composer in worse box than the performer, tho latter a dog's life and few bones. almost closed to anyone not tough enough to be able to DO IT anywhere, any time, no matter what state of digestion or fatigue. Other problm the disproportion, enormous fees and prices at one end, and starvation for anything good that dont fit.[81]

can yu furnish connection with Ll. Wright? Hiler re/ Stewed EEl: "at any rate they give you walls."[82]

tears/ re Joyce in Penguin. or whatever. booHOO, only sold 200,000: can't make any money unless they sell 250.000?[83]

The nu Shitsman/ naturally wd/nt face a CIVILIZED country like Italy/ take example from incult mujik, where capital has been enthroned on the ruins of property.[84] of course the great bleeding is having nation pay rent on its own credit/ believe greece was paying 54% of its taxes to meet debt interest. a few millyum to governors and presidents of Cuba, is a mere flea bite.

p/ 137,[85] minor error: Kibblewhite, not Heppelwhite. (I beleev)

and woTTErbaht the MONETARY sense.?? birth notice of which possibly to be printed privately[86] and just fer a Wyndam studio, ½ hour meditation, consider Gesell/ the monthly tax on UNUSED and therefore not absolutely

at the moment needed paper certificates of debt (i.e. of what is due the bearer).

Anatole (i.e. Asiatic) France end of L'Isle des Ping/ quoted by Ez/ HAS WL really thought about it/[87] Chesterton said "yes, partly" when I asked if he stayed off it in order to keep in touch with his readers. Fordie got to agriculture and trade-routes.

Suppressed books can't be copyright in this country? or were rights sold here also.?[88]

The "Hitler" prob/ only unbias'd account of THAT period. Hv/ recd/ 40 pages of a Tirolese diary, possibly only fair account of THAT recent scene early 1940s.[89]

wonder if any use in speculation re/ dicotomy: WL conditioned by being riz in the rotting/[90] Poss O.M. choosing the sinking, and Ez sticking to the rising (however Holly-Luced crass and etc/) but with some clean sprouts in the middan. waaawkk, 'ear deh eagul sccream.

on the other hand wasn't that Webb-itch, england's winding sheet, partly murkn??[91]

142.[92] yes Ottoman, vid Ambas/ Morgenthau's story. toward the end.

*** p. 143/[93] objective truth// mayn't yu hv/ to include this in action? Doubt if yr/ total exclusion of "truth" from action is a happy phrase, even if yu were driving AT something needing illustration. Gourmont, L'Homme Moyen S/, Veneson. anti-pink. antag/ O.K. mr cummings uses the phrasee "canaille litteraire"/[94] probably this INCLUDÉS the dam lot, lables or no lables.

Malraux is no damgood??[95] (this is a queery, not an assertion, but shd/ hardly expect good chick from bad egg, . . again queery?

The clear definition of ANY pt/ of view is useful TO them az is capable of defining a pt/ of view.

p 145/[96] oh the GAWDDDam hrooshunz, always a bore, and now a universal pestilence. Czar's aunt (and Mr Proust. damn the pair of 'em)[97] Can't at moment recall frogs *talking* of women. wonder if it was all *printed* in the old 1 fr/ edtns?[98]

curious that Rebecca cd/ be so perceptive[99] (then, at least,) and NOT be better.) or get better.

surely Max Ernst was the fount/ or do yu take him as grandad of Dada not of sur-real.[100] clue in v. early study of NATURAL forms. WL ever read any Agassiz (esp/ re/ Classifications?) 25 years ago Max must hv/ painted better than Dali (less commercial acumen.) Did the novel end with Ernst' "Femme aux cent tetes"?[101] vurry interestin' in nanny case.

[LETTER FOUR]

WL/ items/ unconnected p. 156[102]
trifling exception: Matisse 8 by 7/ plaster cast of Wenus di Milo torse, along
wiff stepladder (ef I merember rightly) Santayana: "Muss. has done more
for Rome than three Napoleons" (could have, or would hv/ . . . fergit end
of sentence.)[103] a lot WAS built, and a lot dug out, restored and tidied. Patron
can only MAKE up to quality of best available workmen.

inferiority cx/ in a puke like Eden, adding rage and desire to blot out
superior quality of cultural urge. and god rot Churchill, pig face, and soul
of a sow.

wonder what's left of new Piazza in Brescia.[104]

Gilder jr/ very much concerned that MODELS for mass product (tea cups,
whatnot) be best design obtainable. (as sd/ these are scattered items) p 157.[105]

Picasso basicly humourist since (. . . date in blank) shall we say since 1930,
(or earlier)? "th bloomin' jaoker" qt/ fr/ Davis the supertramp.[106]

158/ and of course they DIDN'T (line 4)[107] in Italy, but as the denizens
of the boot were, to brit, mere wops/ nobody heard that they didn't.

and blimee, pleased to see Jimmy's forelock emerging.[108]

wotter deuce is "le curé deguisé"[109] like in real life? the prudent O.M. deleted
him from Faber's edtn/

Guicciardini[110] more intelligent than Old Nic? also Herb/ of Cherbury
got hold of one bit of solid.

ever read any Sophokles (even in rotten trans/?

161/[111] oh them frawgs.

was Macchiavel very intelligent? register considerbl doubt. I shd/ think
Caesare[112] was prob/ more intelligent. (not saying this as untempered
eulogy.)

know of any GOOD debunking of Montaigne?[113]

How yu goin'ter DEfine the struggle fer ORDER??? not too MUCH of it,
of course.

any theories as to oblivion of Agassiz, AFTER he had stirred up quite a
good deal of mental life?[114]

useful to distinguish between "power" and "authority".[115] purpose of law:
to prevent coercion. very hard to keep words inside specific bounds and
measures.

RESPONSIBLE, or irresponsible personal rule? or ANY-ersonal rule.[116]
Undoubtedly Muss's humanity gets under brit/ skin, even yours, the dam
dago. no I distinguish/ it aint his humanity that gits under yrs/ its that he
was a wop/ which is the last advice I got from another of 'em, at a given date.

what about the term degradationist, fer them to whom it applies.

Turning back to 1913/-18 value of WL's crit or dislike/ gt/ comfort to get
ANY clear objection to a bit of writing that is not based on idiocy or mere
gangster politics. ANY specific objection for a reason, an how often does
one get any real crit??

278

Sc/ I. Aeschylus Promethus.[117]
celular technique is defensive (O.KAY) but also more than. and of course
you DO, a least edderkate, waaal mabbe that is all. p 168[118]
169/[119] no no NO, it was NOT european, it was frog and brit precicely
because Italy did NOT lose appetite for heroism, and germany even sprouted
Hitler Jugend that didn't drink OR smoke (to the total bewilderment of urbane wops) that the dirt of EDENism, the fharts of Shitwalia, (or no lay off
even the Sits/)[120] but the total mufflisme of the Brit/ governing punks/ got
so anti-wop. The sheer personal vanity of Eden being one of yr/ worst bits
of luck. Tho history presents few more repulsive mugs than Winston's. (if
seen from anywhere outside yr unright little untight.
171[121] yes, yes, the minute that war 1919 was OVER England sank into
black mud/ imperfectly registered in Cantos 14/15. by even so notorious
a patron of [deleted: the bottle and chocolats] candy-box. I dunno as they
found out they were DEBTORS. Consols had become a habit/ symbol of
solidity and all Britn/ stood for. and yet it was in Wien that dirty ole Freud
discovered his a.h. (hold on, chronology out, he did that before 1914.)
cinemMUGG in N.Y. to Sig/a A,. personally known[122] "Tell Mussolini
he is a fool not to take our films, if he dont we'll make war on him and MAKE
him take 'em.
Money war/ even Barney B/[123] sez they all are. yu mean england came
out no longer top stinker (creditor)
the ideology merely Barin (boring) Ruse. McCulloch throwing the bullok.
Joad the Toad. Lard Thamuel wheezing britshit.[124] all yu can hold is, that
there was more ideological top dressing
/most successful war/ never before so much DEBT. england got the
socialism. america the militarism. V. day. the goddamned Tory has merely
pushed the Junker to Westen moreSo.[125] Hold it No that is inexact. But . . .
Tu, l'as voulu, M. Georges Dindin.[126] (not personally, but Winston stinks
like the at/bom his total desire wd/ be expressed in bigger and bumber. That
wus the particular J, Bull that yu onfortunately did NOT kill.
yr/ great shits refused to debate on the air DURING the hellMess. if they
hadn't lied like Englanders the Huns wd/ hv/ had NO propahanda. Mr Beerbohm, about 1937: "It'll get worse."[127]
let me segnaler: Ecrits de Paris.[128] saligaud, salonard sans Jules
p. 175/[129] yes, that's that dhirty "Magnificat". Xtn/ disorder, mumbojumbo
hymnology, "an' sail thru BLOODY seas" Rugby song, or only chapel?
180[130] dunno quite how you are going to get yr orientals OUT of yr bloody
ONE world/ or what advantage trying to THINK one damn Rooseveltian
hell before yu begin, say, with a Europa, via M's suggestion to start on Italy,
Austria, Hungary France/ seeing that England was determined to bitch
Europe at least, in trying to bleed "the ends of the earth". The oriental question is how yu git up a hill, IF yu are the bottom, without starting from the
latter.
admit this is not a DIRECT reply to yr/ kite. (yu r quotin Hen Ford to
gt/ eggstent) wot it comes to/ yu had NOT been thru course of Confucian
sprouts, when yu wrote A. o B. R.[131] lumping N. China. S. china, mohammeds and hindoos. it is no privilege to plow thru post renaissance muck,
to the middle ages and thence to Aristotl/ who is inferior to K'ung.[132] but

our generation hadn't much choice of route/ and yu, as yu note, got yr/ bleating blathering mujiks before yu had been lambasted with Sophokles and Aristophanes. or Ari/   and if Plato has anything up on the other kind of orient, wot is it? the rational wd/ have been a privilege *for him* but he was fairly allergic, there being a lot of logic chopping in his vicinity. (oh well say MIGHT, instead of wd/)

loose expression/ as always yu r driving AT something, but that page might be re-looked-at. 181[133]

bottom pp/ good.

[LETTER FIVE]

W.L.

p. 185[134] az to sheep // wo'r bot th olde Egyptian formula: "Know by the head of Pharoah, that ye are all SWINE." I admit that was a shephered, not a would-be. another heckler: what % of the blighters desire intelligent (or ANY) conversation?

considerabl number of yanks seem to be worried about "more primitive conditions" not realizing that many of same are such as might seem ASPIRA-TION to anyone who had gleams. Meaning the yank being nearer to SOME crudities, is more afraid of losing his gadgets, etc.

I suspect the man of science is the worse form of moron; killyloo bird in so far as he does NOT look ahead to any general landscape but only squirts his eye thru a tube.

Danton Walker colum[135] this a.m. sez 20 March/ that nit Bertie hiring a press agent.

Still got yr/ british bee in leaving out Benito who managed quite a bit of modeling. and, god damn it, some of it will stick despite the brit/ neckties. He was certainly super all the god dam Montales and canaille litterarie,[136] and Corriere, in that peninsula. AND WROTE better, he and Farinacci than these slimes. of course living in the glooms of Britain, yu do have an almighty mass of the uncivilizable on yr/ neck. (184)[137]

Portagoose no sooner got in Goa (a.d. 1500 an wotever) than they started digging up spice trees, to keep up the price. of pepper etc/

compulsion is the pest// simple proposition to make education voluntary . . . . MAKE it . . I mean the proposition/ the more compulsory they make it, the more they make it NON-educ/ and per force EXCLUDE all the educative elements from their dhirty curricula/ and it kills curiosity . . which teletype dont.

and make lame excuses
for flatulent Muses.

Nabisco/[138] WL/ wuz recommended, after suggestion had been asked, to something almost a Nabisco/ they took Ortega and Gasses.

(wot about yu n Maritan, so far only the pixchoor)

p. 185, pp 3/[139] not counting end of last pp left over from p. 184 perfectly fascist, in historic sense of what WAS, in woptalia.

waaal, I spose Oro et Lav/[140] will git printed, but will WL look at it. qt/ not all liberals are usurers, why are all usurers liberals?

WL diminishes grip by omission of certain factors/ as the whole of the goddam university press etshitera omits about 30 historic facts, and EVERYTHING that might tend to direct attention toward them. may be, or hv/ been necessary prelude to being printed at all in Shitain. which gloomy isle did after all produce Maggie Carta and Blackstone. BUT did choose Laski[141] and a very dirty further set of demigrants and certainly hoisted up the pewkiest lot of punks imaginable to rule over it.

they cant GET the prefabs/ and fer WHY? cause they wont read even the small Gesellite pamphlet[142] telling HOW it cd/ be done without twisting anyone arms, OR wrist.

AND the perversion of words continues, after 175 years the SLIMES and Sloppress does not admit that Jeff/ and Adams never suggest equality save in sense of no-privilege under the law. Of course most of the good in Blackstone has been blacked OUT by B. 18s or whatever in Eng/ and the sewage here.

2 hour day NOT archaic, but premature/ of course WHEN they got *orario unico*[143] (4 or 5 hours) in Italy, the bgr/z at once started copping two jobs apiece/ but that is no more unpreventable than parking in prohibited spaces. AND is a problema monetaria[144] ANYhow. or almost so. naturally only Webbite[145] sadism wd/ want to drive the baseball fans to a AWT shoal. as yu were about to say. in next pp/

and why not DELOUSE yr/ list of professions?[146]

yu'll hv/ get a better image/ there are no unpointed pyramids or cones. tho the matter may be homogenius from base to apex.[147]

as to statues, it shd/ hv/ been seated/ as yet no one has pulled the chain. p. 188.[148]

Goethe's sense of humour not extended to latin original of the term.[149] a tremendous amount of craft survives the machine and grows with it, e.g. in printing technique (NOT the art printer, or the arty, but the bloke who actually uses the press, tho he may not rise to composition of page lay out. The goddam wop IS more civilized and less reducable to muck than the britan. talking of people not the popinjays.

WL view is natural in an ambience of SEDIMENT/ drained down to London 1951// less applicable to the prairie-dogs and wholly irresponsible squirils/ which are cert/ nearer to mind of "America" despite the 50 or more million of swill that has poured over it when the european chain was pulled, and the plug estracted from near eastern or E. of Poland etc/ drain pipe. they are NOT stolid, the damYanks, just plumb irresponsible, with no need to have irresponsibility conferred upon them.

wd/ assist the un-undersigned to know name of commender p. 190 first pp/ after the first division line.[150] (not idle queery. . am trying to understand at least a FEW of the partially literate.

murka/ possibly more no-track, than one track 191[151] slick g fools have been deriding most of the seriously good points in U.S. constitution for at least 40 years/ following, with time lag, the '90s flippancy.

Lady Gregory[152] called the little ¼th kike/ "Edw the Caresser." and a decent Englander in 1915: "Russia is an ally that STICKS in my throat." but he had been outside the Island, as far as the Taj. qt; nos autem cui mundus est patria.[153] Gertie[154] a yittisch assault syntacticly on the english language. tradition hailed as invention by Parisites.

195/[155] "difficult"? ehj, I beleev "awkward" is the word now used. YES, this ought to bang IN TO quite a number of blokes that WL hasn't yet got INTO. not wholly due to timelag, tho partly. Trust WL notes that "Patria Mia" has been printed in ChiKaGo,[156] quite unimportant essay/ but the LAG is of interest. WL got any 37 year lags? WL/ prob didn't notice the two RUSSES coming in to investigat Rebel Art Centre.[157] qt "BUT yu are

IN-DI-vidualists! Naive son of the Rockies: Yes, what the hell did yu expect?" (E.P. Naiveté incarnate/ NO strategy.) They sank into total Russian sadness and went silently AWAY, for EVER. Protagonist VERY young at the time. Mebbe WL wd/ hv/ been cagier? all of which belongs, of course, to one's mental biography. chronology etc/ it was perfectly true at that time.

GET Adams letters to Waterhouse. Title "Statesman and Friend.[158] JOHN, not J.Q.A.

practical suggestion (not az WL ever takes 'em). The HUDSON pays well. de Angulo certainly good company.[159] NOT WL's specific job, and plenty of hard WORK needed in and ON London. But some notice of the yankee disease, phase 1920-50/ all that cause of the 37 year time lag/ the second-rateness of the descriptive INaccurate crito-profs/ WOULD be distinctly useful, or mebbe only approx-useful let "MIGHT be useful," worth a chance. echo of "How my dear friend . . . . eh . . . . HOWells!"[160] Can etc. . "I Presume"[161] was a dam good job but did not (by its nature) touch on the drear waste of dead printed matter filed during that trentennio. need we say by whom? in the bibliotecarial archives. But BEING RULED seems likely to need some calculation as to the BY what/ the alternative to the muscovite. the pacto-derms. S.O.S.

200[162] does John talk like THAT, or only when he tykes iz pen in 'and? or is it his burlesque? wot he means is perfectly so. "engaged on" . . . . gwad 'ow they do it . . .

of course it dont matter WHICH editor kicked out Campbell's rev/[163] it was potentially ALL of 'em. but still grampaw likes to know DETAIL. sorry I didn't get the pamphlet at the time/ but yu didn't want too many allies. didn't even get a notice of it. tho I had subscribed the 3 quid.

Oiks[164] reports no less than the O.M. gittin smacked fer Yittismo/ mebbe he'll hv/ to move his catapults to the OUTSIDE and start siege operations ALso. but seemz unlikely to reach that breech. DDP/ reports Faber censored Letters LESS than Haircutt hd/ dun.[165] The van D/ preface to am/ edtn/ inserted unbeknownst to Paige might INTEREST WL on the pathology side. Not worth NOTICE save in sanctity of the'ome. Sfar azi kno' THAT one never been playd on le Sieur de WynDAMMM.

"bodyguard"/ never appreciated the USE of Hulme[166] till he was no longer there, and the punks took over unopposed control. Damn the time lag on "The New Paideuma"/ printed in Berlin befo deh (las' i.e. most recent) war. yes p. 203/[167] and are yu about to show WHO is workin the tar babby?

Hem's views are or WERE v. strongly, that no mention shd/ be made PUBLICLY, of that "unfortunate "Torrents".[168] sorry to crash into any of yr/ rare enthusiasms. however he DID write it, and v. timely it wuz. but now a rarity, almost as the oeuvres of Le Sieur McAlmon.[169] in fact q. as much so.

I dont think Italy in the ventennio ever had UNMITIGATED state capitalism.[170] it was called "a mixed economy" which phrase prob/ enraged communists "on deh Powery." I mean the Boss openly called it a MIXED economy. impure the word. wd/ anyone else have DARED?

[LETTER SIX]

WL/

problem of Hem VERY difficult. mebbe his interest in politika was not only small[171] but that it diminished? That is too strong a statement. vury hard/ probm/ to analyze, vide his last he dont LIKE "committing regiments" do that come under the heading of pollyTicks? Wot does BOb say?[172] He might answer you, and be flattered by the enquiry. Why dont yu send BOTH of 'em "Rude As."? Idiot habit of sending review copies to stinking PAPERS, and not, as continental author wd/ do, to PEOPLE. try W.C. Williams, 9 Ridge Rd. Rutherford. N.J. it wd/ get some notice in print somewhere, I beleev.

Arthur is NOT the same in all European tongues.[173]

Muss/ looked (as now documented) to a SANE progress toward a Europa/ 1931/ saw the two colossi Russia and US/ and suggested diffidently, a union starting via Austria, Hungary, Laval's France. The smeared Vidkun suggsted a nordic league/ mentionable perhaps ONLY in Italy after Os Mos/ printed the proposal.[174] Yu'r in the same issue of the B.U.Q. [*With arrow from "two colossi" etc. above:*] Unions without effacement of characters, I beleev.

ref/ the Lute of Gassir.[175] NOT Hart Crane. as pathology. Tate's pat on the back for the swarthy professor.

209/[176] Own countrymen/ fiddlesticks, in the sense that countrymen had little to do with it/ but profiteers ALL. "evrybody" who knew anything KNEW German rearmament was being financed/ axis and tripartite MADE in London. and that sow Winston admitting LATER its un-necessity. Had England behaved TO Italy as anything but the most stinking and pimping Cad/ Mus cd/ have prevented, and wd/ at least have delayed it. a war delayed 20 years is NOT *that* war, but another one murdering a different bi'lin' of combattants/ tho Winston's phosphorus bombs fell on the ladies and kids as well.

Absolutely BLIND to the map of Europe/ NO call for appeasment. M/ did NOT appease the first lunge toward Vienna, he blocked it and "nobody asked (him) and nobody thanked (him)   rudimentary horse sense re balance of power. known since Talyrand. p 209[177]

M/ recognized a pathological hysteric at FIRST interview. "quest' uomo è completamente PAZZO"/[178] But the shitains did everything to drive the hysteric nuts. Not one intelligent move on the part of England. and SNOBISM in excellsis, worse than the roman nobs/ blacksmiff's sons dont have TIES (Etonian) titful Tony no asset.[179] Just like the Brits/ did NOT, we take it, cOmmend the Code Napoleon *WHEN* it was compiled. that much TIME element does have something to do with honour and decency. let alone horse sense. I don't object to even the two preceding terms. Yu reduce the problem to England and Germany. oversimplification. now, of course, purely academik. The blithering IMBECILITY of London, and imbecility PLUS ignorance of the american stinkers . . .

Yu hv/ just tried to think 40 millyum wops off the map. as fer CHD,[180] did he ever know there was a map OF EUROPE?? vs/ which Fuller,[181] re/ wops in Abys/ "No other troops in the world could have done it."

yr/ spirtual home,[182] onforchoonately HAD in 1906, some mujiks in it. cant believe yu ever suffered from CONtemporary france. yu wd/ hv/ be VERY archaic. RABELAIS 1495-1553. The slimy Montaigne 1533-92. YU need that 40 years to be happy in froggery. 38 begob/ p. 209[183]

it was a USURERS' war. Never heard of yr/ illness 1932-/6[184]

re/ qt/ J. Adams: nothing more dangerous than preventing a war.[185]

NO/ NO/ yu gotter have a little states' rights/[186] gone too far toward centralization and snooping./ that wd/ NOT AGAIN mean secession. here yu are in realm of conjecture without ENOUGH american feel.

also the WHOLE constitution was shipped up the river in 1913. yu are without data. Get to Del Mar/ Wot Lincoln did was stopped by assassination/ and finally died about 1878, but nation not wholly enslaved till a few month before Aug 1914. Yu wanna jump to top of mountain without walking up. retrospect. Chas Ricketts 1914: "Oh Yeats, what a pity they cant ALL of them be beaten."[187] which of course they WERE/ but the little shyster shocked the unsophisticated y.m. at that time.

no, it did NOT sedulously ANYthing.[188] "americans offer $, frogs a woman, but fer wop parachutist enough to pin up notice IT IS ABSOLOOTLY forbiden to lean or jump thru this orifice." I know personally a wop/ "radiola Cipolli"[189] so called from flow of his speech. HE got on O.K. in rhoosia. first thing he did was slug a policeman. they KNEW that cd/ NOT be political.

a lot of mass technique was Teddy Roosevelt. from wearing rough rider slouch hats in 1898, to east side political meeting attended in 1910 or '11. eye-witness.

and wot abaht Lacedaemon.[190] (rromantic word, but so only because of misty history. perhaps. anyhow they had iron money, distempered so's to be no use as iron. these are spare facts, not prooves of a TEEyory. nor sorted and combed out to fit one.

bobby-sox/[191] what is max/m profit age fer bullocks? IF contrary to american conditioning, you ripen above the cervix. yes, yes, the child actor in Hollywood/ age group of the 150 millyum. and apparently the population was only 100 millyum in 1914.

215/[192] sounds like Irita. held up my How to Read for at least six months/ only Fordie's pressure got it into print. Hold it/ I see it taint Irita/

end of assignment

Notes

[1] Maurice Barrès, Edouard Berth, Leon Bloy, Charles Maurras, Charles Péguy, Georges Sorel, discussed by Lewis in chapter VI, pp. 32-46 above.

[2] Lewis discusses Benda on pp. 32-35 above; he does not anywhere say Pound translated *La trahison des clercs*, nor did Pound do so. The boost Pound gave Benda was the review of his novel *Belphegor* in the *Atheneum*, 9 July 1920.

[3] Lord Rothermere (and before him his brother Lord Northcliffe) was owner of England's largest chain of newspapers at the time, including the *Daily Mail* and the *Evening News*.

[4] "The saddest words: it might have been" — Pound's Spanish paraphrase of Whittier's famous lines, *not* to be found in Juan Ramon Jimenez, whose book of poems, *Animal de Fondo* (1949), Pound also refers to in Canto 90.

[5] Ion S. Munro, Rome correspondent for the *Morning Post*.

[6] The context indicates that p. 34 (i.e. p. 38 this edition) is meant.

[7] *Studio Integrale* (Rapallo, 1942) is the Italian translation by Pound and Alberto Luchini, with facing Chinese text, of Kung's *The Great Digest*. Pound's "first VERY poor version" was published in Seattle in 1928. Pound's translation of the *Confucian Analects* appeared in the *Hudson Review*, 8 (1959): 9-52 and 237-87.

[8] The Pound-instigated Square Dollar Series, run by T. D. Horton and John Kasper, published *Gists from Agassiz* and Del Mar's *Barbara Villiers or A History of Monetary Crimes* in Washington D.C. in the early 1950s. A volume of Blackstone was projected but never appeared. Rev. Henry Swabey was a long-time correspondent of Pound's and a friend of Lewis's.

[9] Henri Gaudier-Brzeska, the French-born sculptor and Pound's close friend and Vorticist colleague from 1913 until his death in 1915, frequented the Bibliotheque Nationale in Paris before he moved to London in 1910. In 1953 Pound recollected that it might have been Gaudier who first told him of Leo Frobenius, the German anthropologist. See Guy Davenport, "Pound and Frobenius" in *Motive and Method in the Cantos of Ezra Pound* (New York, 1969).

[10] An affectionate reference to Ford Madox Ford.

[11] "Doug" is Major C. H. Douglas, the originator of Social Credit, which Pound advocated as the only sane economic system. (See Kenner's *The Pound Era* [Berkeley, 1971] for further details.) Silvio Gesell, German economist, was the inventor of "stamp scrip," a device intended to insure the circulation, not the hoarding, of currency.

[12] Pound put the proposition to the American philosopher George Santayana in a letter of December 1949. Santayana replied, 'That is true of English and even in part of German speculation, but not of the traditional philosophy which has never died out, in the Church and in many individuals" (*Letters of Santayana*, ed. Daniel Cory [New York, 1955], p. 393).

[13] Kung's "four tuan" are the four fundamental principles of Confucianism — love, duty, propriety, wisdom. In a 1952 addendum to his *Guide to Kulchur*, Pound writes of its first edition,

> While "Kulch" was still in the press E.P. noticed that "before pore Ari was cold in his grave" the compilers of the so-called "Magna Moralia" had already omitted TEXNE ["skill in art, in making things" — *Kulchur*, p. 327] from the list of mental faculties given in the Nichomachean Ethics. E.P. wished to include this observation but a member of the British firm of Faber thought "it would do him no good at Oxford."

The Faber director referred to was F. V. Morley whom Pound dubs "whalo" because of Morely's habit in the thirties of signing on with whalers for his summer holidays (letter to Bryant Knox from D. G. Bridson, 1 Oct. 1980).

[14] Unidentified.

[15] The *Meridiano di Roma* is the Fascist daily to which Pound contributed many articles from 1939 to 1943. According to Noel Stock, the issues in which Pound wrote of his visit to Mussolini were excluded from the U.S. mails (*The Life of Ezra Pound* [New York, 1970], p. 390).

[16] "The state is the spirit of the people." Pound is referring to Lewis's discussion of Edouard Berth: "A State is . . . a society organised for war" (p. 39 above).

[17] Basil Bunting lived for a while in Rapallo in the early thirties, where he first began studying Persian. He continued his researches into Persian poetry and folklore while in Iran during World War II.

[18] Ezra Pound, trans., *Confucius: The Unwobbling Pivot & The Great Digest* (Norfolk, Conn., 1947). Pound's comments can be found on p. 95 of the 1969 New Directions edition *Confucius: The Great Digest: The Unwobbling Pivot: The Analects.*

[19] For *esprits purs* (pure spirits), see Lewis's comment, p. 39 above. Jo Adonis is an alias of Jo Doto, the gambling syndicate boss indicted in 1951. Frank Costello was dubbed "the boss of the New York underworld." When in 1946 the State Harness Racing Commission threatened to close the Roosevelt Raceway on Long Island because of bookmaking operations, the Raceway's head, George Levy, paid Costello $60,000 to "take care of" the Commission's complaints. Asked by a Senate Committee if that wasn't a little like "taking candy from a baby," Costello replied, "I want to meet the man that would turn down $60,000" (*New York Times*, 18 March 1951, Sec. IV, pp. 1-2E).

[20] See p. 45 above. In his biographical sketch for the New Directions *Selected Poems* (1949), Pound insists that his thoughts were turned to economics and the causes of war as early as 1918.

[21] "Who benefits?"

[22] Probably a sketch for the portrait (now lost) exhibited at the Goupil Gallery in 1919. See Walter Michel, *Wyndham Lewis: Paintings and Drawings* (Berkeley, 1971), plate 45.

[23] See p. 56 above. A. R. Orage, editor of the *New Age* from 1908 to 1922, tried to "save Ez" from Lewis's philosophical influence: "Mr. Lewis is for creating a 'Nature' of his own imagination. I am for idealizing the nature that already exists. . . . It is worth quarrelling about" (Wallace Martin, *"The New Age" Under Orage* [New York, 1967], p. 247).

[24] See p. 56 above. Somerset Maugham's novel of 1936.

[25] See p. 59 above.

[26] All names familiar to Joyce students.

[27] In the Spring 1922 issue of the *Little Review*, Pound marked "the end of the Christian era" and proclaimed the birth of a new pagan period, "YEAR 1 p.s.U" (post scriptum *Ulysses*, presumably). The cryptic abbreviation p.t.c may perhaps stand for *post tempore Christi*, "after the Christian era."

[28] Jaime de Angulo, physician, anthropologist, and writer, was a keen student of Jungian analytical psychology. For his contact with Pound, see Raymond L. Neinstein, Letter, *Paideuma*, 5 (1976): 499.

[29] See p. 60 above.

[30] See p. 60 above.

[31] Sir William Blackstone's *Commentaries on the Laws of England* (1765-69), commended as a cultural "sextant" in *Guide to Kulchur.*

[32] Gerhart Hauptmann, the German dramatist, spent several months a year in Rapallo. It was probably at a gathering in his home that Pound heard Emil Ludwig, the prolific popular historian, talking about Lloyd George.

[33] Henry Morgenthau, American ambassador to Turkey under Woodrow Wilson, wrote his recollections of the post in *Ambassador Morgenthau's Story* (1918).

[34] Pound has been reading four sets of memoirs: (1) *I Was There* (1950) by Admiral William Leahy, Roosevelt's Chief of Staff; (2) *The Making of Nicholas Longworth: Annals of an American Family* (1933) by Clara Longworth Comtesse de Chambrun, whose husband was French ambassador to Rome from 1933 to 1936; (3) *The Memoirs of Cordell Hull* (1948), Secretary of State from 1933 to 1944; and (4) the *Stilwell Papers* (1948) of General Joseph Warren Stilwell, Chiang Kai-shek's Chief of Staff and commander of U.S. troops in China and Burma, 1942.

[35] See p. 66 above.

[36] See p. 66n above.

[37] A cartoon by David Low reproduced opposite p. 65 of the first edition of *Rude Assignment*, entitled "Would You Oblige Me with a Match Please?", depicts a swarthy uniformed Mussolini asking Anthony Eden, shown formally dressed in morning clothes and seated contemplating his own photograph, for a light for the bomb which he has placed under Eden's chair.

[38] See p. 70 above.

[39] See p. 70 above, paragraph 1. "Studies in Contemporary Mentality" was a series of articles in *The New Age* (16 Aug. 1917 to 10 Jan. 1918) in which Pound surveyed contemporary periodicals. See *Selected Prose*, p. 332, where Pound mentions Flaubert doing the same.

[40] See p. 70, paragraph 3 above. Presumably this paragraph reminds Pound of Mencius, Confucius's successor. For John Adams, one of Pound's civilization builders, see "The Jefferson–Adams Letters as a Shrine and a Monument," *Selected Prose*, pp. 147-58.

[41] Apropos of Lewis's remarks (pp. 70-71) on the hostile reception given his books of the thirties warning of impending war.

[42] Hesse is now an internationally-known Pound scholar. Pellizzi, president of the Fascist Institute of Culture, was a friend of Pound's for some twenty years (see Charles Norman, *Ezra Pound* [New York, 1969], p. 387). Paige edited Pound's *Selected Letters* (1951). Gabriella Mistral won the Nobel Prize for Literature in 1945.

[43] Lewis mentions (p. 79 above) that Shaw and Wells are representative of social critics "belonging as a rule to no Party"; Pound reminds him they were Fabian socialists. Arnold Bennett, author of *The Old Wives' Tale* (1908), criticized Fabianism under the pen-name Jacob Tonson in the pages of *The New Age*. Burns and Oates Ltd. is the London Catholic publishing firm.

[44] Benjamin Disraeli (Prime Minister from 1874 to 1880), whose political novels *Coningsby* (1844), *Sybil* (1845), and *Tancred* (1847) had diagnosed "the condition of England" and denounced those responsible for the rise of the national debt.

[45] P. 81 above. But as before (see note 6), Pound probably misread the first edition's "73" as "75," a mistake the typeface invites.

[46] Leopold II (1747-1792), grand duke of Tuscany from 1765-1790, initiated beneficial economic, cultural and religious reforms.

[47] *The Book of Mencius* and *The Great Digest, The Unwobbling Pivot* and *The Analects* of Confucius are "the four books," asserts Pound, that "contain answers to all problems of conduct that can arise" (*Kulchur*, p. 352).

[48] See p. 81 above.

49 Luigi Einaudi, later to become president of Republican Italy, published anti-Fascist periodicals such as his *Rivista di storia economica* (Turin), which the Fascist regime tolerated (see Charles F. Delzell, *Mussolini's Enemies* [Princeton, 1961], p. 96).

50 Roberto Farinacci was Secretary of the Fascist Party in 1925 and Minister of State in 1938. "Gerarchs" are top officials of the Fascist Party.

51 "Against the current." Orage printed some of Max Beerbohm's cartoons in *The New Age* but apparently not all those submitted.

52 Pound is responding to Lewis's indignant remarks about George Orwell (Chapter XV above). Orwell had contracted tuberculosis in 1938. The Chilean poet Pablo Neruda was a political enemy of Orwell's, but his comment has not been located.

53 Ford's father, Francis Hueffer, wrote *The Troubadours: A History of Provençal Life and Literature in the Middle Ages* (1878). "Preraph" is Pre-Raphaelite.

54 Lewis's Chapter XVI discusses Four Power meetings in the post-war world; Pound offers his pun.

55 "Disappearance without trace" (properly *verschwinden*). Lewis mentions William C. Bullitt, U.S. ambassador to the Soviet Union, on p. 91 above.

56 Arthur Cecil Murray (Lord Ellibank), *At Close Quarters* (1946), a work illuminating the close associations that existed for war-making purposes between the heads of the British and American government during the first World War.

57 Alice Roosevelt Longworth, daughter of Teddy Roosevelt and wife of Nicholas Longworth (see note 35 above). Pound "wanted to get through to her," feeling she had political power (letter to Bryant Knox from James Laughlin, 30 January 1979).

58 See p. 96 above.

59 Woodrow Wilson's 1913 banking and tariff reforms were responsible for the Federal Reserve Act, which Pound denounces later in this latter.

60 It is unclear what Pound was intending to enclose.

61 White House correspondent for the *Washington Times* in the thirties and forties.

62 T. S. Eliot, who received the Order of Merit from King George VI in 1948.

63 See p. 100 above.

64 "If you want a government of usurers, at least let them be Bolivian [i.e. local] usurers rather than international usurers" (source unknown).

65 On December 23, 1913, the U.S. Federal Reserve System was created and all national banks were compelled to join. The United States, rather than issuing its own money, now had to borrow from the Reserve Bank and pay interest — provided from tax money — on the loan. This, Pound maintained, was a direct infringement of the Constitution, which stipulated that "Congress shall have power . . . to coin Money [and] regulate the Value thereof" (see Pound, *Impact: Essays on Ignorance and the Decline of American Civilization*, ed. Noel Stock [Chicago, 1960], p. 51).

66 Lewis misspells "Madox" on p. 121 of the original edition. The error is corrected in the present edition.

67 Pound refers to the line, "Truth has no place in action" (p. 138 in the present edition).

68 See the Yeats letter on pp. 136-37 above. Pound had written in 1937 that "A 'movement' or an institution lives while it searches for the truth. It dies with its own curiosity. *Vide* the death of Moslem civilization. *Vide* the very rapid withering of Marxist determinism. Yeats burbles when he talks of 'withering into the truth' ["The Coming of Wisdom with Time" (1910)]. You wither into non-curiosity" (*The Selected Letters of Ezra Pound*, ed. D. D. Paige [New York, 1971], p. 76).

69 See p. 138, last paragraph. Sir John Lavery was a British portrait painter and member of the Royal Academy.

[70] "Museum of Oriental Art" (properly *orientalische*).

[71] See pp. 129-30 above, where Lewis discusses his own paintings. "Vorticism," Pound remarked to Donald Hall, "as distinct from cubism, was an attempt to revive the sense of form — the form you had in Piero della Francesca's *De Prospettiva Pingendi*, his treatise on the proportions and composition" (Interview in *Writers at Work*, 2nd series [New York, 1965], p. 44).

[72] See p. 143 above.

[73] Pound praised the German pavilion at the Venice Biennale in a 1942 radio broadcast (see *"Ezra Pound Speaking": Radio Speeches of World War II*, ed. Leonard W. Doob [Westport, Conn., 1978], p. 194). Horace Brodzky was a London-based Australian painter whom Pound regarded as an "amiable bore with some talent" (see B. L. Reid, *The Man from New York: John Quinn And His Friends* [New York, 1968], p. 248).

[74] See pp. 142-43 above. The Omega Workshop was created by the Bloomsbury critic and painter Roger Fry. Lewis joined the group in 1912 but left within two years to found the Rebel Art Centre.

[75] "Outside of Italy."

[76] "Of our days."

[77] Maurice Vlaminck is the French Fauvist painter and Cézanne disciple whom Pound highly regarded. Pound repeats Vlaminck's epigram in *Impact* (p. 81) and cites part of it in Canto 80.

[78] Pound met Marinetti, the founder of Italian Futurism, on a number of occasions and, like Lewis — who attacks Marinetti's "dynamism" (p. 144 above) — grew opposed to his principles. Marinetti fought on the Russian front in his late sixties.

[79] Lewis cites Marinetti's alleged wealth in connection with the fruits of coterie mutual publicity on p. 139 above. Pound's quote (QT) is from Mussolini and is found also in *Jefferson And/Or Mussolini: L'Idea Statale: Fascism as I Have Seen It* (New York, 1970), p. 76. On Picabia, see Andrew Clearfield, "Pound, Paris, and Dada," *Paideuma*, 7 (1978): 113-40.

[80] See p. 144 above.

[81] Lewis mentions musicians on p. 144.

[82] See p. 145 above. Hilaire Hiler was a painter and London friend of Pound's. "Stewed EEl" is the Rooseveltian New Deal.

[83] See pp. 145-46 above.

[84] See p. 146 above.

[85] See p. 148 above. Pound is accurate in his correction. Mrs. Kibblewhite's home was the meeting place of a circle including Pound, Lewis, Gaudier, Aldington, Herbert Read, and T. E. Hulme. (See William C. Wees, *Vorticism and the English Avant-Garde* [Toronto, 1972], p. 44.) The error has been corrected in the present edition.

[86] See Chapter XXV above. Pound may have in mind one of the Del Mar monographs which T. D. Horton (see note 8) was about to print privately.

[87] See p. 149-50 above. Pound's "it" refers to "causes of war." Pound quoted the passage from Anatole France's *Penguin Island* (1908) in "America and the Second World War" (1944) (see *Impact*, pp. 184-96). Pound is referring to Ford's *The Great Trade Route* (1937).

[88] See p. 150 above.

[89] Pound is referring to Lewis's *Hitler* (1931); Lewis's later *The Hitler Cult* (1939) had not yet been read by Pound. The diary is that of Pound's daughter Mary de Rachewiltz, who lived in the Italian Tyrol during the war (letter to Bryant Knox from D. G. Bridson, October 1980). See her autobiography *Discretions* (1971).

[90] See bottom of p. 150 above. The "rotting" is the Notting Hill area of London, where Lewis grew up and lived most of his life. (Pound called it "Rotting Hill" and Lewis used this title for his novel of 1951 about the cultural and political decay of England.) T. S. Eliot, the Possum, chose "sinking" England; Pound himself stuck to the "rising" U.S., despite its corruption by journalism (Henry Luce, publisher of *Time* and *Life*) and Hollywood.

[91] Beatrice Webb, wife of the Fabian Sidney Webb, was American born. Lewis mentions her fleetingly on p. 153 above.

[92] See p. 154 above. The end of *Ambassador Morgenthau's Story* (see note 34 above) is devoted to a condemnation of the Turkish (Ottoman) Empire's persecution of its subject people, especially the Armenians and Greeks.

[93] See p. 155 above.

[94] "Literary rabble" – Cummings's particular use of the phrase has not been discovered. Remy de Gourmont, the French poet and novelist, was for Pound "a great man of letters" and a source of intellectual clarity. For Pound's satirical poems "L'Homme Moyen Sensuel" and the "Poems of Alfred Venison," see *Personae* (New York, 1971).

[95] Mentioned on p. 155 above.

[96] See p. 157 above.

[97] See p. 159 above. Proust is not mentioned by Lewis at this point.

[98] See p. 159 above.

[99] In her review of *Tarr* (see p. 161 above).

[100] See p. 167 above, where Lewis fails to mention Ernst among the "Paris surrealists."

[101] *La Femme 100 têtes* (1929) is one of Ernst's pictorial novels consisting of over a hundred collages.

[102] See p. 170 above.

[103] Probably said in conversation when Pound met Santayana in Venice (see *Letters of Ezra Pound*, p. 334). The quotation is repeated in Canto 100.

[104] Probably a reference to the Piazza della Vittoria in Brescia designed in 1932 by Piacentini, the popular Fascist-period architect.

[105] See p. 171 above. Gilder is unidentified.

[106] Probably in conversation with W. H. Davies, author of *The Autobiography of a Supertramp* (1908).

[107] See p. 172, line 4 above.

[108] Presumably James Whistler, mentioned by Lewis on p. 172.

[109] "The disguised priest" – Cocteau's housekeeper's phrase about Jacques Maritain, who is pictured with Lewis in the photograph facing p. 160 of the first edition. See Canto 77 (p. 472) and Canto 80 (p. 505) for further uses of this phrase applied to Maritain. The Faber edition of the *Pisan Cantos* (1949) censors the name on p. 58 and p. 95.

[110] Francesco Guicciardini (1483–1540), a Florentine political philosopher, was a friend of Machiavelli (see pp. 175ff. above). Pound associates Lord Herbert of Cherbury, the 17th century Platonist, with Machiavelli in *Selected Prose*, p. 305.

[111] See p. 175 above.

[112] Cesare Borgia (1467-1507) is praised in Canto 30 for his intelligence in maintaining a printing press.

[113] Lewis mentions Montaigne on p. 176 above.

[114] In reference to Lewis citing Darwin on p. 176 above.

[115] See pp. 176-77 above.

[116] Lewis discusses "personal rule" on p. 177 above.

[117] Presumably referring to the power of Zeus in chaining Prometheus (see Chapter XXXI above).

[118] See p. 182 above.

[119] See p. 183 above.

[120] The Sitwells.

[121] See p. 185 above.

[122] Olivia Rossetti Agresti, daughter of William Michael Rossetti, edited an economic journal for the Fascist government. She helped Pound work some of his writings into Italian and maintained contact with him during his confinement in St. Elizabeths (see Mullins, *This Difficult Individual*, pp. 193-4).

[123] Bernard Baruch (1870-1965), the American financier and businessman whom Pound attacked in numerous writings from 1934 to 1956.

[124] In reference to Lewis's "Number Two was not a money-war but ideological" (p. 186 above). Barin Ruse is Brains Trust, the B.B.C. program of the 1940s referred to by Pound in broadcast #77 of *"Ezra Pound Speaking"* (ed. Doob), p. 280. Donald McCullough was question master; the philosopher C. E. M. Joad was a regular member of the panel. Lord Samuel was Chancellor of the Exchequer. "Boring" seems to be Pound's judgement of the program.

[125] See p. 186 above.

[126] "You asked for it." A tag from Moliere's play, *George Dandin* (1668). The atom bomb is mentioned by Lewis on p. 186. Lewis attacked "John Bull" from the pages of his Vorticist magazine *Blast* (1914 and 1915).

[127] Presumably in conversation. Beerbohm lived in Rapallo at the time.

[128] The French literary magazine which Pound received at St. Elizabeths (see Dudek, *Some Letters*, pp. 48-50). *Saligaud:* filthy swine. Lewis uses *salonard* (social climber) on p. 187 above.

[129] See p. 189 above.

[130] See p. 194 above.

[131] *The Art of Being Ruled* (1926), discussed by Lewis on pp. 191ff. above.

[132] Lewis has contrasted the subjectivity of the "Oriental — the Indian or the Japanese" with the "rational disciplines inherited by the European from the classic world" which produces the "privilege" of a consciousness "stamped with the objectivity of the rational."

[133] See p. 195 above.

[134] Lewis speaks of "sheep" on p. 183 (p. 198 above). (Pound again misreads the first edition's "3" as a "5.")

[135] A syndicated columnist of the forties and fifties, who later gathered his perspectives in *Guide to New York Nitelife* (1958). Bertie: presumably Bertrand Russell.

[136] "Literary rabble." Eugenio Montale is the Nobel prizewinning poet. Corriere: presumably the Milan paper, *Corriere della Sera*. For Farinacci, see note 50.

[137] See p. 199 above.

[138] Lewis's mention of Unesco in the footnote to p. 200 above prompts Pound to mention some apparently inside story where Ortega y Gasset (1883-1955) was given some "biscuit" (perhaps the honorary doctorate from the University of Glasgow) instead of Lewis.

[139] See, p. 200, paragraph 3 above.

[140] Pound's *Oro e lavoro* (Rapallo, 1944), published in London by Peter Russell as *Gold and Work* (1952).

[141] Harold J. Laski, Professor of Political Science at the London School of Economics from 1926 to 1950, is mentioned by Lewis on p. 201.

[142] *The Natural Economic Order* (San Antonio, Texas, 1934; translated from the sixth German edition). For Gesell, see note 11.

[143] Responding to Lewis's remark at the bottom of p. 201 and top of p. 202. *Orario unico:* the government employee work hours (8:00–2:00) instituted by Mussolini, still in use today.

[144] "Monetary problem."

[145] For the Webbs, see note 91 above. AWT shoal: art school (see p. 202, line 1 above).

[146] See p. 202 above, where Lewis's list includes "the money-lender."

[147] See p. 202 above.

[148] See p. 203 above, where Lewis is referring to a statue of President Roosevelt.

[149] See p. 204 above, where Lewis extends Goethe's use of the term "machine" to describe the "unconscious," mechanical man.

[150] See p. 205 above.

[151] See p. 206 above.

[152] The Irish dramatist, folklorist, and friend of W. B. Yeats. Lewis mentions "Edward the Peacemaker" (King Edward VII) on p. 207 above. The "decent Englander" is possibly T. E. Lawrence.

[153] "We, however, for whom the world is our homeland."

[154] Gertrude Stein.

[155] See p. 210 above.

[156] Pound, *Patria Mia* (Chicago: Ralph Fletcher Seymour, 1950).

[157] After his break with the Omega Workshops (see pp. 132-34 above), Lewis created the avant-garde Rebel Art Centre, in which Pound soon became involved (see Wees, *Vorticism*, pp. 68-70).

[158] John Adams, *Statesman and Friend: Correspondence of John Adams with Benjamin Waterhouse, 1784-1822*, ed. Worthington C. Ford (Boston, 1927). J. Q. A. is John Quincy Adams.

[159] The *Hudson Review* was then publishing Pound and at his instigation had accepted some of de Angulo's work (see note 28 above for de Angulo).

[160] Presumably in conversation with the American novelist William Dean Howells.

[161] Lewis's *America, I Presume* (1940). Pound seems to be picking up on Lewis's remarks about the "social decay" of the thirties (p. 216 above).

[162] See p. 215 above, where Lewis quotes letters from Augustus John and Richard Aldington.

[163] See p. 216 above.

[164] Unidentified: presumably a British correspondent reporting news of T. S. Eliot.

[165] Harcourt, publisher of the U.S. edition of Pound's *Letters* (1950), edited by D. D. Paige. Van D: Mark Van Doren.

[166] In reference to Lewis's function as "public bodyguard," as he phrases himself (p. 216). T. E. Hulme was a "bulwark against malicious criticism," capable of "kicking a theory as well as a man downstairs," Jacob Epstein points out in his foreword to Hulme's *Speculations: Essays on Humanism and the Philosophy of Art* (New York, 1971), p. vii.

[167] See p. 218 above.

[168] See p. 218 above, where Lewis mentions Hemingway's *Torrents of Spring* (1926).

[169] Robert McAlmon (1895-1956), the American expatriate writer and friend of Pound.

[170] See p. 219 above. Boss: Mussolini, the dictator.

[171] See p. 219 above.

[172] Presumably Robert McAlmon again.

[173] See p. 220, paragraph 3, above.

[174] Vidkun Quisling was the Norwegian Nazi collaborator. Oswald Moseley was leader of the British Fascist movement, whose organ was the *British Union Quarterly*, in the first issue of which (1937) contributions by Pound, Lewis, and Quisling appear.

[175] Gassir's Lute, the story from Frobenius's *African Genesis*, is also remembered in the *Pisan Cantos*. Allen Tate, the literary critic, was a friend of the poet Hart Crane. The "swarthy professor" is unidentified.

[176] See p. 224 above.

[177] See p. 224 above. Charles Maurice de Talleyrand (1754-1838), the French statesman, is cited in Cantos 44, 50, 62, 70.

[178] "This man is completely mad" — said to be Mussolini's comment on Hitler at their first meeting in 1934.

[179] Anthony Eden was a product of Eton, the British public school.

[180] Presumably C. H. Douglas.

[181] Presumably General J. F. C. Fuller, the military strategist.

[182] I.e., France; see p. 224, paragraph 6, above.

[183] P. 224 above.

[184] See p. 225, fifth new paragraph, above.

[185] See p. 210 above, where Lewis recounts "the personal loss entailed . . . by my stand against war."

[186] See p. 226 above.

[187] Charles Ricketts was a set and costume designer for Yeats. The quotation is also found in *Kulchur*, p. 188, and *Letters*, p. 46.

[188] See bottom of p. 228 above.

[189] This personal acquaintance is not recorded elsewhere.

[190] Sparta, not mentioned by Lewis.

[191] See p. 229 above.

[192] See p. 230 above. Irita Van Doren's role in the publication of *How to Read* is referred to in *Pound/Ford: the Story of a Literary Friendship*, ed. Brita Lindberg-Seyersted (New York, 1982), pp. 89-93.

[LETTER ONE]

W.L.

ASSIGNMENT   , hv/ impression it is best of yr/ theoretico-dogmatics.
but not yet finished , and \'theo-dog' may apply only to first part.

Cert/ good clearing of cloacae/ ▓▓▓▓▓▓H i▓▓▓▓▓ interim notes
as I read // too fatigued to wait) holding stuff in what's left
of head/

Naow as swell as kicking them goddam punks/ wot about
noting the few ideas that Ez has occasionally set down/
az Ez never did fall for any of them punks that got a

great deal too much attention BEFORE W.L. fetched out his tardy

insecticide. (Incidentally can't remember having translated

Benda's ("La Traison,") but believe am first to mention or boost

the dratted little negative (Dial time) and sent fisst copy

of La Traison to London... BECAUSE of the desolation and lack
of anything much better in Paris /

credit fer noting the FLOP of froggery at fairly early date.
*** wd/ be timely in view of PRESENT circs/ and Fascist lable
to note the KIND of Fascismus Ez talked of (sticking to K'ung
and Johnnie Adams , and providing a DAMsite better historic view
thaI Toynbee / and NEVER falling fer the Fabian concrete mixer.
///

What about a W.L. analysis of the SOUND ideas , the positives
during the past 40 years/
                        submerged by the crap /
and of course the crap DES CLERCS providing the Rothermeres etc
with the avalanche material which has damn well submerged/
most everything else.   Note Jimenez title " Animal di Fondo "

not exactly with this bearing , but not rotten.

#la mas triste palabra ; habria podido ser ... waaal , wot bout
picking up the IDEAS that WOULD have been useful if
every time , let us say , purely fer example , Muss said he

needed PEACE. fer the London BMM Slimes to report it as " WAR
Speech "
or Ian Monro saying he had to watch EVERY pair of words in his
news , cause IF it waz posbl/ they wd/ take out a phrase, #twist
the meaning and use it as headline. (#ll this ref/ p. 54 and
thaaar abouts.#   Also the TIMEliness of certain sentences

in my Studio Integrale AT the date that trans/ of K'ung was
printed in chink and wop bilingual.   I spose I ought to have
INSISTED more on that text/ but we were not in geographic vicinage
in 1927 or whenever I got the first VERY poor version into print.
  ▓▓▓ Also look at the Analects/ if Hudson Rev/ hasn't
sent it to you , I#ll ax 'em to.
)

2/ O.K yu shd/ HAVE read all that crap , and got out the bug-powder,
but what about ʸⁱ reading a few serious authors ? Blackstone,
Agassiz, and especially Del Mar (ask Swabe fØr copies on loan , or
see what is in the Briʰh Mouseum.) Alexander Del Mar, almost
everything except the " Science of Mon"/ that was a bit off his
beat .. and in the less competent part of his mind... bothered
by mistranslation of Ari/ etc. I spose, incidentally, that
Frobenius was the bloke Gaudier had been reading in the Bib/Nat/

                    anyhow, time W.L. started looking for solid stuff .
another distinction : what one CAN believe ᵛ⁵ₐₙₔ all this crap, the

cures deguiseʃs try to hoax people into thinking that they believe
W.L. having at one time EATEN a lot of wind and dust, might have
edged rancour over time wasted. Even the fat man, with all his

fuzz , had a few right lines/ too bad he never got to Doug/ who
was good diagnostician, but not sufficiently anti-bugrocrat. Hence
POST-gesellite ratiocination.

Might say ENG PASSANG/ that ole Santayana gave ground on proposition :
no philosophy in the occident since gorNoze when , only philo-epistemology. K'ungs four tuan ⁺ʲ superior to Aristøtl (even before the
disciples castrated him, but removing teXne from his list. Drop
from Nic/ Ethics, to Magna Moralia (which whalo-Morely didn't want
to add to Kulch , saying wd/ do me no good at Cowslip(no, that is
spelled Oxford.
Incidentally it took a Chinee to look up the EXACT spot in Erigena
where he plugs fer right reason as source of authority. wot we
need is more COLLYboRation.

Important item in Meridiano d'Italia 11 Feb/ re Idea Luce per l'Europa.
dunno ø how to get copies of whole series. BUT sometime W.L. might
reflect that woptalia was the ONLY place where one COULD print certain
facts. Ole Meridiano di Roma stopped in U.S. post , for economic
ideas./// which is how close the MUZZLE wuz øn is Roosenpoops hellhole.

" The state is organized fear " that is anti-fascist. or at least
anti M's " lo stato e lo spirito del popolo ". Certainly LESS
fear in Rapallo over 25 year period than any where else, unless
up in the Bunter's Persia. or some such./ If I ever git another edtn/
of Pivot thru the press, kindly ref/ the two or three comments
by the translator.

esprits purs/ sorry yu missed (if yu did) Jo Adonis or Costello
" whadda I wanna see iz th' guy that'ud turn down $60,000. "
** Ez gittin ready to KICK some of them az has sposed he never THOUGHT
anything of interest , merely because he refrained from emitting
general statements before he had collected enough specific data to
know what a general statement might mean. finger (or nose) exercise :
List some of the shysters(past and recent)
                                    whom Ez never did fall
for. Including Neitsch (save fer rhetoric in Zar/a) Bergson, Sorel, Pascal.
          A lot of false dilemma in all this occidental crap.
and Mencius met, I shd/ say em, about ALL the main varieties
of nit-wit, and classified em.

3/ demur, re/ p. 41 Assignment / suggest W.L. insert word " BEFORE
1914" (after 1917 at least there wd/ seem to hv/ been considerbl
attention to war as product of economic stink, a designed activity.
Alex the Gt/ paid his soldiers debts, and died QUITE bloody dam soon
after, less than six weeks if I remember rightly , from MYS(ehem)sterious
causes. Try the test cui bono BOTH to war and to that greatest of
fakes Original sin.(the idea of orig.s.) After all W.L's first sketch
for first portrait of Ez/ was a Holbinian cine-star , and W.L.
cdn't stand it, tho he prob/ forgets the eggspesiion on his mug
 as he destroyed it (in fact how CD/ he hv/ knowd the eggspression
as there warnt not wall mirror , and he cdn't hv/ held a
pocket glass while operating on that delicate water colour.

                              ad interim ,

            and strictly anonymous communique

prob/ more to follow
azI procede thru deh woik.

[LETTER TWO]

W.L.
    FOR the Wreek-ord (re/ p 52) I recall Yeats re/ WL/
" PoWWnd's evIL genius " / both he and Ørage trying to separate
or save Ez/ FORD never (let me say NEVER) made any such etc/
and , of course, no such KIND of machination could have entered
his occiput. Oøage argued on point of philosophic coherence/ and
our opposite directions at the time. Fact that mind better be ALIVE
than dead , didn't convince him.
  What is " Cakes and Ale" ?
Shd/ think Joyce's mind was formed in Dublin/ unlikely to hv/ been
influenced by HHH Dung when so far thru Ulyss/ Did J/ ever read /ˈbut
any Whitehead / ? Did yu evr hear him mention anyone bят Dujardins,
Vico, Svevo and Mr Dooley ? not that it matters a dam/ Book had to
be PUT over, fer practical reason/ but cert/ I sd/ it was an END
not a start/ P.S.U. after that FINISH/ period of rot , p.t.c
what he may have absorbed later, when he READ nothing gornoze/
american slang via his children.
      Pity de Angulo hasn't left (so far as I kno) andy
orderly statement re Dung (spell it wiff a Y , milorrr)

WL seems to hv/ lured the J/ into serious discussion of something.
Cant recall that I EVER did/ tho must have approached it at
times/ prob/ because I never rose to his mention of names such as
Vico o.ᴜ Dujardin/ etc/ One up to Humb/ Woof.

been trying to get a BR/ highly respected stud/t legal"philos "
to do a condensed Blackstone / all the parts containing principles
or necessary history/ blighter hedges/ \ mebbe WL could do it/
 Ez simply not got physical force/ or proGODDAMcrastinates
purpose of law : to prevent coercion by either by force or by fraud.
fer garzache start putting some of the essential concepts into
circulation.
civilization NOT a one man job. HH
ef I cd/ purrsuade yu to give some serious attention to PIVOT ....
not think of it as merely heathen chinoiserie.

mHHHH mania for having so many laws that they cannot be executed
without crushing taxation/ hiring cops to protect people from
themselves.

wHHH wash up the puppytician// That detritus Em/Ludwig at
Hauptman's talking about LLard George .
(parenthesis , ever read the elder Morgenthau's " Amb/Morg's Story " ?
very clever lubricator. also what he does NOT include.

identical zones of ignorance in Leahy , MMe de Chambrun,Hull, and even
Stilwell,
Has WL/ ANY excuse for the existence of a smear like Croce ??
on any grounds save that " gawd made him , having nothing else to do" ? (o.k. Ez iz a emotional , or dont cheat his own nose.)

NOTE / a faculty of the olfactory sense is that it does not have to
come into direct contact with a thing , in order to discern certain
properties of it. Thanks fer them kind words re/ Plat and Heg. p.62
feetnut.

keep down the taxes and the central govt/ cannot become a goddamned
nuisance BOTH at home and abroad.

for credit/ ref/ Ez/ necessary both trust AND mistrust.

had never thought about Low : a great and dirty criminal, tho possibly
sincere in his ignorance. P. 65. pp/l. O.K. first Confucian statement
so far in WL. (? or hv/ I missed one ?) AND nobody but Orage ever
seemed to twig wot Ez/ wuz at in ' Studies in Contemporary Mentality.'
even tho Flaubert had started it.

p.65 pp/3 , as sd/ Mencius.

J.Adams : " nothing more dangerous than preventing a war".

GET a review copy to Eva Hesse , Munich-Schwabing , Bauerstr/ 19.iii

probably most intelligent reviewer on the continent. Do yu see 'Ecrits
de Paris ? ' Also rev/ cop. to Camillo Pellizzi 12 via di Villa Albani.
                                                                    Roma

and why not to D.D.Paige , casella 30, Rapallo. it wd/ also reach
Gabriella Mistral via DDP/ as she is in Rap/

weren't both Shaw and Wells stinking fabians ? and Bennett(Arnold)
a better mind ? at least when he wrut Old Wives(french derivative but..)

Did either Sh/ or Wl/ criticise fabianism, with ALL its filth? Pore
ole Fordie did NOT swallow it . or milk Burrns and Oats.

Neither did the bgrs/ crit/ the REAL rulers, tho Dizzy had pointed
to them.
 Partisans both / split minds , Shaw and Bertie never having tied up
to the missing halves.

mebbe Wells was split above the midriff / horizontal not perpendic/
split ??

Dont believe serfs had much or ANYthing to do with it. (p. 75)

Shaw and Wells-bellz merely of the rising, not of the slopping-down party.
WL. might ref/ the Leopoldine Reforms mid xviii th.

YU damn well measure the times yu are right against Mencius and
the other 3 of the 4 Books.

no it is NOT fascism / it may be (p. 75 bottom) nazism or Berlinism,

but it was neither theory nor fact in Italy. where Croce and that
Cambridgified mutt Einaudi , esp/ the latter had a publishing house
and nasty britified publications. just DUMB. but tolerated.

        fascism rising out of guild ideas , and of balances
mixed economy etc/etc/ and Farinacci very true in saying putt
the 25 top gerarchs together and each one will be found with
a different idea of WHICHHHWHHHWHHHHHH of the corporate state.
   and of course D.Low never disagreed with his owners.

3

newspaper caricature   per nesessita , the voice of a large HMB
herd , herded by the owners.

when a little squirt like Max DOES a caricature contra corrente
it stays privately on Orage's wall.   which aint fer suppressin' Low
but for giving someone a chance to talk back/
                                                Which they do NOT

get in Shitain. (birds nest in the shrubbery on the dung-heap ,
or pershaps we shd/ say " once nested ".)

Mr Orwell , a LOUSE. Neruda noticed this also. physically
diseased (extenuation ....)

turning backward to Fordie again   accepted him as delayed preraph/

son of bloke wot wrut on Troubs/ who had curious theatric letch
to dress up as a tory WITH a large income. None of us ever
had anymercy   on the hang over from his earlier nerve brakdown
or then had faintest understanding of what that meant.

Pow-wowers (why didn' yu say it first ?) yu can hv/ it. I aint
in position to shoot it.   Most of these observations are in
past works , whence WL at lib/ to take 'em for any useful purpose.
WITHOUT perusing sd/ scripts/ and wop-print.

The beastly Bullitt , by the bay , had, incidentally, been woke up
but not disinfected by the spurloss verschwindet of 5 intimates
some time before 1939. MHHMHMHM   The perfect pus-sack .

Hv. yu read Col Murray's " At close quarters " ?

Why dont yu send a copy of Rude to Alice ?

                              strictly anynonnymouse
                                   ad interim.

not obsession, but to keep it together/ re Fordie AGAIN/
in perspective / measured against the successful fakers ?

some decent ideas are THERE in his books/ NOT out of date
in fact his politica vs/ Shw/ Wel/Bertie/ and the goddam lotuvum

before, contemporary or since ?

cert/ much more intelligent than Joyce / reach excede grasp

man too waak to FINISH certain jobs , but not to swinish as
                                                    so
to pretend they dont exist.

[LETTER THREE]

W.L.

p. 92 IN-NO-Vation . me foot / return to pre 1914
when passports only needed for sloughs such as Rhoosia and Turkey.
pre/ 1919 . how many Ez letters to the Paris Tribune. denouncing the
first step toward universal bondage/ well , not the first
but a dirty one. And COULD Ez/ get ANY highbrow support , or

make people see ANY disuse in pissports, visas (at $10) and the
bank-stooge Woodie-cod-face) aldse coin (same coins)
good in Frog/ Baviere. Swiss, Ausstria and Woptalia. The eggstent
to which the occident has rotted in 35 years vurry amazink.

BJenda , forget in which rotten frog sheet/ must be six years ago
saying : Yourup does not WANT to be united. W̶t̶h̶.̶ ̶a̶l̶s̶o̶ ̶p̶o̶l̶t̶e̶
e̶n̶d̶/̶ ̶p̶r̶i̶n̶t̶e̶d̶ ̶4̶ ̶y̶e̶a̶r̶s̶. Earl Godwin/ got to seeing Am/ inkum
snoopers only one step from police state/ dowto ROT of police, dowe
to laws to prevent people being themselves. and inkum. ONLY mechanism
left to govt/ to get taxes WITHOUT honest money system.
            what yu can do is to stimulate COMMUNICATION between
intelligent men in different places/ did the O.M. ever git over

feeling that anything from E. of Suez is something out of a zoo ?

World State no enemies ? nuts/ And for why / because a son of pig
at 3000 miles remove knows less of what any local need is/ and
gets more and more abstract with the distance/
Si quieren un goberno di usureros , por lo menos un gobierno
di usureros Bolivianos, y no un gobierno di usureros internacionales.
van a l'il realism , please, re the U.S.

                                                    IF
or specify / world state AFTER and without. senza/. Local control
of local purchasing power   power
cd/ be guaranteed against monopoly of the press by archswine.

WL didn't notice END of U.S. consterooshun on Dec 23 / 1913.
almost no news of the event leaked to europe , and not much to
the yankoboobs?
Oh goRRRRd/ I didn't mean to mention F/ again , 'ow cd/ vu

disturbe the ghost. YU hv/ spelled Madox wiff TWO DDs.
      I dont mind. and he was indubitably born to suffer,

that being his A.1. series A. corn.
                                            or were
P. 128/ pp/ l last line : AN' thaaar'z whaar vu're wrong.
and mebbe ho ok up on the other end of W.B.Y's bumbusted Bhuddism
" withering into ".

next pp/ and pp/ 3 O.K.

ov course it AIN'T "difficult to believe" , fer anyone whose

memory goes back that far. Yr/ eggspression re/ Gaudier was
" the Lavery of sculpture ". , all of which purity was
highly stimulating to such of yr/ contemporaries as cd/
take it. (possibly not a very heavy force at the polls.)

Gaudier re my mantlepiece glass box : Museu für orientalsiche Kunst ,
ever looked at Pier della Francesca's De(something or other, probably
                              Proportione) Pingendi ?

well   well, here is some real fascismo/ using the term not as
pejorative,but simply in ref/ historic fact as to what DID happen
and happen with considerable amelioration of product. IN ITALY.
          and may add that the last dhirty Biennale I was inveighled
into looking at showed the damned Hun pavillion as the decent one/
all other furrin exhibits a mess/ sub Brodsky etc. really
diseased. And be it said the wops pampered a lot of rats
but what of it , the general level of technique improved and a considerable
amount of sincere effort went into it on part of qualified non-painters
who worked at the selection. Damn sight better than Bun-Pips and Omega
am'mosphere. The favoured did NOT appreciate , having had no

eggsperience fuori d'ITalia, and the omitted nacherly squealed, or
mumbled. And a few efficient blokes with a market suffered not at all
from the competition(stimulus). Results cert/ much better than in

Frogland de nos jours/   crit/ shd/ oobserve chronology/
i.e. when one place rots and another sprouts.

Good deal in Vlaminck's : intelligence is internat/ , stupidity, national
and art is LOCAL.

did I say that Marinetti asked my op/ re/ something on his wall about
5 ft by 7. Pointed out that yu cd/ shift various hhh chunks
from here to there , in short introduced subject of COMposition .
His Eccellenza quite surpried , a new view of the subject
not previously in his etc.

          Yet he was useful. Went , at advanced age , off to combat
like various other big pots . Got no credit , as his " friends" sd/ it
was just fer advertisment. HHHHHHHH all'o'wich relates to the
Kulchurl level.

coterie/state. QT' : a membership card in this party does NOT confer
literary and artistic genius on the holder. Doubt if Marinetti was
millionaire. Shd/ think /F/ Piccabia must hv/ had nearly as much.

Yus, yus, a vurry useful work, or shd/ be if some of the points can
be rammed into the bleating booblik.

might NAME whom they wanted to keep poor.
composer in worse box than the performer , tho latter a dog's life
and few bones. almost closed to anyone not tough enough to be
able to DO IT anywhere, any time, no matter what state of digestion
or fatigue. Other probm/ the disproportion , enormous fees and prices
at one end, and starvation for anything good that dont fit.
          can yu furnish connention with Ll. Wright ??
Hiler re/ Stewed EEl : " at any rate they give you walls ".

tears / re Joyce in Penguin. or whatever. booHOO , only sold 200,000 :
cant make any money unless they sell 250.000?

The nu Shitsman/ naturally wd/nt face a CIVILIZED country like
Italy / take example from SHVVHHH incult mujik , where
capital has been enVHHHHH enthroned on the ruins of property.

GUHHHHHHHHHHHHHHHHH of course the great bleeding is having
nation pay rent on its own credit/ believe greece was paying 54%
of its taxes to meet debt interest. a few millyum to governors
and presidents of Cuba , is a mere flea bite.

3/

p/137 , monor error: Kibblewhite , not Heppelwhite. (I beleev)

an ·woTTErbaht the MONETARY sense.?? (birth notice of which possibly to be printed privately
and just fer a Wyndam studio, ½ hour meditation, consider Gesell/
the monthly tax on UNUSED and therefore not absolutely at the moment
needed paper certificates of debt(of what is due the bearer) .
i.e.
Anatole(i.e Asiatic) France end of L'Isle des Ping/ quoted by Ez/
HAS WL really thought about it/ Chesterton said " yes, partly"
when I asked if he stayed off it in order to keep in touch with hh his
readers. Fordie got to agriculture and trade-routes.

Suppressed books can't be copyright in this country ? or
were rights sold here also.?
The "Hitler " prob/ only unbias'd account of THAT period. Hv/ recd/
40 pages of a Tirolese diary, possibly only fair account of THAT
recent scene early 1940s.

wonder if any use in speculation re/ dicotomy: WL conditioned by being
riz in the rotting / Poss O.M. choosing the sinking , and Ez
sticking to the rising(however Holly-Luced crass and etc/) but

with some clean sprouts in the middan. waaawkk , 'ear deh eagul sccream.
on the other hand wasn't that Webb-itch , england's winding
sheet, partly murkn ??
142. yes Ottoman , vid Ambas/ Morgenthau's story. toward the end.

n't
*** p.143/ objective truth// mayNot yu hv/ to include this in
action ? Doubt if yr/ total exclusion of " truth" from action is a happy
phrase, even if yu were driving AT something needing X illustration.

Gourmont, L'Homme Moyen S/ , Veneson. anti-pink . antag/ O.K.

mr cummings uses the phrase " canaille litteraire"/ probably this INCLUDES
the dam lot , lables or no lables.

Malraux is no damgood ?? (this is a queery, not an assertion , but
shd/ hardly expect good chick from bad egg , ...again queery ?
p 145 / oh the GAWDDDam hrooshunz , always a bore,and now a

The clear definition of ANY pt/ of view is useful TO them az is
capable of defining a pt/ of view.

universal pestilence . Czar's aunt (and Mr Proust. damn the
pair of 'em.) Cant at moment recall frogs talking of women.

wonder if it was all printed in the old lfr/ edtns ?

curious that Rebecca cd/ be so perceptive(then yy, at least ,) and
NOT be a better .) or get better.
surely Max Ernst was the fount/ or do yu take him as grandad of Dada
not of sur-real. clue in v. ¢/ early study of NATURAL forms.
WL ever read any Agassiz (esp/ re/ Classifications ?)
25 years ago Max must hv/ painted better than Dali (less commercial
acumen.) Did the novel end with Ernst' " Femme aux cent tetes "?
vurry interestin' in nanny case.

[LETTER FOUR]

WL/ items/ unconnected p. 156

trifling exception : Matisse 8 by 7 /   plaster cast of Wenus
di Milo torse, along wiff stepladder (ef I merember rightly)
Santayana: HMWH "Muss. has done more for Rome than three Napoleons "
(could have, or would hv/ ... fergit end of sentence.)
a lot WAS built , and a lot dug out, restored and tidied. Patron
can only MAKE up to quality of best available workmen.

inferiority cx/ in a puke like Eden , adding rage and desire
to blot out superior quality of cultural urge. and god rot
Churchill, pig face. and soul of a sow.

wonder what's left of new Piazza in Brescia .

Gilder jr/ very much concerned that MODELS for mass product
(tea cups, whatnot) be best design obtainable. (as sd/ these
                           are scattered items)   p 157.

Picasso basicly humourist since (... date in blank)
shall we say since 1930 ,(or earlier)? " th bloomin' jacker"
                              qt/ fr/ Davis the supertramp.
158/ and of course they DIDN'T   (line 4) in Italy, but
as the denizens of the boot were , to brit, mere wops/ nobody
heard that they didn't.

and blimee , pleased to see Jimmy's forelock emerging.
         wotter deuce is " le cure deguisé " like in real life ?
the prudent O.M. deleted him from Faber's edtn/

Guicciardini more intelligent than Old Nic ? also Herb/ of Cherbury
got hold of one bit of solid.

ever read any Sophokles(even in rotten trans/ ?

161 / oh them frawgs.

was Macchiavel very intelligent ?   register considerbl doubt.

I shd/ think Caesare was prob/ more intelligent. (not saying this
                 as untempered eulogy.)

know of any GOOD debunking of Montaigne ?

How yu goin'ter DEfine the struggle fer ORDER   ???
         not too MUCH of it, of course   .

any theories as to hhhh oblivion of Agassiz , AFTER he had stirred up
     hh quite a good deal of mental life ?
useful to distinguish between " power " and " authority ".

purpose of law : to prevent coercion .

                           very hard to keep words inside
specific bounds and measures.

RESPONSIBLE, or irresponsible personal rule ? or ANY-ersonal rule .
Undoubtedly Muss's humanity gets under brit/ skin
                the dam dago .   skin , even yours

no I distinguish / it aint his humanity that gits under yrs/

its that he was a wop / which is the Ahhh last advice I got
from another of 'em, at a given date.

what about the term deMYH degradationist, fer them to whom it applies.
Turning back to 1913/-18 value of WL's crit or dislike / gt/ comfort
to get ANY clear objection to a bit of writing that is not based
on idiocy or mere gangster politics. ANY specific objection
for a reason. an how often does one get any real crit ??

Sc/ I. Aeschylus Promethus.

celular technique is defensive (O.KAY) but also more than.

and of course you DO (edderkate fer one thing), waaal mebbe that is
all. p I 68
169 / no no NO , it was NOT european , it was frog and brit

precicely because Italy did NOT lose appetite for heroism ,
and germany even sprouted Hitler Jugend that didn't drink OR

smoke (to the total bewilderment of urbane wops) that the dirt
of EDENism , the fharts of Shitwalia, (or no lay off even
the the Sits/) but the total mufflisme of the Brit/ governing

punks/ got so anti-wop. The sheer personal vanity of Eden
being one of yr/ worst bits of luck. Tho history presents few more
repulsive mugs than Winston's. (if seen from anywhere outside
yr unright little hhhh untight.   171

yes, yes, the minute that war was OVER England sank into black
mud/ imperfectly registered in Cantos 14/15. bv even so notorious
I dunno as they found out they were DEBTORS . Consols had become
a habit / symbol of solidity and all Britn/ stood for. and yet it
was in Wien that dirty ole Freud discovered his a.h.
(hold on , chronology out , he did that before 1914.)

candy-box
a patron of tHMHISHHHx
HHHBHXXXXMXXXMHHHH

cinemaMUGG in N.Y. to Sig7a A,. personally known
" Tell Mussolini he is xa fool not d to take our films , if he dont
we'll make war on him and MAKE him take 'em.
                                    Money war/ even Barney
B/ sez they all are. yu mean england came out no longer top
stinker (creditor)
                      the ideology merely Berin Xuse. McCulloch throwing
the bullok . Joad the Toad, Lard Thamuel wheezing britshit.
all vu can hold is. that there was more ideological top dressing

/ most successful war / never before so much DEBT.
england got the socialism . america the militarism. V. dav.
the goddamned Torv has merely pushed the Junker to Westeyn moreSo.

3 No that is inexact. But ... yHHMMHH

Tu , l'as voulu , M.Georgés Dindin.(not personally, but Winston stinks
like the at/bom/ his total desire wd/ be expressed in bigger and
bumber. That wus the particular J,Bull that yu onfortunately
did NOT kill.

yr/ great shits refused to debate on the air DURING the hellMess.

if they hadn't lied like Englanders the Huns wd/ hv/ had NO
propahanda. Mr Beerbohm , about 1837 ; 'll get worse. "

let me segnaler : Ecrits de Paris. saligaud, salonard
sans Jules

p.175/ yes, that's that dhirty " Magnificat". Xtn/ disorder,
mumbojumbo hymnology ," an' sail thru BLOODY seas ",
Rugby song, or only chapel ?

180 / dunno quite how yu are going to get yr orientals OUT of yr
bloody ONE world/ or what advantage trying to THINK one damn
Rooseveltian hell before yu begin,say,with a Europa , via M's
suggestion to start on Italy, Austria, Hungary France/ seeing that
England was determined to bitch Europe at least,in trying to
bleed " the ends of the earth". The oriental question is how yu
git up a hill , IF yu are the bottom , without starting from the latter.

admit this is not a DIRECT reply to yr/ kite.

(yu r quotin Hen Ford to gt/ eggstent) / wot it comes to/ yu
had NOT been thru course of Confucian sprouts, when yu wrote A.o BR. R.

4./lumping N.China. S.china, mohammeds and hindoos. it is no privilege
to plow thru post renaissance muck , to the middle ages and
thence to Aristotl/ who is inferior to K'ung. but our generation
hadn't much choice of route/ and yu, as yu note , got yr/ bleating
blathering mujiks before yu had been lambasted with Sophokles and Aristoph
—anes. or Ari/ and if Plato has anything up on the other kind
of orient, wot is it ? the rational wd/ have been a privilege for him
but he was fairly allergic, there being a lot of logic chopping in
his vicinity. (oh well say MIGHT , instead of wd/)
loose expression/ as always yu r driving AT something, but
that page might be re-looked-at. 181
bottom pp/ good.

[LETTER FIVE]

W.L. p. 185

az to sheep // wo'r bot th olde Egyptian formula : Know by the
head of Pharoah, that ye are all SWINE.
        I admit that was a shephered, not a would-be.

 another heckler : what % of the blighters desire intelligent (or ANY)
conversation ?

considerabl number of yanks seem to be worried about " more primitive
conditions " not realizing that many of same are such as might
seem ASPIRATION to anyone who had gleams. Meaning the yank
being nearer to SOME crudities , is more afraid of losing his
gadgets, etc.

I suspect the man of science is the worse form of moron ; killyloo
bird in so far as he ░░HHHHH does NOT look ahead to any
general landscape but only squirts his eye HHWHHHHHHWHH thru a tube.
Danton Walker colum this a.m. / sez / 20 March/ that nit Bertie hiring
a press agent .
Still got yr/ british bee in leaving out Benito who managed quite
a bit of modeling. and, god damn it, some of it will stick
despite the brit/ neckties. He was certainly super all the
god dam Montalés and canaille litterarie , and Corriere , in that
peninsula. AND WROTE better , he and Farinacci than these slimes.

of course living in the glooms of Britain , yu do have an almighty mass
of the uncivilizable on yr/ neck. (184)

Portagoose no sooner got in Goa (1500 an wotever) than they started digging
up spice trees , to keep up the price.of pepper etc/

 compulsion is the pest// simple proposition to make education
voluntary .... MAKE it .. I mean the proposition /
the more compulsory they make it , the more they make it NON —educ/ and
 per force EXCLUDE all the educative elements from their dhirty
 curricula / and it kills curiosity .. which teletvpe dont .
                and make lame excuses
                for flatulent Muses .
Nabisco / WL/ wuz recommended , after suggestion had been asked, to
        something almost a Nabisco/ they took Ortega and Gasses.
(wot about vu n Maritan , so far only the pixchoor)
p. 185 , pp 3/ not counting end of last pp left over from p. 184
        perfectly fascist, in historic sense of what WAS , in woptalia.
                waaal , I spose Oro et Lav/ will git printed, but will
WL look at it. qt/ not all liberals are usurers , why are all usurers
liberals ?
        WL diminishes grip by omission of certain factors /
as the whole of the goddam university press etchitera omits
about 30 historic facts , and EVERYTHING that might tend to

2 to direct attention toward them.

may be, or hv/ been necessary prelude to being printed at all in
shitain.
          which gloomy isle did(produce Maggie Carta and Blackstone.
BUT did choose Laski and and a very dirty further set of
demigrants and. certainly hoisted up the pewkiest lot of punks
imaginable to rule over it.

they cant GET the prefabs/ and fer WHY ? cause they wont
read even the small Gesellite pamphlet telling HOW it cd/
be done without twisting anyone arms, OR wrist .

AND the perversion of words continues, after 175 years the SLIMES
and Sloppress does not admit that Jeff/ and Adams never suggest
equality save in sense of nox-privilege under the law.

Of course most of the good in Blackstone has been blacked OUT
by B. 18s or whatever in Eng/ and the sewage here.

2 hour day NOT archaic, but premature / of course WHEN they
got orario unico (4 or 5 hours) in Italy , the bgr/z at once
started copping two jobs Z a piece/
                                but that is no more
unpreventable than parking in prohibited spaces. AND is a
problema monetaria ANYhow. or almost so.

                                     naturally only Webbite
sadism wd/ want to drive the baseball fans to a AWT shoal.
as yu were about to say. in next pp/
and why not DELOUSE yr/ list of professions ?

yu'll hv/ get a better image / there are no unpointed pyramids
or cones. tho the matter may be homogenius from base to apex.

as to statues , it shd/ hv/ been seated/ as yet no one has pulled
the chain. p. 188.

Goethe's sense of humour not extended to latin original of the term.

a tremendous amount of craft survives the machine and grows with it,
e.g. in printing technique (NOT the art printer, or the arty, but
the bloke who actually uses the press, tho he may not rise to
composition of page lay out. The goddam wop IS more civilized
and less reducable to muck than the britan. talking of
people not the popinjays.

WL view is natural in an ambience of SEDIMENT/ drained down to
London 1951 //
              less aplicable to the prairie-dogs and wholly
irresponsible squirils/ which are cert/ nearer to mind of
"America" despite the 50 or more million of swill that has
poured over it when the european chain was pulled , and the plug
estracted from near eastern or E. of Poland etc/. drain pipe.
      they are NOT stolid , the damYanks , just plumb

3/ just plum/ irresponsible, with no need to have irresponsibility
conferred upon them.
wd/ assist the un-undersigned to know name of commender p. 190
first pp/ after the first division line. (not idle queery.. am
trying to understand at least a FEW of the partially literate.
        murka/ possibly more no-track , than one track ⟨191⟩
slick g fools have been deriding most of the seriously good points
    in U.S. constitution for at least 40 years/ following
with time lag, the '90s flippancy. Lady Gregory called the little
½th kike/"Edw the Caresser. " and a decent Englander in 1915 : " Russia
is an ally that STICKS in my throat. " but he had been outside
the Island, as far as the Taj. EMMHHMHMMM qt; nos autem cui
mundus est patria. Gertie a yittisch assault on the english language.
tradition hailed as invention by Parisites. syntacticly.
        195 / "difficult"? ehj , I beleev" awkward " is the word now used.
YES, this ought to bang IN TO quite a number of blokes that WL hasn't
        yet got INTO. not wholly due to timelag, tho partly. ℰ
trust WL notes that MHMM"Patria Mia" has been printed in ChiKaGo, quite
unimportant essay / but the LAG is of interest . WL got any
37 year lags ? WL/ prob didn't notice the two RUSSES
coming to investigat Rebel Art Centre. qt" BUT vu are IN-DI-vidualists !
(E.P.) Naive son of the Rockies : Yes, what the hell did yu expect ? "
Naivete´ incarnate/ NO strategy.⟩ They sank into total Russian sadness
and went silently AWAY , for EVER. Protagonist VERY young at
the time. Mebbe WL wd/ hv/ been cagier ? all of which
belongs , of course, to one's mental biography. chronology etc/
it was perfectly x true at that time.
        GET Adams letters to Waterhouse. Title" Statesman and
Friend. JOHN , not J.Q.A.
practical suggestion (not az WL ever takes 'em). The HUDSON pays well.
de Angulo certainly good company. NOT WL's specific job, and plenty
of hard WORK needed in and ON London. But some notice of the
yankee disease, phase 1920 -50 / all that cause of the 37 year
time lag/ the second-rateness of the descriptive INaccurate hhh
crito-profs/ WOULD be distinctly useful , or mebbe only approx-useful
let "MIGHT be useful,"worth a chance. echo of" How my dear friend
.... eh .... HOWells ! " Can etc.. " I presume"was a dam good job
but did not(by its nature) touch on the drear waste of dead
printed matter filed during that trentennio. need we say by whom ?

in the bibliotecarial archives. But BEIN G RULED seems likely
to need some calculation as to the BY what/ the alternative to the
muscovite. the pachy-derms . S.O.S.
⟨200⟩ does John talk like THAT, or only when he tykes iz pen in 'and ?
or is it his burlesque ? wot he means in perfectly so.
    " engaged on " .... gwad 'ow they do it ...

of course it dont matter WHICH editor kicked out Campbell's rev/
it was potentially ALL of 'em. but still grampaw likes to know DETAIL.
        sorry I didn't get the pamphlet at the time / but yu didn't want
too many allies.

4 / didn't even get a notice of it. tho I had subscribe\ the   3 quid.
Oiks reports no less than the O.M. gittin smacked fer Yittismo/
mebbe he'll hv/ to move his catapults to the OUTSIDE and start
siege operations ALso. but seemz unlikely to reach that breech.
DDP/ reports Faber censored Letters LESS than Haircutt hd/dun.

The van D$ preface to am/ edtn/ inserted unbeknownst to Paige might
INTEREST WL on the pathology side. Not worth NOTICE save
in sanctity of the'ome. Sfar azi kno' THAT one never been playd

on le Sieur de WynDAMMM.

" bodyguard"/ never appreciated the USE of Hulme till he was no longer
there, and the punks took over unopposed control. Damn.the time lag on
" The New Paideuma" / printed in Berlin befo deh (las' i.e. most recent)
war.

yes p. 203 / and are vu about to show WHO is workin the tar babby ?

Hem's views are or WERE v. strongly , that no mention shd/ be
made PUBLICLY , of that "unfortunate " Torrents ". sorry to
crash into any of yr/ rare enthusiasms. however he DID write
it , and v. timely it wuz. but now a rarity . almost as the oeuvres
of Le Sieur McAlmon. in fact q. as much so.
I dont think Italy in the ventennio ever had UNMITIGATED state
capitalism. it was called " a mixed economy " which phrase prob/
enraged communists "on deh Powery. " I mean the Boss openly called
it a MIXED economy. impure the word . wd/ anyone else have DARED ?

[LETTER SIX]

WL/
prob% of Hem VERY difficult. mebbe his interest# in politika
was not only small but that it diminished ? That is too strong
a statement. vury hard/ prob/ to analyze , vide his last
he dont LIKE " committing regi#ments "

                                    do that come under
the heading of pollyTicks ?

                               Wot does BOb say ? He might answer
you , and be flattered by the enquiry .

Why dont yu send BOTH of 'em " Rude As. " ?
Idiot habit of sending review copies to stinking PA#ERS , and
not , as continental author wd/ do , to PEOPLE.
try W.C.Williams, 9 Ridge Rd. Rutherford . N.J.
it wd/ get some notice in print somewhere , I beleev.

Arthur is NOT the same in all European tongues.

Muss/ looked (as now documented) to a SANE progress toward a
Europa/ 1931/ saw the two colossi Russia and US/ and suggested
diffidently , a union starting via Austria,Hungarv , Laval's
France. The smeared Vidkun suggsted a nordic league / mentionable
perhaps ONLY in Italy after Os Mos/ printed the proposal. Yu'r
in the same issue of the B.U.Q.
Unions without effacement of characters , I beleev.

ref/ the Lute of Gassir. NOT Hart Crane. as pathology. Tate's
            pat on the back for the swarthy professor.

209/ Own countrymen / fiddlesticks , inthe sense that
            countrymen had little to do with it / but profiteers ALL.
"evrybody " who knew anything KNEW German rearmament was being
finance/ axis and tripartite MADE in Loch on. and that sow Winston
admitting LATER its un-nenessity.
Had England behaved TO Italy as anything but the most stinkingand
pimping Cad/ Mus cd/ have prevented, and wd/ at least have delayed it.

a war delayed 20 years is NOT   t h a t   war , but another one
murdering a different bi'lin' of combattants/ tho Winston's
phosphorus bombs fell on the ladies and kids as well.

Absolutely BLIND to the map of Europe/ NO call for appeasment.
M/ did NOT appease the first lunge toward Vienna . he blocked it
and " nobody t##### asked (him) and nobody thanked (him)
rudimentary horse sense re balance of power. known since Talyrand. p

2/ M/ recognized a pathological hysteric at FIRST interview.

" quest' uomo e completamente ⟩PAZZO "/ But the shitains
did everything to drive the hysteric nuts. Not one intelligent
move on the part of England.

                              and SNOBISM in excellsis . worst than
the roman ▨▨▨▨ nobs/ balcksmiff's sons dont have TIES (Etonian)
titful Tony no asset. Just like the Brits/ did NOT , we take it ,
cOmmend the Codé Napoleon WHEN it was compiled.

                              that much TIME element
does have something to do with honour and decency. let alone
horse sense. I dont object to even the two preceding terms .

Yu reduce the problem to Engalnd and Germany. oversimplification.

now of course, purely academik. The blithering IMBECILITY of London ,
and imbecility PLUS ignorance of the american stinkers ...

Yu just tried to think 40 millyum wops off the map.
as fer CHD , did he ever know there was a map OF EUROPE ??

vs/ which Fuller , re/ wops in Abvs/ " No other troops in the world
    could have done it. "

yr/ spiritual home, onforchoonately HAD in 1906, some mujiks in it.
cant believe yu ever suffered from CONtemporary france.
yu wd/ hv/ be VERY archaic. RABELAIS 1495-1553. The slimy
Montaigne 1533-92.

                    YU need that 40 years to be happy in froggery.
38 begob/   p. 209
it was a USURERS' war.   Never heard of yr/ illness 1932-/6
re/qt/ J.Adams : nothing more dangerous than preventing a war.

NO/ NO/ yu gotter have a little states' rights / gone too far
toward centralization and snooping./ that wd/ NOT again mean
secession.   AGAIN
 here yu are in realm of conjecture without ENOUGH american feel.

also the WHOLE constitution was shipped up the river in 1913.
yu are without data. Get to Del Mar/ Wot Lincoln did was
stopped by assassination/ and finally died about 1878 , but
nation not wholly enslaved till a few a month before Aug 1914

Yu wanna jump to top of mountain without walking up.
retrospect. Chas Ricketts 1914 :

3/"Oh Yeats, what a pity they cant ALL of them be beaten.
which of course they WHEH WERE / but the little shyster
shocked the unsophisticated y.m. at that time.
     noW it did NOT sedulously ANYthing. "(americans offer
$, frogs a woman , but fer wop parachutist " enough to pin up notice
IT IS ABSOLOOTLY forbiden to lean or jump thru this orifice."

I know personally a wop / " radiola Cipolli " so called from
flow of his speech. HE got on O.K. in rhoosia. first thing he
did was slug a policeman. they KNEW that cd/ be phhh political.
    a lot of mass technique was Teddy Roosevelt. from wearing
rough rider slouch hats in 1898, to east side poly meeting attended in
1910 or '11. eye-witness.

and wot abaht Lacedaemon.(rromantic word , but so only because
of mistv history. perhaps. anyhow they had iron money , distempered
so's to be no use as iron.

          these are spare facts , not prooves of
a TEEvory. nor sorted and combed out to fit one.

bobbv-sox / what is max/m profit age fer bullocks ?

WꞰꞰ꞉꞊꞉꞉꞊꞉꞉꞊꞉꞉꞊꞉꞉꞊꞉꞉꞊W IF contrary to american
conditioning, you ripen above the cervix.

yes, yes , the child actor in Hollywood / age group of the 150 millyum.
and apparently the pop/ was only 100 millyum in 1914.
215 / sounds like Irita. held up mv How to Read for at
least six months/ only Fordie's pressure got it into print.
Hold it/ I see it taint Irita/
            end of assignment

AFTERWORD

BY

TOBY FOSHAY

I

IN the first week of July, 1946, Lewis submitted a proposal to Hutchinson & Co. for an autobiographical book of 70,000 words provisionally titled "Story of a Career".[1] In editorial conference on July 10, Hutchinson accepted the proposal and decided on an offer of £400 advance for the book.[2] On August 10, Lewis was sent the editorial agreement. It called for a book of 90,000 words with an advance of £500. Surprisingly, it named the date of delivery of the MS as November 1946 (changed at Lewis's request from October 31). This was surely an optimistic expectation on the part of both parties, even given Lewis's considerable capacity for rapid work. The contract also specified that Lewis was to provide an index and at least 16 illustrations, and that he would give Hutchinson the first offer on his next book.[3]

On October 29, Lewis was still hoping to deliver the MS to Hutchinson by the end of November. But by November 13, he wrote to Allen Tate, then at Henry Holt & Co. in New York, that he had been held up by "journalism, broadcasting and now by flu." He promises to send the MS for consideration by Henry Holt when it is complete. On November 19, Lewis was struck by a motorcycle while crossing the street in front of his building. It resulted in what he called "a hole in his leg" and forced him to keep it stretched out on a chair. It took almost three weeks to heal. As a result of the flu and the accident, Lewis by December 5 had pushed on his date of completion to late January.[4]

Lewis submitted the MS by late March or early April of 1947.[5] He must have worked at an intense if not a feverish pace. "I am trying to do a hundred things at once — finish a long book, journalism, broadcasting, business with lawyers etc. etc.," he wrote in January. Clearly, it was not as if he had nothing else on his mind during this period. On February 3, Hutchinson wrote turning down Lewis's proposal of a small illustrated book on Gwen and Augustus John. He was also at this point in the heat of his squabble with Poetry London over the publication of *America and Cosmic Man*, necessitating a long letter of self-defence to his solicitors on February 10.[6] Lewis also made two BBC broadcasts in January and March, 1947, on "Liberty and the Individual" and "A Crisis in Thought". The latter described the impact made on him by his early reading of the 19th century Russian novelists; in revised form it was included in *Rude Assignment* as Chapter XXVII, "The Puritans of the Steppes".

Instead of the 70,000 words originally proposed and the 90,000 words subsequently agreed upon, Lewis produced a MS of some 110,000 words in eight months. Taking into account illness, accident and his other active interests, this is a truly impressive performance. Lewis continuously described

Rude Assignment as "my big book" and as a work "of great importance to me". In a letter to his friend and patron Sir Nicholas Waterhouse, he maintains that "every line is carefully written."[7] *Rude Assignment* emerges in this context as Lewis's most significant literary effort between the appearances of *The Revenge for Love* in 1937 and *Self Condemned* in 1954.

By April 18, Hutchinson was sending Lewis their legal advisor's comments on "Ascent of Parnassus", as the MS had now been titled.[8] The lawyer's comments show an extreme vigilance, as was no doubt necessary, on behalf of his client's interests. The most innocuous of Lewis's observations (and some not so innocuous) are subjected to cautions. To the query concerning what the lawyer describes as "the attack on Orwell" (see Chapter XV), Lewis responds quite rightly that it was Orwell who had attacked *him*. But Lewis's responses show him very willing to cooperate with the lawyer's suggestions by making changes in wording and tone. Despite this, a misunderstanding not of Lewis's making arose. After the submission of his responses to the lawyer's queries, K. H. Webb, Lewis's Hutchinson contact, wrote back: "I am sorry that you omitted to make the necessary alterations in the first place as requested by our Advisor as he reads all our books for libel and knows just how far we can go." Lewis contacted Webb immediately and she replied that she hadn't known that the MS was still at Hutchinson's and not available for Lewis's revisions. But Lewis correctly observed in a subsequent letter that he had not been requested to make the revisions but rather asked to respond to the lawyer's queries, which he had promptly done in an accommodating way. Orwell he insisted on being allowed to answer, although he agreed to delete the term "slander" ("which I did not know was slanderous").[9] Here the matter dropped.

By late June, Allen Tate at Henry Holt in New York had received the MS, to which Lewis had given the title *The Politics of the Intellect* for its American appearance. According to Lewis: "My publisher here takes a disgustingly large commission if *he* sells the book and 6 weeks ago got an American publisher interested." But, not only for economic reasons, Lewis would rather have Henry Holt publish it. By the end of July, Tate was "very unhappy" to communicate the refusal of this "very powerful and moving book". Nobody at Henry Holt anticipated a sale of more than 1000 copies at the very most. Tate pronounced himself "very close to all the controversies of which you were the center back in the 20's and 30's" but added that, since the war, "the younger generation are looking in other directions." Lewis was clearly stung by what he called "the manner you have found of communicating to me the news of the refusal of my book". He made two "rejoinders", the first of which, at least (perhaps intentionally), quite misconstrues Tate's letter, however tactless it may have seemed:

> (1) I have no recollection of being a center back in any team of which you were a member. (2) I do not remember any occasion on which I followed automatically 'the direction' taken by people around me — nor, I believe I am right in saying, has it been your habit to do so in the past, whatever may be your procedure now. — But why provoke such rejoinders? If a New York firm does not wish to publish a book of mine, there is nothing new in that.[10]

In July, Lewis had offered Hutchinson *America, I Presume* (New York, 1940) for English publication. They refused it "in view of the great hold-up in production" and the two books, one in process and the other commissioned, which they were already doing of Lewis's. They were agreeable to it being published elsewhere.[11] By December Lewis was writing of his discouragement with the publishing situation — it was paying pre-war money. "There is my big novel *has* to be finished. Once that is done I am through with books." This big novel, then titled *The Victory of Albert Temple*, was the second book commissioned by Hutchinson. Lewis had described the book in a letter to Hutchinson on May 29. It was not to be a satire like *The Apes of God* but "a straight novel, a normal narrative, as much as 'Tarr' for instance." By June 11, Lewis had submitted a synopsis, but the novel became a cause of contention between himself and Hutchinson as it dragged on, never to be finished.[12]

Also by December, 1947, the MS of *Rude Assignment* is at the printers, but Lewis writes to them on December 23 to make some important revisions in Part III. He finally decides, he says, on *The Ascent of Parnassus* as title. By January 13, "proofs are pouring in for my big book," but money worries result in him hardly having the "heart" to correct them. On April 15, Lewis writes that the book is to appear in September, "but there is a labour and paper blockage, which may delay it a little."[13] He corrects another set of proofs in June.[14] In August, Lewis wrote to J.E. Palmer at the *Sewanee Review*, with whom he was trying to publish Chapter VI of *Rude Assignment* as an article, that the book "is supposed to be published by Christmas." In an effort to place the article (which was eventually rejected): "Perhaps I should add," he said, "that there is no possibility of 'Rude Assignment' being published in the U.S." By September, Lewis's American friend and agent, Felix Giovanelli, was negotiating with Doubleday for the publication of *America and Cosmic Man*, with an option on Lewis's next book "whatever it is".[15]

On September 10, 1948, Lewis was doing the index to *Rude Assignment*, but the illustrations were still being chosen on December 18. Things were moving slowly. In March, Lewis was trying to get a decision from Augustus John on the use of John's portrait of the young Lewis in *Rude Assignment*. Lewis wants a decision "as soon as may be: my publisher already grinds his teeth at my delays and procrastinations."[16] Lewis was later to have every reason to grind *his* teeth at Hutchinson's delays.

As mentioned, Lewis had tried to publish Chapter VI of *Rude Assignment* as an article in the *Sewanee Review* under the title "Do Intellectuals Exist?" The editor, John Palmer, was extremely cautious, submitting the piece to "opposition" readers because of its complexity. In September of 1948, Palmer returned the article, claiming it departed too far from their editorial line. The opposition readers were no less than Jacques Maritain and Etienne Gilson; Maritain was too busy for a formal reply, while Gilson was against doing "refutations". In March, 1949, Palmer wrote to explain more fully the decision not to publish "Do Intellectuals Exist?" With Maritain he did not get so far as an agreement to read the piece. Gilson, however, did read it, finding it "so incoherent" that, were he the editor, he "would not touch it with a ten foot pole." There follows an extract from the correspondence from

Gilson in which he explains his harsh view. Lewis's reply to Palmer's letter was remarkably buoyant:

> Your correspondent is most fierce and contentious — I am glad his "ten-foot pole" is not a *lance*, and I a knight (however thick my armour) against whom this fiery paladin is driving in the Lists. — However, his only valid weapon, ultimately, is the human reason (by him oh how subjectively wielded): and in this merely dialectical field, although I brandish no "ten-foot pole", I feel I shall prevail, because his reasoning is as fallacious as it is noisy.

Also in March, Lewis finally submits the index to *Rude Assignment* that he had begun the previous September, "not that it is much use sending it in, as my poor book seems indefinitely held up."[17]

Meanwhile in the U.S., Giovanelli had been trying to interest a journal in doing a special issue on Lewis. He had a supporting letter for the project from T.S. Eliot, in which Eliot referred to Lewis as "one of the very few writers of incontestable genius in our time." Since his return from Canada after the war, Lewis had been trying to arrange a lecture tour in America that would support a visit there. He had also been fishing for an academic post that would make a more permanent removal there possible. By April, 1949, a philosophy teaching post had been arranged for him at Bard College. But by April 12, he writes Eliot that he begins to be wary of the demands on his time that teaching philosophy would entail, leaving him very little for his own writing. On May 9, Lewis writes to turn down the philosophy post, offering himself instead as "resident artist" or "cultural expert".[18]

Lewis had been preparing feverishly for months for the May opening of the successful Redfern Gallery retrospective. On May 10, he received a letter from his friend Heath that the latter had left Hutchinson. "The place is quite impossible," he says. "Luckily your book is practically finished but please insist on seeing the jacket before it goes to press — they make the most hideous mistakes, mainly due to ignorance." In June, Lewis heard from Giovanelli that he had "received a couple of inquiries about *Rude Assignment* in the wake of Gotham Book Mart ad offering delivery at $8.50 a copy. Do tell me what is with that title."[19]

"What was with that title" is very difficult to say. The paper and labour problems that Lewis had previously cited may have issued in very slow production levels at Hutchinson. For certain, they were not eager to get the book onto the market, because it was to be a year and a half yet before it appeared.

In the meantime, Lewis was still trying to sell the book in America. Doubleday felt that "it would be an enormous mistake to publish RUDE ASSIGN-MENT on the heels of AMERICA AND COSMIC MAN." The latter had not sold to expectation. They had hoped that the next book from Lewis would be the novel in progress (*The Victory of Albert Temple*); if successful, "it would make the ground fallow for the autobiography." Lewis was sorry that Doubleday did not "like" *Rude Assignment* but was appreciative of the desire for a further option. "The trouble with that . . . is that I must at least have a try at selling *Rude Assignment* and no publisher would take it if I were not prepared to give him an option on my next book." He proclaims his lack of understanding of the American book market and asks quite humbly for the nature of Doubleday's objections to his autobiography. "Do not spare my feelings please."[20]

298

In February, 1950, the illustrations were in proof. In May, Lewis received a request from a Stockholm publisher for the Swedish rights and a copy of *Rude Assignment*. Nothing further came of this inquiry. The idea of a paper shortage as responsible for the hold-up of the book is supported by Hutchinson's inability to get the paper Lewis had requested for his design for the jacket of *Rude Assignment*. On October 17, Mrs. Webb wrote that they would be "publishing the book at long last in November." She takes the opportunity to remind Lewis of his promise of *The Victory of Albert Temple*, for which they paid him an advance of £225 in June, 1947. On November 10, 1950, Hutchinson finally mailed Lewis a copy of the book, and Lewis responded: " 'Rude Assignment' has been sent me. Have you seen it? It is a kind of war-time type and paper is it not? . . . As to the novel, I was naturally deeply discouraged by the hold-ups, and after that my eyes began to be a prime obstacle."[21]

Lewis's eyes had begun to deteriorate rapidly in late 1949. In January, 1950, he had all his teeth extracted, a favorite cure-all at that period, but irrelevant to Lewis's condition, and of course very painful. The diagnosis of pituitary tumor was finally confirmed a month later, but his age and the danger of the operation made Lewis postpone it, making visits to Swiss and Swedish specialists in June. In August, X-ray therapy seemed to aggravate his condition. By April, 1951, blindness was near complete and Lewis published his moving valediction as painter and art critic, "The Sea-Mists of the Winter", in the *Listener* in May.[22]

The period surrounding the appearance of *Rude Assignment* was an extremely serious one for Lewis. There can be very few documents in modern letters as dignified and dispassionate as "Sea-Mists". In self-confrontation Lewis was, throughout his life, on his best footing. It was confrontations with others which so often roused the over-didactic in him. But it is clear that *Rude Assignment*'s appearance partook of a momentous narrowing of Lewis's conditions, a confinement, however, which issued in some of his finest work, notably *Self Condemned*. But then *Rude Assignment* is a serious book and deepened (if it did not, by nature, extend) Lewis's audience in the fifties.

A month after the appearance of *Rude Assignment*, Lewis wrote to Mrs. Webb with a complaint about the availability of review copies: "I will pass over the *production* of the book as now a new disservice to me (and to your firm) has come to light." This was the failure to send a review copy to Lewis's friend and mentor at the *Listener*, J. A. Ackerley. Webb replied that a copy had in fact been sent to the *Listener* and she included a list of 75 journals to which review copies had been issued. Also in December, H. G. Porteus, friend and author of the early book on Lewis, wrote that *Rude Assignment* "I consider contains many valuable and important statements, not presented in a form likely to be fairly dealt with by the average editor or reviewer." However, a few months later, he was "glad to see that *Rude Assignment* had a pretty fair press."[23]

Two months after its appearance, *Rude Assignment* had sold 1580 copies of 2500 printed, and a reprint of 1000 copies had been issued. Three years later, Hutchinson had received an offer for the remainder stock and asked Lewis if he wanted any of the 164 bound copies (and 248 sheets) that were left.[24] At 3200 plus copies, *Rude Assignment* had a respectable if modest sale and must have done Lewis's reputation considerable good.

Lewis received some warm responses to *Rude Assignment* from friends. John Rothenstein wrote that it "gave me, as your writings always do, a bracing [word] of your aggressive sanity." I. A. Richards wrote: "I have been reading *Rude Assignment* with delight — not unmixed with those runnels of awe which you command." Lewis replied to Richards that he was "tremendously pleased . . . by your references to 'Rude Assignment'."[25] In the same letter Lewis referred gratefully to Richards' attempt to gain him the Bollingen Prize, which was not to succeed.

Despite his blindness, Lewis was working on his novel for Hutchinson, *The Victory of Albert Temple*. In September, Mrs. Webb was actively pursuing him, asking for the MS or the return of the advance of £225 "as soon as possible". Lewis responded with an apology for the delay in completing the book, explaining that he had lost his sight and been interrupted as well by the treatment necessitated by the condition. "But now I am working extremely hard, and all the time, on your book, and hope to finish it in one month." Webb replied that she was pleased that he was working hard on the book, but made no acknowledgment of Lewis's blindness. Four months later, the book was still "hanging fire" and Webb called again for the return of the advance, since Lewis could not give a definite delivery date. Lewis continued to work on the novel. In December of 1956, Hugh Kenner was negotiating with New Directions for its publication under the title *Twentieth Century Palette*. By February, 1957, Kenner had notified New Directions that the MS was on its way.[26] But in the previous December Lewis had entered hospital with his final illness. By March, death had proved itself the only successful obstacle to his lifelong pursuit of art.

In 1952, Lewis had made a final serious attempt to place *Rude Assignment* with an American publisher. Henry Regnery in Chicago, who brought out a reprint of *The Revenge for Love* in 1952 and American editions of *Rotting Hill, Self Condemned* and *The Demon of Progress in the Arts*, was very keen about *Rude Assignment*: "a wonderful book and an important one. I want to bring it out in the fall of next year, and to make a real 'blast' with it." Regnery had a plan to interest a wealthy friend, Jack Blodgett, in the book so that he would contribute ($3000 to $5000) to advertising that would make a splash. Again, after initial enthusiasm, cold feet ensued. Regnery wrote a month later: "I am most impressed with *Rude Assignment* but it might be better to publish something else before this." Lewis replied:

> So let me begin with "Rude Assignment". It is a biography of my books. The great objection to it in an American bookshop is just that the bookseller would snort that he knows nothing about most of these books and his readers, feeders on "Forever Amber" would feel about "The Apes of God", "The Art of Being Ruled", as a Scottish crofter would about Birds' Nest Soup or a French dish of snails. "Rude Assignment" is of great importance to me, and has been of great service to me: but I am not so conceited as to recommend it for America. But I may be wrong.[27]

Lewis would no doubt be pleased that this new edition of *Rude Assignment* originates in America.

II

IN *Rude Assignment*, Lewis systematically subordinates purely autobiographical matter, which, he says, "has no place here really" (p. 150). At the end of Part II, "Personal Background of Career", he explains: "It had been my intention to continue the personal record, as an accompaniment to the career-narrative, up to the outbreak of world war ii," but, "I found that in surveying the landscape from 1925 onwards that book after book occupied ninety per cent of the area, and all that was important in it" (pp. 150-1). This distinction between "personal record" and "career-narrative" is an important one. The sub-title to the first edition of *Rude Assignment* was "A Narrative of My Career Up-to-Date", so that it is clear that Lewis intended the book to be a treatment of the objective rather than the subjective conditions of his life.

But, as he explains in the "Introduction":

> This is not, as I have said, purely an account of a career, however. It has not been primarily to speak of my work that I have undertaken to write this book. Indeed, it would never occur to me to pass my time so unprofitably as in the indulgence of an historic mood. — Certainly it is about my work, and especially that side of it which has raised up difficulties for its author. But it is also about *the nature of this type of work*, and about the paradoxical position of the workman — not myself alone — engaged in it. And, more personally, it is about my thinking (as illustrated in my work and otherwise) which has resulted in my life being so difficult a one to live. Lastly, this book is itself a work — a new work (pp. 11-12; Lewis's emphasis).

Rude Assignment is, then, not only a narrative, even an objective one, but the treatment of a *type*, a treatment necessarily as analytical as narrative in focus. Lewis presents the "narrative" of his career in order to *represent*, to typify, the work of the artist and writer in the contemporary world. It is within this representative treatment, also, that he is able to isolate "more personally" what has "resulted in my life being so difficult a one to live." It is precisely his sense of himself as *typical*, he later says, that led to what he calls a "paradox" and to much misunderstanding of his views. The "originality" which he so often asserted "did not seem peculiar to me as an *individual*" (p. 212).

Lewis discusses this *detachment* from self elsewhere in *Rude Assignment* (p. 76), and is very careful to explain that it is not impersonal observation:

> For the whole virtue of accurate observation is that it is a *person* observing. . . . No person, of course, is capable of perfect detachment: the effort to attain it would damage the observation. But a group does not observe at all: it *acts*. That is how it thinks. To think is to be split up (Lewis's emphasis).

The individual subject, then, is split up by a paradox at the heart of the effort to think rather than merely act. As he says at the end of the long passage quoted above: "Lastly, this book is itself a work — a new work." The process of autobiographical reflection is in fact creative; it produces a new split between the subject and the past self which he attempts to represent — another self emerges through the autobiographical act of detached (but personal) self-observation.

"This book," Lewis writes, "necessarily deals with politics — because politics has been used as a lever for attacks upon me, so, *although it is not the real issue*, the gravamen of the charges it is my business to refute belongs to politics, or is semi-political" (p. 106; my emphasis). But Lewis had earlier observed of politics: "The moment you go over into them, from some other department of life, using the rational approach — which would be the correct one elsewhere — you get into difficulties. You are in a different medium altogether" (p. 65). It is this fundamental irrationality in politics, its inability to sustain the detached observation necessary to thought, and therefore its immersion in action for its own sake, which has made it a representative issue *but not the real one* in Lewis's career. The real issue has been thought itself and the inherently paradoxical condition which it produces in artistic creation.

Artistic politics, and general politics for the sake of art, play a conspicuous role in Lewis's career and they make their impact felt on the shape of *Rude Assignment* as well. On the artistic side, it is the libellous nature of three of Lewis's books in the thirties which led to their suppression. Lewis would like to tell the full tale of those suppressions but is prevented by the legal battle which would surely result (p. 150). He threatens to deposit a "Supplement" (see pp. 13 and 150) in libraries in London and Washington, to be opened in fifty years' time, which would fully reveal the circumstances (apparently it was never written). The more purely political issue was a handling of Lewis's disastrous response to Hitlerism, also in the thirties. Two fragmentary drafts of chapters on this misadventure survive and are included in this edition as Appendix II.

Also included here as Appendix I is a remarkably candid draft of Chapter XXI, "How One Begins", which demonstrates the process by which Lewis achieved the final, less personal and more typical, published version. This early version of one of the most strictly autobiographical chapters is fascinating and revealing and makes one wish that Lewis had felt more comfortable in "indulging a purely historic mood". We learn in detail about the sloth and anti-bookishness of his public school and Slade days. It is revealed how little Lewis availed himself of formal artistic or academic training. We learn the hitherto unknown fact that Lewis was actually deprived of his scholarship and sent down from the Slade. His revelation in Chapter XXVII of the impact of the Russian novelists on his early development is made correspondingly more vivid when we realize that he read very little indeed previous to their discovery, and the "crisis" which it brought on.

Lewis's decision to revise away the strictly autobiographical in favour of a representative treatment of his career is well in keeping with one of the dominant tendencies throughout his work. Lewis formulated this approach doctrinally in *Men Without Art* (pp. 115-28) as the classical, external approach to art. *Men Without Art* is a work which in fact shows affinities to *Rude Assignment* in Lewis's use of himself, as satirist, as the representative modern writer. Indeed, autobiography in the *Rude Assignment* pattern can be seen as integral to a significant cross-section of Lewis's *corpus*. Other than the obvious example of autobiography in *Blasting and Bombardiering* — a much more relaxed and chatty narrative than *Rude Assignment* — *Wyndham Lewis the Artist, The Writer and the Absolute* and, on the fictional side, *The Wild Body, Tarr, Rotting Hill* and *Self Condemned* attest to the strength of the autobiographical impulse in Lewis's work. Within Lewis's pictorial oeuvre, the tendency toward self-reflection and analysis is visible in his numerous self-portraits, representative examples of which illustrate the present edition. The reappearance of the hitherto practically unobtainable *Rude Assignment* will perhaps contribute to a reconsideration of this aspect of Lewis's exceptional, and exceptionally varied, artistic effort.

Notes

[1] This proposal has survived in draft form. Consisting of two handwritten pages, it was recently discovered at Cornell among the *Rude Assignment* MSS.

[2] K. H. Webb (Hutchinson) to WL, 10 July 1946; unpublished letter in the Cornell Lewis Collection. Hereafter, unless otherwise indicated, all letters are unpublished and in the Cornell Collection.

[3] Hutchinson to WL, 10 Aug 1946; contract also at Cornell.

[4] WL to Augustus John,, 29 Oct 1946; unpub. section of Cornell letter which appears in the *The Letters of Wyndham Lewis*, ed. W. K. Rose (London: Methuen, 1963), p. 399 (hereafter referred to as *Letters*); WL to Allen Tate, 13 Nov 1946; WL to Sir Nicholas Waterhouse, 19 Nov 1946; WL to Geoffrey Grigson, 5 Dec 1946; WL to Tate, 5 Dec 1946.

[5] By April 18, Hutchinson's legal advisor had read the MS and submitted his queries. Also, in a letter to Tate dated simply April, 1947, WL says of the MS: "It was handed in here two days ago." By April 27, WL had a further chapter to add to the MS (the longish Ch. VI) as well as an *envoi*. By May 28, the MS was complete including the revisions suggested by Hutchinson's lawyer. See WL to Webb, 27 April 1947 and to Waterhouse, 29 May 1947.

[6] WL to Felix Giovanelli, 26 Jan 1947; WL to W. Mitchell, 10 Feb 1947. See Jeffrey Meyers, *The Enemy: A Biography of Wyndham Lewis* (London: Routledge, 1980), p. 294; hereafter Meyers.

[7] WL to Waterhouse, 29 May 1947.

[8] Only the first 9 of 12 (based on WL's numbered replies) of the lawyer's comments have survived (at Cornell).

[9] Webb to WL, 7 May 1947; WL to Webb, 11 May 1947.

[10] Tate to WL, 1 July 1947; WL to Tate, 4 July 1947; Tate to WL, 31 July 1947; *Letters* #367. Lewis takes Tate's phrase "center back in the 20's and 30's" as a football metaphor and imputes the accusation that he had followed other people's "directions", which Tate had surely not intended.

[11] It was not republished in WL's lifetime.

[12] WL to Waterhouse, 10 Dec 1947; WL to Webb, 29 May 1947; WL to F. W. Heath (Hutchinson), 11 June 1947. Lewis's description in the May 29 letter identifies the novel as *Twentieth Century Palette*, a bulky unfinished MS in the Cornell archive.

[13] WL to Fisher and Knight, 23 Dec 1947; WL to Waterhouse, 13 Jan 1948 — during the correcting of proofs, Lewis decided on the title *Rude Assignment*; Lewis to David Kahma, 15 April 1948.

[14] The situation with surviving sets of proofs of *Rude Assignment* is complicated and can only be gone into briefly here. There are three complete sets of proofs in the Lewis Collection at Cornell. However, the Catalogue of the Collection speculates on the date of 1950 for one set, which on closer examination is proved to be a duplicate of the set dated in the Catalogue 7 & 8 Jan 1948. Both these sets are in fact stamped consecutively 1, 2, 12, 13, 14 and 15 Jan, bundles of pages obviously having been sent to Lewis as they were pulled. The set dated 7 and 8 Jan in the Catalogue is marked #1 in blue pencil on the date-stamped pages while that dated 1950 is marked in red #2. A comparison of the revisions in the two sets of Jan 1948 and that dated (correctly in the Cat.) 17 June 1948 with the final published text produces confusing results. The set of 17 June sometimes incorporates the changes of set #1 and sometimes of set #2 while the final version sometimes ignores the alterations made in this third set of 17 June and chooses an earlier version. The situation is somewhat clarified by the discovery of 3 sheets only of a set of page proofs amongst one of the galley sets. These sheets (of the final pages of the book) include a (printed) footnote which does not appear in any of the three earlier sets. By the time page proofs had been drawn off, Lewis had clearly made further revisions. Whether these revisions were made on a fourth set of galleys or on an initial set of page proofs is not known. The precise character of the revisions in the various sets of proofs is a question too vexed with detail to be entered into here. Suffice it to say that deleted matter often expressed more individual views and opinions which Lewis must later have felt too much personalized his treatment of issues.

[15] WL to John Palmer, 3 Aug 1948; Giovanelli to WL, 20 Sept 1948.

[16] WL to Giovanelli, 10 Sept and 18 Dec 1948; Wl to John, 7 March 1949.

[17] Palmer to WL, 26 July and 21 Sept 1948 and 9 March 1948 — Palmer also communicated in this last letter, however, that he wished to publish WL's "The Rot", later to appear in *Rotting Hill*; WL to Palmer, 18 March 1949; WL to Mr. Houldgate, 22 March 1949.

[18] Giovanelli to WL, 25 March 1949; WL to Theodore Weiss, 2 April 1949; WL to Eliot, 12 April 1949; WL to Edward Fuller, 9 May 1949.

[19] Heath to WL, 10 May 1949; Giovanelli to WL, 22 June 1949.

[20] John Sargent (Doubleday) to WL, 23 Aug 1949; WL to Sargent, 6 Nov 1949.

[21] Bokförlaget Natur och Kultur to WL, 9 May 1950; Hutchinson to WL, 2 Oct 1950; Webb to WL, 17 Oct 1950; Hutchinson to WL, 10 Nov 1950; WL to Webb, n.d.

[22] For a full treatment of Lewis's blindness, see Meyers, pp. 300-5.

[23] WL to Webb, n.d.; Webb to WL, 14 Dec 1950; Porteus to WL, 3 Dec 1950 and 15 April 1951.

[24] Webb to WL, 22 Jan 1951; Hutchinson to WL, 28 May 1954.

[25] Rothenstein to WL, 16 May 1951; Richards to WL, 22 March 1951; WL to Richards, 9 April 1951.

[26] Webb to WL, 14 Sept and 8 Oct 1951, 5 March 1952; WL to Webb, 3 Oct 1951; Kenner to WL, 2 Dec 1956 and 6 Feb 1957.

[27] Regnery to WL, 5 Sept and 29 Oct 1952; WL to Regnery, n.d.

INDEX

[This is the Index to the text of *Rude Assignment* substantially as printed in the first edition. Though doubtless authorized by Lewis, it may not have been compiled by him, since it contains both corrections of errors that remained in the text (it lists "Barr, Jnr., Alfred" whereas the text had "Robert") and new errors unlikely to have been made by Lewis (it indexes his reference to Francisco Suarez, the theologian, as being to André Suarès, the French writer). These mistakes are corrected here, as are a couple of typographical errors. Otherwise, only such changes have been made as are necessitated by repagination and by the emendations to the text already listed in full above.]

J

James, Henry, 20, 107, 113, 144
Jefferson, Thomas, 64, 97, 198, 226
Jehovah's Witness, 192
John, O.M., Augustus D., 49, 53, 126-9, 215
Jonson, Ben, 48
Joyce, James, 28, 44-5, 48-9, 58-62, 114, 123, 131
Jung, Dr. C. G., 59-60

K

Kafka, Franz, 180, 233
Kaiser, 185
Kameneff, 219
Kant, Emanuel, 96
Karamazovs, The, 157
Keats, John, 21, 45, 131
Kelmscott Press, 201
Kibblewhite, Mrs., 148
Kierkegaard, Sören, 157
Kipling, Rudyard, 118, 229
Kirstein, Lincoln, 233
Klee, Paul, 28
Koestler, Arthur, 92
Kotelenko, 108
'Kreutzer Sonata, The,' 157
Kropotkin, Prince P., 25
Kutuzov, Marshal, 157

L

La Bruyère, Jean de, 34
Lamb, Henry, 124
'Language, Truth and Logic,' 43
Lansbury, M.P., George, 93
Laski, Prof. Harold, 80, 95-6, 201
Lawrence, D. H., 20, 28, 48, 114, 191, 218-9, 221
Lawrence, T. E., 20, 45, 150
League of Nations, 88
'Leatherstocking,' 117
Lechmere, Miss Kate, 135
'Left Wings over Europe,' 71-2, 226
Leicester Galleries, The, 140, 145
Leonardo da Vinci, 114
Lerroux, A., 234
Lesbos, 191

'Lettres Provinciales,' 34
Levin, Harry, 58-62
Library of Congress, 150
'Lilas,' The, 159
Linatti, Carlo, 221, 235
Lincoln, Abraham, 93, 226
'Lion and the Fox, The,' 174-83, 209-10
Lippmann, Walter, 102
"Little Minister, The,' 237
Livingstone, Dr., 111
London Library, The, 200
Loredano, Doge Leonardo, 53
Louvre, The, 119
Low, David, 48-9, 57, 82, 193, 215
Luisa, Queen Maria, 53

M

MacArthur, General, 93
MacDonald, Ramsay, 193
Machiavelli, Niccolò, 65-8, 75-6, 153, 176-8, 182, 219
Maine, Henry, 68
Malatesta, Sigismondo, 52
Malraux, André, 34, 155, 234
Manchester Museum, 139
Marat,.J.-P., 233
Marinetti, F. T., 139, 178-9
Maritain, Jaques, 35
Maritain, Raissa, 35
Marx Brothers, 159, 230
Marx, Karl, 38, 191
Maugham, Somerset, 57, 131
Mauriac, André, 48, 230
Maurier, Daphne du, 28
Maurras, Charles, 35-6, 39-40
May, Phil, 48
'Méfaits des Intellectuels, Les,' 32-42
'Men Without Art,' 222
'Mendiant Ingrat, Le,' 132
Meredith, George, 48
Michelangelo (Buonarroti), 29, 115, 127
Middleton, 118
Millais, Sir John Everett, 20
Milton, John, 28-9
Mitchison, Naomi, 140
Modigliani, Amedeo, 145
Molotov, Vyacheslav, 72, 87, 105
Montaigne, Michel de, 125, 176

Printed in September 1984 in Santa Barbara & Ann Arbor
for the Black Sparrow Press by Graham Mackintosh
& Edwards Brothers Inc. Design by Barbara Martin.
This edition is printed in paper wrappers; there
are 400 cloth trade copies; & 226 numbered deluxe
copies have been handbound in boards by Earle Gray.

WYNDHAM LEWIS (1882-1957) was a novelist, painter, essayist, poet, critic, polemicist and one of the truly dynamic forces in literature and art in the twentieth century. He was the founder of Vorticism, the only original movement in twentieth century English painting. The author of *Tarr* (1918), *The Lion and the Fox* (1927), *Time and Western Man* (1927), *The Apes of God* (1930), *The Revenge for Love* (1937), and *Self Condemned* (1954), Lewis was ranked highly by his important contemporaries: "the most fascinating personality of our time . . . the most distinguished living novelist" (T. S. Eliot), "the only English writer who can be compared to Dostoievsky" (Ezra Pound).

Toby Foshay is a Social Sciences and Humanities Research Council of Canada Doctoral Fellow at Dalhousie University, Halifax, Nova Scotia, writing his thesis on subjectivity in Wyndham Lewis. In addition to articles on Joyce and Yeats and on critical theory, he has published *John Daniel Logan: Canadian Man of Letters.*

Bryant Knox is a former high school teacher, college and university instructor who holds a Masters degree in English from Simon Fraser University. He has written previously on Ezra Pound and Charles Olson, and is working on a pictorial presentation of "Charles Olson's Yucatan." He has also studied and travelled extensively in Mexico and lectures professionally on pre-Hispanic art and culture. He lives with his wife and two daughters in Burnaby, British Columbia.

LEE COUNTY LIBRARY SYSTEM

3 3262 00121 3484

B
Lewis
Lewis
Rude assignment

DISCARD
LEE COUNTY LIBRARY
107 HAWKINS AVE.
SANFORD, N. C. 27330